COLLINS
COMPLETE GUIDE TO
IRISH WILDLIFE

Paul Sterry

Collins

HarperCollins Publishers Ltd.
1 London Bridge Street
London SE1 9GF

WilliamCollinsBooks.com

Collins is a registered trademark of HarperCollinsPublishers Ltd.

First published in 2004
This edition reissued in 2010

20
10 9

A catalogue record for this book is available from the British Library.

ISBN: 978-0-00-734951-7

Collins uses papers that are natural, renewable and recyclable products made from
wood grown in sustainable forests. The manufacturing processes conform to the
environmental regulations of the country of origin.

Edited and designed by D & N Publishing, Hungerford, Berkshire
Printed and bound in China by RR Donnelley APS

CONTENTS

INTRODUCTION 4

MAMMALS 20

BIRDS 32

REPTILES 94

AMPHIBIANS 94

FISH • FRESHWATER 96

FISH • SEASHORE 100

INSECTS • BUTTERFLIES AND MOTHS 104

INSECTS 122

SPIDERS 152

MOLLUSCS 156

TERRESTRIAL AND FRESHWATER CRUSTACEANS 166

SEASHORE CRUSTACEANS 168

OTHER TERRESTRIAL AND FRESHWATER INVERTEBRATES .172

OTHER SEASHORE INVERTEBRATES 174

TREES AND SHRUBS 178

WILD FLOWERS 190

WATER PLANTS AND HORSETAILS 264

GRASSES, RUSHES AND SEDGES 266

LOWER PLANTS 276

FUNGI 288

GLOSSARY 298

FURTHER READING 301

NATURAL HISTORY SOCIETIES 302

PICTURE CREDITS 303

INDEX 304

INTRODUCTION

In the big picture of the natural world, Ireland looks like a small place. You could well be forgiven for thinking that not a lot happens here. I thought that too, once, but since I began making radio programmes about Ireland's flora and fauna a decade or so ago, I now know that Ireland is beautiful, unique and as natural as her people. I have also had the pleasure of learning much more about our wildlife through working with experts such as Dr Richard Collins, whose work on Mute Swans has contributed to our understanding of Europe's largest bird and who has guided my hand in writing this introduction.

Ireland is an offshore island of Europe's largest offshore island, Britain. Situated in the warm waters of the Gulf Stream, wafted by moist westerly winds, it is a land both of moderation and of extremes. Although it is one of the world's windiest countries, Ireland has an exceptionally mild climate. The average temperature in the coldest months is seldom lower than 4°C while the average for the warmest month is 17°C. The area under forest is smaller than that of any European country apart from Iceland, and its population, although increasing, is still small. It is often said that Ireland has fewer animals and plants than its neighbour, Britain, from which it is separated by the Irish Sea. However, Britain is three times larger than Ireland. For its size, Ireland has an equally diverse and fascinating flora and fauna.

PHYSICAL FEATURES

This saucer-shaped island comprises a flat central plain, surrounded by mountains, the highest rising to 1,041 metres above the sea. The Shannon, the longest river in Ireland and Britain, flows down through the centre of the country. Lough Neagh, in the north, is one of the largest lakes in Western Europe. Ireland's west coast, open to the ravages of Atlantic storms, has fjord-like indentations and spectacular cliffs.

THIS BOOK

Collins Complete Irish Wildlife Photoguide is the first comprehensive identification guide to Ireland's flora and fauna. All the plants, fungi and animals that are likely to be encountered on the island of Ireland, are featured. Only rarely observed plants and animals have been omitted.

Each species is described and illustrated by a photograph. Where possible, similar species are featured on the same page of the book so that immediate comparisons can be made. Descriptions are concise and should be read in conjunction with the photographs.

Although the book is primarily concerned with field identification, some understanding of Ireland's natural history may be helpful. So let's take a look at its most important features over the next few pages.

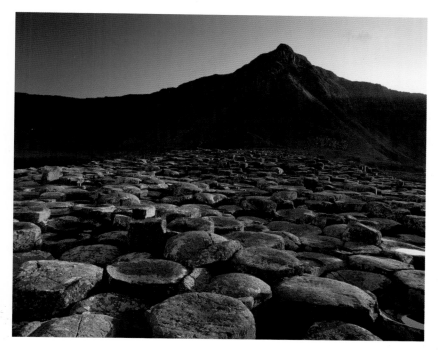

Basalt columns at the Giant's Causeway are a dramatic element in Ireland's complex and ancient geological heritage.

THE NATURAL HISTORY OF IRELAND

IN THE BEGINNING

The foundations of the island were laid when the American and European continental plates collided some 450 million years ago. The plates then separated again, and the void between them became the Atlantic Ocean. The remains of this ancient rift are still evident today; old rock formations in Ireland have the same composition as those of Newfoundland in Canada. The rocks on which the island would eventually be built were submerged in the ocean for long periods and the limestone base of Ireland's central plain was laid down under the sea until, around 300 million years ago, a land vaguely resembling the Ireland of today began to emerge.

ICE AGES

Over the last two million years or so, the world has been subjected to a series of ice ages. Great ice caps covered much of the northern hemisphere, including all but the southernmost fringe of Ireland. The ice advanced and retreated at least six times, and on each occasion the animal and plant communities were annihilated. The last incursion was at its peak about 22,000 years ago, when Ireland was covered by a blanket of ice up to a kilometre thick in places.

At the height of the cold period, so much water was locked up in the ice caps that sea levels were 120 metres lower than they are today. Then the ice began to melt. The sea levels rose as the melt waters flowed from the ice-cap. By about 15,000 years ago, they had risen to within 90 metres of today's levels, and a sub-arctic tundra landscape, surrounded by mountain glaciers, appeared. The small rounded hills, known as drumlins, which are common in Ireland, are heaps of spoil piled up and left behind by the moving ice. Rivers, flowing under the ice, laid down deposits of gravel, known as eskers.

THE FIRST PLANTS AND ANIMALS
Towards the end of the last ice age, Britain and Ireland were part of a peninsula joined to the European mainland. When the ice retreated, plants and animals moved into the peninsula. Lichens and mosses arrived first, and then Arctic and alpine plant species followed.

Around 13,000 years ago, grasslands covered much of Ireland and the landscape probably resembled that of present-day Greenland. The Mountain Hare and Stoat may have arrived then. Ireland soon had Reindeer, Arctic Foxes and Lemmings, and the grasslands were the perfect habitat for our most celebrated animal, the Giant Irish Deer.

IRELAND BECOMES AN ISLAND
Water from melting ice continued to raise the level of the sea until, about 12,000 years ago, the land-bridge between Ireland and Britain disappeared, one of the most momentous ecological events in the island's history. But the bridge between Britain and Europe still remained intact, so Ireland was cut off from mainland Europe much earlier than Britain was cut off.

Immediately after the warm period, the country became colder again. The grasslands declined during this mini ice age and many plant and animal species, including the Reindeer, Lemming, Arctic Fox and Giant Irish Deer, perished and became extinct. This cold spell ended around 11,000 years ago and Juniper and birch forests began to thrive in the milder climate. A thousand years later, Hazel had become the dominant plant, and following this, Oaks and elms began to spread throughout the island. Scots Pine thrived on the poorer soils and on the lower slopes of the mountains.

The Irish Sea was no barrier to some creatures. Birds had little difficulty reaching our shores, and seals, whales and dolphins visited the coast. Those fish able to tolerate both fresh and salt water, such as salmonids, lampreys and the Eel, colonised our rivers and lakes. But land animals could not cross the sea, so only those that had arrived before the disappearance of the land-bridge, and which had managed to survive the subsequent cold spell, remained.

THE ARRIVAL OF MAN

When the first people arrived around 9,000 years ago, Ireland was 95 per cent forest, and had only a restricted range of plants and animals. The earliest people were hunter-gatherers, who lived on fruit, fish and wild animals, but their activities probably had little impact on the numbers of wild creatures or on the environment as a whole.

THE FIRST FARMERS

People started farming in Ireland around 6,000 years ago. It is not known whether farming arrived with a new wave of people or whether those already here adopted a farming lifestyle, but its arrival heralded the most profound change that Ireland had experienced since becoming an island. The farmers burned forests to make clearances for crop cultivation and for keeping livestock. The area of forest destroyed was probably very small and their main crops were wheat and barley.

When areas of trees are felled, the ground is fertile and can be cultivated. However, the soils are soon washed away by rain and the farmers are forced to cut down more forest. The cleared areas gradually become waterlogged,

Ireland's mosaic of wetland and moorland habitats, seen here at Slieve Blinniau, owes its existence in part to the activities of Man.

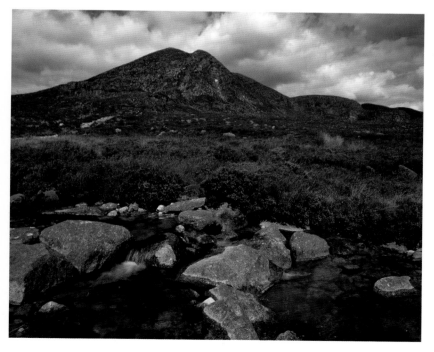

leading to the formation of bogs. Although Ireland's blanket bogs probably resulted from forest clearances, rainfall was also a factor. So the climate became wetter over time, causing the extinction of the island's most widely distributed conifer, the Scots Pine.

By AD 1,000, all of the denser forests had gone. The loss of its trees had profoundly changed the landscape. The exposed mountains were cloaked in blanket bog. Many lakes became fens. Dead vegetation piled up in the fens, outstripping the ecosystem's ability to break it down. The plant roots lost contact with the ground water and the fens became raised bogs. Around 16 per cent of today's Ireland is bog: the great Bog of Allen, in counties Offaly and Kildare, covered an area of over 6,000km^2.

Social changes also affected the landscape. In ancient Ireland, land was held tribally so there was little need to enclose farmland. All this changed with the arrival of the Normans, in the 12th century, who began to create hedges by cutting back the wildwood and planting saplings. The large hedges between town-lands, the territories of great landowners, date from this time.

MODERN TIMES

In the 18th century, exotic trees such as Beech, Lime and the first American conifers were planted in the great estates of Ireland. It was a time of great social change and, by the end of the century, the human population was increasing rapidly. There were eight and a half million people in Ireland at the outbreak of the great famine in 1845, the largest population the country has ever sustained. The famine and its aftermath reduced the population to five million.

Following this, the great estates were broken up and the land distributed to small farmers. An extensive network of new hedges was needed to mark the boundaries of such holdings. Mixed farming required further enclosures, with hedges mainly of Blackthorn and Hawthorn, to keep livestock off the tilled areas.

The 19th and 20th centuries saw the destruction of almost all of the great Turloughs of Connaght in, often pointless, drainage schemes. Turloughs, an Irish word meaning 'dry lake', are lakes with a limestone base, which dry out in summer, filling again in winter.

Peat has been a traditional fuel source in rural Ireland but, until the 20th century, it was extracted at a renewable rate. Harvesting was mechanised during the 1950s and most of the great bogs of the midlands were destroyed to supply peat to power stations.

In the 1950s, the practice of planting fast-growing American conifers commenced. Trees covered about 1 per cent of the country at the beginning of the 20th century. By the end of the century, 9 per cent of the land was forested, much of it with Sitka Spruce and Lodgepole Pine.

In recent years, mechanised farming has led to the removal of hedges in the interests of farming efficiency, and herbicides and insecticides are being widely used. Organo-chlorine residues drastically reduced the numbers of

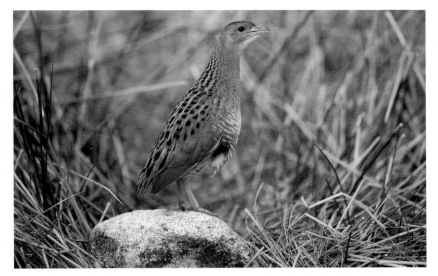

Despite a massive reduction in numbers in recent decades, Ireland is still the best place in northwest Europe to see Corncrakes.

birds of prey in the 1950s and 60s, but, fortunately, controls on pesticides have saved Ireland's Peregrines from extinction. Such changes in farming practice may be to blame for the demise of Ireland's Corncrake population. Only a small relict population survives in the west and midlands. The Grey Partridge is at the verge of extinction. Overgrazing has also caused problems for wildlife: blanket bog was overgrazed by sheep during the 1980s, and in overgrazed areas of the west of Ireland, the soils were washed from the mountains leaving a barren rocky landscape.

SOCIAL ATTITUDES
At the beginning of the 20th century, Ireland had one of the best-documented natural histories in the world. But, following the foundation of the Irish Free State in 1921, there was a period of neglect. An interest in nature was seen as belonging to an alien ascendancy culture. The impoverished new State, confronting enormous political and social problems, had little interest in the natural environment.

With rising educational levels, and particularly with the advent of television in the 1960s, attitudes began to change. A large, mainly urban based, conservation movement developed. Natural history societies and field groups thrived. 'Green' issues are now part of the mainstream of Irish political life, and entry to the European Union in 1973 made the country subject to European environmental directives.

PLANT AND ANIMAL GROUPS

Scientists and naturalists divide plants and animals into groups, members of which have characters in common with one another. The species included in this book have been organised into these widely accepted groups and the accompanying notes detail their most distinctive features. The coloured symbols to the left of the page correspond to those used throughout the book as thumbnail indicators of page subjects.

VERTEBRATE ANIMALS
Animals with backbones, which comprise:

 Mammals: warm-blooded animals, which have hairy skins; give birth to live young, which are subsequently suckled by the mother.

 Birds: warm-blooded animals whose skins are covered with feathers, these aiding heat regulation and allowing flight; all birds lay eggs.

 Reptiles: cold-blooded animals with scaly skins, which breathe air. The young develop inside eggs, which, in some species, hatch within the body of the female.

Amphibians: cold-blooded animals with soft, moist skins capable of absorbing oxygen from water; some also have lungs and can breathe air. Often found on land but most breed in water, laying eggs, which grow as larval tadpoles before metamorphosing into miniature adults. Some give birth to live young or lay eggs on land.

 Fish: cold-blooded animals that live in water throughout their lives; all the species use gills to extract oxygen from water. In most species, the skin is covered with scales and fins facilitate swimming.

INVERTEBRATE ANIMALS
Animals without backbones, which include:

      Arthropods: the most numerous group of animals and one which is characterised by the presence of an external skeleton and paired, jointed limbs. Members include insects, spiders, crustaceans and allies, millipedes and centipedes. Insect groups dealt with in this book include butterflies and moths, grasshoppers and bush-crickets, dragonflies and damselflies, earwigs, bugs, lacewings, caddis flies, flies, ants, wasps, bees and beetles; crustacean groups covered include crabs, lobsters and barnacles.

Molluscs: soft-bodied animals that are found on land, in fresh water and in the sea. Some molluscs protect their bodies by producing hard shells, while this feature is absent or much reduced in slugs, sea slugs and octopuses.

 Coelenterates: radially symmetrical, soft-bodied creatures that include sea anemones, jellyfish and freshwater hydras.

Segmented worms: examples of which are found in soil, fresh water and in the sea. The body is soft, segmented and often bears bristles to aid movements as with earthworms and marine annelid worms.

Echinoderms: animals which are radially symmetrical, mostly organised into five rays. Some members have bodies protected by a hard shell comprising armoured plates with spines. Included in the book are sea urchins, starfish and brittlestars.

Sponges: primitive, aquatic animals whose bodies have external vents and are covered in minute pores.

HIGHER PLANTS

Distinguished from animals by the presence of the green pigment chlorophyll, which is used to manufacture food from sunlight energy, water and carbon dioxide; oxygen is produced as a by-product of this chemical reaction known as photosynthesis. Higher plants come in all shapes and sizes and are separated into two groups:

  Flowering plants: plants whose reproductive structures are borne in flowers; their seeds are enclosed in structures known as fruits, a term which, for botanists, is not confined to conspicuous and edible forms. Flowering plants covered in this book include deciduous and some evergreen trees, shrubs and wildflowers.

 Grasses, rushes and sedges are grouped separately.

 Conifers: mostly sizeable, evergreen plants whose reproductive structures are borne in cones; the seeds lack a seedcoat.

LOWER PLANTS

These lack the complex reproductive structures of higher plants and are generally smaller and less robust. Among those included in this book are the following:

Algae: primitive aquatic plants. Many are microscopic and not covered in this book but the larger seaweeds are included.

Mosses: primitive land plants, which lack roots and whose stems bear simple leaves.

Liverworts: primitive land plants, which are usually broad and flattened, anchored to the substrate by root-like structures.

Lichens: unusual organisms that exist as a symbiotic relationship between a fungus and an alga. Usually form encrustations on rock or bark.

Clubmosses: small, simple plants with upright stems which bear numerous narrow leaves. Clubmosses bear a passing resemblance to miniature conifers.

Horsetails: perennial plants that comprise an underground stem or rhizome from which arise upright stems bearing whorls of narrow leaves.

Ferns: easily recognised during their spore-producing stages which are large and robust and have a vascular system and roots.

FUNGI

Although formerly considered to be part of the plant kingdom, many scientists now place fungi in a group separate from both plants and animals. They lack the photosynthetic pigment chlorophyll, which characterises plants, and are thus unable to make their own food; nutrition is obtained instead from organic matter via the thread-like hyphae, which comprise the bulk of the fungal organism. The familiar mushrooms and toadstools are merely the reproductive structures of the fungi.

FLORA

Ireland's naturally occurring plants and animals came from Europe, mostly through Britain. Of our 815 flowering plants, 15 are not found in Britain. Ten of these are of Iberian origin but just how they came to be here remains a mystery. Twenty-six plants are of Arctic-alpine origin and have been here since the retreat of the ice. There are 78 native ferns, 21 broad-leaved native trees and two native conifers. A third conifer, the Scots Pine, became extinct, but was reintroduced and is usually regarded as a native.

MOSSES, LIVERWORTS, FUNGI, ALGAE AND LICHENS

In Ireland's mild climate with persistent rainfall, the mosses and liverworts have thrived: some 759 species have been recorded to date and there are 23 species of sphagnum moss alone. At the time of writing some 3,500 fungi, 1,050 lichens and 1,400 algae have been identified.

FAUNA

Many animals have been introduced to Ireland by man: of the 22 land mammals, at least 13 were introduced. In an isolated island environment, with a restricted range of species, there is less competition and many creatures have come to occupy different or wider ecological niches than their cousins elsewhere. The Irish version of the Mountain Hare, for example, is not confined to high ground, but occurs throughout the island. Many animals have become subtly different from their European cousins.

There are some 50 mammal species, including the whales, dolphins and seals, and 425 bird species recorded to date. Only about half of these can be regarded as genuinely Irish birds. There are no endemic species but the Irish forms of the Jay, Coal Tit and Dipper are unique.

The Viviparous Lizard is Ireland's only land reptile, although the Slowworm, recently introduced to the Burren area of County Clare, may well become established there. Five species of marine turtle occur as vagrants off the Irish coast. Ireland has three amphibians, only one of which, the Smooth Newt, is thought to be native. The origin of the Natterjack Toad is uncertain. It may have been accidentally introduced, but this view has been challenged. Twenty-seven freshwater fish species are found here. The Pollan, a relative of the Salmon, is found in Irish lakes and nowhere else in Europe. A unique sub-species of Shad inhabits the lakes of Killarney. The human need for a diverse food supply led to the introduction of a many alien fish species. The number of invertebrates is unknown. To date, over 15,000 have been identified. The most famous Irish invertebrate is the Kerry Slug, which is of Iberian origin.

HABITATS

In spring, the limestone region known as the Burren offers the botanist an extraordinary array of wild-flowers in a moon-like landscape against the backdrop of the Atlantic Ocean. The country has outstanding seabird breeding colonies, with hundreds of thousands of seabirds converging on our islands and mainland cliffs. In winter, ducks, geese, swans and wading birds crowd into internationally important wetlands. In addition, Ireland has some of the last remaining peat-bogs of Europe.

SEABIRD COLONIES
Little Skellig, off the coast of County Kerry, holds 26,000 pairs of Gannets. Only St Kilda, in the Outer Hebrides, has a greater number. The Blasket Islands, also in Kerry, are the world stronghold of the European Storm-petrel.

WETLANDS
The mild winter climate attracts hundreds of thousands of wildfowl and wading birds from Europe, Iceland and the Canadian Arctic. The pale-bellied race of the Brent Goose winters in Ireland as does the Icelandic population of Whooper Swans. A large proportion of Iceland's Redshanks and Black-tailed Godwits visit Ireland in winter.

THE BURREN
'Buireann', in Irish, means a rocky area. The Burren, about 800km^2 in extent, consists of low bare limestone hills, interspersed with bare rocky pavements. The pavements are dissected by deep vertical cracks, which provide a range of micro-habitats. This region of Counties Clare and south Galway is renowned for its wild flowers, including plants from southern Europe and Alpine-Arctic regions. Their occurrence close together in one small region is truly remarkable.

FARMLAND
Modern farming practice has taken its toll on wildlife. Agricultural chemicals have wiped out the wild flowers and reduced the range and abundance of invertebrates. Destruction of hedgerows has greatly reduced the cover for mammals and birds. The seed-eating birds have declined drastically in numbers, the shortage of insect larvae making it difficult for birds to raise their young. The Corncrake, the only Red Data listed bird species in Ireland, is a farmland bird that is now confined to a few island and mainland areas of the west and the callows of the Shannon. Fewer than 200 pairs of Corncrakes now breed here.

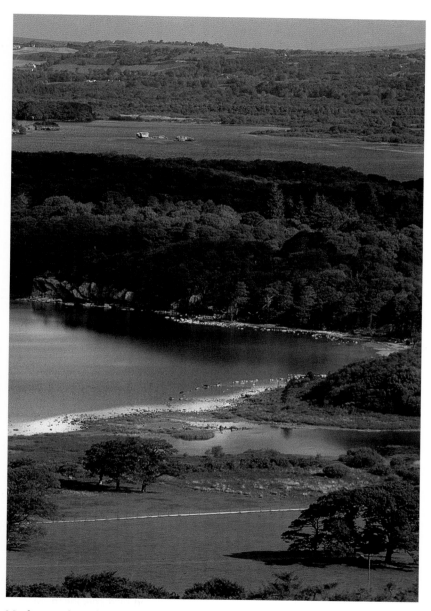

Muckross Lake. Wherever you go in Ireland, you are never far from water.

Badgers, which feed largely on earthworms, are common in Irish farm-land. The animal has been identified as a vector of tuberculosis in cattle and culling of Badgers has commenced in some areas.

WOODLANDS

Little of Ireland's original woods remain. In recent decades, American conifers have been widely planted. Young trees support tits, warblers and finches. Irish woodlands have particularly high densities of Goldcrests.

There are no woodpeckers in Ireland although some arrive as vagrants. The Irish Jay, however, is a unique sub-species, shyer and darker in colour than its cousins elsewhere. The Pine Marten, once close to extinction, is now relatively common in scrub and woodland areas in the west of the country. Contrary to widely held belief, there are no Weasels in Ireland. Red Squirrels have been displaced by the introduced Grey Squirrels throughout much of Ireland, but in coniferous forests, the Reds have managed to hold their own.

MOUNTAIN AND MOORLAND

Mountainous districts, such as those of Wicklow, Connemara and West Mayo, support Meadow Pipits, Skylarks and Ravens. As elsewhere in Europe, the numbers of Irish birds of prey declined during the post-war period when organo-chlorine pesticides, the best known of which is DDT, were widely used. Controls on such chemicals have led to a marked improvement in raptor numbers.

CITIES AND TOWNS

Foxes are now more common in urban areas than in rural ones. The intro-duced Grey Squirrel has colonised city parks. The Phoenix Park in Dublin, the largest urban park is the world, has a fine herd of Fallow Deer, which were introduced in the 17th century.

PLACES TO VISIT

KILLARNEY NATIONAL PARK

The Killarney National Park has a unique Oak wood with an understorey of Yew. The Strawberry Tree, Killarney Fern and Irish Spurge are found within the park. Purple Hairstreak butterflies frequent the woodlands.

Killarney's Red Deer herd is particularly ancient and, unlike herds else-where in Ireland, has not been contaminated by introduced animals. The Killarney Shad, a member of the herring family, is found only in Killarney's lakes. This is a sub-species of the Twaite Shad, which arrived here in post glacial times.

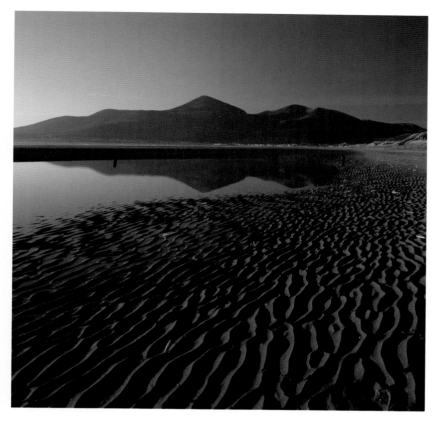
The Mourne Mountains still retain a feeling of real wildness.

GLENVEAGH NATIONAL PARK
The Glenveagh National Park, in Donegal, has fine blanket bog and lakeland habitat. It is the location of a Golden Eagle restoration project. Young eagles, imported from Scotland, are being released in the park in an attempt to re-establish the species here.

BULL ISLAND
Bull Island, only 6km from the centre of Ireland's capital city, is an internationally important nature reserve. Each winter, its mud-flats and salt-marshes hold some of the largest concentrations of wildfowl and wading birds in the country. The birds have become accustomed to people and are particularly easy to observe. There is a small interpretative centre on the island, just beyond the central causeway.

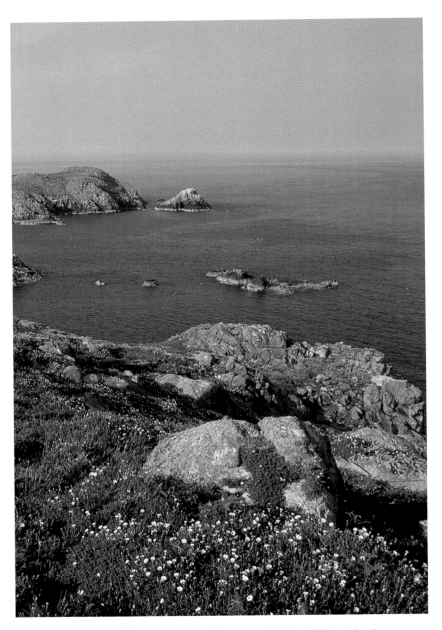

For seabirds galore and stunning coastal flowers, visit Great Saltee Island.

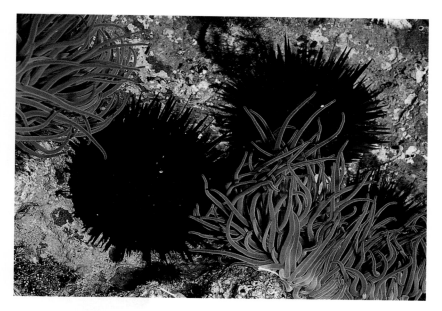

Purple Sea Urchins occur in huge numbers on the shores of Lough Hyne.

WEXFORD WILDFOWL RESERVE
The Wexford Slobs are home to half the entire World population of Greenland White-fronted Geese between the months of September and March. A reserve, jointly owned by the Wildlife Service and BirdWatch Ireland, has been established north of Wexford town. There are bird-watching hides and a viewing tower.

IRELAND'S EYE
Eleven seabird species, including Gannets, breed on Ireland's Eye, near the village of Howth in County Dublin. Boats take visitors to the island at weekends throughout the summer.

GREAT SALTEE
Great Saltee in County Wexford has spectacular seabird colonies and a Grey Seal rookery. Boat trips are available from Kilmore Quay.

LOUGH HYNE
This marine nature reserve, in County Cork, is only 1km^2 in extent. This sea lough contains several thousand species of marine plants and animals, including the Purple Sea Urchin, which occurs in huge numbers along its northern shore. The lough also supports rare species of fish, such as Couch's and Red-mouthed Gobies.

HEDGEHOG *Erinaceus europaeus*   Length 16–26cm
Familiar and unmistakable nocturnal mammal. At home in urban settings and often seen as a road casualty. Will come to food in the garden. If alarmed, rolls into a ball, protected against most potential predators by its spines. Hibernates typically from October to March. Widespread and locally common throughout.

PYGMY SHREW *Sorex minutus*   Body length 6cm
Ireland's smallest mammal. Continually searches for insects, spiders and snails. Favours hedgerows, field borders and woodlands. Tail length two-thirds that of the body length. Common and widespread throughout the region.

BANK VOLE *Clethrionomys glareolus*   Body length 9–11cm
An introduced rodent and the region's only vole species. It can be recognised by its reddish brown coat and rather short tail. Found in woods and hedgerows and restricted, in Ireland, to the SW where it is only locally common.

WOOD MOUSE *Apodemus sylvaticus*   Body length 7.5–11cm
The common mouse of woods, hedgerows and mature gardens and an important prey item for many native predators. Fur is dark yellowish brown above and whitish below. Mainly nocturnal and it may venture indoors in winter. Found throughout Ireland.

HOUSE MOUSE *Mus musculus*   Body length 7.5–10cm
Formerly common and widespread but now comparatively scarce and local. Usually associated with people, both on farmland and in towns. Grey-brown fur distinguishes it from the Wood Mouse. Mainly nocturnal and fairly vocal. Likely to be encountered in almost any urban site or arable farm in Ireland.

BROWN RAT *Rattus norvegicus*   Body length 22–27cm
Reviled by many because of its association with disease and its choice of habitat. In reality, numbers reflect wastefulness of modern society, rats thriving on refuse and discarded food. In this respect at least, it could be said to be serving a useful function. Burrows and swims well. Common and widespread throughout.

RED SQUIRREL *Sciurus vulgaris*   Body length 20–28cm
Our only native squirrel species. Easily told by orange-red fur and presence of ear tufts; tail usually paler than body, sometimes almost white. Has disappeared from some of its former range but spreading thanks to forestry. Widespread and locally common.

GREY SQUIRREL *Sciurus carolinensis*   Body length 25–30cm
Introduced from N America. Occurs in woodland but also found in urban sites such as parks. Fur can look reddish during summer months, but never has ear tufts. Has economic impact in commercial forests. Widespread but distinctly local.

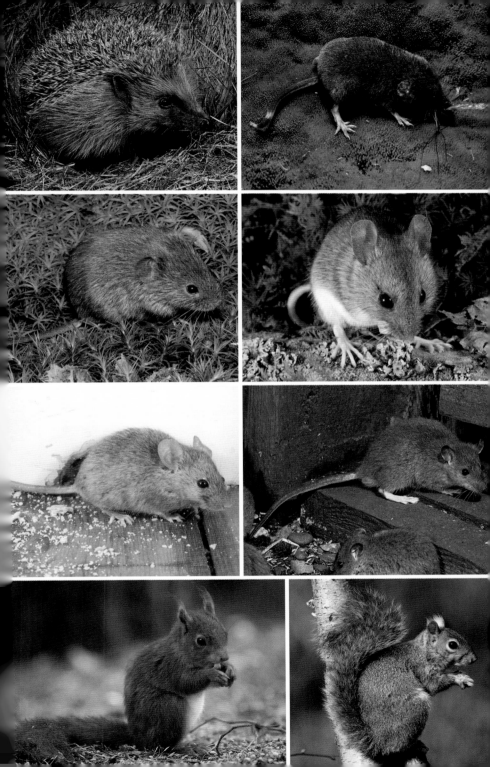

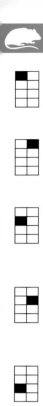

RABBIT *Oryctolagus cunniculus*   Body length 35–40cm
Introduced in Middle Ages but now a common and conspicuous countryside mammal despite depredations of myxomatosis. Often numerous enough to cause serious damage to crops and natural vegetation. Lives socially in extended warrens. Most active from dawn to dusk. Found in most lowland areas of Ireland.

IRISH MOUNTAIN HARE *Lepus timidus hibernicus*   Body length 50–65cm
Distinguished from Rabbit by its proportionately much longer legs. Summer coat is reddish brown; in winter this becomes mottled with white. Favours upland moors although descends to lower altitudes in harsh winter weather. Widespread and locally common.

STOAT *Mustela erminea*   Length 35–40cm
Confusingly, often referred to as a 'Weasel'. Note the long, sinuous body and the distinctive black tip to tail. Coat colour orange-brown above with clear demarcation from white underparts. Some N individuals turn white in winter, retaining black tip to tail. Sometimes located by pinpointing anguished squeals of rabbit prey, a favourite food. Found throughout Ireland.

AMERICAN MINK *Mustela vison*   Length 42–65cm
An unwelcome alien that has become established after escaping from fur farms during past few decades. Dark brown fur makes confusion with otter possible but mink's smaller size, slimmer build and proportionately shorter tail help distinguish it. Invariably associated with water where it feeds on waterbirds, fish and waterside small mammals. Found throughout Ireland.

PINE MARTEN *Martes martes*   Length 65–75cm
Truly arboreal, favouring coniferous forests. Excellent climber, ability and confidence shown to best effect when in pursuit of Red Squirrel prey among treetops. Recognised by reddish brown coat and creamy yellow throat and chest. Shy and largely nocturnal. Easily overlooked but locally not uncommon.

OTTER *Lutra lutra*   Length 95–130cm
Superbly adapted to amphibious lifestyle, occurring in both coastal waters and on rivers and lakes. Dives may last for several minutes. Feeds mainly on fish but also eats sea urchins around coasts. Persecution from fishing interests, hunting and habitat destruction have caused a decline in numbers. However, it is still locally common in suitable habitats across Ireland.

FOX *Vulpes vulpes*   Length 100–120cm
Common but justifiably wary of man given history of persecution of this species. Easily recognised by dog-like appearance, orange-red fur and bushy, white-tipped tail. Gives birth and spends much of daytime in underground 'earth'. Widespread throughout Ireland. Has colonised urban areas in recent years.

BADGER *Meles meles*   Length 80–95cm
Recognised by black-and-white facial stripes. Common, but unobtrusive and largely nocturnal habits make it easy to overlook. With care, easily watched emerging from underground sett at dusk. Very fond of peanuts but slugs and earthworms important in natural diet. Found across Ireland in wooded farmland.

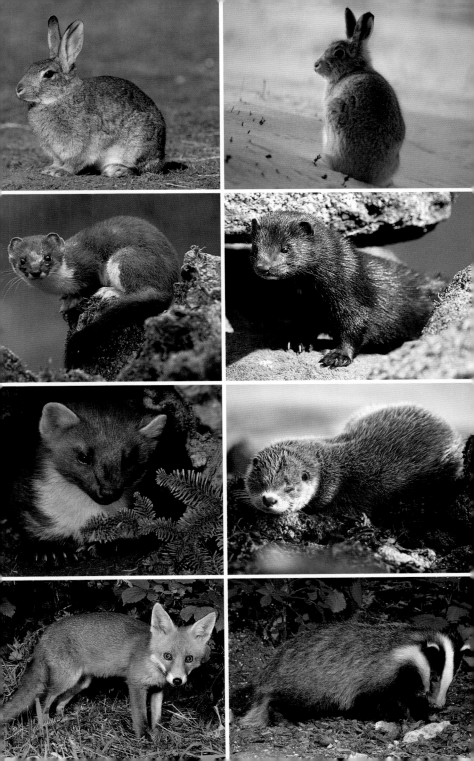

LESSER HORSESHOE BAT *Rhinolophus hipposideros*   Wingspan 22–25cm
Distinguished from other Irish bat species by the horseshoe-shaped 'nose leaves' (fleshy outgrowths from side of nose) and absence of a tragus (pointed inner ear outgrowth). During summer months, uses caves and cellars for daytime roost. Active for much of the night in search of moths. Wingbeats fast and fluttering. In winter, hibernates deep in caves, sometimes in considerable numbers. Found in W Ireland.

LEISLER'S BAT *Nyctalus leisleri*   Wingspan 30–34cm
Medium-sized bat with broadly triangular ears that are rounded at the tip. Fur is rather long and rufous brown; close inspection reveals individual hairs to be dark at the base but pale at the tip. Associated with woodland, roosting in summer in tree holes and crevices. Flight is fast and typically at, or above, height of tree canopy. Locally common throughout.

WHISKERED BAT *Myotis mystacinus*   Wingspan 19–22cm
Relatively small bat with rather narrow, triangular and pointed ears; the tragus is narrow and straight. Fur is rather long and shaggy, brown above and whitish grey below. Favours a mosaic of pockets of woodland, grassland and water. Often roosts in buildings in summer months; hibernates typically in cellars and caves. Typically flies relatively low to the ground and often patrols hedgerows. Widespread and locally common.

DAUBENTON'S BAT *Myotis daubentoni*   Wingspan 23–27cm
Medium-sized bat with comparatively short ears. Frequently associated with water and seen flying low over lakes, ponds and canals just as dusk is falling. Also feeds along woodland rides. Chirps can be heard by those with good hearing. In summer, roosts, sometimes in colonies, in hollow trees and tunnel entrances. In winter, hibernates in caves, mines and cellars. Widespread and fairly common in Ireland except the SW.

NATTERER'S BAT *Myotis nattereri*   Wingspan 25–30cm
Medium-sized bat with comparatively large ears and a well-developed tragus. Wings pale in flight. Has brownish fur and fringe of hairs on wing membrane between legs. Generally favours wooded habitats but also found near water and in towns. In summer, roosts during day in hollow trees, caves and sometimes even lofts and buildings; sometimes colonial. In winter, hibernates in caves, tunnels and mines. Widespread and fairly common.

BROWN LONG-EARED BAT *Plecotus auritus*   Wingspan 23–28cm
As name suggests, has very long ears with well developed tragus. Seen in silhouette, outline of ears can clinch identification. Found in a range of habitats including gardens, woods and farmland. Flies throughout night and sometimes in daytime. Will hover to pick insect off vegetation. In summer, roosts in hollow trees and lofts. In winter, hibernates in cellars and caves. Widespread and locally common.

PIPISTRELLE BAT *Pipistrellus pipistrellus*   Wingspan 19–25cm
The commonest Irish bat and also the smallest. Its brown fur is variable in tone. Common in woodland and farmland but also often seen in towns where it roosts in lofts and buildings. Emerges just after sunset and has jerky flight pattern and fluttering wings. Found throughout Ireland. Scientists now split the species into two – the Soprano Pipistrelle (*P. pygmaeus*), which also occurs in Ireland, has a 55kHz sonar call; that of the Common Pipistrelle is 45kHz.

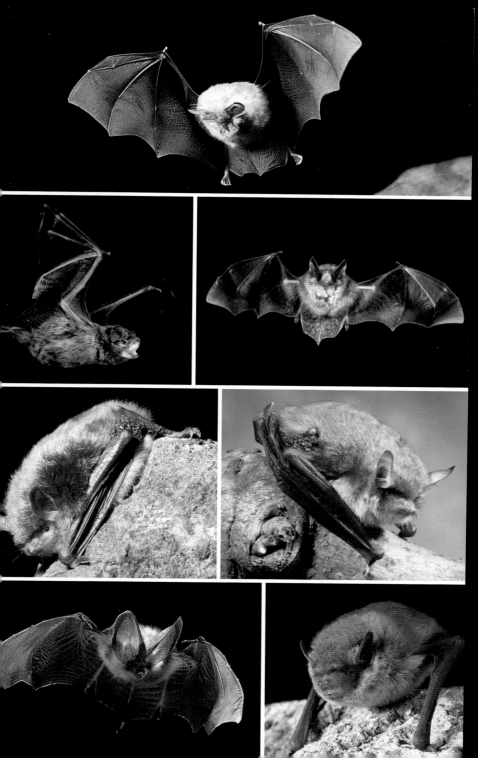

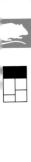

FERAL GOAT *Capra hircus* Shoulder height 50–60cm
Although not native to Ireland, domesticated goats have long been kept for milk, meat and skin. In many parts of the region, feral populations have become established as a result of escapes or deliberate releases from captivity. Populations have persisted in remote and rugged areas to which the animal is ideally adapted. Goats are nimble-footed on crags and precipitous cliffs. Occurs in range of colours but coat usually a mixture of grey, black and brown. Both sexes have horns, larger in male than female.

FALLOW DEER *Dama dama* Shoulder height 85–95cm
Introduced from mainland Europe by Normans but now well established in many parts of Ireland and generally the commonest deer. Kept as a parkland animal, becoming accustomed to man. Away from protection, often hunted and is wary and shy. Parkland animals often selected for pale, dappled coats but elsewhere animals with dark coats predominate. Prefers to live in medium-sized herds and favours wooded areas; sometimes on farmland in summer months. Young born in spring. Rut occurs in October accompanied by barking coughs of males. Male only has antlers which, in mature animals, have broad, flattened tips.

RED DEER *Cervus elaphus* Shoulder height 1.15–1.20m
An imposing animal and Ireland's largest native land mammal. Male (stag, A) is larger than female (hind, B) and has well developed, branching antlers. These are shed each February, reappear in the spring and become larger with each successive season. Summer coat is reddish brown but appears more grey-brown in winter. Lives in separate-sex herds for much of year and spends much of daytime resting or wallowing in mud. Most active from dusk to dawn. Annual autumn rut accompanied by roaring, bellowing sounds from stags. Restricted to wild terrain and commonest in Kerry, Donegal and Wicklow.

SIKA DEER *Cervus nippon* Shoulder height 75–80cm
Introduced to Ireland from its native range in Asia. Now established as feral populations in several locations, chiefly in Wexford, Wicklow, Kerry, Tyrone, Fermanagh and Limerick. In winter, appears uniformly grey-brown in colour but, in summer, acquires reddish brown coat beautifully marked with white spots. Head appears narrow and pointed compared to other deer species. Female lacks antlers. Those of male are narrow and poorly branched; these are shed in April. Favours areas of woodland and farmland and typically found in isolated populations.

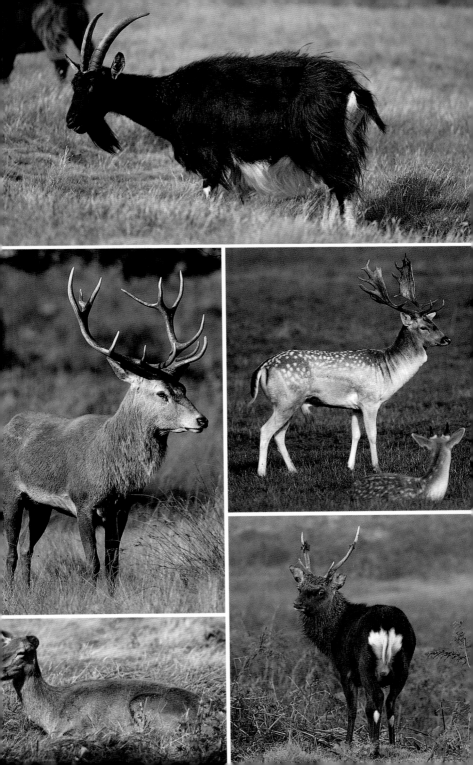

COMMON SEAL *Phoca vitulina*   Length 1.8–2m
The smaller of our two seal species, females being appreciably smaller than males. Compared to Grey Seal, has rather rounded disc-like face with short snout. Coat colour is variable but usually some shade of grey or white with darker spots. Favours shallow, sheltered coastal waters and estuaries. Females give birth on land but pups can swim straight away. Dives well for fish, submerging for up to 10 minutes.

GREY SEAL *Halichoerus grypus*   Length 2.5–3m
A large mammal, streamlined in water but cumbersome on land. Frequently seen 'bottling', with head and neck clear of water. Males (A) up to 0.5m longer than females and much heavier. Both sexes have rather dog-shaped appearance to head; male has a particularly thick neck and convex profile. Coat colour extremely variable but usually some shade of blue-grey; background colour of male generally darker than that of female. Both sexes show irregular and individually unique pattern of blotches and spots on coat. Comes ashore to mate and give birth. Pups (B) born in autumn and generally remain on land for two to three weeks. Common off W coast of Ireland but persecuted by fishermen in some areas.

MINKE WHALE *Balaenoptera acutorostrata*   Length 8–10m
Smallest baleen whale and the only one regularly seen in coastal waters. Locally common off W coast. At close range, diagnostic white spot on flippers can be seen in clear water. Seldom breaches but occasionally lunge-fishes at surface. Head is rather triangular in outline with ridge from snout to blowhole. Fin pronounced and curved. Tail not raised prior to diving. Blow is small and easily missed.

HUMPBACK WHALE *Megaptera novaeangliae*   Length 13–16m
Large and impressive whale with extremely long (3.5–4.5m) flippers, a small dorsal fin, ridged back and well-developed throat pleats. Often raises its tail when it dives. Regularly breaches, lifting almost entire body clear of water. Passes W coast in small numbers on migration, mainly autumn and early winter. Seldom seen close to land.

FINBACK WHALE *Balaenoptera physalus*   Length 17–19m
Second largest living animal. A fast-swimmer with a streamlined body. Seldom stays at surface for long. Features to look for are the tall spout, the relatively small fin, set well back on the body, and asymmetrical colouring on head: lower right jaw is white, lower left is dark. Passes the W coast on migration but seldom comes close to land.

SPERM WHALE *Physeter catadon*   Length 8–11m
Large whale with a disproportionately large, barrel-shaped head. Lower jaw is narrow and toothed. Dorsal fin is tiny but note the 'bumpy' back. Single blowhole directs spout forward and to the left. Associated with deep water where it dives for squid. Seen mainly in offshore waters. Dead specimens are sometimes washed up.

KILLER WHALE *Orcinus orca*   Length 5–9m
The largest 'dolphin'. Noted for its distinctive black, grey and white markings and for the tall dorsal fin (most impressive in males). Feeds mainly on fish, seals and other cetaceans. Typically seen in small groups ('pods'). Occasional around the coast, sometimes lingering where the feeding is good.

LONG-FINNED PILOT WHALE *Globicephala melas*   Length 3–6m
Rather long and slender 'dolphin' with a bulbous head, long flippers and a prominent, curved dorsal fin. Typically seen in schools of 10 or more individuals which occasionally loiter in relatively shallow inshore waters. Fairly common from spring to autumn.

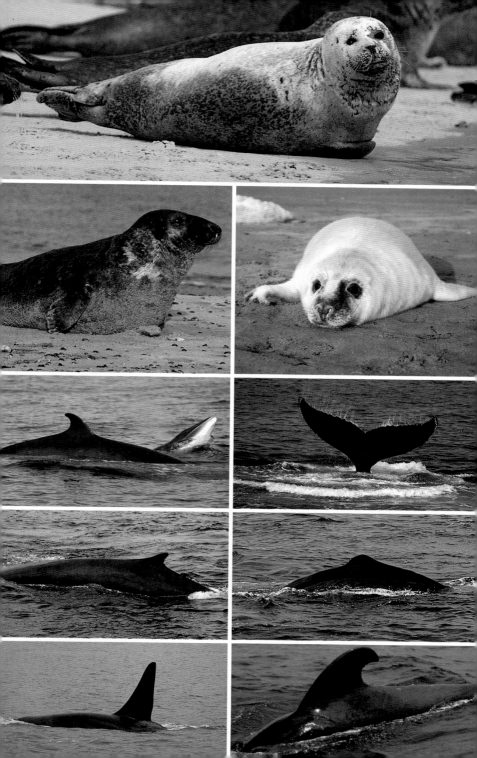

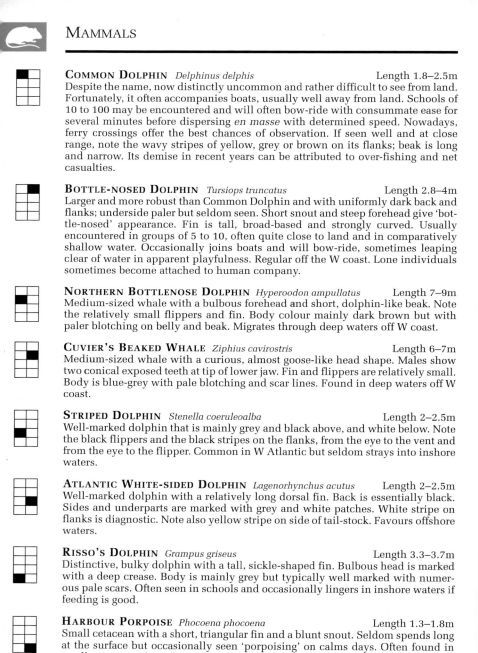

COMMON DOLPHIN *Delphinus delphis*   Length 1.8–2.5m
Despite the name, now distinctly uncommon and rather difficult to see from land. Fortunately, it often accompanies boats, usually well away from land. Schools of 10 to 100 may be encountered and will often bow-ride with consummate ease for several minutes before dispersing *en masse* with determined speed. Nowadays, ferry crossings offer the best chances of observation. If seen well and at close range, note the wavy stripes of yellow, grey or brown on its flanks; beak is long and narrow. Its demise in recent years can be attributed to over-fishing and net casualties.

BOTTLE-NOSED DOLPHIN *Tursiops truncatus*   Length 2.8–4m
Larger and more robust than Common Dolphin and with uniformly dark back and flanks; underside paler but seldom seen. Short snout and steep forehead give 'bottle-nosed' appearance. Fin is tall, broad-based and strongly curved. Usually encountered in groups of 5 to 10, often quite close to land and in comparatively shallow water. Occasionally joins boats and will bow-ride, sometimes leaping clear of water in apparent playfulness. Regular off the W coast. Lone individuals sometimes become attached to human company.

NORTHERN BOTTLENOSE DOLPHIN *Hyperoodon ampullatus*   Length 7–9m
Medium-sized whale with a bulbous forehead and short, dolphin-like beak. Note the relatively small flippers and fin. Body colour mainly dark brown but with paler blotching on belly and beak. Migrates through deep waters off W coast.

CUVIER'S BEAKED WHALE *Ziphius cavirostris*   Length 6–7m
Medium-sized whale with a curious, almost goose-like head shape. Males show two conical exposed teeth at tip of lower jaw. Fin and flippers are relatively small. Body is blue-grey with pale blotching and scar lines. Found in deep waters off W coast.

STRIPED DOLPHIN *Stenella coeruleoalba*   Length 2–2.5m
Well-marked dolphin that is mainly grey and black above, and white below. Note the black flippers and the black stripes on the flanks, from the eye to the vent and from the eye to the flipper. Common in W Atlantic but seldom strays into inshore waters.

ATLANTIC WHITE-SIDED DOLPHIN *Lagenorhynchus acutus*   Length 2–2.5m
Well-marked dolphin with a relatively long dorsal fin. Back is essentially black. Sides and underparts are marked with grey and white patches. White stripe on flanks is diagnostic. Note also yellow stripe on side of tail-stock. Favours offshore waters.

RISSO'S DOLPHIN *Grampus griseus*   Length 3.3–3.7m
Distinctive, bulky dolphin with a tall, sickle-shaped fin. Bulbous head is marked with a deep crease. Body is mainly grey but typically well marked with numerous pale scars. Often seen in schools and occasionally lingers in inshore waters if feeding is good.

HARBOUR PORPOISE *Phocoena phocoena*   Length 1.3–1.8m
Small cetacean with a short, triangular fin and a blunt snout. Seldom spends long at the surface but occasionally seen 'porpoising' on calms days. Often found in small groups. Relatively common in inshore waters but numbers reduced as a consequence of modern fishing activities.

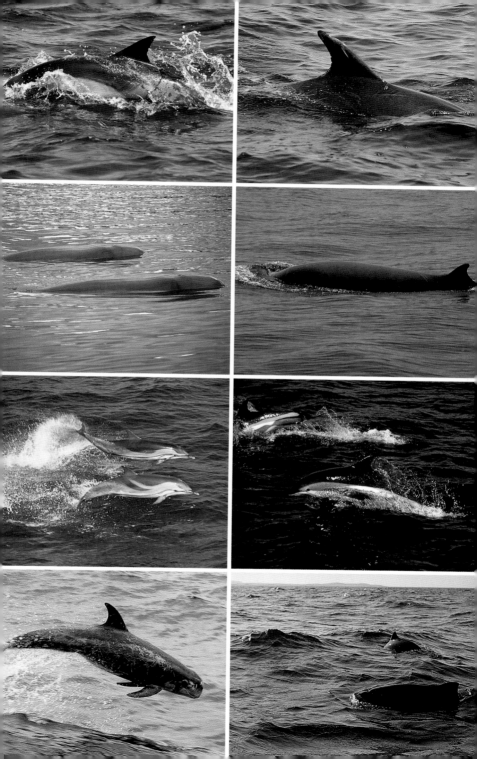

BIRDS

BLACK-THROATED DIVER *Gavia arctica*   Length 60–70cm
Large, robust waterbird that swims buoyantly. Dives frequently and well for fish. Sexes similar. In winter, has mainly blackish upperparts and white underparts; white 'thigh' patch often visible at water level. In summer (sometimes seen in the region), unmistakable with blue-grey head and nape, black throat and black and white stripes on side of neck. Belly and underparts white, wings and upperparts black with chequerboard of white spots on back. Scarce winter visitor to inshore waters, mainly in E.

GREAT NORTHERN DIVER *Gavia immer*   Length 75–85cm
Large and majestic waterbird with a massive bill. Swims and dives well for fish. Summer plumage (sometimes seen in region) has dark head and neck with banded white band on sides. Back is blackish with white spots and breast and underparts are white. Winter bird has darkish upperparts and white underparts. Favours bays and inshore waters. Fairly common winter visitor, especially to W.

RED-THROATED DIVER *Gavia stellata*   Length 55–65cm
Slim, elegant build. Dives well in search of fish. Characteristically holds head and dagger-like bill uptilted. In summer plumage, elegant with blue-grey face and sides to neck, red throat and black and white streaks on nape. In winter, has mainly dark grey upperparts and pale underparts; delicate speckling of white spots on back visible only at close range. Breeds on small lochs in NW Ireland, always within flying range of sea for feeding. More widespread and numerous in winter, in sheltered inshore seas.

GREAT CRESTED GREBE *Podiceps cristatus*   Length 46–51cm
Slender waterbird with long, thin neck. Looks strikingly black and white at a distance although upperparts mainly grey-brown and underparts white. In summer, both sexes acquire prominent orange-rufous ruff and show crest to dark cap. In winter, loses ruff but retains dark cap and suggestion of crest. Builds floating nest among emergent vegetation on lakes. Breeds throughout Ireland. In winter, often around coasts.

SLAVONIAN GREBE *Podiceps auritus*   Length 31–38cm
Dumpy and compact grebe with straight bill. Stunning in breeding plumage (A) with black face, striking golden-yellow ear tufts and plumes, brick-red neck and underparts, and black back. In winter (B), looks black and white with dark cap, nape and back, and pale underparts. Beady red eye seen at close range. Essentially a scarce winter visitor but breeding plumage birds are occasionally seen in late spring.

BLACK-NECKED GREBE *Podiceps nigricollis*   Length 28–24cm
Distinguished at all times from Slavonian Grebe by uptilted bill and steep forehead. In breeding season has black head, neck and back with striking yellow ear tufts. In winter, has dark cap, cheeks, nape and back, and whitish underparts. Rare and erratic breeder in N Ireland. Widespread in winter in coastal seas.

LITTLE GREBE *Tachybaptus ruficollis*   Length 25–29cm
Smallest Irish grebe. Common and widespread. In breeding plumage, has chestnut on cheeks and neck with lime-green spot at base of bill; plumage otherwise brownish except for white powderpuff of feathers at rear end. In winter, has mainly dark brown upperparts and buffish underparts. Nests on ponds, canals and slow-flowing rivers. Presence often indicated by whinnying call. In winter, also on reservoirs around sheltered coasts.

32

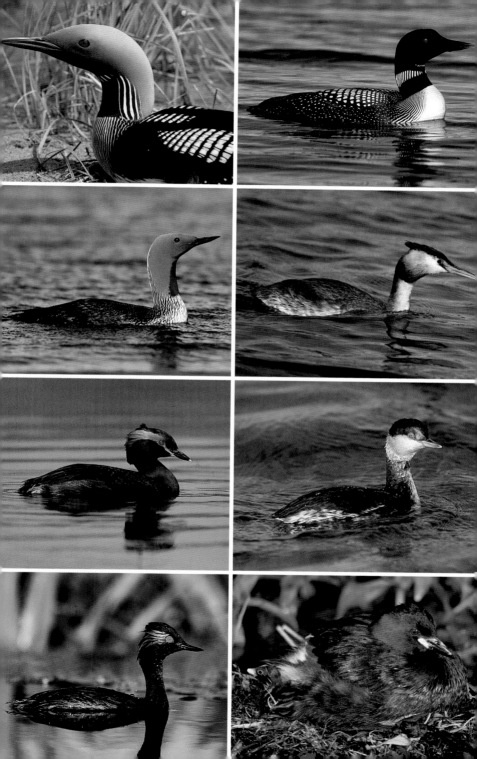

FULMAR *Fulmarus glacialis* Wingspan 1.05–1.10m
Has stiff-winged, gliding flight pattern. Back and upperwings blue-grey but plumage otherwise mostly white except for dark smudge behind eye. When seen closely at nest, note tube nostrils and bill plates. Common around most coasts.

MANX SHEARWATER *Puffinus puffinus* Length 30–38cm
Flies low over water on stiffly held wings showing, alternately, almost black upperparts then white underparts as it banks and glides. Comes ashore to breed in burrows only after complete darkness has fallen. Breeding colonies found on remote islands. Seen at sea from May to September off W and S coasts, and from ferries.

GREAT SHEARWATER *Puffinus gravis* Length 45–50cm
Appreciably larger than Manx Shearwater. Has a dark cap separated from the otherwise dark upperparts by a white collar; note also the white uppertail coverts. Underparts are white. Passes through NW Atlantic in late summer and autumn.

SOOTY SHEARWATER *Puffinus griseus* Length 40–50cm
Medium-sized and narrow-winged seabird. Looks dark at a distance but in good light note the mainly sooty brown plumage and silvery underwing coverts. Glides well. Passes through NW Atlantic in late summer and autumn.

EUROPEAN STORM-PETREL *Hydrobates pelagicus* Length 14–18cm
Smallest Irish seabird. Sooty brown plumage looks completely dark except at very close range. White rump distinctive. Patters feet on water when feeding but otherwise employs strong, direct flight. Occurs in Irish waters from May to September. During daytime, always far out to sea. Visits breeding colonies only after dark.

LEACH'S STORM-PETREL *Oceanodroma leucorhoa* Length 18–20cm
Marginally larger than European Storm-petrel and with longer wings and a forked tail. Note the faint grey upperwing panel. Flight pattern is rather variable, often gliding and switching direction. Seen mainly in autumn gales on W coasts.

GANNET *Morus bassanus* Wingspan 1.65–1.80m
Largest Irish seabird. Has long, narrow wings and cigar-shaped body. Adult recognised by pure white body with black wingtips. Juvenile has dark brown plumage speckled with white dots. Breeds colonially on inaccessible cliffs or rocky islands. Otherwise, only seen at sea. Plunge-dives after fish.

CORMORANT *Phalacrocorax carbo* Length 80–100cm
Large, dark seabird with long, hook-tipped bill. In summer, adult has white patch on face and on thighs; in winter, thigh patch lost and face appears grubby. Juvenile has dark brown upperparts and whitish underparts. Breeds on cliffs and islands on sheltered coasts. In winter, seen on estuaries, reservoirs and rivers.

SHAG *Phalacrocorax aristotelis* Length 65–80cm
Similar to Cormorant but smaller and with green, oily sheen visible in good light. Adult has narrow yellow patch at base of bill, most apparent in breeding season when crest on forehead also seen. Juvenile has dark brown upperparts and pale but grubby underparts. Found throughout year on rocky coasts. Frequently seen perched on rocks with wings outstretched to dry.

GREY HERON *Ardea cinerea* Length 90–98cm
A familiar large, long-legged resident wetland bird. Adult has dagger-like yellow bill and black crest of feathers. Head, neck and underparts otherwise whitish except for black streaks on front of neck and breast. Back and wings blue-grey. Has slow, flapping wingbeats and holds neck folded in hunched 's' shape. Juvenile similar to adult but markings less distinct and plumage more grubby in appearance. Often seen standing motionless for hours on end. Call a harsh and distinctive *frank*. Nests in loose colonies.

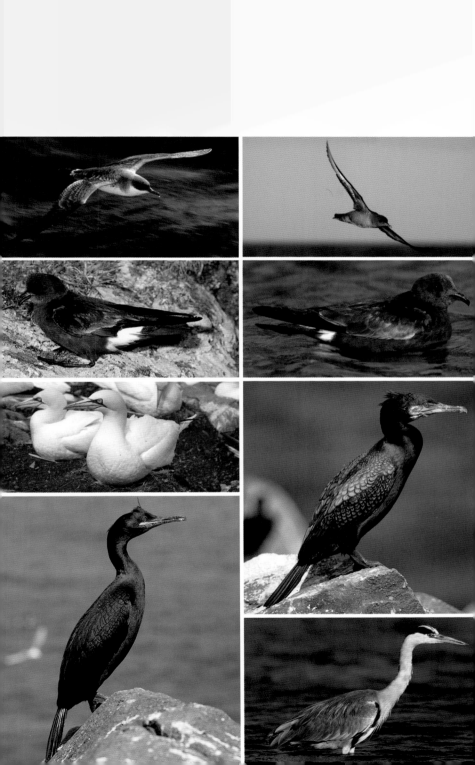

BITTERN *Botaurus stellaris*   Length 70–80cm
Seldom seen due to retiring nature and excellent camouflage afforded by streaked, buffish brown plumage in reedbed habitat. When seen resting, bird has dumpy, hunched appearance. If alarmed, however, adopts upright, sky-pointing posture. Occasionally seen briefly in flight, flying low over tops of reeds on broad, rounded wings and with legs trailing. Invariably associated with extensive, undisturbed reedbeds although harsh winter weather occasionally forces birds into more open wetlands. Feeds mainly on fish and amphibians but will take waterside small mammals too. Scarce winter visitor.

SPOONBILL *Platalea leucorodia*   Length 80–90cm
A scarce visitor to coasts, mainly in E. Often stands for extended periods with bill tucked under wings and then can be confused with resting Little Egret or even Mute Swan if long, black legs not visible. Unmistakable at other times when long, flattened bill with spoon-shaped tip can be seen; bill is black with paler tip in adult but dull pinkish in juvenile. At all times has pure white plumage but breeding adult usually shows dirty yellow flush on breast and around base of bill. Feeds by wading through shallow water, sweeping bill from side-to-side. In flight, has long, bowed wings and keeps head and neck extended with legs trailing. Characteristically flies with shallow wingbeats and extended glides; wings of adult pure white but dark-tipped in juveniles. Food items include small fish, crustaceans, aquatic insect larvae and tadpoles.

LITTLE EGRET *Egretta garzetta*   Length 55–65cm
Formerly classed as a rarity in Ireland, this species is now a regular visitor to many estuaries and coastal waterways. Indeed, it has bred recently in the S, nesting alongside Grey Herons. Unmistakable, pure white, heron-like bird with black, dagger-like bill and long neck. Legs long and black with plastic-yellow feet, these often not visible if bird is wading. In breeding season, acquires head plumes and trailing plumes on back. In flight, trailing legs and yellow feet conspicuous; neck held in hunched 's' shape. Active feeder, often chasing after fish in shallow water and stabbing with great accuracy. At other times, may rest in a hunched-up posture with head and bill hidden, when it could be confused with a swan.

MUTE SWAN *Cygnus olor*   Length 1.50m
Large, distinctive waterbird. The commonest swan in Ireland and the country's only resident species. Adult has pure white plumage, black legs and orange-red bill; black knob at base of bill is smaller in female than male. Young cygnets often seen accompanying mother. Later in season, full-grown juvenile has buffish brown plumage and dirty pink bill. When swimming, bird usually holds neck in elegant curve. In flight, has broad wings and shallow but powerful wingbeats which produce characteristic, throbbing whine; birds otherwise silent. Nests beside lakes and rivers. In winter, also on estuaries and sheltered coasts.

WHOOPER SWAN *Cygnus cygnus*   Length 1.50m
A local winter visitor to Ireland from breeding grounds in Iceland; seen mainly from October to March. Similar size to Mute Swan but has black and yellow bill, triangular in profile; yellow wedge extends beyond nostrils. Holds neck upright. Usually seen in medium-sized flocks comprising many family groups; juvenile birds have pinkish buff plumage and pinkish white bills. Feeds on arable land and in wetlands.

BEWICK'S SWAN *Cygnus columbarius*   Length 1.15–1.25m
The smallest Irish swan. A winter visitor from October to March from Siberian breeding grounds. Adult is pure white with a black and yellow bill, triangular in profile; yellow on bill less extensive than on Whooper Swan and barely reaches nostrils. Juveniles have pinkish buff plumage and pinkish bill; arrive in Ireland and remain together as family parties among larger flocks. Most birds return to traditional wintering sites. Harsh winter weather sometimes forces wintering birds to wander.

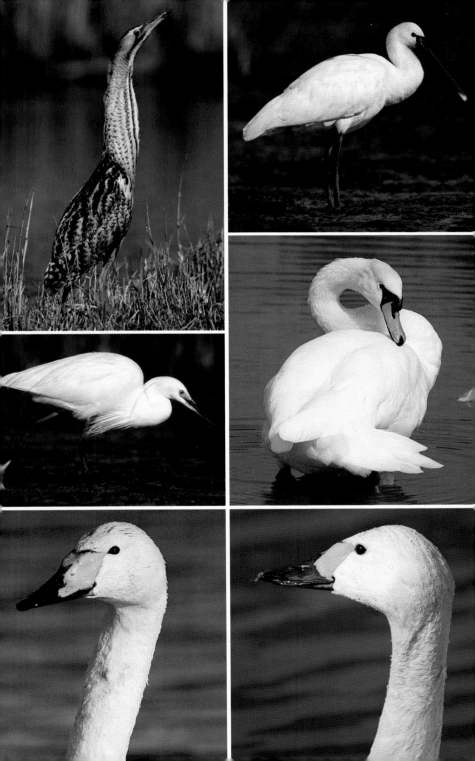

BIRDS

BRENT GOOSE *Branta bernicla*   Length 56–61cm
Winter visitor to Ireland from Arctic breeding grounds; present from October to March. Adult has black head and neck with small white collar; juvenile lacks collar in first half of winter. Pale-bellied race (from Spitzbergen and Greenland) (A) predominates; dark-bellied race (from Siberia) (B) turns up occasionally. Found on estuaries and sheltered coasts. Seen in large, noisy flocks.

BARNACLE GOOSE *Branta leucopsis*   Length 58–69cm
Small, well-marked goose. Winter visitor from Arctic breeding grounds. Seen from October to March usually in large, noisy flocks which utter loud, barking calls. Vast majority of birds return to traditional wintering grounds. Adult has white face, black neck, barred dark grey upperparts and paler barred underparts; juvenile similar but markings less distinct. Flocks feed on coastal grassland and often roost on mudflats. Greenland population winters mainly in Ireland.

CANADA GOOSE *Branta canadensis*   Length 95–105cm
Large, unmistakable goose. Native range is N America but introduced and now established as a resident breeding bird. Has white cheeks on otherwise black head and neck. Body mainly grey-brown except for white under stern; juvenile similar but markings less distinct. Nests beside wetlands. Outside breeding season, seen in flocks on lakes and grassland. In flight, utters loud, disyllabic trumpeting calls.

GREYLAG GOOSE *Anser anser*   Length 75–90cm
Largest of the so-called grey geese and the only one which breeds in Ireland. Precise natural range confused by presence of numerous feral populations. Population swollen in winter, from October to March, by migrants from Iceland; these birds favour coastal grassland and farmland. Has grey-brown plumage which is barred on back and belly; has white stern and dark, wavy feather ridges on neck. Irish birds have pink legs and orange-yellow bill; birds from E Europe (seen occasionally) have pink bills. In flight, has blue-grey panel on leading edge of inner wing.

PINK-FOOTED GOOSE *Anser brachyrhynchus*   Length 60–75cm
A small, compact goose. Bill rather small and shows variable pink band towards tip. Head and neck chocolate-brown, grading to buffish brown on breast and belly. Stern white and back and wings grey. As name suggests, legs and feet pink. A scarce winter visitor from Arctic breeding grounds, present from October to March. In flight, wings look quite pale; flies in extended 'v' formations uttering higher pitched calls than other grey geese. Usually seen in flocks and favours areas of grassland and stubble fields; sometimes seen on wetlands or saltmarshes.

BEAN GOOSE *Anser fabilis*   Length 65–85cm
Superficially similar to Pink-footed Goose but much bulkier and with orange, not pink, band on the more robust bill. Head and neck chocolate-brown grading to paler brown on breast and belly. Stern white and back and wings dark brown; legs bright orange. A scarce winter visitor to Ireland from Arctic breeding grounds; present from October to March. Seen in small flocks, usually grazing on areas of grassland or stubble fields. In flight, looks darker-winged than other grey geese and utters nasal cackling call. Scarce but regular visitor to N and S Ireland.

WHITE-FRONTED GOOSE *Anser albifrons*   Length 65–75cm
Distinctive grey goose. Winter visitor from Arctic breeding grounds, present from October to March. Has brown, barred plumage, darkest on head, neck and back. Stern white and belly has variable, thick black bars; legs orange-yellow. Adult has characteristic white blaze on forehead, absent in juvenile. Birds from Greenland predominate in Ireland and have mainly orange-yellow bills; birds from Siberia (seen occasionally) have pink bills. In flight, utters barking, rather musical calls. Although local, where it does occur it is usually common and seen in flocks of hundreds or even thousands. Visit the Wexford Slobs for particularly good numbers.

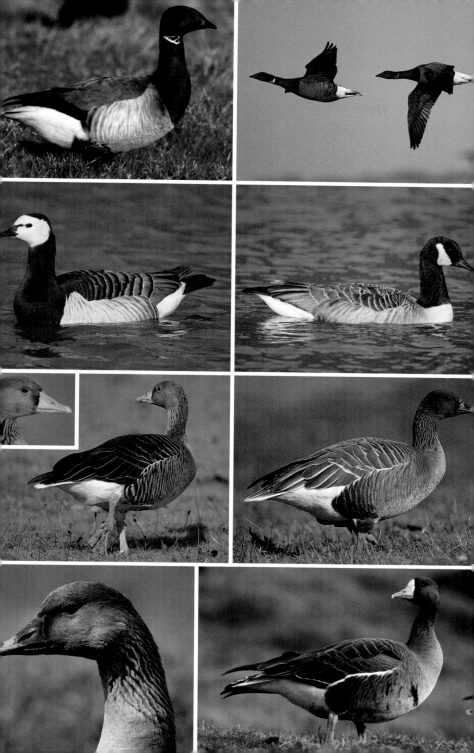

SHELDUCK *Tadorna tadorna*　　　　　　　　　　Length 58–65cm
A large, goose-sized duck with distinctive markings. Adult has glossy green head and upper neck which looks black in poor light. Plumage otherwise mostly white except for orange chest band and black on wings. Legs pinkish red and bill bright red, that of male having knob at base. In flight, looks very black and white. Juvenile has white and buffish brown plumage, the patterning reminiscent of that of adult. Favours coastal habitats including estuaries, mudflats and sheltered coasts where invertebrate food items common. A common breeding bird in undisturbed areas, nesting in burrows. After hatching, black-and-white ducklings follow parents onto mudflats. Common around coasts of Ireland.

MALLARD *Anas platyrhynchos*　　　　　　　　　Length 50–65cm
Widespread and familiar duck. Colourful male (A) has yellow bill and green, shiny head and neck separated from chestnut breast by white collar. Plumage otherwise grey-brown except for black stern and white tail. Female (B) has orange bill and mottled brown plumage. In flight, both sexes have blue and white speculum (patch on trailing edge of inner wing). Resident throughout Ireland in a wide variety of wetlands; often on urban ponds and lakes where usually tame.

GADWALL *Anas strepera*　　　　　　　　　　　Length 46–56cm
Locally common dabbling duck. Breeds locally but more widespread and numerous as a winter visitor. Both sexes have white on speculum, best seen in flight. Male has dark bill and pale brown head. Plumage otherwise grey-brown except for diagnostic black stern, prominent when bird upends to feed. Female similar to female Mallard and best identified by association with male or from glimpse of white speculum. Favours lakes, reservoirs and gravel pits.

WIGEON *Anas penelope*　　　　　　　　　　　Length 45–57cm
Scarce breeding species but locally common winter visitor. Male has orange-red head with yellow forehead, pinkish breast and otherwise finely marked, grey plumage; characteristic black and white stern. In flight, male has bold white wing patch. Reddish brown female best told by association with male. Favours mudflats and saltmarsh; locally also on inland wetlands. Male's *wheeoo* call is evocative of winter estuaries.

TEAL *Anas crecca*　　　　　　　　　　　　　Length 34–38cm
Ireland's smallest duck. Local and rather scarce breeding species but a widespread winter visitor from September to April. Male (A) has chestnut-orange head with yellow-bordered green patch through eye. Plumage otherwise finely marked grey except for black-bordered yellow stern. Grey-brown female (B) best identified by small size and association with male. Green speculum in both sexes. Favours freshwater marshes and estuaries. Rises almost vertically when alarmed.

SHOVELER *Anas clypeata*　　　　　　　　　　Length 44–52cm
Long, flattened bill characteristic. Male striking with green head, black and white on body and reddish chestnut flanks. Female mottled brown. Both sexes have green speculum and pale blue panel on forewing. Scarce breeding species but common winter visitor. Favours wetlands and flooded grasslands.

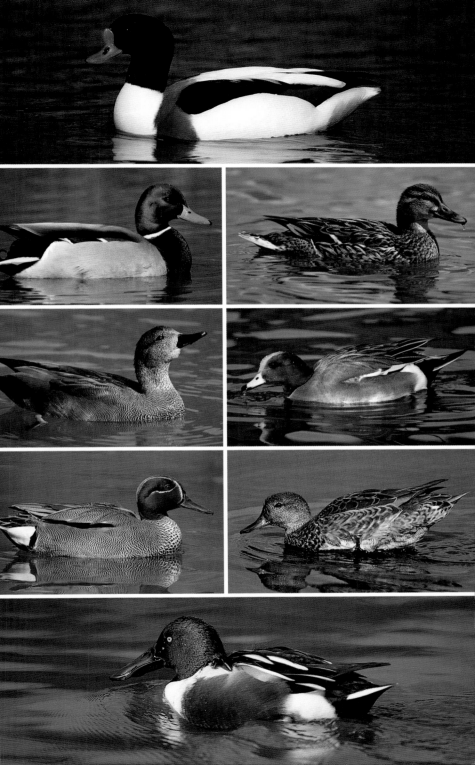

GARGANEY *Anas querquedula* Length 37–41cm

The region's only summer migrant duck. Arrives from African wintering grounds in March and stays until August. Male has reddish brown head and broad white stripe above and behind eye; breast brown but plumage otherwise greyish. Mottled brown female similar to female teal and best told by association with male or by blue forewing panel, seen in male as well. Breeds in very small numbers in wetland but seen more regularly as a passage migrant. Male has distinctive rattling call.

PINTAIL *Anas acuta* Length 51–66cm

Scarce breeding species but widespread and locally common winter visitor. Male is striking with chocolate-brown head and nape, and white breast forming stripe up side of head. Plumage otherwise finely marked grey but shows cream and black at stern and long, pointed tail, often held at angle. Mottled brown female shares male's long-bodied appearance. In winter, found on estuaries, lakes and freshwater marshes.

TUFTED DUCK *Aythya fuligula* Length 40–47cm

Familiar and distinctive diving duck. Widespread and common year-round resident, numbers augmented in winter by continental birds. Male appears black and white but purplish sheen to head visible in good light; has tufted crest. Female has brown plumage, palest on flanks. Shows suggestion of crest and sometimes white at base of bill; latter feature is never as extensive as on female Greater Scaup. Both sexes show yellow eye and black-tipped grey bill. Favours lakes and gravel pits, sometimes in urban settings. Nests in waterside vegetation.

GREATER SCAUP *Aythya marila* Length 42–51cm

Locally common winter visitor to Ireland. Superficially similar to Tufted Duck but larger. Male (A) has rounded, green-glossed head which lacks tufted crest; has dark breast, white belly and flanks, grey back and black stern. Female (B) has brown plumage, palest on flanks, and shows conspicuous white face patch. Usually seen in single-species flocks in coastal waters. Occasionally on coastal lakes and pools, particularly if forced to move by severe weather.

POCHARD *Aythya ferina* Length 42–49cm

Common winter visitor to Ireland but scarce as a breeding species. Male is unmistakable with reddish orange head, black breast, grey flanks and back, and black stern. Female has brown head and breast and grey-brown back and flanks; usually shows pale 'spectacle' around eye. Bill of both sexes dark with pale grey band towards tip. In flight, wings of both sexes look rather uniformly grey-brown. Usually seen in medium- to large-sized flocks and often mixes with Tufted Duck. Dives well and often. Favours lakes and reservoirs.

EIDER *Somateria mollissima* Length 50–70cm

Distinctive and attractive seaduck with large, wedge-shaped bill forming continuous line with slope of forehead. Male (A) has mainly black underparts and white upperparts except for black cap, lime green on nape and pinkish flush on breast. Female (B) is brown and barred. Immatures and moulting adults variably black and white. Found mainly on rocky shores where mussels and other molluscs common. In summer, females often accompanied by 'creche' of youngsters. Breeds mainly along N coasts. In winter, range extends further S.

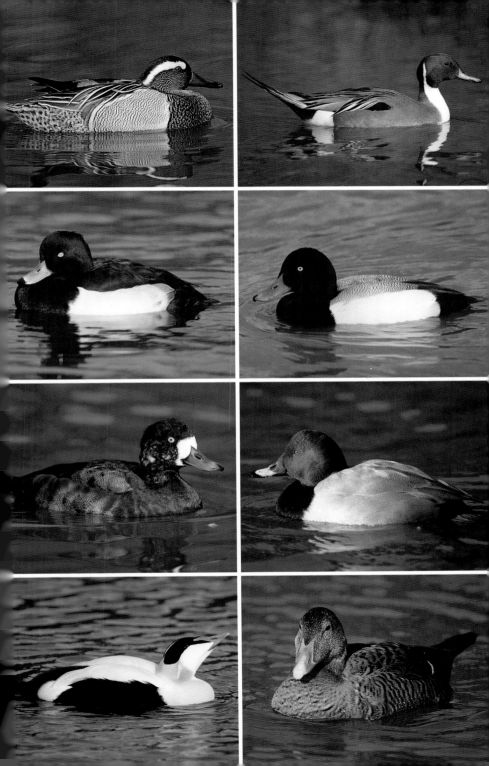

COMMON SCOTER *Melanitta nigra*   Length 44–54cm
Locally common winter visitor to coastal waters and a scarce breeding species. Male is only all-black Irish duck; yellow ridge on bill visible only at close range. Female has mainly dark brown plumage but has noticeably pale cheeks. Invariably seen in flocks out to sea. Dives well after crustaceans and molluscs, especially mussels. In flight, often forms long lines of birds flying low over the water.

VELVET SCOTER *Melanitta fusca*   Length 51–58cm
Appreciably larger than Common Scoter with which it often mixes. Male has mainly all-black plumage but white eye, white patch under eye and yellow patch on bill are visible at considerable distance. Female brownish but with pale patches at base of bill and on cheek. Both sexes have distinctive white wing patch, sometimes visible when swimming but most obvious in flight. Scarce winter visitor.

GOLDENEYE *Bucephala clangula*   Length 42–50cm
Distinctive diving duck, male (A) with mainly black and white plumage; has rounded, green-glossed head with yellow eye and conspicuous white patch at base of bill. Female (B) has grey-brown body plumage separated from dark brown head by pale neck. Both sexes show white on wings in flight. Scarce breeding bird but a common winter visitor, found on lakes and coasts.

LONG-TAILED DUCK *Clangula hyemalis*   Length 40–47cm
Attractive diving duck. Winter visitor from northern breeding grounds between October and March. Male characterised by long, narrow tail and has mainly black and white plumage with buffish wash on face and pink band on bill in winter (A) occasionally seen in summer plumage (B) when head, neck and breast all-black except for pale patch on face. Female lacks male's long tail streamers and has brown and white plumage, darker on head and neck during summer months. Invariably found on coastal waters in restless flocks. Sizeable flocks seen only off the N.

GOOSANDER *Mergus merganser*   Length 58–66cm
Large, elegant sawbill duck, almost exclusively associated with fresh water. Male is unmistakable with red, serrated-edged bill, green-glossed head, white body and black back. Looks very white at a distance but close view reveals feathers to be flushed with delicate shade of pink. Female also has reddish bill but head is orange-red with shaggy crest; body plumage greyish, palest on breast. Both sexes show considerable amount of white on wings in flight. Swims buoyantly. Scarce winter visitor.

RED-BREASTED MERGANSER *Mergus serrator*   Length 52–58cm
Both sexes have shaggy crest on back on head. Male has narrow red bill, green head, white neck and orange-red breast; flanks grey and back black. Female has red bill, dirty orange head and nape except for pale throat, and greyish buff body plumage. Immature male resembles female. In flight, both sexes show white speculum broken by black line; male also has large patch of white on forewing. Nests in tree holes beside rivers. In winter, widespread around sheltered coasts and estuaries.

SMEW *Mergus albellus*   Length 38–44cm
Small but stunning sawbill duck. Irregular winter visitor. Recorded mainly between November and February if severe weather affects mainland Europe. Unmistakable male (A) looks pure white at a distance but closer view reveals black patch through eye and black lines on breast and back. Female (B) and immature birds known as 'redheads' and have orange-red cap and nape contrasting with white cheeks and throat; body plumage grey-brown. Favours fish-rich waterbodies.

RUDDY DUCK *Oxyura jamaicensis*   Length 35–43cm
N American species with small feral populations. Compact, dumpy diving duck with short, stiff tail often held cocked at an angle. Male has orange-chestnut body plumage, white stern, white cheeks and black cap; bill is a striking plastic-blue colour. Female has mainly grey-brown plumage with paler cheeks.

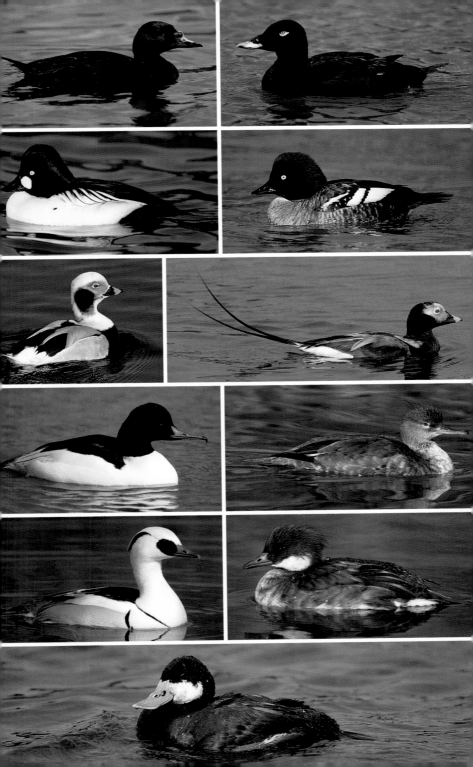

OSPREY *Pandion haliaetus* Wingspan 1.45–1.60m
Impressive fish-eating raptor, usually seen near water. A scarce passage migrant in the region. In flight, looks superficially gull-like with pale underparts and long, narrow wings; shows dark primary feathers and dark carpal patch. Upperparts brown except for pale crown. Catches fish by plunging into water, talons first.

RED KITE *Milvus milvus* Wingspan 1.45–1.65m
Told in flight by long, bowed wings and deeply forked tail, constantly twisted to aid flight control. Seen perched (A), bird looks reddish with pale grey head; yellow feet and black-tipped yellow bill only visible at close range. Seen from below in flight (B), shows reddish chest, pale grey patches on wings and grey tail; from above, tail looks red and wings brown with dark flight feathers. Scarce and occasional visitor.

SPARROWHAWK *Accipiter nisus* Wingspan 60–75cm
Common and widespread raptor. Recognised by relatively short, rounded wings and proportionately long, barred tail. Male appreciably smaller than female and has blue-grey upperparts and barred reddish brown underparts. Female has grey-brown upperparts and pale underparts with narrow brown barring. Catches small birds in flight by low-level, surprise attacks. Formerly heavily persecuted by gamekeepers but now protected and numbers are recovering to former levels. Year-round resident of woodland and farmland.

GOSHAWK *Accipiter gentilis* Wingspan 1–1.15m
Similar in silhouette to Sparrowhawk but much larger. Male noticeably smaller than female but both sexes have grey-brown upperparts and pale underparts with dark barring. Staring yellow eyes, white stripe over eye and yellow legs only visible at close range. Usually seen circling high above when white under-tail feathers often fluffed out. Favours extensive forests. Medium-sized birds such as Woodpigeons are caught in flight. Scarce and occasional visitor.

BUZZARD *Buteo buteo* Wingspan 1.15–1.25m
Formerly much persecuted despite fact that diet comprises mainly earthworms and carrion in many areas. Draws attention to itself in flight with mewing calls. Rides thermals with ease on broad, rounded wings, held in 'v' shape when soaring. Perches for long periods on posts and dead branches. Plumage colour extremely variable but usually some shade of brown; wings barred and tail uniformly banded. Prefers farmland for feeding with nearby woods for nesting. Locally common only in N.

HONEY-BUZZARD *Pernis apivorus* Wingspan 1.35–1.50m
Superficially similar to Buzzard but underparts paler; shows dark carpal patches on wings. Tail proportionately longer with two broad bands near base and broad, dark terminal band; these features separate it from Buzzard. In flight, head appears narrow, pointed and pale. Soars on flat wings. Scarce passage migrant, mainly along E coast.

GOLDEN EAGLE *Aquila chrysaetos* Wingspan 1.90–2.5m
A huge raptor. Adult soars on long, parallel-sided wings that are constantly flexed as bird rides upcurrents. Tail relatively long. Against sky, adult looks uniformly dark. Immature shows white patch at base of tail and on wings. Brown plumage and golden-yellow mane seen only on perched birds at close range. Scarce and occasional visitor to NE.

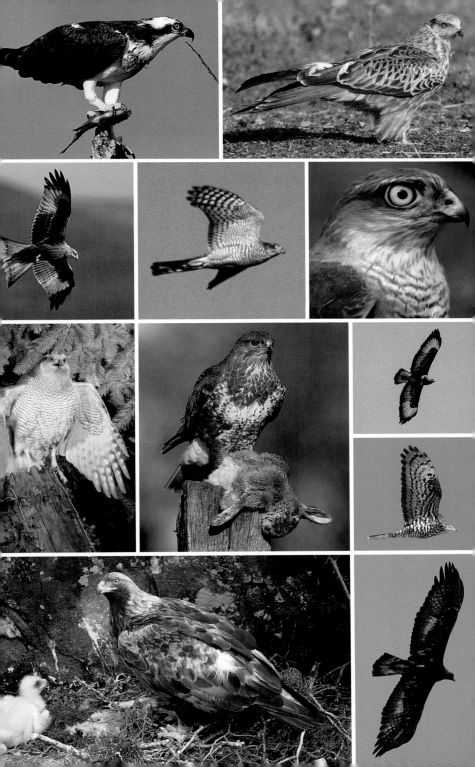

MARSH HARRIER *Circus aeruginosus*　　　　　　Wingspan 1.10–1.25m
Associated with wetlands, particularly extensive reedbeds. Flies at slow speed just above tops of reeds, occasionally stalling to drop on prey. Long-winged and long-tailed. Male reddish brown except for blue-grey head and grey, unbarred tail; in flight, has grey and reddish brown areas on wings and black wingtips. Female dark brown except for pale leading edge to wing and pale cap and chin. Scarce passage migrant.

HEN HARRIER *Circus cyaneus*　　　　　　Wingspan 1.0–1.20m
Scarce, but the most likely harrier species to be seen in Ireland. Male has pale blue-grey plumage except for white belly, white rump and black wingtips. Female and immature (A and B) brown with barring on wings and tail, and white rump. Favours expansive areas of heathland, moor and grassland. Flies low and at slow speed, often quartering ground in search of small mammals and birds. Breeds on upland moors and winters mostly at lower elevations, numbers swollen by continental birds. Uses communal winter roosts.

MONTAGU'S HARRIER *Circus pygargus*　　　　　　Wingspan 1.0–1.20m
Both sexes superficially similar in size and appearance to corresponding sex of Hen Harrier. Male (A) has blue-grey plumage but with less-pronounced white rump than male Hen Harrier and with single dark bar on upperwing and two dark bars on underwing. Female (B) has pale brown plumage with barring on wings and tail. Scarce passage migrant, typically seen flying low over coastal grassland.

PEREGRINE *Falco peregrinus*　　　　　　Wingspan 95–115cm
Ireland's most impressive falcon. Formerly rare but now rather widespread. Adult has dark blue-grey upperparts and pale, barred underparts; face shows characteristic dark mask. Juvenile has browner plumage with streaked underparts. Sometimes seen perched on rocky crag but more usually spotted in flight with broad, pointed wings and relatively long tail. Soars with bowed wings but stoops on prey such as pigeons with wings swept back. Locally common on cliffed coasts; less so in upland areas inland.

HOBBY *Falco subbuteo*　　　　　　Wingspan 70–85cm
Small but elegant falcon. Adult has dark blue-grey upperparts and pale, dark-streaked underparts. At close range, dark moustachial markings, white cheeks and reddish orange 'trousers' visible. In flight, has anchor-like outline with narrow, swept-back wings and long tail. In spring, hunts dragonflies over lakes. Later in season, catches birds such as Swallows on the wing. A scarce passage migrant.

MERLIN *Falco columbarius*　　　　　　Wingspan 60–65cm
Ireland's smallest raptor. Male (A) has blue-grey upperparts and buffish, streaked and spotted underparts. Female (B) has brown upperparts and pale underparts showing large, brown spots. Seldom soars but more usually seen flying low over ground in dashing flight, in pursuit of prey such as Meadow Pipits. Perches on rocks and fenceposts for long periods. Breeds on upland moors. In winter, many birds move S to coastal districts.

KESTREL *Falco tinnunculus*　　　　　　Wingspan 65–80cm
Ireland's commonest and most familiar raptor and the only one that habitually hovers and hunts along roadside verges. Male has spotted, orange-brown back, blue-grey head and blue-grey tail with terminal black band. Female has barred, brown plumage. Nests in trees and on cliff ledges but also in man-made settings such as window ledges on office blocks. Feeds primarily on small mammals but takes insects in summer months.

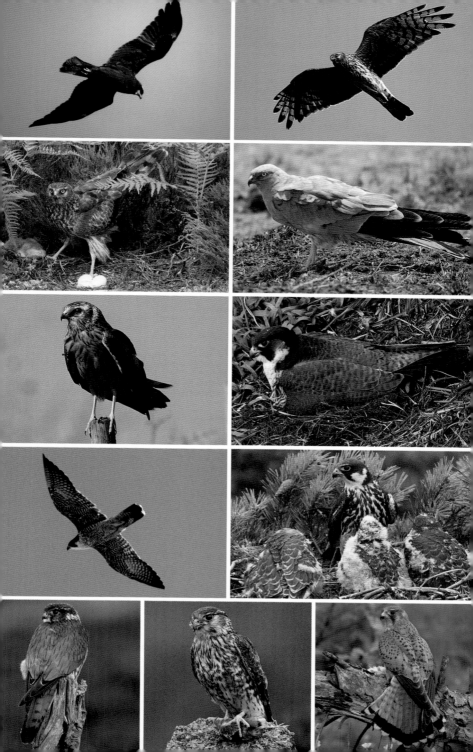

RED GROUSE *Lagopus lagopus* ssp. *scoticus*　　Length 37–42cm
Familiar gamebird of heather moorland. Male has chestnut-brown plumage and conspicuous red wattle over eye. Female has marbled, grey-brown plumage. Takes to the air explosively and, in flight, both sexes show uniformly dark wings; wingbeats rapid but interspersed with long glides. *Go-back go-back go-back* call evocative of moorland.

PHEASANT *Phasianus colchicus*　　Length 53–59cm
Introduced from native Asia but now well established and numbers continually boosted by release of captive-bred birds for shooting. Adult male (A) familiar and unmistakable with red wattle, blue-green sheen on head, orange-brown body plumage and long, orange tail; some birds show white collar. Female (B) is mottled buffish brown with shorter tail than male. Feeds on shoots, seeds and invertebrates. Widespread and common.

GREY PARTRIDGE *Perdix perdix*　　Length 29–31cm
A scarce and declining gamebird. Grey plumage is finely marked. Male has orange-buff face, dark chestnut mark on belly, maroon stripes on flanks and streaked back. Female similar but markings less distinct. Usually seen in small groups feeding in arable fields. When disturbed, birds take to air with whirring, noisy wings.

WATER RAIL *Rallus aquaticus*　　Length 23–28cm
Shy and retiring wetland species whose pig-like squealing calls are heard more than bird itself is seen. Has long, reddish bill, reddish legs and mainly blue-grey underparts and reddish brown upperparts; shows black and white barring on flanks. Favours extensive reedbeds, marshes and overgrown margins of water-cress beds. Local breeding species but more widespread in winter due to influx of continental birds.

CORNCRAKE *Crex crex*　　Length 27–30cm
Has declined catastrophically in recent years and now confined to a few areas in the W. Summer visitor from May to September. Sandy brown plumage; in flight, shows chestnut on wings and dangling legs. Favours hay meadows that are undis-turbed during nesting season; early rolling of grassland or cutting for silage largely responsible for species' decline. Male's *crek-crek* call uttered tirelessly throughout night. Bird is shy and difficult to observe.

MOORHEN *Gallinula chloropus*　　Length 32–35cm
Widespread and familiar wetland bird. Often wary but in urban areas can become rather tame. Adult has brownish wings but otherwise mainly dark grey-black plumage. Has distinctive yellow-tipped red bill and frontal shield on head, white feathers on sides of undertail and white line along flanks. Legs and long toes yellowish. Juvenile has pale brown plumage. Swims with jerky movement and with tail flicking; in flight, shows dangling legs.

COOT *Fulica atra*　　Length 36–38cm
Often found in similar habitats to Moorhen but easily told by all-black plumage and white bill and frontal shield to head. Has lobed toes which facilitate swim-ming. Utters distinctive, loud *kwoot* call. Feeds by upending or making shallow dives in water but also grazes waterside grass. Builds mound nest of waterplants often in full view. Common year-round resident of lakes and freshwater marshes. Numbers boosted in winter by influx of continental birds; then forms large flocks.

OYSTERCATCHER *Haematopus ostralegus*　　Length 43cm
Distinctive and noisy wader. Widespread around coasts. Favours undisturbed shores for nesting. More widespread outside breeding season on beaches and estuaries; sometimes roosts in large flocks. Has distinctive black and white plumage with white wingbars seen in flight; winter birds have white half-collar. Long pinkish legs. Stout red bill used to feed on molluscs.

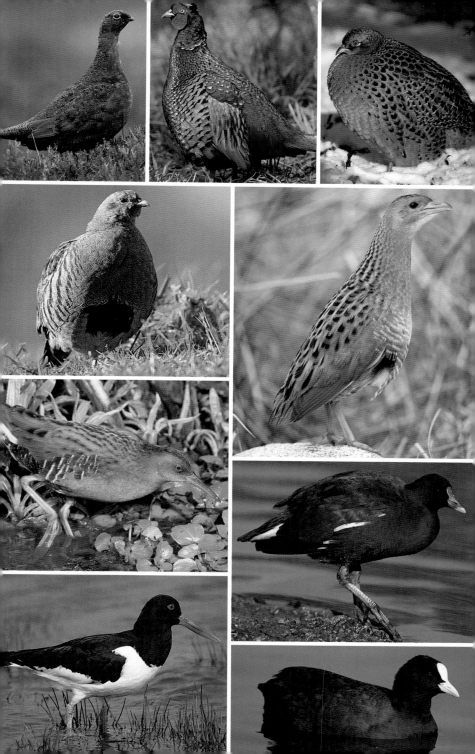

AVOCET *Recurvirostra avosetta*   Length 43cm
Easily recognised by black and white plumage, long, blue legs and long, upcurved
bill that is swept from side-to-side through water when feeding. Favours shallow
saline lagoons and estuaries. Scarce winter visitor. Symbol of RSPB.

LAPWING *Vanellus vanellus*   Length 30cm
Formerly more numerous but still common in many parts of Ireland. Breeds on
undisturbed farmland and on moors and open country throughout. N birds move
S outside breeding season and, in winter, population is boosted by influx of continental birds. Looks black and white at a distance but in good light has green, oily
sheen on back; winter birds have buffish fringes to feathers on back. Spiky crest
feathers longer in male than female. In flight, has rounded, black and white wings
and flapping flight. Loud *pee-wit* call.

RINGED PLOVER *Charadrius hiaticula*   Length 19cm
Small, dumpy wader associated mainly with coastal habitats. Breeds on sandy
and shingle beaches but excluded from some areas by human disturbance. Outside breeding season, found on estuaries, mudflats and beaches. Adult has sandy
brown upperparts and white underparts with continuous black breast-band and
collar. Black and white markings on face and white throat and nape. Legs orange-
yellow and bill orange with black tip. Juvenile similar but dark markings less distinct and has dull legs and dark bill. Shows white wingbar in flight at all ages.
Feeds in distinctive manner, usually running along beach as if powered by clock-
work and then standing still for few seconds before picking food item from sand.
Frequently utters soft *too-it* call.

GOLDEN PLOVER *Pluvialis apricaria*   Length 28cm
Both sight and sound of this species are evocative of desolate upland areas that
are favoured during breeding season. Male in breeding season (A) has spangled
golden upperparts with white on underparts and black belly grading to greyish on
neck and face; breeding birds from N Europe with black face, neck and belly
sometimes seen on migration. Female has similar upperparts to male but less distinct dark markings on underparts. Winter birds (B) lose black on underparts. In
flight, shows white 'armpits' at all times. Nests on moorland. Winters throughout
much of Ireland, mainly on farmland; flocks sometimes mix with Lapwings.
Numbers boosted at this time by influx of birds from continent. Flight call *peeoo*.
Song haunting and fluty.

GREY PLOVER *Pluvialis squatarola*   Length 28cm
Non-breeding visitor from high Arctic nesting grounds, present usually from September to April. Almost exclusively coastal, favouring estuaries and mudflats. In
winter plumage (A), looks grey overall, with upperparts spangled black and white
and underparts whitish. Juvenile birds can have buffish wash to upperparts leading to confusion with Golden Plover. Stockier Grey Plover shows black 'armpits'
in flight at all times. Birds in breeding plumage (B) sometimes seen in spring and
autumn and have striking black underparts, separated from grey upperparts by
band of white. Trisyllabic *pee-oo-ee* call is like human wolf-whistle. Generally
solitary. Feeds in plover manner: runs for several yards, tilts forward and remains
still before leaning forward to pick morsel from mud.

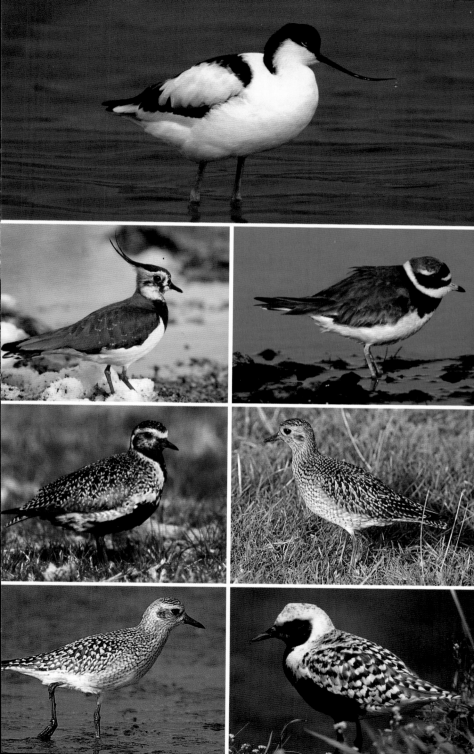

DUNLIN *Calidris alpina*   Length 17–19cm
A local but fairly common breeding species on moors in NW but an abundant, flock-forming winter visitor to most estuaries and mudflats where it is generally the most numerous species of wader. Variable in terms of body size and bill length but bill usually long and slightly downcurved. Winter bird (A) has rather uniform grey upperparts and white underparts. In breeding season (B), shows chestnut-brown back and cap, streaked underparts and black belly. Juvenile has dark spots on flanks with grey, black and chestnut on back. Call *priit*.

CURLEW SANDPIPER *Calidris ferruginea*   Length 19cm
Very similar to Dunlin but has more markedly downcurved bill and conspicuous white rump, latter best seen in flight. Scarce passage migrant, mainly in autumn *en route* from Arctic breeding grounds to African wintering range. Most birds seen are juvenile with pale-edged feathers on back giving scaly appearance, and white belly and buffish breast. In winter, adult bird has grey upperparts and white underparts. In breeding plumage, head, neck and underparts become orange-red; both adult plumages are occasionally encountered in migrants.

LITTLE STINT *Calidris pusilla*   Length 13cm
Tiny wader, recalling miniature, short-billed Dunlin. Scarce passage migrant, most records are of juvenile birds in autumn. Favours margins of freshwater pools mainly near coasts. Constant and frantic activity is a clue to identity. Juvenile has chestnut-brown upperparts and cap, white underparts, and distinctive buff patch on shoulder; usually shows white 'v' on back. Adult seen comparatively rarely in region: in winter, has grey upperparts and white underparts; acquires reddish orange wash to head and neck in breeding plumage.

KNOT *Calidris canutus*   Length 25cm
Non-breeding visitor to estuaries and mudflats and present from September to April. Seen mostly in winter plumage with uniform grey upperparts and white underparts. Bill black and comparatively short; legs dull yellowish. Juvenile similar but buffish and pale feather margins on back give scaly appearance. Brick-red breeding plumage birds sometimes seen in spring and autumn. In winter, forms large flocks which fly in tight formation.

SANDERLING *Calidris alba*   Length 20cm
Common winter visitor to sandy beaches around Ireland, present from September to April. At a distance, winter bird looks very white; at close range shows grey upperparts, white underparts, black 'shoulder' patch, and black legs and bill. Invariably seen in small flocks running at great speed and feeding along edge of breaking waves. Usually tolerant of human observers. Confusing, reddish brown breeding plumage birds sometimes seen in spring and autumn.

PURPLE SANDPIPER *Calidris maritima*   Length 21cm
Widespread but local winter visitor, present from September to April; commonest in N and W. Recalls dumpy Dunlin but has yellow-based bill, yellow legs, blue-grey upperparts and pale underparts. Favours rocky shores and headlands, feeding in small, unobtrusive flocks just where waves are breaking. In spring, acquires purple sheen to grey feathers that can only be seen at close range.

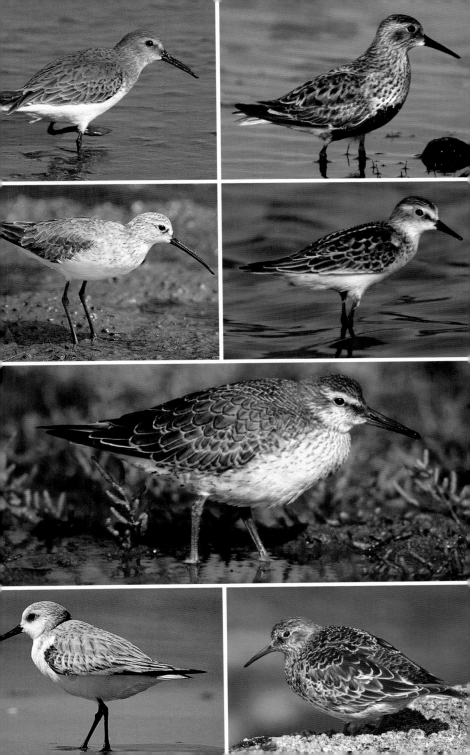

REDSHANK *Tringa totanus*   Length 28cm
Local but fairly common resident breeding species but a numerous winter visitor.
Utters a loud, piping alarm call. Easily recognised by its red legs and long, red-
based bill. Plumage mostly grey-brown above and pale below with streaks and
barring; plumage more heavily marked in breeding season. In flight, shows white
trailing margin to wing. In breeding season, favours flood meadows, marshes and
moors. In winter, mainly coastal.

SPOTTED REDSHANK *Tringa erythropus*   Length 30cm
In non-breeding plumage, superficially similar to Redshank but larger and with
proportionally longer red legs and red-based bill. Breeds in Scandinavia and seen
in Ireland as a passage migrant and occasional winter visitor. Winter and incomplete breeding plumage birds (A) have pale grey upperparts and whitish underparts. Breeding plumage adult (B) sometimes seen on migration and easily
recognised by almost all-black plumage. In flight, all plumages have uniform grey-
brown wings. Flight call distinctive *chewit*.

GREENSHANK *Tringa nebularia*   Length 30–31cm
Attractive, long-legged wader. Passage migrant and local winter resident. In all
plumages, has yellowish green legs and long, slightly upturned bill with grey
base. Winter adult is pale grey above with white underparts; in breeding plumage,
some feathers on back have dark centres. Juvenile has brownish upperparts. In
flight, all birds show uniform wings and white rump and wedge up back. Feeds
in deliberate, probing manner. Flight call a distinctive, trisyllabic *tchu-tchu-tchu*.

PECTORAL SANDPIPER *Calidris melanotos*   Length 19–22cm
Recalls a Dunlin but note the yellow legs. Most records occur in autumn and
relate to juveniles that have grey, brown and black feathers on the back, all with
pale margins; these align to form striking white stripes. The face, neck and breast
are streaked but there is a clear pectoral demarcation from the clean white underparts. Rare visitor from N America. Favours freshwater pools and marshes.

BUFF-BREASTED SANDPIPER *Tryngites subruficollis*   Length 18–20cm
Rare visitor from N America, mostly in autumn. Looks overall pale buff but back
feathers are rather dark greyish with pale margins creating a scaly appearance.
The pale buffish head, and whitish eyering, emphasise the rather large, dark eye.
Note the yellow legs. Favours short grassland.

GREEN SANDPIPER *Tringa ochropus*   Length 23cm
Fairly common passage migrant and a local but regular winter visitor to S from
September to April. Always seen near fresh water. When flushed looks black and
white with striking white rump; flight usually accompanied by yelping, trisyllabic call. Has curious gait, constantly bobbing body up and down. Straight bill
and yellowish green legs seen at close range.

WOOD SANDPIPER *Tringa glareola*   Length 20cm
Similar to Green Sandpiper but has longer, yellow legs. Scarce passage migrant to
shallow wetlands, mostly in August and September with juvenile birds predominat-
ing. Has brownish, spangled upperparts, brightest in juvenile birds, and a pale belly.
In flight, shows conspicuous white rump. White tail has narrow terminal bars, these
greater in extent than on Green Sandpiper. Underwings are mostly white whereas on
similar Green Sandpiper these are black. Flight call is a distinctive *chiff-chiff-chiff*.

COMMON SANDPIPER *Actitis hypoleucos*   Length 20cm
Summer visitor to N and W, nesting near river or lake margins. Occurs elsewhere on
passage. Scarce wintering species, mainly on coasts in S. Small, plump-bodied
wader with rather elongated tail end. Upperparts warm brown and underparts white;
clear demarcation between dark breast and white belly. Usually adopts horizontal
stance and constantly bobs body. Flies on bowed, fluttering wings low over water.

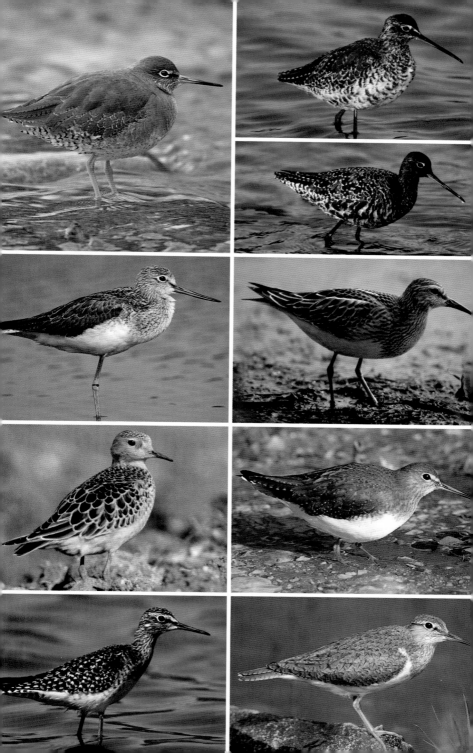

CURLEW *Numenius arquata*   Length 53–58cm
Widespread year-round resident with numbers boosted by influx of continental birds in winter months. The commonest large wader with a long, downcurved bill. Plumage mainly grey-brown with streaked and spotted underparts and pale belly. In flight, wings uniformly dark brown but shows white rump and wedge on lower back; tip of tail has dark, narrow barring. Breeds on damp grassland and moors. In winter, usually found on coasts, preferring estuaries and mudflats. Uses long, blue-grey legs to wade in deep water and bill to probe for worms. Utters *curlew* call and has a bubbling song.

WHIMBREL *Numenius phaeopus*   Length 41cm
Superficially similar to Curlew but appreciably smaller and with distinctive head pattern comprising two dark lateral stripes on otherwise pale crown. Presence also detected by bubbling call, usually of seven notes descending slightly in pitch from start to finish. A rather scarce passage migrant in spring and autumn, almost always on coasts and favouring both rocky shores and sheltered estuaries. Winters in Africa. Song is rather confusingly similar to that of Curlew.

BLACK-TAILED GODWIT *Limosa limosa*   Length 41cm
Large, long-legged wader with incredibly long, very slightly upturned bill that is pinkish at base. In all plumages, recognised in flight by black tail, white rump and conspicuous white wingbars. In winter plumage, has rather uniformly grey-brown upperparts and pale underparts. In breeding plumage, acquires orange-red wash to head and neck with feathers on back having black centres. Juvenile has buffish wash on neck and breast. Rare breeding species favouring flood meadows. Locally common, flock-forming migrant and winter visitor to mudflats and estuaries; in winter, widespread except in N.

BAR-TAILED GODWIT *Limosa lapponica*   Length 38–42cm
Superficially similar in outline to Black-tailed Godwit but with more dumpy appearance. Easily told in flight in all plumages by uniformly dark wings and white rump grading to narrow-barred tail. Passage migrant and winter visitor from high-Arctic breeding grounds. Juvenile and adult in winter have rather curlew-like plumages, grey-brown above and pale below; upperparts more strongly marked in juvenile birds. Breeding plumage birds, with brick-red on head, neck and underparts, sometimes seen in late spring or early autumn. Locally common on estuaries and coastal grassland, mainly from September to April.

TURNSTONE *Arenaria interpres*   Length 23cm
Common, non-breeding visitor to coasts all around Ireland. Can be seen in most months but majority of birds arrive from August onwards and stay until late April. Unobtrusive and well camouflaged and so easily overlooked. Winter adult and juvenile variably marked with black, brown and white on upperparts, usually showing clear demarcation between dark breast and white underparts. In breeding plumage, has orange-brown feathers on back and black and white markings on head. Legs reddish orange. Bill short and triangular; effective when turning stones and tideline debris in search of sandhoppers.

RUFF *Philomachus pugnax*   Length 23–29cm
Very variable wader; proportionately small head its most consistent character. Male in breeding plumage (A) has coloured facial warts, ruff and head plumes, used in communal display. Each male is slightly different but ruff feathers usually uniform black, white or chestnut. Outside breeding season, male recalls smaller female (Reeve, B) with grey-brown upperparts, pale underparts, dark bill and dull orange legs. Buffish juvenile has pale feather margins on back giving scaly appearance. Passage migrant and scarce winter visitor near coasts.

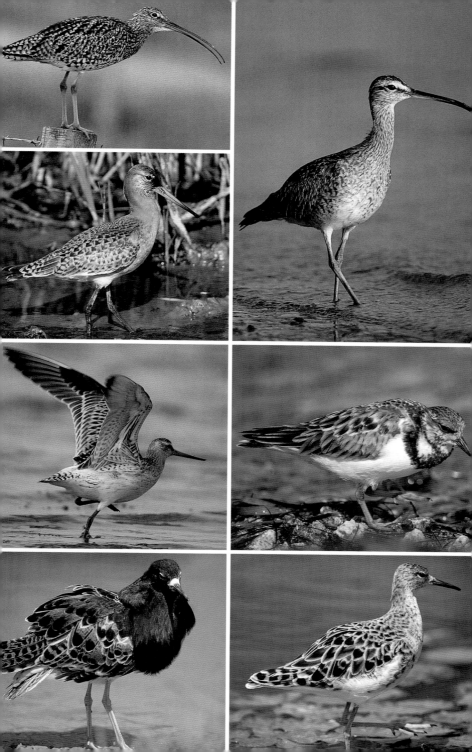

GREY PHALAROPE *Phalaropus fulicarius*   Length 20–21cm
Charming and unusual wader. Typically seen swimming, often spinning rapidly
or picking insects off water surface. Scarce passage migrant, mostly in autumn, and
very occasional winter visitor to Ireland. Oceanic outside breeding season and so
most usually seen near coasts during or after severe gales. Small groups sometimes seen flying past headlands in W of Ireland; storm-driven birds may feed on
coastal pools, sometimes further inland. Usually tame. Mainly seen in winter
plumage with grey upperparts, white underparts and black 'panda' mark around
eye. Brick-red breeding plumage birds seen only very rarely.

RED-NECKED PHALAROPE *Phalaropus lobatus*   Length 18cm
In winter plumage, similar to Grey Phalarope and best told by needle-like bill and
more black and white appearance. In breeding season, female has white throat
and red neck; male similar but duller. Habitually swims. Rare and erratic breeder
in N Ireland. Present on breeding grounds from May to August. Favours coastal
moorland pools; often difficult to see among emergent vegetation. Tame but easily disturbed at nest and protected by law. Oceanic outside breeding season and
most frequently seen around Irish coasts as a scarce passage migrant and rare winter visitor.

WOODCOCK *Scolopax rusticola*   Length 34cm
Dumpy, short-legged, long-billed wader. Marbled chestnut, black and white plumage
affords superb camouflage among fallen leaves. Large eyes placed high on head
give bird almost complete all-round vision. Nests on ground in woodlands
throughout Ireland; camouflage and habit of sitting tight make it difficult to see.
Easiest to observe on spring evenings when male performs 'roding' display over
treetops; presence also indicated by soft duck-like calls and explosive squeaks.
Feeds mostly between dusk and dawn, probing damp ground for worms. Resident
Irish birds joined by continental visitors in winter.

SNIPE *Gallinago gallinago*   Length 27cm
Easily recognised, even in silhouette, by dumpy, rounded body, rather short legs
and incredibly long, straight bill. Feeding method characteristic: probes vertically
downwards with bill in soft mud, in manner of sewing machine. In good light,
has buffish brown plumage, beautifully patterned with black and white lines and
bars; has distinctive dark stripes on head. Locally common breeding species on
marshy ground and moors in many parts of Ireland. More widespread in winter
and found in a range of wetland habitats; resident Irish birds are then joined by
visitors from N Europe. Utters one or two *kreech* calls when flushed. Performs
'drumming' display in breeding season, humming sound produced by vibrating
tail feathers.

JACK SNIPE *Lymnocryptes minimus*   Length 19cm
Appreciably smaller than Snipe. Bill shorter than relative but plumage similar
although stripes on head more distinctive. Fairly common winter visitor to
marshes in Ireland from October to March. Easily missed because feeds unobtrusively among vegetation and very reluctant to fly, preferring to crouch motionless
until danger passes. If flushed, however, rises silently and drops back into cover
after short distance. Pumps body up and down as it walks.

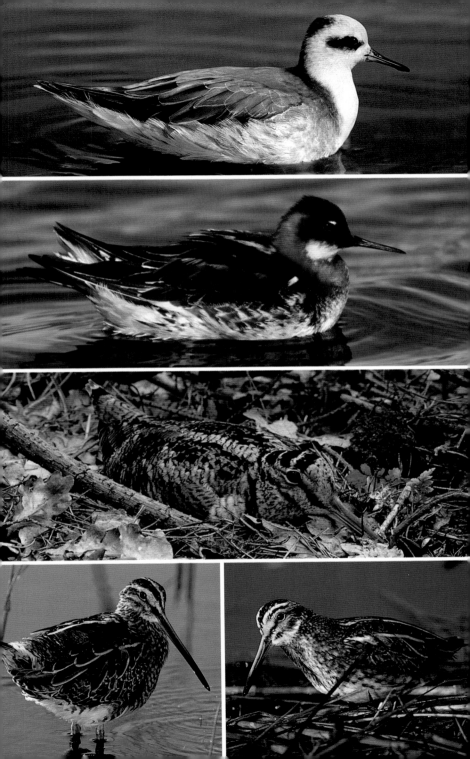

BLACK-HEADED GULL *Larus ridibundus*   Length 35–38cm
The most numerous small gull in Ireland. Plumage varies according to age and time of year but at all times easily recognised in flight by white leading edge to wings. Adult has grey back and upperwings, white underparts, red legs and a reddish bill. In winter (A), has dark smudges behind eye but in summer (B) acquires chocolate-brown, not black, hood. Juvenile birds, seen in late summer, have marbled brown and grey upperparts; in first-winter plumage, shows dark-tipped pinkish bill with grey and brown on upperwings. Breeds beside upland lakes and on coastal marshes. Outside breeding season, found on a wide range of freshwater habitats as well as around coasts. Will visit urban areas and frequents car parks and ornamental lakes; also follows ploughs on arable land.

MEDITERRANEAN GULL *Larus melanocephalus*   Length 36–38cm
Scarce but increasingly frequent visitor to Ireland, mostly in S and E. Superficially similar to Black-headed Gull but separable in all plumages with care and experience. Most consistent features of adult are pure white wings. In winter (A), has dark smudges around eyes but in summer (B) acquires black hood, eyes defined by white 'eyelids'. Blood-red bill is stouter than that of Black-Headed and has dark band near tip. In first winter, similar to first-winter Black-headed but dark streaks on head and white 'eyelids' give menacing look to face. In second winter, similar to winter adult but, at rest, shows dark tips to primaries. Outside breeding season, often found with Black-headed Gulls.

LITTLE GULL *Larus minutus*   Length 28cm
The world's smallest gull. Has buoyant, tern-like flight and favours coastal and marine habitats outside breeding season. Does not nest in Ireland but seen as an uncommon passage migrant in spring and autumn. Also occurs as a scarce and erratic winter resident in Irish Sea. Small size is always a good character when seen with Black-headed Gulls, but adult Little Gull's sooty black underwing is its most diagnostic feature; wings look rounded and have narrow, white trailing margin. In winter, has dark smudges on face but in summer acquires dark hood; legs and bill reddish at all times. Juvenile has striking black bars along wings and black-tipped tail; can be confused only with juvenile Kittiwake.

COMMON GULL *Larus canus*   Length 41cm
Despite name, generally not our most numerous gull. Recalls small version of Herring Gull, adult having grey back and upperwings with white body plumage. Otherwise white, although in winter back of head and nape have dark streaks. In flight, black wingtips show white spots. Legs greenish yellow and bill yellow in summer but duller in winter with dark band near tip. First-winter bird has bands of grey, brown and black on upperwings. Breeds mainly in N and NW Ireland, mostly on the coast but sometimes inland beside fresh water. In winter, widespread around most coasts and also feeds inland, sometimes following ploughs with Black-headed Gulls; outside breeding season, resident Irish birds joined by influx of migrants from N Europe. Calls include a nasal *heeow*.

KITTIWAKE *Rissa tridactyla*   Length 41cm
Visit almost any Irish seabird colony and you will not need to be told this bird's name. Loud *kittee-wake kittee-wake* calls ring from the cliffs and are highly evocative of coasts of Ireland. Adult (A) easy to recognise with blue-grey back and otherwise white body plumage; bill yellow and legs and feet black. In flight, recalls adult Common Gull but wingtips pure black, as if dipped in black ink. Immature (B) is striking in flight with black zigzag markings on upperwings, black nape band and black tip to tail. Arguably, our only true seagull, with non-breeding period spent entirely at sea; confident flight even in the roughest weather. Nests mostly on precipitous cliff ledges overhanging sea.

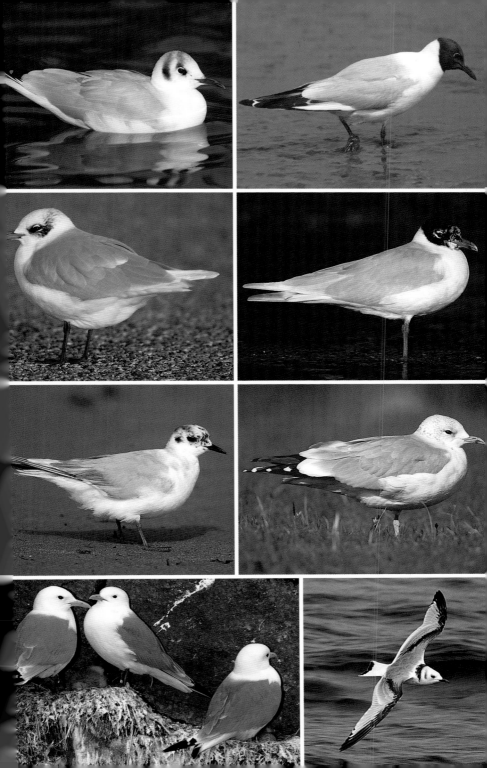

RING-BILLED GULL *Larus delawarensis*   Length 42–48cm
A medium-sized gull from N America; intermediate in character between Herring and Common Gulls. Adult has grey back and upperwings but otherwise plumage is white. Note the yellowish legs and eyes; bill is yellow with a black subterminal band. Immature birds resemble their Common Gull counterparts but the back is paler grey and note the stouter bill. Mainly coastal; a rare visitor.

HERRING GULL *Larus argentatus*   Length 56–66cm
A familiar and noisy bird, generally the most numerous large gull species. Common around coasts of Ireland but also inland at rubbish tips. Adult has blue-grey back and upperwings with white-spotted, black wingtips; body otherwise white but sometimes has dark streaks on nape in winter. Legs pink and bill yellow with orange spot near tip. Juvenile mottled grey-brown with dark bill.

LESSER BLACK-BACKED GULL *Larus fuscus*   Length 53–56cm
Similar proportions to Herring Gull but adult has dark grey back and upperwings. Grey tone varies, however, so yellow legs are best diagnostic features; bill yellow with orange spot near tip. In flight, upperwing colour usually a shade paler than black wingtips. Juvenile closely resembles other large gull juveniles with mottled brown plumage; acquires adult plumage over subsequent two years. Colonial breeding species, mostly on W and N coasts. A partial migrant, numbers in winter boosted by birds from N Europe. Mainly coastal but also inland on fields.

GREAT BLACK-BACKED GULL *Larus marinus*   Length 64–79cm
Our largest gull. Superficially similar to Lesser Black-backed but always looks more bulky and has pink, not yellow, legs. Bill massive and upperwings appear uniformly black in flight. Immatures resemble other large gulls of similar ages and best told by size and bulk. Breeds in small numbers around coasts of Ireland; least frequent in E. Laughing call is noticeably deeper than that of other gulls.

GLAUCOUS GULL *Larus hyperboreus*   Length 62–68cm
A winter visitor to Ireland from Arctic breeding grounds in variable numbers. Easiest to see in N with most records between November and February. Marginally smaller than Great Black-backed Gull but adult close in appearance to Herring Gull except for diagnostic white wingtips. Legs pink and bill massive. Immature birds have very pale buffish grey plumage, pale wingtips and dark-tipped pink bills.

ICELAND GULL *Larus glaucoides*   Length 52–60cm
A winter visitor to Ireland in variable numbers and easiest to find between November and March. Similar in all plumages to Glaucous Gull but appreciably smaller with a proportionately smaller bill and longer wings. Adult has mainly grey back and wings but with white flight feathers. Body is otherwise white although head and neck sometimes show dark streaking. Immature birds have extremely pale plumage that acquires adult's grey elements over two years. Mainly coastal.

GREAT SKUA *Catharacta skua*   Length 58cm
Chocolate-brown plumage recalls that of immature gull but relatively large head, bulky proportions and dark legs and bill soon confirm identity. In flight, shows conspicuous white patches near wingtips. Observed around coasts on migration, most easily from headlands in W during onshore gales.

ARCTIC SKUA *Stercorarius parasiticus*   Length 46cm
Buoyant and graceful on the wing. Adult has narrow pointed wings with white patch near tip and shows pointed tail streamers extending beyond wedge-shaped tail. Two different adult plumages: sooty brown dark phase and pale phase with dark cap, back and wings but plumage otherwise white except for yellow-buff wash to nape. Juvenile has chocolate-brown, heavily barred plumage and pointed, wedge-shaped tail. Seen around coasts on migration in spring and autumn. Feeds by parasitising other seabirds.

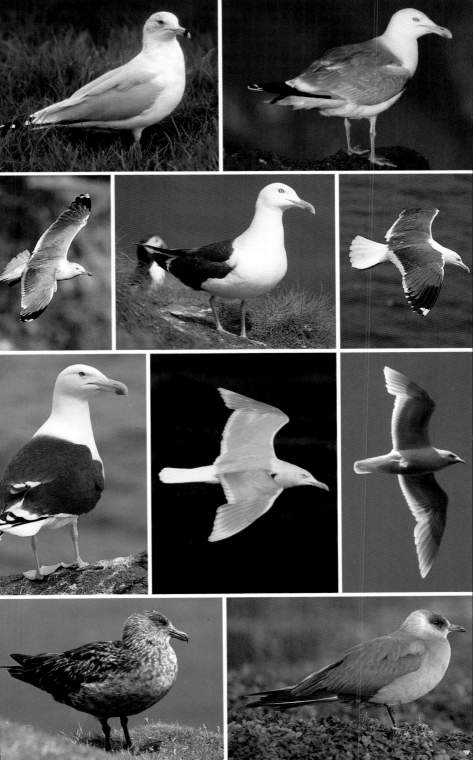

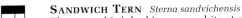

SANDWICH TERN *Sterna sandvichensis* Length 41cm
Elegant seabird, looking pure white at a distance. Summer visitor, seen on coasts from April to September. Easily recognised in flight by powerful, buoyant flight on long, narrow wings and frequently uttered, harsh *churrick* call. Back and upperwing of adult pale grey but plumage otherwise white except for dark crest; in winter plumage, sometimes seen in birds in autumn, loses dark cap but retains black on nape. Legs black and bill black with yellow tip. Juvenile has scaly-looking back and dark bill. Breeds very locally in large colonies on undisturbed sand or shingle beaches around Irish coast.

COMMON TERN *Sterna hirundo* Length 35cm
Common and widespread around coasts of Ireland from mid-April to late August; also seen on large inland lakes and rivers. Appearance typically tern-like with pale grey back and upperparts and otherwise white plumage. Red legs relatively long compared to similar Arctic Tern. Bill orange-red with black tip. Black cap present in summer adult but incomplete in winter plumage. In flight, outer primaries appear dark on upperwing. Juvenile has scaly appearance to back and dark leading edge to inner wing. Colonial nester on undisturbed shingle and sandy beaches. Plunge-dives for surface-feeding fish.

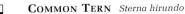

ARCTIC TERN *Sterna paradisaea* Length 35cm
Superficially very similar to Common Tern and told at close range by uniformly blood-red bill and very short, red legs. Underparts pale greyish, becoming paler on throat and cheeks. In flight, wings have a translucent look. Summer visitor to coasts of Ireland from wintering grounds in Antarctic seas. Present from April to September and most numerous in N and W. Breeds in large colonies, mainly on undisturbed shingle and sandy beaches. Plunge-dives for fish. Utters harsh *krt-krt-krt* call at intruders near nest.

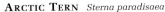

ROSEATE TERN *Sterna dougallii* Length 38cm
Rare breeding tern in Ireland and threatened throughout world range. Rather similar to Arctic and Common Terns but adult has red-based black bill, long tail streamers and pinkish flush to breast and underparts in summer. In autumn, birds usually lack long tail streamers. Looks rather short-winged in flight compared to other terns. Present from May to August at breeding colonies. Sometimes parasitises other terns returning to colonies with fish. Utters distinctive disyllabic call.

LITTLE TERN *Sterna albifrons* Length 24cm
The smallest tern, easily recognised by size and colour alone. At close range, black-tipped yellow bill, yellow legs and white forehead of adult can be seen. Juvenile has dull legs and bill colour and scaly appearance to back. Present around coasts from April to August. A scarce breeding species with scattered colonies around Irish coast. Excluded from many potentially suitable shingle and sandy beaches by human disturbance. Flight buoyant and frequently hovers before plunge-diving into shallow water for small fish and shrimps. Utters raucous *crree-ick* and other calls.

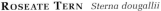

BLACK TERN *Chlidonias niger* Length 24cm
A scarce passage migrant, mostly in May and August. Single birds usually seen but very occasionally occurs in small flocks. Adult in breeding plumage has black body, dark grey wings and white stern and tail. From mid-summer onwards, body plumage of adult white except for black on nape and crown. Juvenile similar to winter adult but feathers on back have pale margins and tail and rump grey. Occurs near fresh water, often reservoirs and lakes. Hunts insects over water with buoyant flight. Could turn up almost anywhere.

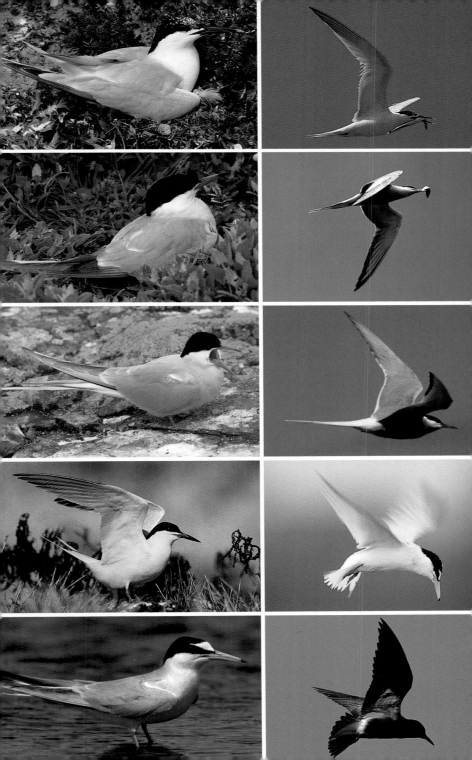

BIRDS

RAZORBILL   *Alca torda*   Length 41cm
Easiest to see at breeding colonies where present from May to August. In summer, has black head and upperparts and white underparts. Bill large and flattened; at close range, vertical ridges and white lines can be seen. In winter, acquires partly white face; spends most of non-breeding period far out to sea and so this plumage seldom seen on healthy or live birds. Flies on whirring wings. Nests among boulders and in rock crevices on cliffed coasts, mainly in N and W Ireland. Because pairs are usually more spaced out, never as visibly numerous as Puffin or Guillemot. Like other auks, suffers badly in oil-spill incidents. Feeds mainly on fish, including sandeels, these carried back to chick in bill.

GUILLEMOT   *Uria aalge*   Length 42cm
A common auk among larger seabird colonies. Where cliff ledges are suitable, hundreds or even thousands of birds sometimes stand side-by-side. Only visits land during breeding season, from May to August, thereafter being found at sea, sometimes in comparatively inshore waters. In summer, can be recognised by chocolate-brown head and upperparts (darker in northern birds than southern ones) and white underparts; bill dagger-like and straight. Some birds show white 'spectacle' around eye. In winter, has white cheeks marked by dark line from eye. Lays single, pear-shaped egg, sometimes on narrowest of ledges. Tiny youngster flings itself into sea to join parents long before it is fully fledged. Breeding colonies mainly in N and W Ireland.

PUFFIN   *Fratercula arctica*   Length 30cm
Endearing and unmistakable seabird, often allowing close and excellent views at colonies. Has mainly black upperparts but dusky white face and white underparts. Legs orange-red and bill huge and flattened, marked with red, blue and yellow. Winter adult and juvenile have grubby-looking faces and smaller, duller bills. Comes ashore only during breeding season from May to August. Nests in burrows on sloping, grassy cliffs and islands, usually in large colonies. In June and early July, returns to burrows carrying several fish, usually sandeels, in bill. Numbers and range reduced in recent years but still very locally common in N and W Ireland. Utters strange, groaning calls.

LITTLE AUK   *Alle alle*   Length 20cm
The smallest auk in Europe. Does not breed in Ireland but seen as a winter visitor, in variable numbers, from its high-Arctic breeding grounds. Winters mainly far out to sea and so usually observed during or after severe gales or prolonged cold weather. In outline, remarkable for seeming to have almost no neck and for its tiny, stubby bill. In flight, body can appear almost spherical with short wings and whirring wingbeats. Winter plumage birds have black cap, nape and back, and white underparts; white lines on wings and tiny white crescent above eye visible only at extremely close range. Makes long, frequent dives and so can be very difficult to find or relocate.

BLACK GUILLEMOT   *Cepphus grylle*   Length 34cm
Distinctive at all times of year. In summer, has mainly sooty black plumage except for striking white patch on wing, conspicuous both at rest and in flight. In winter, upperparts look scaly grey and underparts white; white wing patch still visible but black element of plumage restricted to wingtips and tail. At close range, red legs and orange-red gape can be seen. Usually seen singly or in small groups, often quite close to shore off rocky coasts and jetties. Rather local but occurs around much of Irish coast. Dives well in search of bottom-dwelling fish such as Butterfish. Breeds in fairly small and loose colonies on rocky coasts. Utters high-pitched call.

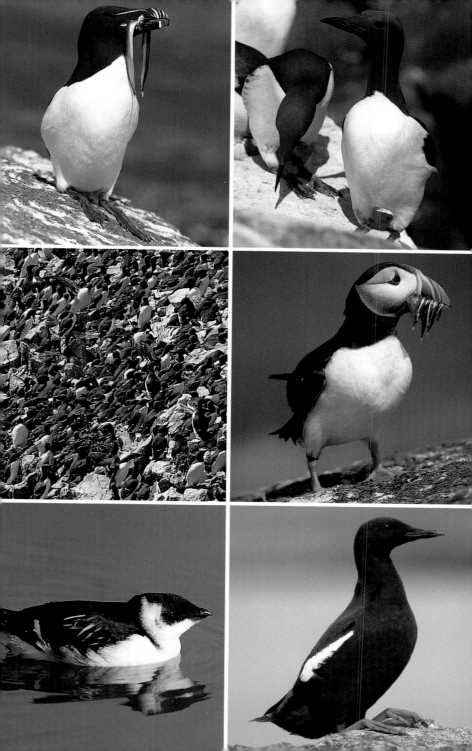

FERAL PIGEON/ROCK DOVE *Columba livia*   Length 33cm
A descendant of native Rock Dove, the Feral Pigeon is now widespread and common, mainly in urban areas. Rock Dove now local and scarce, confined to rocky coasts mainly in N, S and W Ireland. In some parts of Ireland, Feral Pigeon has returned to its ancestral haunts on cliffs. True Rock Dove recognised by blue-grey plumage, two broad, black wingbars, white rump and black-tipped grey tail. A few Feral Pigeons show ancestral-type plumage but most exhibit wide range of additional or alternative colours and features.

STOCK DOVE *Columba oenas*   Length 33cm
A fairly common bird of farmland and open country with scattered woodland. Found locally throughout Ireland and least numerous in N. Plumage lacks any prominent features and species recognised by uniform blue-grey upperparts and lack of white rump and white barring on neck; shows two narrow black wingbars on upper surface of inner wing. Feeds in flocks in arable fields, sometimes with Woodpigeon. Nests in tree holes and, during breeding season, utters diagnostic and repetitive *ooo-look* call.

WOODPIGEON *Columba palumbus*   Length 41cm
A plump, medium-sized pigeon, common and familiar on farmland and increasingly seen in urban areas too. Plumage mainly blue-grey with pinkish maroon on breast. Has distinctive white patch on side of neck and, in flight, shows prominent, transverse white wingbars. When disturbed, flies off with loud clattering of wings. During breeding season sings typical series of *oo-OO-oo*, *oo-oo* phrases. Builds twig nest on horizontal branches; despite apparent fragility, often still intact, and more visible, in winter. Feeds on seeds and shoots.

COLLARED DOVE *Streptopelia decaocto*   Length 32cm
Despite being first recorded in the late 1950s, now common and widespread in most parts of Ireland although seldom far from habitation. A common garden bird in many areas, feeding on lawns and coming to food; often seen in pairs. Has sandy-brown plumage with pinkish flush to head and underparts. Shows dark half-collar on nape. Black wingtips and white outer tail feathers most noticeable in flight. In display, glides on bowed wings. Somewhat irritating song comprises much repeated *oo-oo-oo* phrase. Feeds on seeds and shoots.

CUCKOO *Cuculus canorus*   Length 33cm
Males's familiar *cuck-oo* call heard more often than bird itself is seen for six weeks or so after arrival in late April; female utters bubbling call. Secretive but sometimes perches on fenceposts. In low-level flight, recalls Sparrowhawk. Male and most females have grey head and upperparts, underparts being white and barred. Juvenile and some females have brown, barred plumage, juvenile with pale nape patch. Widespread in Ireland. Nest parasite of songbirds.

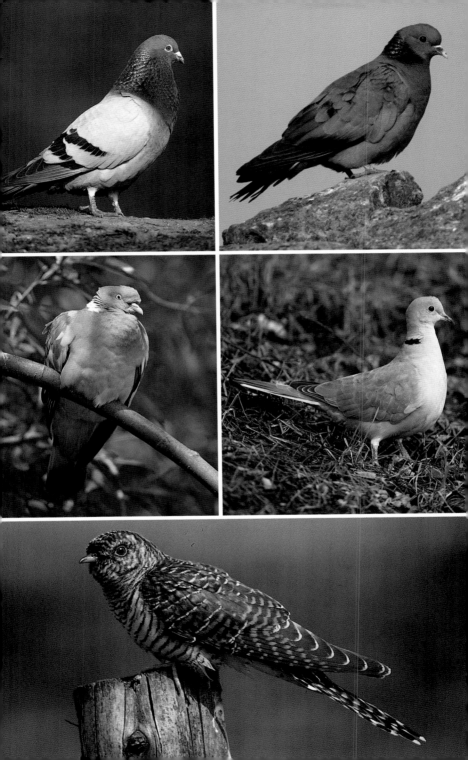

NIGHTJAR *Caprimulgus europaeus* Length 27cm
Nocturnal habits and cryptic markings make this a difficult bird to see in day-time. Brown, grey and black plumage resembles wood bark. Sits motionless on ground, even when closely approached. At dusk, takes to wing and hawks insects. Looks long-tailed and narrow-winged in flight; male has white on wings and tail. Male utters churring song for hours on end at night. Rare summer visitor to S and W, present May–August.

BARN OWL *Tyto alba* Length 34cm
A beautiful owl, sadly decidedly scarce in most areas. Usually seen at dusk or after dark, caught in car headlights, when appears ghostly white; flight leisurely and slow on rounded wings. Only when seen perched can the orange-buff upper-parts, speckled with tiny black and white dots, be appreciated; facial disc heart-shaped and white. Feeds mainly on small mammals located by quartering meadows, farmland and roadside verges; seen all too often as a road casualty. Sometimes nests in tree holes but, as name implies, often uses barns and other buildings and readily takes to nesting platform provided for this purpose. Blood-curdling call one of the most frightening sounds of the countryside at night. Widespread in Ireland although absent from many upland areas.

LONG-EARED OWL *Asio otus* Length 36cm
Active only in complete darkness but, fortunately for birdwatchers, sometimes conspicuous at daytime roosts in winter. Has dark brown upperparts and paler underparts, the whole body, however, being heavily streaked; underwings look very pale when seen in flight. At close range, staring orange eyes and long 'ear' tufts can be seen; these may be raised or lowered, depending on bird's mood. When alarmed, bird sometimes adopts strange, elongated posture. Often nests in dense conifer woodlands. Roosts in similar habitats and occasionally in hawthorn hedges or damp woodland. Widespread in Ireland throughout year although precise distribution poorly known due to difficulty in locating species. Rather silent but young utter calls like rusty gate hinge.

SHORT-EARED OWL *Asio flammeus* Length 38cm
A large and well-marked owl, often seen feeding in daylight. Favours areas of open grassland for hunting small mammals and birds and often perches on fenceposts providing good views for observers. Plumage mainly buffish brown but heavily marked with dark spots and streaks. Seen head-on, round facial disc, short 'ear' tufts and staring yellow eyes are noticeable. Flight is leisurely and slow on long, rounded-tipped wings with pale undersides. Usually quarters ground at low level but displaying birds sometimes rise to considerable heights. Rare in summer. More widespread in winter but still generally scarce.

HOOPOE *Upupa epops* Length 25–29cm
Unmistakable, exotic-looking bird. Note the buffish pink plumage, erectile crest and long, slightly downcurved bill. Black and white patterns on the wings and tail are most striking in flight. Favours short grassland and probes ground for food. Rare passage migrant, seen mainly spring and autumn, typically near coasts.

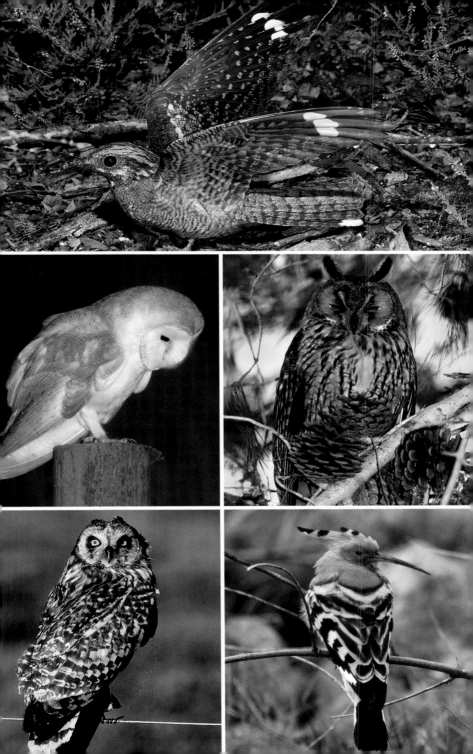

KINGFISHER *Alcedo atthis*   Length 16–17cm
Dazzlingly attractive bird. Has orange-red underparts and mainly blue upperparts; electric blue back seen to best effect when bird observed in low-level flight speeding along river. Invariably seen near water and uses overhanging branches to watch for fish. When feeding opportunity arises, plunges headlong into water, catching fish in bill. Nests in holes excavated in riverbank. Widespread and fairly common on fish-rich rivers and lakes. In winter, sometimes seen on sheltered rocky coasts, especially in cold weather.

SWIFT *Apus apus*   Length 16–17cm
A familiar summer visitor to most of Ireland, present from mid-May to early August. Nests in loft spaces and church roofs. Otherwise spends its entire life in the air. Easily recognised in flight by its anchor-shaped outline and all-black plumage; has paler throat. Tail slightly forked. Parties of Swifts are frequently seen hawking insects above towns and over fresh water. Presence often indicated by loud, shrill screaming. Claws on the tiny feet enable bird to cling to walls. Legs are useless for walking.

SWALLOW *Hirundo rustica*   Length 19cm
A common summer visitor to most of Ireland. The arrival of the first birds in early April heralds the start of spring. Most birds depart for their African wintering grounds in August and September but small numbers often linger late into autumn. Recognised in flight by pointed wings and tail with long streamers; these are shorter in juvenile and female than male. Has blue-black upperparts and white underparts except for brick-red throat and forecrown. Frequently utters its *vit* call in flight and, when perched on overhead wires, male sings a twittering song. Nests under eaves and in barns and sheds, building half cup-shaped nest of mud attached to wall or rafter. Prior to migration in autumn, gathers in sizeable flocks.

SAND MARTIN *Riparia riparia*   Length 12cm
A widespread and fairly common summer migrant to most parts of Ireland. Often one of the first spring migrants to arrive, with small numbers appearing in March, and one of the last to leave, October sightings on coasts in S not being uncommon. Recognised in flight by its sandy-brown upperparts and white underparts with brown breast-band; tail short and slightly forked. Juvenile has pale margins to feathers on back giving scaly appearance. Breeds colonially, birds excavating nest burrow in sandy bank of river. Usually seen feeding around lakes and reservoirs, hawking for insects low over the water, sometimes even picking them from the surface.

HOUSE MARTIN *Delichon urbica*   Length 12–13cm
A familiar and welcome summer visitor to most parts of Ireland; often found breeding in surprisingly urban settings. Most birds present from mid-April to August. Adult easily identified in flight by white underparts and blue-black upperparts showing conspicuous white rump; juvenile similar to adult. As its name suggests, most birds breed on outsides of houses, constructing almost spherical mud nests under eaves and overhangs in loose colonies; in more natural settings, birds sometimes use cave entrances or cliffs as sites for nest construction. Soon after arrival in spring, birds can be seen gathering sticky mud from puddles; this is carried back to nest site and applied, mixed with saliva. Like other hirundines, often seen feeding over freshwater pools and lakes, catching insects in low-level flight. Frequently utters its *prrrit* call in flight. Usually delivers twittering song from overhead wire near to nest site.

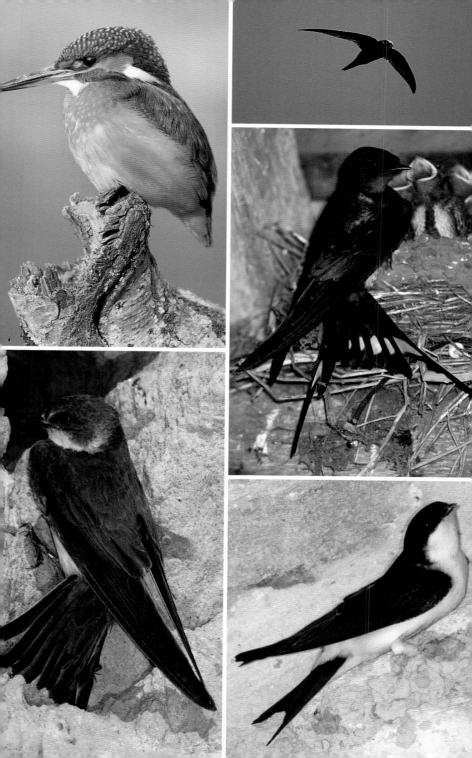

SKYLARK *Alauda arvensis*   Length 18cm
The Skylark's incessant trilling and fluty song, which is often delivered in flight,
can be heard over areas of grassland throughout much of Ireland and in most
months of the year. The bird's plumage is rather nondescript with streaked,
sandy-brown upperparts and paler underparts; note the short, erectile crest,
which is not always apparent. Skylarks are mostly resident in the region but some
N birds move S in winter, forming flocks.

MEADOW PIPIT *Anthus pratensis*   Length 14–15cm
This species has a rather nondescript plumage with streaked brown upperparts
and pale streaked underparts. Note the proportionately rather long tail, the outer
feathers of which are white. The Meadow Pipit is a common resident on open,
grassy areas throughout Ireland; in winter, numbers are boosted by an influx
of birds from northern mainland Europe. Utters a *pseet pseet pseet* call and has
a trilling, descending song, which is delivered in flight but starting from ground
or fencepost.

ROCK PIPIT *Anthus petrosus*   Length 16–17cm
Almost always found within sight of the sea. The Rock Pipit is widespread
around the coast of Ireland. It is larger and darker than its cousin, the Meadow
Pipit, and it has greyish, not white, outer tail feathers. Utters a single *pseest* call
and has a Meadow Pipit-like song delivered in flight from an outcrop on a cliff. It
breeds on rocky coasts, but in winter the Rock Pipit also feeds along beach tide-
lines, sometimes in the company of Turnstones and other waders.

PIED WAGTAIL *Motacilla alba ssp. yarrellii*   Length 18cm
A familiar bird of playing fields, farmland and coastal meadows. The Pied Wagtail's name derives from its black and white appearance and habit of pumping its
tail up and down. It is often seen in bounding flight, uttering a loud *chissick* call.
The female differs from the male by having a dark grey, not black, back. Juvenile
has the black element of the adult male's plumage replaced by grey. Common
throughout the region and often found in towns and villages.

GREY WAGTAIL *Motacilla cinerea*   Length 18cm
Despite its name and the bird's blue-grey upperparts, the lemon-yellow underparts
are this species' most striking feature. Summer male has a black throat, which is
absent in the female and the winter male. The Grey Wagtail is invariably associated with water, and is typically found beside fast-flowing streams and rivers,
where it catches emergent and waterside insects. It perches on boulders, pumping
the tail up and down. Utters a *chsee-tsit* call in flight. Widespread in Ireland.

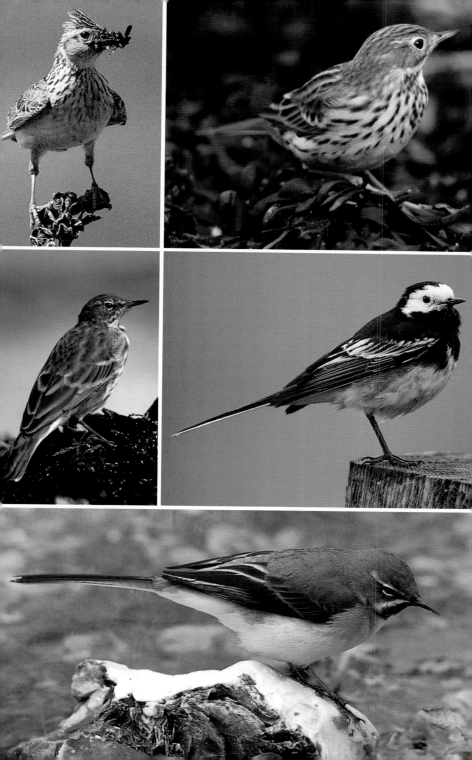

WAXWING *Bombycilla garrulus* Length 18cm

Rare winter visitor in variable numbers from October to March. If berry crop fails in NE Europe, birds are forced to move W to Britain in large numbers, and smaller numbers filter across Irish Sea. Can turn up almost anywhere but most records come from SE and E, often on berry bushes in towns and gardens. Plumage pinkish buff. Has prominent crest, black throat and mask, chestnut undertail and yellow-tipped tail. Wings have white and yellow margins and red, wax-like projections. Trilling call. Starling-like in flight.

STARLING *Sturnus vulgaris* Length 22cm

Familiar urban bird in Ireland, also common in rural areas. Outside breeding season, forms huge flocks which roost in trees or on buildings. Numbers boosted in winter by influx of continental birds. Adult's dark plumage is iridescent in summer (A); in winter (B), acquires numerous white spots. Bill yellow in summer but dark in winter. Juvenile buffish brown. Varied song includes clicks and whistles; also imitates other birds and man-made sounds such as car alarms.

DUNNOCK *Prunella modularis* Length 14–15cm

Common but unobtrusive resident breeding bird in Ireland. Adult has chestnut-brown back, blue-grey underparts, streaked flanks and needle-like bill. Feeds quietly, often on ground, searching for insects and seeds. Most noticeable in early spring when male sings lively, warbler-like song from exposed perch. Call is a thin *tseer*. Favours woods, hedgerows and gardens.

WREN *Troglodytes troglodytes* Length 9–10cm

A tiny bird, recognised by its dumpy proportions, mainly dark brown plumage and habit of frequently cocking tail upright. Generally widespread and common throughout Ireland although numbers plummet during cold winters. Creeps through low vegetation in search of insects and can look rather mouse-like. Song loud, and warbling, ending in trill; has a rattling alarm call.

DIPPER *Cinclus cinclus* Length 18cm

The most likely dumpy, black-and-white bird to be seen perched on boulders in a fast-flowing stream or river. Bobs body up and down and plunges into water to feed on aquatic insects. Chestnut on breast seen at close range. Flight fast and low over water. Widespread in Ireland.

GRASSHOPPER WARBLER *Locustella naevia* Length 13cm

Widespread but local summer visitor to Ireland from May to August. Insect-like, almost mechanical song delivered mainly at dawn and dusk and heard far more often than bird itself seen. Olive-brown, streaked plumage and skulking habits combine to make bird difficult to see in favoured habitat, usually scrubby grassland often with abundant rushes. Occasionally sings in open.

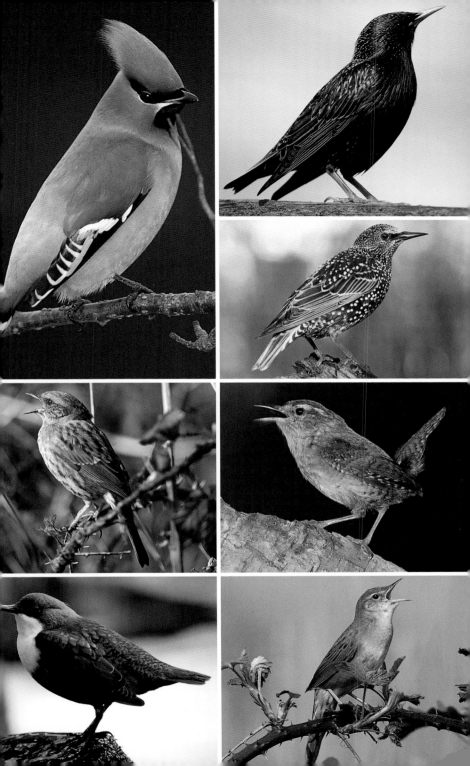

REED WARBLER *Acrocephalus scirpaceus* Length 12–13cm
Almost always associated with reedbeds. Scarce, local summer visitor, from May to August, to suitable habitats mainly along E coast. Singing birds clamber up reeds; chattering song includes some mimetic elements. Has rather nondescript sandy-brown upperparts, paler underparts and dark legs. Constructs woven, cup-shaped nest attached to upright reed stems. Feeds on insects.

SEDGE WARBLER *Acrocephalus schoenobaenus* Length 13cm
A well-marked summer visitor whose harsh, scratchy song is a familiar sound in many wetland habitats. Widespread and fairly common in Ireland, present from May to August. Has noticeably streaked plumage with sandy-brown upperparts and paler underparts; head shows distinctive dark and pale stripes. Favours marshy scrub and reedbeds. Utters *chek* alarm call.

WILLOW WARBLER *Phylloscopus trochilus* Length 11cm
Widespread and common summer visitor throughout Ireland, present from April to September. Adult has olive-yellow upperparts and pale, yellowish white underparts; juvenile has brighter, more yellow plumage. Flesh-coloured legs distinguish silent birds from similar Chiffchaff. Song comprises a tinkling, descending phrase, endlessly repeated by newly arrived birds. Can be found in almost any wooded or partly wooded habitat.

CHIFFCHAFF *Phylloscopus collybita* Length 11cm
Similar to Willow Warbler and distinguished by its song (which gives it its name), dark legs and drabber plumage. Widespread summer visitor to Ireland; early birds arrive in March. Most birds migrate S in autumn but small numbers overwinter in S. Found in woods and scrub. Call *hooeet*, similar to Willow Warbler.

WOOD WARBLER *Phylloscopus sibilatrix* Length 12–13cm
Larger than superficially similar Chiffchaff or Willow Warbler and with brighter plumage comprising olive-green upperparts, yellow throat and white underparts. Distinctive song, likened to coin spinning on a plate, starts with ringing notes that accelerate into a silvery trill. Favours mature woodlands with open understorey. Scarce summer visitor and passage migrant.

GOLDCREST *Regulus regulus* Length 9cm
Our smallest bird. Has needle-like bill, large dark eyes and proportionately large head with seemingly short neck. Upperparts greenish with two pale wingbars and underparts yellowish buff. Adult male has black-bordered orange crown, that of the female being yellow; juvenile lacks adult's crown markings. During breeding season, found in areas of mixed woodland, conifer forests and sometimes in gardens. In winter, becomes more widespread and then seen in deciduous woodland as well.

WHITETHROAT *Sylvia communis* Length 14cm
Locally common summer visitor to many parts of Ireland, present from May to September. A characteristic bird of scrub, overgrown hedgerows and heaths. Male often perches on exposed perch revealing white throat, blue-grey crown, rufous back and wings, and pale underparts with buffish tone on breast. Female drabber. Scratchy song often delivered in dancing song flight. Alarm call a harsh *chek*.

GARDEN WARBLER *Sylvia borin* Length 14cm
A rather nondescript warbler to look at with uniform grey-brown upperparts and paler, buffish underparts. At times, can resemble a Blackcap without the cap colour; has also been likened to a Robin without the red breast. Lack of distinguishing plumage features is more than made up for by song, which is one of the most attractive of all Irish birds; can be confused with Blackcap's song but is even more musical. A scarce summer visitor from May to August. Favours wooded areas with dense undergrowth and mature gardens.

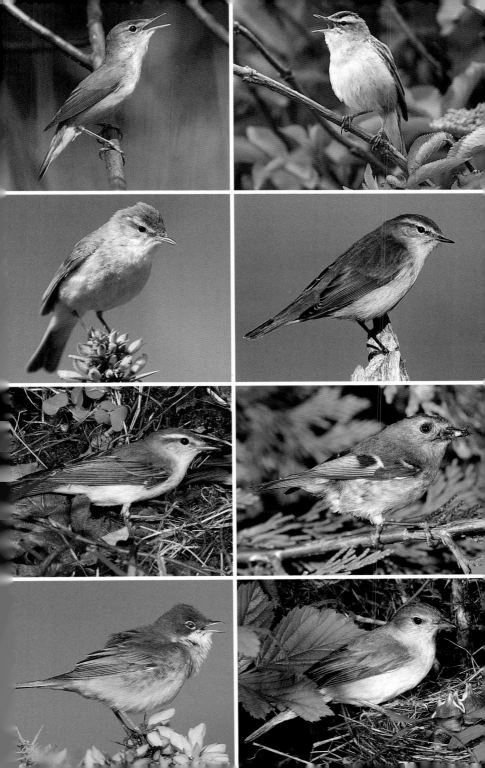

BLACKCAP *Sylvia atricapilla*   Length 14cm
Overwinters in S in very small numbers but seen mainly as a summer visitor, present from April to September. Then widespread in Ireland and common in suitable habitats. Breeds in deciduous woodland. Male has grey-brown upperparts, paler underparts and distinctive black cap; female is similar but has chestnut-brown cap. Male's song attractive and musical with chattering and fluty elements.

SPOTTED FLYCATCHER *Muscicapa striata*   Length 14cm
Fairly common summer visitor to Ireland, present from May to August. Adult has rather undistinguished plumage with grey-brown upperparts, streaked on crown, and paler underparts, heavily streaked on breast; juvenile similar but with spotted breast. Easily identified by upright posture and habit of using regular perch from which to make insect-catching aerial sorties. Often breeds around habitation.

PIED FLYCATCHER *Ficedula hypoleuca*   Length 13cm
Distinctive male (A) is aptly named with black upperparts, white underparts and bold white band on otherwise black wing. Female (B) has black elements of male's plumage replaced by brown. Scarce passage migrant, and rare summer visitor, from May to August; mainly on E coast. Favours open oakwoods. Forages and fly-catches in tree canopy. Male has sweet, ringing song.

STONECHAT *Saxicola torquata*   Length 12–13cm
Small, distinctive resident of gorse- and bramble-covered ground; commonest in W. In breeding season, male (A) is handsome with black head, white on side of neck, dark back, reddish orange breast and pale underparts. Female (B) and winter male have duller plumage. Often perches openly, flicking tail and announcing presence with harsh *tchak* call, like two pebbles being knocked together. Whitethroat-like song sometimes delivered in flight.

WHINCHAT *Saxicola rubetra*   Length 12–13cm
Similar to Stonechat but male has brown, streaked upperparts and conspicuous pale stripe above eye. Female has similar stripe but plumage otherwise similar to that of female Stonechat. A scarce summer visitor, May to September. Favours rank grassland and scrubby slopes. Has *tik tik* call and chattering song.

WHEATEAR *Oenanthe oenanthe*   Length 14–15cm
Summer visitor, present from March to September. Breeds on coastal grassland, moors and heaths; common only in W. Seen on migration around coasts generally. Male (A) has blue-grey crown and back, black mask and wings, and pale underparts with orange-buff wash on breast. Female (B) has mainly sandy-brown plumage. Both sexes show white rump in flight. Perches low and nests in burrow. *Chak* alarm call like pebbles being knocked together.

REDSTART *Phoenicurus phoenicurus*   Length 14cm
Male has black and grey on head and back, and red breast. Female has grey-brown upperparts and orange wash to pale underparts; both sexes have striking red tail. Scarce summer visitor, April to September, and passage migrant. Favours open woodland and wooded heaths. Has ticking alarm call and tuneful, melancholy song.

BLACK REDSTART *Phoenicurus ochrurus*   Length 14cm
Striking red tail is seen in all plumages. Breeding plumage male (sometimes seen) is mainly black and slate-grey. Female and immature male are both grey-brown. A scarce passage migrant and winter visitor, found mainly on S and W coasts.

ROBIN *Erithacus rubecula*   Length 14cm
Adult (A) is familiar red-breasted bird of gardens and woodland. Brown juvenile (B) has streaked upperparts and underparts with crescent markings. Widespread resident throughout Ireland. Alarm call a sharp *tic*. Male sings variation of melancholy song at most times of year. Highly territorial.

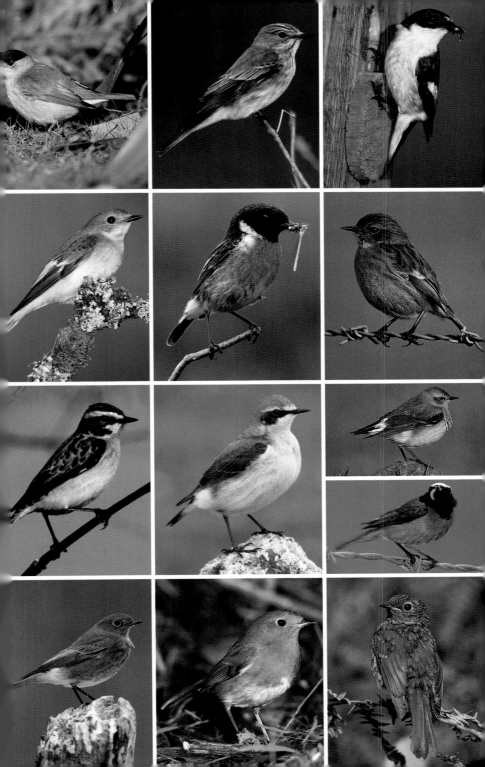

BLACKBIRD *Turdus merula*   Length 25cm
Familiar garden bird in much of Ireland but also found in woodland, farmland
and on moors. Mostly resident but N European birds add to numbers in winter.
Male (A) easily identified by thrush-like appearance and all-black plumage; yellow eyering and bill usually conspicuous. Female (B) and juvenile have brown
plumages. Harsh *tchak* alarm calls often heard at dusk or if prowling cat located.
Male is excellent songster. Feeds on worms, insects, fruit and berries.

RING OUZEL *Turdus torquatus*   Length 24cm
A scarce and local summer visitor to upland districts from late March to September; more widespread, but still scarce, as a passage migrant. Superficially similar
to Blackbird but mainly black male has striking white crescent on breast; at close
range, pale margins to feathers can be seen along with pale patch on wing. Female
has brown plumage, the feathers with conspicuous pale margins giving scaly
appearance; pale crescent on breast less striking than on male. Alert and wary,
found on slopes with broken ground and rocky outcrops. Has loud, fluty song and
tuk alarm call.

FIELDFARE *Turdus pilaris*   Length 25–26cm
A large thrush that is a winter visitor from October to March. Seen in large, flighty
flocks, often mixed with Redwings. Recognised by grey head, chestnut back and
pale, spotted underparts with yellow wash on breast; pale grey rump and white
underwings noticeable in flight. Occurs mainly on farmland. Nomadic and could
turn up almost anywhere in Ireland. Chattering calls often heard, sometimes from
night-migrating flocks.

REDWING *Turdus iliacus*   Length 21cm
A small but attractive thrush with grey-brown upperparts, prominent white stripe
above eye, neatly spotted pale underparts and orange-red flush on flanks and
underwings. Seen mainly as a winter visitor to almost all parts of Ireland from
October to April. Flocks are nomadic and numbers vary from year to year but usually a very common winter bird. Feeds on farmland and in woodland where it
searches for worms and invertebrates. An opportunistic feeder, particularly in cold
weather, and will feast on fallen apples and berries. Has high-pitched *tseerp* call.

SONG THRUSH *Turdus philomelos*   Length 23cm
Familiar bird of gardens and grassland but numbers have declined markedly in
recent years. Easily told from Mistle Thrush by smaller size, more dainty appearance and orange-red underwing. Upperparts warm brown with hint of orange-
buff wingbar and pale underparts well marked with dark spots and with buff
flush to breast. Song loud and musical, phrases repeated two or three times; often
sings at dusk. Flight call a thin *tik*. Widespread resident in Ireland.

MISTLE THRUSH *Turdus viscivorus*   Length 27cm
Distinctly larger than Song Thrush and with white, not orange-buff, underwings.
Upperparts grey-brown with suggestion of white wingbar. Pale underparts with
large, dark spots; in flight, white tips to outer tail feather noticeable. Juvenile has
white, teardrop-shaped spots on back. Widespread and fairly common in Ireland
but never numerous. In winter, individual birds often guard their own berry-bear-
ing bush or tree. Has loud, rattling alarm call. Loud song contains brief phrases
and long pauses; often sung in rain or dull weather.

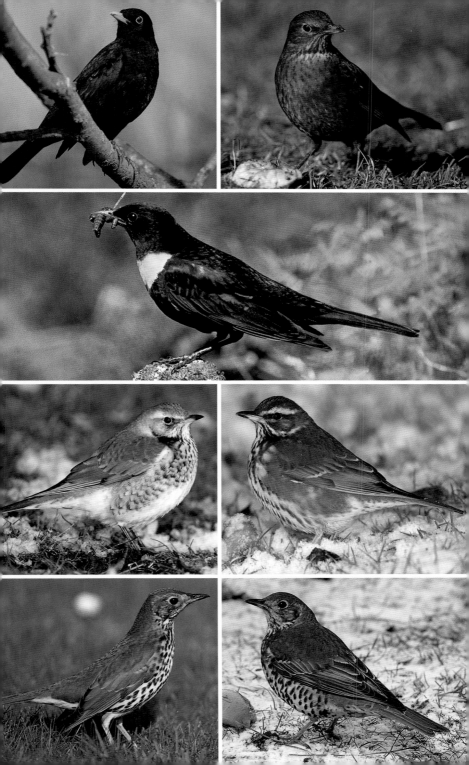

BLUE TIT *Parus caeruleus* Length 11–12cm
Familiar garden resident in most of Ireland, often coming to bird feeders in winter months; a common woodland species as well. Has elements of blue, green and yellow in its plumage with striking dark markings on head; juvenile similar to adult but lacks blue in plumage. Utters familiar, chattering *tserr err err err* call and has whistling song. Nests in tree holes and takes to hole-fronted nestboxes.

GREAT TIT *Parus major* Length 14cm
Common woodland and garden species, appreciably larger than Blue Tit alongside which it is often seen at bird feeders. Has bold black and white markings on head and black bib forming line running down chest, broader in male than female. Underparts otherwise yellow and upperparts mainly greenish. Juvenile has sombre plumage with no white on head. Song is extremely variable but a striking *teecha teecha teecha* rendered by most males.

COAL TIT *Parus ater* Length 11–12cm
A small resident bird. Widespread and fairly common. Has black and white markings on head with conspicuous white patch on nape. Back and wings slate-grey with two white wingbars, and underparts pale pinkish buff. Found in both coniferous and deciduous woodland and will visit feeders in winter. Song *teecha teecha teecha*, higher-pitched and weaker than Great Tit.

LONG-TAILED TIT *Aegithalos caudatus* Length 14cm
Charming resident of woods, heaths and hedgerows, feeding flocks resembling animated feather dusters. Plumage can look black and white but at close range has pinkish wash to underparts and pinkish buff on back. Has tiny, stubby bill, long tail and almost spherical body. Widespread in Ireland.

BEARDED TIT *Panurus biarmicus* Length 16–17cm
Scarce and occasional visitor that has bred in the past. Invariably associated with reedbeds. Has long tail and mainly sandy-brown plumage; male has blue-grey head and conspicuous black 'moustaches'. Sometimes seen in small groups, clambering up reeds or flying, one after the other. Utters distinctive pinging calls.

TREECREEPER *Certhia familiaris* Length 12–13cm
A widespread woodland resident. Unobtrusive and easily overlooked as it creeps up tree trunks. Has streaked brown upperparts, pale underparts and needle-like, downcurved bill. Has high-pitched *tseert* call. Typically feeds by spiralling round and up tree then dropping down to base of adjacent trunk to repeat process. Feeds on invertebrates prised from bark crevices with bill.

YELLOWHAMMER *Emberiza citrinella* Length 16–17cm
Locally common on farmland throughout much of Ireland but least so in N and W. Male is particularly striking with mainly bright yellow head and underparts, and chestnut back and wings; female has more subdued colours and juvenile is sandy-brown and streaked. In spring, male sings well-known song, often rendered *a little bit of bread and no cheese*; also utters a rasping call.

REED BUNTING *Emberiza schoeniclus* Length 15cm
Characteristic of wetland habitats but also in drier areas of farmland too. In breeding season, male has head black except for white moustachial stripes; underparts pale and upperparts chestnut-brown. Male in winter has less distinct black head; female has striking dark moustachial stripes at all times. Has chinking song.

SNOW BUNTING *Plectrophenax nivalis* Length 16–17cm
Scarce passage migrant and winter visitor to coastal districts, mainly in N. In winter, all birds have variable amounts of buffish orange on breast and face, sandy-brown back and white underparts. Unobtrusive when feeding on ground but, in flight, black and white wings are conspicuous. Tinkling flight call.

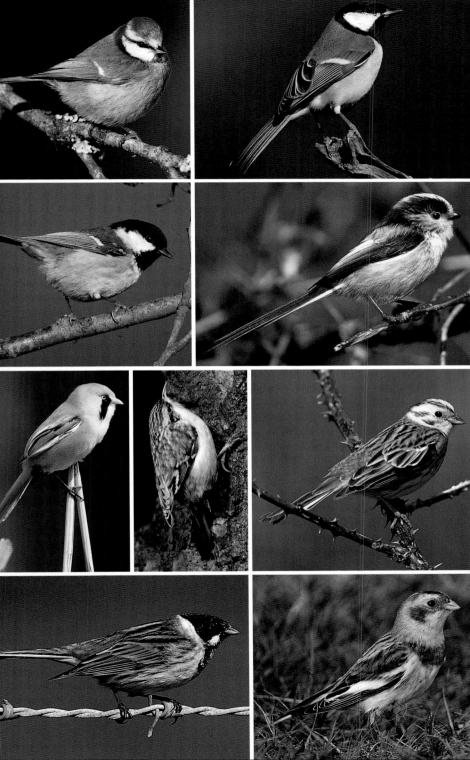

CHAFFINCH *Fringilla coelebs* Length 15cm

One of the commonest and most widespread birds in Ireland, favouring a wide variety of habitats including gardens, parks and woodland; in winter, numbers of residents boosted by influx of N European birds. Colourful male (A) has reddish pink face and underparts, blue crown and chestnut back; female (B) is more uniformly buffish brown but, like male, has prominent white shoulder patch and white wingbar. Song comprises a descending trill with a characteristic final flourish. Call a distinct *pink pink*. Feeds mainly on insects during summer months but seeds taken in winter when often gather into sizeable flocks.

BRAMBLING *Fringilla montifringilla* Length 14–15cm

Autumn passage migrant and widespread and locally common winter visitor to most parts of Ireland. In winter plumage, superficially similar to Chaffinch but always shows orange-buff shoulder patch and on breast and flanks; white rump seen in flight. Female and immature birds have buffish grey face with characteristic dark, parallel lines down nape. Male has dark brown head that in breeding plumage becomes black. Calls including harsh *eeerp*. Seen in flocks, sometimes with Chaffinches, and especially fond of fallen beech mast.

GOLDFINCH *Carduelis carduelis* Length 12cm

One of our most colourful birds and the only one with bright yellow wingbars and a white rump. Adult has red and white on face, black cap extending down sides of neck, buffish back, and white underparts with buff flanks. Juvenile has brown, streaked plumage but yellow wingbars as in adult. Common and widespread resident in Ireland. Favours wasteground and meadows where narrow, pointed bill is used to feed on seeds of thistles and Teasels in particular. Usually seen in small flocks that take to the wing with tinkling flight calls. Male's song is twittering but contains call-like elements.

SISKIN *Carduelis spinus* Length 12cm

Charming little finch. Numerous and widespread during the winter months in Ireland, numbers being boosted by influx of continental birds. In breeding season, distribution is patchier, particularly so in S. Male in breeding plumage has striking yellow and green plumage with black bib and forehead. Female and winter male have more subdued colours but always show two yellow wingbars and yellow rump in flight. Breeds mainly in conifer forests but, in winter, forms flocks which feed mainly on cones of alder and birch. Often mixes with Redpolls in feeding flocks.

GREENFINCH *Carduelis chloris* Length 14–15cm

Widespread throughout most of Ireland. A familiar bird of gardens, parks and farmland but absent from many wooded and upland areas within its range. In full breeding plumage, male is very bright yellow-green but for most of year colours are duller; female has grey-green plumage and juvenile is streaked. All birds show yellow wing patches and have yellow rumps and sides to tail. Bill pinkish and conical, used for feeding on seeds. Outside breeding season, forms flocks which feed on stubble fields and grain spills. Winter visitor to garden bird feeders. Has wheezy *weeeish* call.

BULLFINCH *Pyrrhula pyrrhula* Length 14–16cm

An attractive but unobtrusive resident throughout much of Ireland. Often encountered in pairs. Easy to overlook in the dense cover it favours until its soft but distinctive, piping call is learnt. Male has rosy-pink face and breast, the colour unlike that of any other Irish bird; also shows black cap and blue-grey back. Female similar but with duller colours. Both sexes have characteristic white rump, seen as bird flies away. Found in woodland scrub, hedgerows and mature gardens. Uses stubby bill to feed on insects, seeds and berries; in spring, visits orchards to eat flower buds of fruit trees.

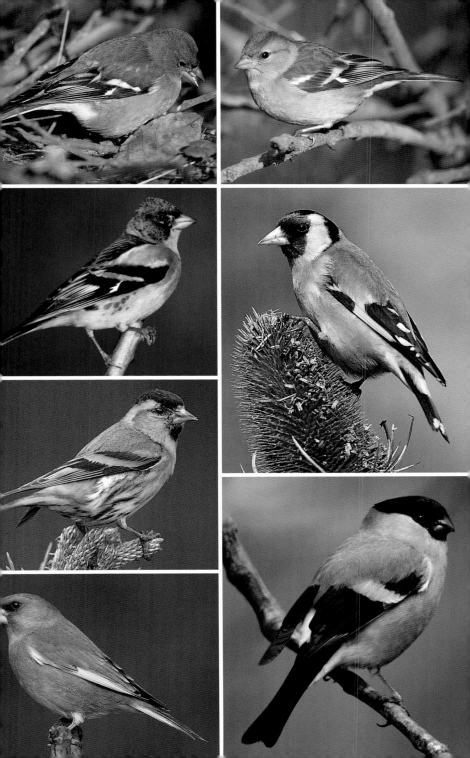

LESSER REDPOLL *Carduelis cabaret*   Length 13–15cm

A small finch with rather variable plumage. Most birds can be recognised by yellowish conical bill, black bib and red patch on forecrown; latter feature absent in some juvenile birds. Has streaked, grey-brown upperparts and pale underparts, streaked on flanks; in breeding season, male has pinkish flush to breast. As a breeding species, occurs locally throughout much of Ireland but distinctly scarce in S. In winter, much more numerous and widespread, thanks to influx of birds from N Europe. Breeds in open woodland but winter flocks mostly in alder and birch, often with Siskins.

TWITE *Carduelis flavirostris*   Length 13–14cm

Superficially Linnet-like but separable with care. Plumage is mainly brown and streaked at all times. Adult male has pinkish rump. Bill is grey in summer but yellow in winter. Found year-round on rugged grassy moors, mainly on W and NW coasts; forms flocks outside breeding season.

LINNET *Carduelis cannabina*   Length 13–14cm

Common and widespread resident throughout much of Ireland. Male has grey head and chestnut back; in breeding season, acquires rosy-pink patch on forecrown and on breast but this feature absent in winter months when male is rather similar to streaked, grey-brown female. Breeds on gorse- or bramble-covered slopes, heaths and scrubby grassland. Male often perches prominently to deliver his twittering, warbling song. Has Greenfinch-like flight call. Forms small flocks in winter.

COMMON CROSSBILL *Loxia recurvirostra*   Length 16–17cm

Has evolved crossed-tipped mandibles to extract seeds from conifer cones, and in particular those of spruces; seldom seen away from mature specimens of these trees. Bizarre bill structure only visible, however, at close range. Male has mainly red plumage, that of female being yellowish green. Often nests as early as February or March and thereafter seen as roving, single-species flocks. Feeds high in trees but visits woodland pools to drink. Flight call a sharp *kip kip*. Presence of feeding birds often indicated by sound of falling cones. Locally common.

HOUSE SPARROW *Passer domesticus*   Length 14–15cm

Widespread in Ireland. Because of affinity for human habitation and farmyards, however, only locally common, being absent from large tracts of land. Male has grey crown, cheeks and rump, chestnut-brown nape, back and wings, pale underparts and black throat. Female rather nondescript with streaked buff and grey-brown plumage. Small groups of birds often encountered sitting on roofs, uttering familiar sparrow chirps. Frequently dust-bathes. Usually nests in roof spaces or holes in walls but occasionally builds large and untidy nest in bush. Where fed in urban parks, can become remarkably tame, taking food from hand.

TREE SPARROW *Passer montanus*   Length 14cm

Scarce and declining resident, commonest in E Ireland but decidedly local even there. Occasionally found on outskirts of villages but more usually associated with untidy arable farms, taking advantage of frequent grain spills along with buntings and finches. Sexes similar and easily distinguished from House Sparrow by chestnut cap and nape, and black patch on otherwise white cheeks; plumage otherwise streaked brown on back with pale underparts. Juvenile lacks black cheek patch. Utters House Sparrow-like chirps but also a sharp *tik tik* in flight. Forms flocks in winter months and sometimes feeds in stubble fields.

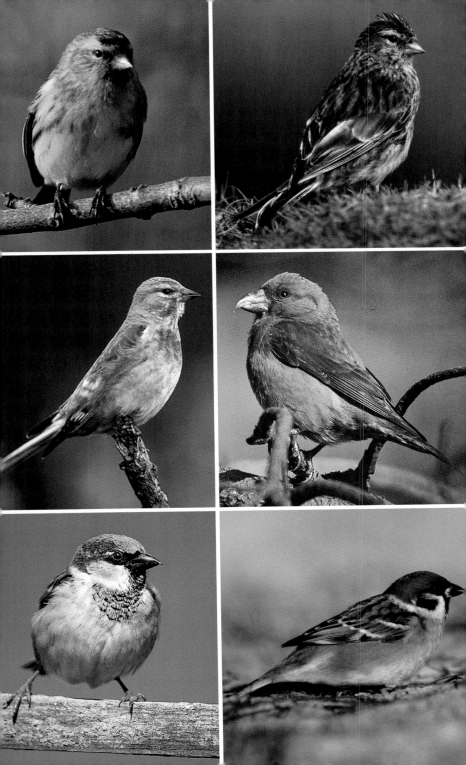

JAY *Garrulus glandarius* Length 34cm
Colourful bird but wary nature ensures that colours seldom seen to best effect. Woodland resident, generally scarce and local in Ireland. Pinkish buff body plumage except for white undertail and rump, latter most conspicuous as bird flies away and emphasised by black tail. Wings have black and white pattern and chequerboard patch of blue, black and white. Utters loud, raucous *kraah* call. Buries acorns in autumn.

CHOUGH *Pyrrhocorax pyrrhocorax* Length 40cm
A Jackdaw-sized bird with glossy, all-dark plumage and bright red legs and long, downcurved bill. Almost exclusively coastal, favouring dry, grassy slopes in summer but sometimes visiting beaches in winter. A local and rather scarce species, found mainly in W and S Ireland. Often nests in sea caves. Outside breeding season, forms flocks. Recognised in flight by broad, 'fingered' wingtips and frequently uttered *chyah* call. Probes ground for insects.

MAGPIE *Pica pica* Length 46cm
Familiar and unmistakable black and white bird. In good light, greenish blue sheen can be seen on rounded wings and long tail. Widespread and often common in much of Ireland. Builds large and untidy twig nest in bushes. Often seen in small groups outside breeding season, frequently uttering loud, rattling alarm call. An opportunistic feeder, taking insects, fruit, animal road kills, young birds and eggs.

JACKDAW *Corvus monedula* Length 33cm
The most familiar small crow. Widespread and common in much of Ireland. Equally at home on farmland or sea cliffs and often encountered in large flocks; aerobatic in flight, frequently uttering sharp *chack* calls. Has mainly smoky-grey plumage; at close range, pale eye and grey nape are obvious. Walks with characteristic swagger. Nests in tree holes and rock crevices, but also in buildings. Omnivorous, opportunistic diet.

RAVEN *Corvus corax* Length 64cm
Appreciably larger than Hooded Crow, with massive bill and shaggy, ruffled throat; plumage has an oily sheen in good light. Often seen in flight; distant bird bears a passing resemblance to Buzzard but recognised by long, thick neck and wedge-shaped tail. Incredibly aerobatic, tumbling and rolling in mid-air. Utters loud, deep *cronk* call. A bird mainly of remote, untamed parts of Ireland, common on rocky coasts.

HOODED CROW *Corvus corone* ssp. *cornix* Length 47cm
Has grey and black plumage. Far less gregarious than either Jackdaw or Rook. Found on farmland, moorland and on coasts. Utters harsh, croaking call. An opportunistic feeder, taking carrion, insects, young birds and eggs. Widespread in Ireland.

ROOK *Corvus frugilegus* Length 46cm
A familiar bird of farmland throughout most of lowland Ireland. Often seen in large flocks feeding in fields or at colonial tree nest sites where noisy and active from early March to May. Glossy black plumage. Adult has bare, white facial patch at base of long bill; absent in immatures.

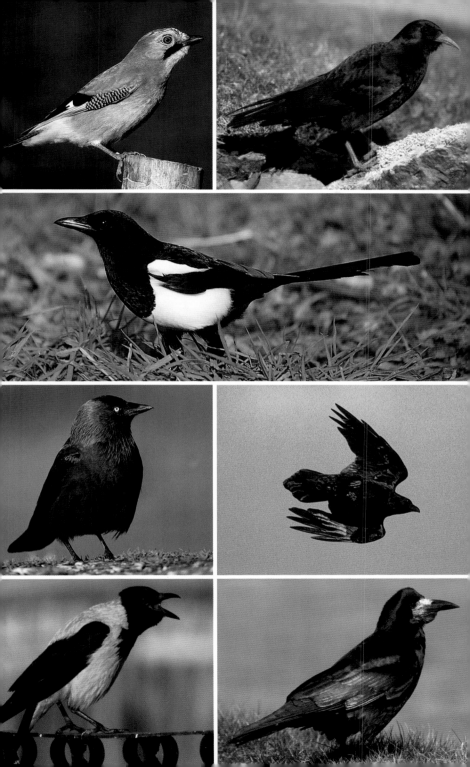

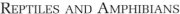

COMMON LIZARD *Lacerta vivipara*   Length 10–15cm
Fond of sunbathing on sunny banks, sometimes several together. Colours and markings rather variable, but usually brown or grey-brown with patterns of dark blotches along length; throat and belly often whitish or reddish. Widespread throughout much of Ireland, favouring areas of dry, short grassland, especially on coastal cliffs, as well as heaths, moors and even warm embankments. Female produces eggs internally but young are born as tiny lizards, mainly during summer months. At all ages, feeds on invertebrates, especially insects. Hibernates from October to March. Can shed tail to fool predators.

SLOW WORM *Anguis fragilis*   Length 30–50cm
Superficially snake-like but in fact a legless lizard. Head and neck barely distinguishable from rest of uniform-diameter body. Tail-end rather blunt-ended, sometimes very much so when tail itself has been shed to distract would-be predator. Most individuals are shiny golden-buff but a few, notably some coastal or island populations, are blue-spotted. Not native to Ireland; those found in Burren area are presumed to have been introduced. Favours hedgerows, grassland, heaths and woodland borders. Hibernates from October to March. Feeds on invertebrates such as slugs and insects.

SMOOTH NEWT *Triturus vulgaris*   Length 8–10cm
Male is particularly well-marked and attractive. In breeding season, shows spotted flanks, undulating crest along back, and orange belly and pale throat with conspicuous spots. Brown female lacks crest; distinguished by spotted, not unspotted, throat. Widespread but rather scarce; the only newt species in Ireland. Found in ponds, ditches and lakes from March to September; thereafter, leaves water and hibernates during winter months under fallen logs and in holes.

COMMON FROG *Rana temporaria*   Length 6–9cm
Introduced to Ireland where distribution is rather patchy. Colour variable but usually greenish brown or olive-buff with darker blotches; shows dark 'mask'. Male has hard swelling on first finger, used to grasp female during mating; throat often bluish in breeding season. Spawning takes place typically in March or April. Mating pairs and masses of frogspawn are a common sight in most ponds. Males utter faint croaking song.

NATTERJACK TOAD *Bufo calamita*   Length 6–8cm
Extremely local and endangered. Restricted to a few sites in SW Ireland. Found on sandy soils, including stablised dunes and golf courses, and breeds in shallow, often quite saline pools. Body is rather flattened with a conspicuous yellow stripe down back. Gathers in pools to spawn in spring, often after heavy downpours. Most active at night when males are very vocal.

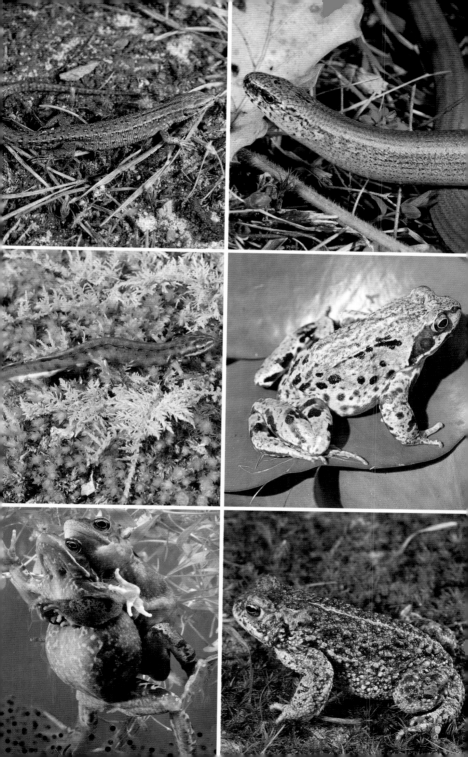

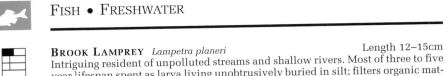

BROOK LAMPREY *Lampetra planeri*   Length 12–15cm
Intriguing resident of unpolluted streams and shallow rivers. Most of three to five year lifespan spent as larva living unobtrusively buried in silt; filters organic matter. Adults seen in April and May after metamorphosing from larvae. These congregate in shallow, stony areas to spawn. Sucker used for attachment and to move stones to create egg-laying site. Adult does not feed; dies after spawning.

RIVER LAMPREY *Lampetra fluviatilis*   Length 30cm
Migratory, adults moving upstream from sea in winter and spring to spawn on gravel beds in rivers. After spawning, adults die but eggs hatch into larvae that spend several years buried in river silt. Following metamorphosis to adult stage, they move to sea until maturity drives them to repeat cycle. Adult attaches to fish with toothed sucker to feed on blood; also eats carrion.

EEL *Anguilla anguilla*   Length up to 1m
Snake-like body ideally suited to life spent among silt and debris at bottom of ponds, lakes and canals. Complicated life history. Spawns in Sargasso Sea and young larvae drift across the Atlantic in the Gulf Stream for three years or so. On reaching our shores, so-called *elvers* migrate up rivers; after several years, become familiar, yellow-bodied eels. Mature, silvery eels migrate to the sea and are sometimes found in estuaries.

ARCTIC CHARR *Salvelinus alpinus*   Length up to 70cm
Member of salmon family. Relict species from last post-glacial era, now mostly confined to land-locked and isolated populations in deep, oligotrophic lakes. Very local in Ireland, most populations being found in the W, from Donegal to Kerry. Body streamlined with small adipose fin. Male has greenish grey upperparts and bright red belly; colours on female much less intense.

ATLANTIC SALMON *Salmo salar*   Length up to 1.20m
Large and impressive when mature. Much of adult life spent at sea but returns to fast-flowing, healthy rivers in Ireland to breed. Moves upstream from November to February when rivers in full spate. Adult (A) jumps clear of water to overcome waterfalls. Spawns in shallow gravel beds after which most adults die. Young fish (B) migrate to sea after two years or so in fresh water.

BROWN TROUT *Salmo trutta*   Length 50–80cm, often much smaller
A familiar and popular sport fish. Widespread and often common both in fast-flowing, unpolluted rivers and streams, and in stream-fed lakes. Known in two forms: Brown Trout which spends entire life in fresh water and Sea Trout which only ventures up rivers to breed. Both forms spawn in shallow water on gravel beds. Young spend first year or so in nursery stream before moving downstream to larger river (Brown Trout) or to sea (Sea Trout). Feeds mainly on invertebrates.

PIKE *Esox lucius*   Length 30–120cm
Superb predator. Takes invertebrates when small but larger Pike will tackle other fish and even young waterbirds. Marbled green and brown markings afford it excellent camouflage when lurking among water plants. Streamlined shape and broad tail enable fish to perform lightning attacks on prey that are engulfed in huge mouth and retained by numerous sharp teeth. Favours weedy lowland lakes and large, slow-flowing rivers. Widespread in Ireland.

CARP *Cyprinus carpio*   Length 25–80cm
Introduced but long-established in lakes in Ireland. Ancestral form has golden-olive colour and even-sized scales; also seen as so-called Leather and Mirror Carp. Feeds on bottom-living invertebrates and plants.

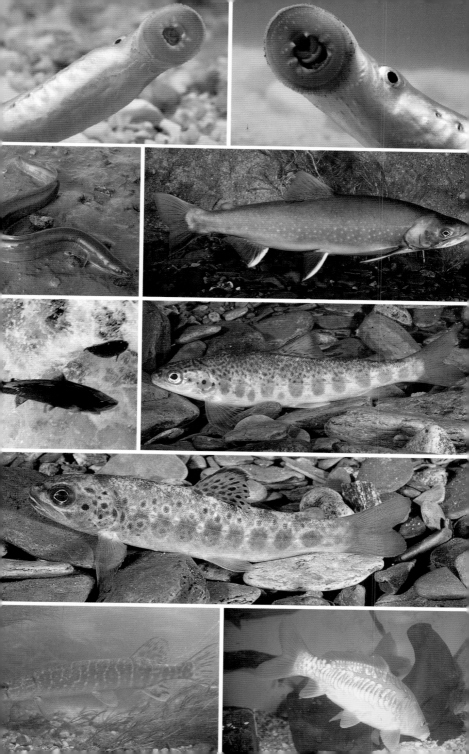

GUDGEON *Gobio gobio* Length 7–15cm
Bottom-dwelling fish of fast-flowing rivers and streams in Ireland. Has well-developed barbels which help detect invertebrate prey among sand and gravel. Shoal-forming during summer months.

 ROACH *Rutilus rutilus* Length 10–25cm
Has silvery appearance and reddish fins; dorsal fin lies above pelvic fins. Rather local in Ireland (confusingly, the more numerous Rudd is sometimes called 'Roach'). Favours lakes and rivers.

 RUDD *Scardinius erythrophthalmus* Length 20–35cm
Superficially similar to Roach but usually has deeper body and golden tinge to flanks. Fins reddish, the dorsal fin lying behind point of origin of pelvic fins. Found in lakes and rivers in Ireland. Shoal-forming.

 MINNOW *Phoxinus phoxinus* Length 4–10cm
Small but attractively-marked fish of fast-flowing streams but also occasionally lakes too. Rather local in Ireland. Shoals seen in shallows in summer months but these move to deeper water in winter.

 PERCH *Perca fluviatilis* Length 25–40cm
Distinctive fish of rivers and lakes throughout Ireland. Greenish body shows broad, vertical dark stripes. Has two separate dorsal fins, the first very spiny; other fins usually red. Shoals when small.

 STONE LOACH *Nemacheilus barbatus* Length 5–10cm
Charming and bizarre fish with well-developed barbels around mouth. Widespread but often overlooked in gravel-bottomed, unpolluted streams and rivers throughout Ireland. Bottom-dwelling species.

 THREE-SPINED STICKLEBACK *Gasterosteus aculeatus* Length 4–7cm
Beloved of small boys and a familiar resident of both streams and brackish waters. Recognised at all times by its three dorsal spines. Silvery for most of year but, in breeding season, male acquires red belly and bluish dorsal sheen.

NINE-SPINED STICKLEBACK *Pungitius pungitius* Length 2–4cm
Recognised by its usually nine (sometimes ten) dorsal spines and elongated tail stock. Occurs both in fresh water and brackish conditions around coasts. Widespread in Ireland.

COMMON BREAM *Abramis brama* Length 30–50cm
An extremely deep-bodied, laterally flattened member of the carp family. Note the hump-backed appearance and bronzy brown colour. Widely established in weedy lakes and slow-flowing rivers.

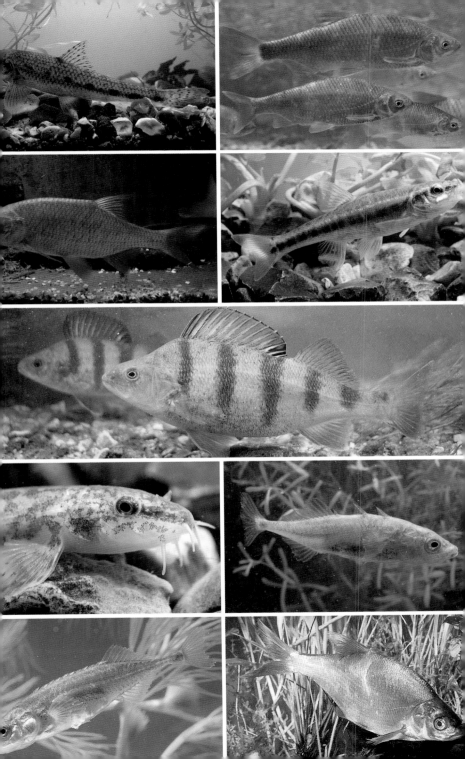

LESSER SPOTTED DOGFISH *Scyliorhinus canicula*   Length up to 60cm
Common and widespread fish around the coasts of S Ireland. Occurs mainly in offshore waters but also sometimes in comparatively shallow seas off muddy shores and the mouths of estuaries. Well-marked with a rough skin. So-called 'mermaid's purses' (egg-cases of this species) often washed up on shores.

THORNBACK RAY *Raja clavata*   Length up to 50cm
Has a distinctive, diamond-shaped outline. Skin rough and with conspicuous spines down back and on dorsal surface of muscular tail. Fairly common and widespread off coasts of Ireland. Favours muddy and sandy seabeds and sometimes found trapped in pools at very low tide on expansive shores at estuary mouths.

CONGER EEL *Conger conger*   Length up to 2m, often shorter
Extremely muscular, snake-like fish whose skin lacks scales and is variable in colour. Favours rocky coasts, often in deep water but sometimes shallow enough seas to be found at extreme low water hidden among rocks. Upper jaw just longer than lower jaw. Common and widespread around coasts of Ireland.

WHITING *Merlangius merlangus*   Length up to 50cm
Relative of the Cod, often common in inshore waters over muddy or sandy seabeds. Body comparatively narrow and has upper jaw longer than lower jaw. First of two anal fins is long, starting mid-way along first dorsal fin and ending level with end of second dorsal fin. Sometimes seen while snorkelling but often in deeper water.

POLLACK *Pollachius pollachus*   Length up to 1m
Fairly common and widespread fish around rocky shores of Ireland. Easily seen while snorkelling off suitable coasts in summer months. Can also be viewed in clear water from jetties and piers, and in rocky gullies. Has Cod-like appearance and lateral line which curves smoothly over pectoral fin.

FIVE-BEARDED ROCKLING *Ciliata mustela*   Length up to 20cm
As name suggests, has five barbels around mouth. Body elongate with long dorsal and anal fins. Common and widespread around coasts of Ireland. Lives in shallow water on muddy and sandy shores, sometimes in intertidal zone. Can be found by turning over rocks and debris on estuaries and mudflats at low tide.

GREATER PIPEFISH *Syngnathus acus*   Length up to 50cm
Bizarre little fish with worm-like body and elongate, snout-like mouth. One of several, similar species and best told by large size, when adult, and tapering, curved snout which is longer than length of rest of head. Common among seaweed and rocks in shallow water around coasts of Ireland.

THICK-LIPPED GREY MULLET *Chelon labrosus*   Length up to 50cm
One of a complex of closely related Grey Mullet species. Body has grey, silver appearance and lip of upper jaw is very thick. A common fish of estuaries and shallow, sheltered coasts; congregates around outfalls of power stations and sewage treatment plants. Widespread around Irish coasts except in N.

BASS *Dicentrachus labrus*   Length up to 60cm, often smaller
Common and widespread around coasts of Ireland. When small, often found in shoals near mouths of estuaries and in shallow, sheltered water. Larger specimens often solitary off shingle or rocky shores, sometimes in deep water. Young fish often show pinkish tinge but become more silvery-grey with age.

CORKWING WRASSE *Crenilabrus melops*   Length up to 15cm
A beautiful fish. Variable colours and patterns but usually mainly blue with deep pink patterns and lines. Favours clean, rocky coasts. Sometimes found in rock pools but easy to see in calm water darting among seaweed in rocky gullies. Widespread around coasts of Ireland and common except in N.

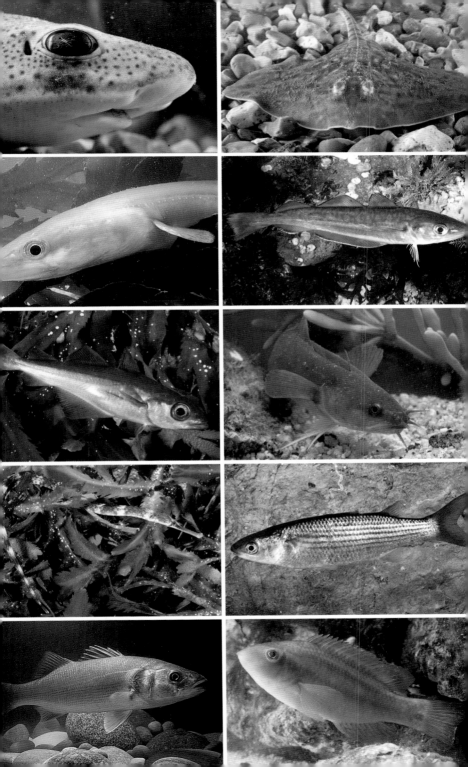

Butterfish *Pholis gunnellus*   Length up to 15cm
Widespread around coasts of Ireland and commonest in N. A bottom-living species found among rocks and seaweed on otherwise sandy or muddy seabeds. Has elongate body with long dorsal and anal fins, continuous at tail-end. Sometimes found in pools at low tide. Important food of Black Guillemot.

Common Blenny *Blennius pholis*   Length up to 10cm
Delightful little fish of rocky shores. Common and widespread in suitable habitats around coasts of Ireland, particularly numerous in W. Found among stones and seaweed in rocky gullies on lower shore; sometimes trapped in rock pools at low tide. Colours variable but usually mottled greenish brown.

Rock Goby *Gobius paganellus*   Length up to 19cm
A large-headed fish of rocky shores around coasts of Ireland. Often found among seaweed and stones at low tide and frequently trapped in rock pools at low tide. Characteristically has dark bands along length of otherwise usually pale brown body. Can be very difficult to see among rocks until it moves.

Grey Gurnard *Eutrigla gurnardus*   Length up to 30cm
A distinctive fish with a tapering body and pectoral fins partly divided into three feeler-like rays, used in sensory detection. Usually lives near rocky outcrops on muddy or sandy seabeds and sometimes found near pier and jetty supports at very low tides. Widespread around Irish coasts, commonest in S.

Father Lasher *Myxocephalus scorpius*   Length up to 15cm
Squat little fish with proportionately large, spiny head and tapering body. Body usually mottled grey-brown but often darker. Mouth rather large and gill covers spiny. Found among seaweed and stones on otherwise muddy or sandy seabeds. Common on suitable coasts around Ireland. A bottom-dwelling species.

Lumpsucker *Cyclopterus lumpus*   Length up to 40cm, often much smaller
Curious, rather round-bodied fish. Young specimens typically mottled or marbled yellow-buff and brown but older fish rather grey above and reddish below. Usually found on rocky shores and can survive in turbulent waters, clinging to rocks with sucker formed by modified pelvic fins. Commonest on S coasts.

Common Sea-snail *Liparis liparis*   Length up to 10cm
A strange little fish with a rather tadpole-like appearance. Profile smooth with oval outline. Body colour variable but usually reddish grey. Anal fin fused with tail fin. Found mainly on muddy and sandy shores, often among rocky outcrops. Widespread around coasts of Ireland, commonest in SW.

Cornish Sucker *Lepadogaster lepadogaster*   Length up to 6cm
Another strange-looking fish with flattened, tadpole-like appearance and rather pointed snout. Body colour usually reddish. Has two bluish, eye-like markings on back of head behind true eyes. Lives on rocky coasts, often in shallow water. Clings to rocks using sucker formed by modified pelvic fins. Commonest in SW.

Sole *Solea solea*   Length up to 25cm
One of the classic flatfish, easily recognised by its oval outline and very short tail whose fin is not separated from dorsal and anal fins by any distinct tail stock. Lives on sandy and muddy seabeds, often in shallow water in estuary and river mouths. Common and widespread around coasts of Ireland.

Flounder *Platichthys flesus*   Length up to 17cm
Flatfish with rounded-oval outline and long dorsal and anal fins separated from tail fin by distinct tail stock; dorsal fin starts near eye. Colour rather variable but usually mottled brown on upperside and pale on underside. Common and widespread on muddy and sandy seabeds around coasts of Ireland.

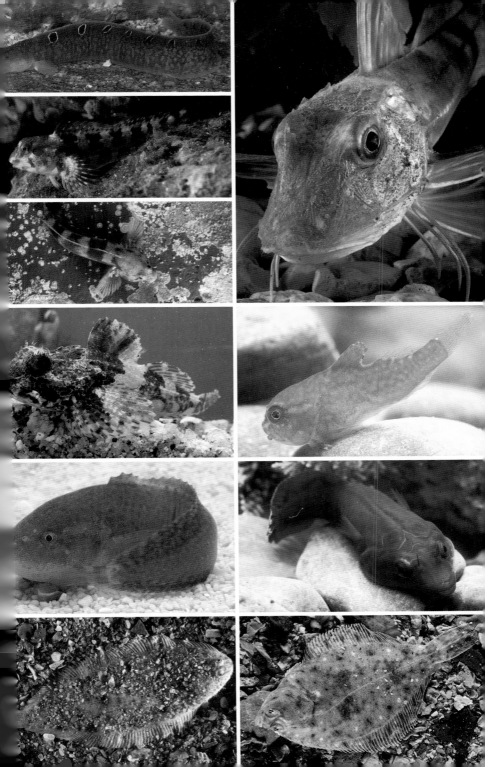

LARGE WHITE *Pieris brassicae*   Wingspan 60mm
Underwings yellowish. Upperwings creamy-white with black tip to forewing; female also has two spots on forewing. Flies May–September. Foodplants of its black and yellow caterpillars include cabbages and other garden brassicas.

SMALL WHITE *Pieris rapae*   Wingspan 45mm
Smaller and commoner than Large White. Underwings yellowish. Upperwings creamy-white with dark tip to forewing; female has two dark spots on forewing. Flies April–May and July–August. Caterpillars feed on cabbage and other brassicas.

GREEN-VEINED WHITE *Pieris napi*   Wingspan 45–50mm
Common wayside butterfly. Similar to Small White but veins on upperwings dark and greyish green on underwings, particularly hindwing. Caterpillars eat Garlic Mustard and other wild crucifers. Double-brooded, seen in spring and mid-summer.

ORANGE-TIP *Anthocharis cardamines*   Wingspan 40mm
Attractive spring butterfly, flying April–June. Male's orange patch on dark-tipped forewing absent in female; hind underwing of both sexes marbled green and white. Larvae feed mainly on Cuckoo-flower. Widespread in Ireland.

RÉAL'S WOOD WHITE *Leptidea reali* **& WOOD WHITE** *L. sinapis*   WS 40mm
Both are delicate-looking with rounded wings and feeble flight; forewings dark-tipped, most noticeably on upper surface. Fly May–July in two broods. Réal's Wood White is widespread but local in Ireland; Wood White occurs only in Burren.

BRIMSTONE *Gonepteryx rhamni*   Wingspan 60mm
Herald of spring. Single-brooded. Summer adults hibernate and emerge from February onwards on sunny days. Uniquely-shaped wings. Male's brimstone-yellow colour unmistakable. Paler female can be mistaken for large white in flight.

CLOUDED YELLOW *Colias crocea*   Wingspan 50mm
Summer migrant in variable numbers. Sometimes breeds but does not survive winter. Fast-flying and active. Dark-bordered upperwings yellow in female, orange-yellow in male. Both sexes have yellow underwings with few dark markings.

SMALL TORTOISESHELL *Nymphalis urticae*   Wingspan 42mm
Common and familiar garden and wayside species. Sun-loving. Seen on wing March–October with two or three broods. Upperwings marbled orange, yellow and black; underparts smoky-brown. Gregarious caterpillars feed on Common Nettle.

PAINTED LADY *Vanessa cardui*   Wingspan 60mm
Summer migrant to flowering meadows in variable numbers; most numerous near coasts. Sometimes breeds but does not survive winter. Upperwings marbled pinkish buff, white and black. Underwing colour buffish, pattern as upperwing.

RED ADMIRAL *Vanessa atalanta*   Wingspan 60mm
Adults hibernate in small numbers but seen mostly as summer migrant to Ireland, sometimes in good numbers. Underwings marbled smoky-grey, upperwings black with red bands and white spots. Commonest July–August. Larvae feed on nettle.

PEACOCK *Inachis io*   Wingspan 60mm
Common in Ireland except in N. Visits garden flowers. Adult flies July–September and again in spring after hibernation. Underwings smoky-brown but maroon upperwings have bold eye markings. Caterpillars feed on Common Nettle.

PEARL-BORDERED FRITILLARY *Boloria euphrosyne*   Wingspan 42mm
Sun-loving butterfly of woodland glades. Very local in Ireland. Flies May–June. Underside of hindwing shows seven silver spots on margin and two in centre. Caterpillar feeds on violets.

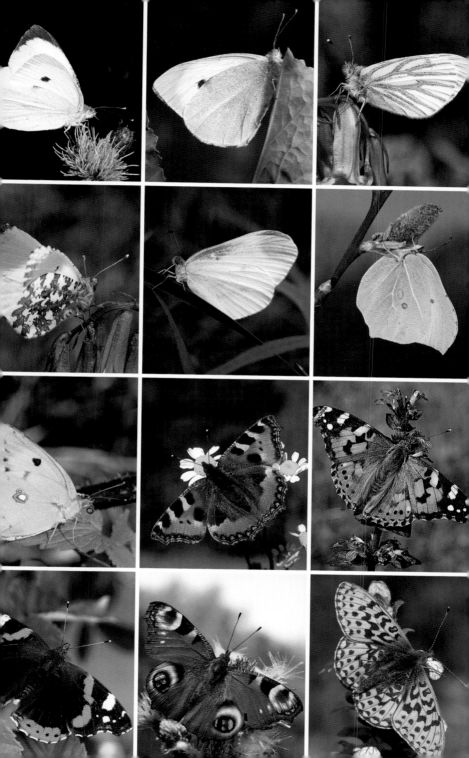

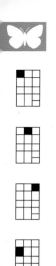

DARK GREEN FRITILLARY *Argynnis aglaja*   Wingspan 60mm
Widespread and locally common in Ireland. Flies July–August and seen on sand dunes and downs. Fast and powerful flier, visits thistles and knapweeds. Caterpillars feed on violets. Underside of hindwing has greenish scaling.

SILVER-WASHED FRITILLARY *Argynnis paphia*   Wingspan 60mm
Locally common woodland species in Ireland. Upperwings well-marked orange-brown; underside of hindwing has silvery sheen. Sun-loving adult fond of Bramble flowers; flies June–August. Larvae feed on violets.

MARSH FRITILLARY *Euphydryas aurinia*   Wingspan 40–50mm
Widespread but very local in Ireland. Flies May–June but only active when sunny. Beautifully marked wings. Favours damp heaths and moors but also dry chalk grassland. Larvae feed on Devil's-bit Scabious and plantains.

SPECKLED WOOD *Pararge aegeria*   Wingspan 45cm
Widespread but local woodland butterfly. Double-brooded, flying April–June and July–September. Favours clearings and fond of sunbathing. Upperwings dark brown with pale markings; underwings rufous brown. Caterpillars feed on grasses.

WALL BROWN *Pararge megera*   Wingspan 45cm
Widespread but local on grassy heaths and coasts. Orange-brown colour creates fritillary-like appearance but shows small eyespots on wings. Double-brooded, flying April–May and July–September. Larva feeds on grasses.

GRAYLING *Hipparchia semele*   Wingspan 50mm
Favours warm, dry places including sea cliffs, heaths and dunes. Widespread in Ireland but commonest near coasts. Invariably sits with wings folded and angled to cast the least shadow. Flies June–August.

RINGLET *Aphantopus hyperantus*   Wingspan 48mm
Widespread in Ireland and found in grassy places. Flies June–July. Has smoky-brown wings, darker on males than females, with variable numbers of small eyespots. Caterpillars feed on various grasses.

GATEKEEPER *Maniola tithonus*   Wingspan 40mm
Wayside and hedgerow butterfly, flying July–August. Locally common in S and E Ireland. Often feeds on bramble flowers. Upperwings smoky-brown with orange markings and paired eyespot on forewing. Caterpillars feed on grasses.

PURPLE HAIRSTREAK *Favonius quercus*   Wingspan 38mm
Extremely local. Flies July–August around tops of oaks on which caterpillars feed. Has purple sheen on upperwings. Underwings grey with hairstreak line.

LARGE HEATH *Coenonympha tullia*   Wingspan 38mm
Found on acid moors where larval foodplant, White Beak-sedge, common. Occurs locally in Ireland. Flies June–July in sunny weather. Underside of hindwing grey-brown; forewing orange-brown with small eyespot.

SMALL HEATH *Coenonympha pamphilus*   Wingspan 30mm
Widespread in Ireland. Caterpillars feed on grasses and adult invariably found in meadows and on downs and dunes. Double-brooded, flying mainly May–June and August–September.

MEADOW BROWN *Maniola jurtina*   Wingspan 50mm
Widespread but rather local in Ireland. Favours all kinds of grassy places; flies June–August. Upperwings brown; male has small orange patch on forewing containing eyespot; orange patch larger in female (A). Pupa (B) among grasses.

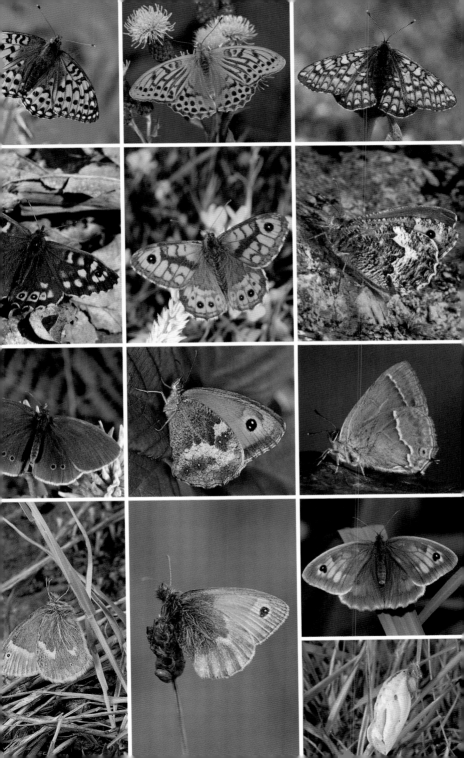

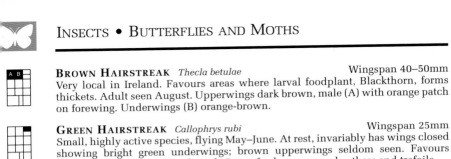

INSECTS • BUTTERFLIES AND MOTHS

BROWN HAIRSTREAK *Thecla betulae*   Wingspan 40–50mm
Very local in Ireland. Favours areas where larval foodplant, Blackthorn, forms thickets. Adult seen August. Upperwings dark brown, male (A) with orange patch on forewing. Underwings (B) orange-brown.

GREEN HAIRSTREAK *Callophrys rubi*   Wingspan 25mm
Small, highly active species, flying May–June. At rest, invariably has wings closed showing bright green underwings; brown upperwings seldom seen. Favours heaths, cliffs and downland scrub. Larva feeds on gorses, heathers and trefoils.

COMMON BLUE *Polyommatus icarus*   Wingspan 32mm
Locally common in grassy places across Ireland. Flies April–September in successive broods. Male has blue upperwings, female's being generally brown. Underside grey-brown with dark spots. Larva feeds on trefoils.

HOLLY BLUE *Celastrina argiolus*   Wingspan 30mm
Silvery in flight. Violet-blue upperwings seldom seen well. Rests showing white, black-dotted underwings. Mainly S and E Ireland. Two broods, flying April–May, laying eggs on Holly, and August–September, laying eggs on Ivy.

SMALL BLUE *Cupido minimus*   Wingspan 25mm
Small and highly active. Local in Ireland, mainly in S. Occurs where larval foodplant, Kidney Vetch, common, often on chalk grassland. Flies June–July. Upperwings smoky-brown, male with purplish iridescence. Underwings grey.

SMALL COPPER *Lycaena phlaeas*   Wingspan 25mm
Attractive, open country species. Flies May–September in two or three broods. Variable orange and dark brown on upperwings. Underwings have similar patterns to upperwings but dark brown replaced by grey-buff. Larva feeds on Sheep's Sorrel.

DINGY SKIPPER *Erynnis tages*   Wingspan 25mm
Moth-like appearance with buzzing flight and dark grey-brown upperwings; underwings reddish brown. Sexes similar. Flies May–June and favours meadows and rough ground. Local and rather scarce in Ireland.

BROWN HOUSE MOTH *Hofmannophila pseudospretella*   Length at rest 10mm
A frequent and unwelcome visitor to houses. Adult usually found in vicinity of stored natural fabrics and foods on which eggs are laid and larvae feed. Seldom flies but prefers to scuttle along floor.

MOTHER OF PEARL *Pleuroptya ruralis*   Wingspan 35mm
Flies June–August and frequently comes to light. Flight weak. Has mother of pearl sheen to wings at certain angles. Common and widespread throughout Ireland. Found in meadows, wasteground and overgrown hedgerows.

WHITE PLUME MOTH *Pterophorus pentadactyla*   Wingspan 28mm
Distinctive moth with white, dissected, feather-like wings. Often seen resting among low vegetation in daytime. Flies from dusk onwards and often attracted to light. Flies May–August. Caterpillar feeds on Hedge Bindweed. Common and widespread.

GHOST MOTH *Hepialus humuli*   Length at rest 25mm
Favours meadows and grassy hedgerows. Groups of pure white males engage in dancing display flights at dusk. Female has buffish yellow wings with orange streaks. Widespread and often common throughout much of Ireland. Flies June–August.

FIVE-SPOT BURNET *Zygaena trifolii*   Wingspan 35mm
Distinctive, day-flying moth with red hindwings and five red spots on otherwise metallic greenish blue forewings. Favours damp meadows and fairly common and widespread in Ireland. Flies July–August.

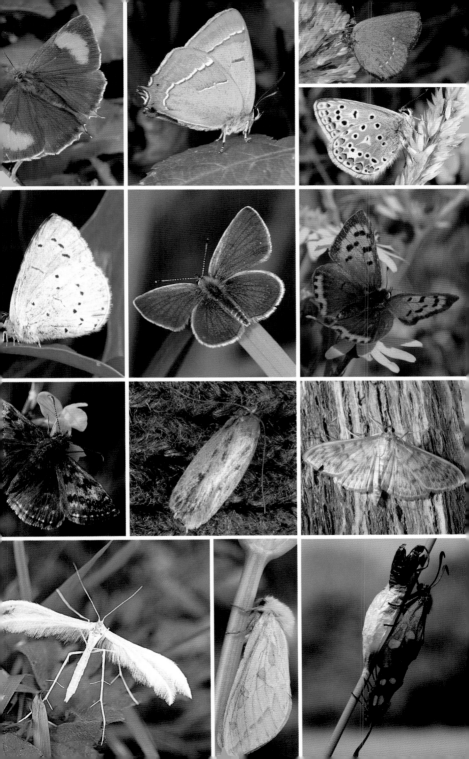

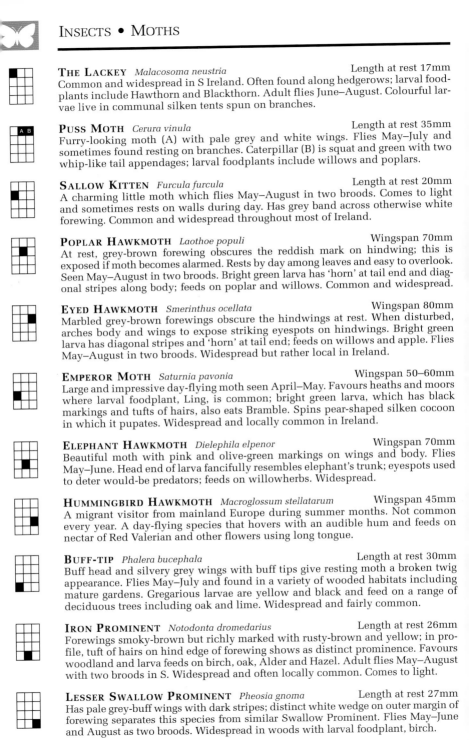

THE LACKEY *Malacosoma neustria* Length at rest 17mm
Common and widespread in S Ireland. Often found along hedgerows; larval food-plants include Hawthorn and Blackthorn. Adult flies June–August. Colourful larvae live in communal silken tents spun on branches.

PUSS MOTH *Cerura vinula* Length at rest 35mm
Furry-looking moth (A) with pale grey and white wings. Flies May–July and sometimes found resting on branches. Caterpillar (B) is squat and green with two whip-like tail appendages; larval foodplants include willows and poplars.

SALLOW KITTEN *Furcula furcula* Length at rest 20mm
A charming little moth which flies May–August in two broods. Comes to light and sometimes rests on walls during day. Has grey band across otherwise white forewing. Common and widespread throughout most of Ireland.

POPLAR HAWKMOTH *Laothoe populi* Wingspan 70mm
At rest, grey-brown forewing obscures the reddish mark on hindwing; this is exposed if moth becomes alarmed. Rests by day among leaves and easy to overlook. Seen May–August in two broods. Bright green larva has 'horn' at tail end and diagonal stripes along body; feeds on poplar and willows. Common and widespread.

EYED HAWKMOTH *Smerinthus ocellata* Wingspan 80mm
Marbled grey-brown forewings obscure the hindwings at rest. When disturbed, arches body and wings to expose striking eyespots on hindwings. Bright green larva has diagonal stripes and 'horn' at tail end; feeds on willows and apple. Flies May–August in two broods. Widespread but rather local in Ireland.

EMPEROR MOTH *Saturnia pavonia* Wingspan 50–60mm
Large and impressive day-flying moth seen April–May. Favours heaths and moors where larval foodplant, Ling, is common; bright green larva, which has black markings and tufts of hairs, also eats Bramble. Spins pear-shaped silken cocoon in which it pupates. Widespread and locally common in Ireland.

ELEPHANT HAWKMOTH *Dielephila elpenor* Wingspan 70mm
Beautiful moth with pink and olive-green markings on wings and body. Flies May–June. Head end of larva fancifully resembles elephant's trunk; eyespots used to deter would-be predators; feeds on willowherbs. Widespread.

HUMMINGBIRD HAWKMOTH *Macroglossum stellatarum* Wingspan 45mm
A migrant visitor from mainland Europe during summer months. Not common every year. A day-flying species that hovers with an audible hum and feeds on nectar of Red Valerian and other flowers using long tongue.

BUFF-TIP *Phalera bucephala* Length at rest 30mm
Buff head and silvery grey wings with buff tips give resting moth a broken twig appearance. Flies May–July and found in a variety of wooded habitats including mature gardens. Gregarious larvae are yellow and black and feed on a range of deciduous trees including oak and lime. Widespread and fairly common.

IRON PROMINENT *Notodonta dromedarius* Length at rest 26mm
Forewings smoky-brown but richly marked with rusty-brown and yellow; in profile, tuft of hairs on hind edge of forewing shows as distinct prominence. Favours woodland and larva feeds on birch, oak, Alder and Hazel. Adult flies May–August with two broods in S. Widespread and often locally common. Comes to light.

LESSER SWALLOW PROMINENT *Pheosia gnoma* Length at rest 27mm
Has pale grey-buff wings with dark stripes; distinct white wedge on outer margin of forewing separates this species from similar Swallow Prominent. Flies May–June and August as two broods. Widespread in woods with larval foodplant, birch.

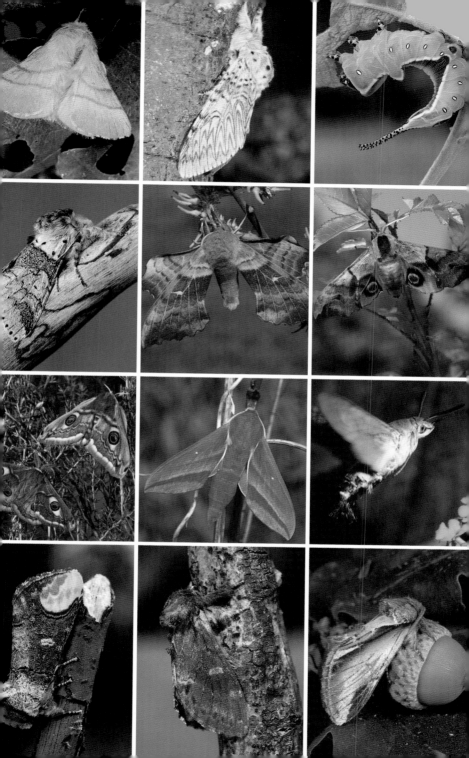

PEBBLE PROMINENT *Eligmodonta ziczac*   Length at rest 25mm
Buffish brown forewings have grey-brown fingernail-like mark near tip and white patch on leading edge. Larva feeds on Sallow, willow and Aspen. Adult flies May–June, sometimes August as second brood. Widespread in woodlands.

PALE PROMINENT *Pterostoma palpina*   Length at rest 30mm
In profile, greyish brown wings show prominences along back; palps project at head end and tufted tip to abdomen protrudes beyond wings. Flies May–August. Favours woodlands and hedgerows where larval foodplants, Sallow and Aspen, grow.

PALE TUSSOCK *Calliteara pudibunda*   Length at rest 30mm
Attractive, hairy moth (A) with grey or greyish buff wings. Associated with wooded areas where yellow and black, hairy larva (B) feeds on birch, oak, lime and other deciduous trees. Locally common in S and W Ireland. Flies May–June.

THE VAPOURER *Orgyia antiqua*   Length of male at rest 16mm
Male has chestnut forewing with conspicuous white spot on trailing edge; flies July–September. Wingless female sometimes seen near clusters of eggs laid on bark of deciduous trees and shrubs. Larva has tufts of yellow and black hairs.

YELLOW-TAIL *Euproctis similis*   Length at rest 24mm
Pure white moth exposes yellow-tipped abdomen when alarmed. Favours woods and hedges where larval foodplants, various deciduous shrubs, are common. Flies June–August. Hairy larva is marked with black and red.

RUBY TIGER *Phragmatobia fuliginosa*   Length at rest 22mm
Has reddish forewings which conceal pink or grey hindwings at rest. Widespread and often common. Adult flies May–June, sometimes August in second brood. Favours meadows and grassy hedgerows.

GARDEN TIGER *Arctia caja*   Wingspan 65mm
Familiar and widespread moth, found in most habitats. Flies July–August. Often comes to outdoor lights around houses. Dark-spotted orange hindwings concealed by forewings unless moth disturbed. Hairy larva feeds on wide range of plants.

WHITE ERMINE *Spilosoma lubricipeda*   Length at rest 28mm
Attractive moth whose white wings bear conspicuous black spots. Yellow and black abdomen usually concealed by wings at rest. Widespread and common in most habitats. Flies May–July and comes to light. Larva eats wide variety of plants.

MUSLIN MOTH *Diaphora mendica*   Length at rest 23mm
Male reddish buff, female white; both sexes have black spots on wings. Night-flying male comes to light; female often diurnal. Common and widespread in meadows. Larval foodplants include dandelions and plantains. Flies May–June.

THE CINNABAR *Tyria jacobaeae*   Length at rest 22mm
Recognised by red and charcoal-grey wings (A). Flies May–July, usually at night but also during day. Widespread and common in meadows and on coasts. Orange and black striped larvae (B) feed mainly on Ragwort; usually seen in small groups.

COMMON FOOTMAN *Eilema lurideola*   Length at rest 25mm
Widespread and locally common in Ireland. Flies July–August and favours wooded habitats. Larva eats lichens on the bark of trees and shrubs. Moth rests with wings rolled lengthways in somewhat caddisfly-like manner.

ROSY FOOTMAN *Miltochrista miniata*   Length at rest 14mm
Attractive little moth with rosy-orange forewings bearing black spots. Rests with wings pressed close to surface on which it is clinging. Favours wooded areas; larvae feed on lichens on tree bark. Occurs in SE Ireland.

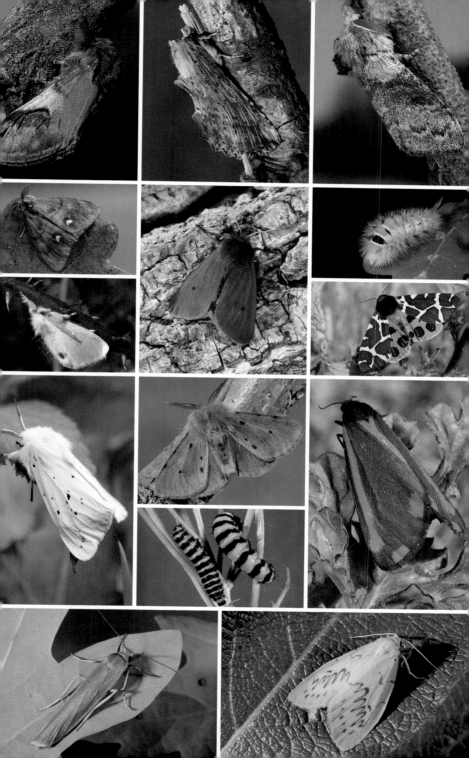

HEART AND DART *Agrotis exclamationis*   Length at rest 20mm
So-called because of dark markings on forewings. Widespread and extremely common; often the most numerous moth recorded at traps. Flies May–July. Larva eats a wide range of plants and adult found in gardens, meadows and woodland.

TRUE LOVER'S KNOT *Lycophotia porphyrea*   Length at rest 16mm
Small but well-marked moth but with ground colour of forewing rather variable. Flies June–August. Favours heathy places and open woods where larval food-plants, Ling and Bell Heather, grow. Widespread in Ireland.

BROAD-BORDERED YELLOW UNDERWING *Noctua fimbriata*   Length at rest 25mm
At rest, variably marked forewings obscure yellow and black hindwings. Moth is easily disturbed, however, needing little encouragement to fly even in daytime. Seen July–September. Widespread and common. Larva eats wide range of plants.

LARGE YELLOW UNDERWING *Noctua pronuba*   Length at rest 25mm
Similar to *N. fimbriata* but forewings more marbled and yellow hindwings with only narrow black border. Flies June–September. Common and widespread in Ireland in gardens, meadows and woods. Larva eats almost any herbaceous plant.

BROOM MOTH *Ceramica pisi*   Length at rest 22mm
Ground colour of forewing rather variable. Has characteristic pale spot on hind edge of forewing, the spots on both wings meeting when moth at rest. Widespread and fairly common. Flies May–June. Larva feeds on Broom and many other plants.

HEBREW CHARACTER *Orthosia gothica*   Length at rest 20mm
Common and widespread in Ireland. Flies March–April and comes to light. Recognised by dark mark on wings having semi-circular section removed as if by hole-punch. Found in woods and gardens. Larva feeds on variety of plants.

BROWN-LINE BRIGHT-EYE *Mythimna conigera*   Length at rest 21mm
Markings on reddish brown wings accurately described by name. Flies June–August. Widespread and often common in much of Ireland. Found in meadows and grassy hedgerows, the larva feeding on various species of grasses.

COMMON WAINSCOT *Mythimna pallens*   Length at rest 20mm
Has straw-coloured forewings, the veins of which are white; white hindwings usually hidden at rest. Widespread and locally common. Flies June–October in two broods. Favours meadows and hedges. Larva feeds on various grass species.

THE SHARK *Cucullia umbratica*   Length at rest 32mm
Unusually shaped moth sometimes found resting on frayed wooden surfaces in daytime. Flies May–July. Locally common in S Ireland; less so further N. Favours rough meadows and wasteground. Larva eats Sow-thistles.

POPLAR GREY *Acronicta megacephala*   Length at rest 20mm
Has grey forewings well-marked with darker lines and well-defined pale circle; pale hindwings usually hidden at rest. Favours parks, gardens and woods. Flies May–August. Larva eats poplars and willows. Widespread but local.

GREY DAGGER *Acronicta psi*   Length at rest 23mm
Easily recognised by pale grey forewings bearing distinctive black dagger-like markings. Common and widespread in Ireland. Flies June–August and favours woodland. Colourful larva feeds on deciduous shrubs and trees.

THE MILLER *Acronicta leporina*   Length at rest 20mm
Ground colour of forewing varies from pale to dark grey and typically shows jagged black transverse line from leading edge. Flies April–June and found in woodland. Hairy larva feeds mainly on birch but also on other deciduous trees.

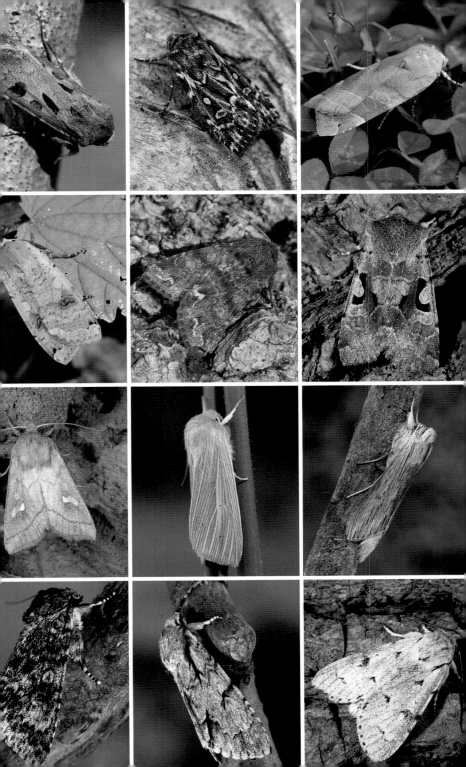

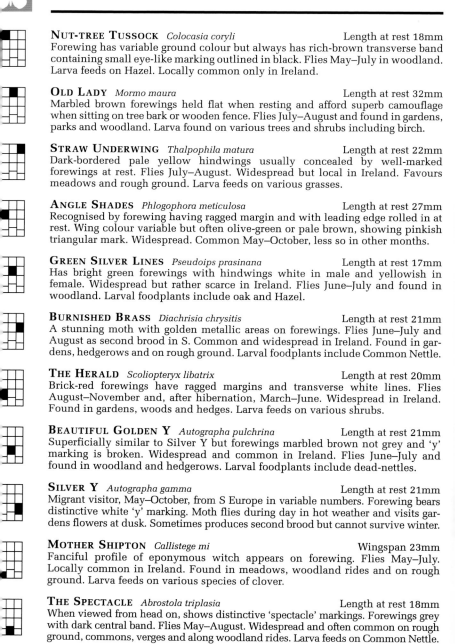

NUT-TREE TUSSOCK *Colocasia coryli*　　　　　Length at rest 18mm
Forewing has variable ground colour but always has rich-brown transverse band containing small eye-like marking outlined in black. Flies May–July in woodland. Larva feeds on Hazel. Locally common only in Ireland.

OLD LADY *Mormo maura*　　　　　Length at rest 32mm
Marbled brown forewings held flat when resting and afford superb camouflage when sitting on tree bark or wooden fence. Flies July–August and found in gardens, parks and woodland. Larva found on various trees and shrubs including birch.

STRAW UNDERWING *Thalpophila matura*　　　　　Length at rest 22mm
Dark-bordered pale yellow hindwings usually concealed by well-marked forewings at rest. Flies July–August. Widespread but local in Ireland. Favours meadows and rough ground. Larva feeds on various grasses.

ANGLE SHADES *Phlogophora meticulosa*　　　　　Length at rest 27mm
Recognised by forewing having ragged margin and with leading edge rolled in at rest. Wing colour variable but often olive-green or pale brown, showing pinkish triangular mark. Widespread. Common May–October, less so in other months.

GREEN SILVER LINES *Pseudoips prasinana*　　　　　Length at rest 17mm
Has bright green forewings with hindwings white in male and yellowish in female. Widespread but rather scarce in Ireland. Flies June–July and found in woodland. Larval foodplants include oak and Hazel.

BURNISHED BRASS *Diachrisia chrysitis*　　　　　Length at rest 21mm
A stunning moth with golden metallic areas on forewings. Flies June–July and August as second brood in S. Common and widespread in Ireland. Found in gardens, hedgerows and on rough ground. Larval foodplants include Common Nettle.

THE HERALD *Scoliopteryx libatrix*　　　　　Length at rest 20mm
Brick-red forewings have ragged margins and transverse white lines. Flies August–November and, after hibernation, March–June. Widespread in Ireland. Found in gardens, woods and hedges. Larva feeds on various shrubs.

BEAUTIFUL GOLDEN Y *Autographa pulchrina*　　　　　Length at rest 21mm
Superficially similar to Silver Y but forewings marbled brown not grey and 'y' marking is broken. Widespread and common in Ireland. Flies June–July and found in woodland and hedgerows. Larval foodplants include dead-nettles.

SILVER Y *Autographa gamma*　　　　　Length at rest 21mm
Migrant visitor, May–October, from S Europe in variable numbers. Forewing bears distinctive white 'y' marking. Moth flies during day in hot weather and visits gardens flowers at dusk. Sometimes produces second brood but cannot survive winter.

MOTHER SHIPTON *Callistege mi*　　　　　Wingspan 23mm
Fanciful profile of eponymous witch appears on forewing. Flies May–July. Locally common in Ireland. Found in meadows, woodland rides and on rough ground. Larva feeds on various species of clover.

THE SPECTACLE *Abrostola triplasia*　　　　　Length at rest 18mm
When viewed from head on, shows distinctive 'spectacle' markings. Forewings grey with dark central band. Flies May–August. Widespread and often common on rough ground, commons, verges and along woodland rides. Larva feeds on Common Nettle.

RED UNDERWING *Catocala nupta*　　　　　Wingspan 65mm
Black-barred red underwings usually concealed at rest by marbled grey and brown forewings; they are revealed when moth is disturbed. Flies August–September. Extremely rare.

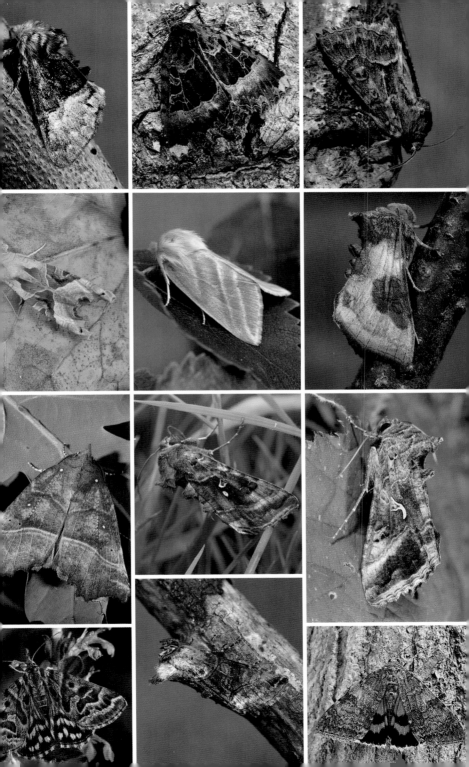

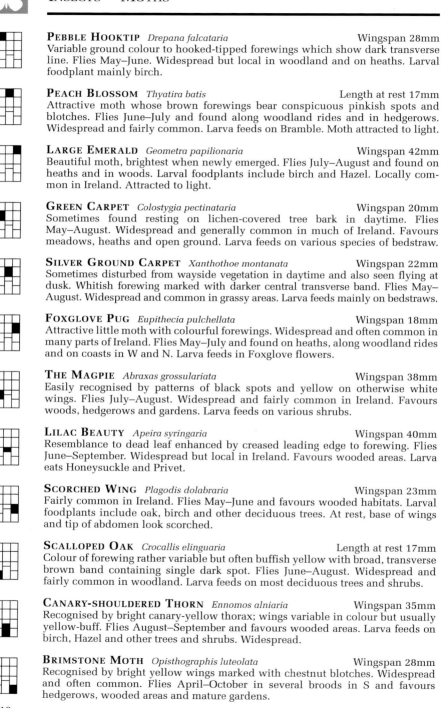

PEBBLE HOOKTIP *Drepana falcataria* Wingspan 28mm
Variable ground colour to hooked-tipped forewings which show dark transverse line. Flies May–June. Widespread but local in woodland and on heaths. Larval foodplant mainly birch.

PEACH BLOSSOM *Thyatira batis* Length at rest 17mm
Attractive moth whose brown forewings bear conspicuous pinkish spots and blotches. Flies June–July and found along woodland rides and in hedgerows. Widespread and fairly common. Larva feeds on Bramble. Moth attracted to light.

LARGE EMERALD *Geometra papilionaria* Wingspan 42mm
Beautiful moth, brightest when newly emerged. Flies July–August and found on heaths and in woods. Larval foodplants include birch and Hazel. Locally common in Ireland. Attracted to light.

GREEN CARPET *Colostygia pectinataria* Wingspan 20mm
Sometimes found resting on lichen-covered tree bark in daytime. Flies May–August. Widespread and generally common in much of Ireland. Favours meadows, heaths and open ground. Larva feeds on various species of bedstraw.

SILVER GROUND CARPET *Xanthorhoe montanata* Wingspan 22mm
Sometimes disturbed from wayside vegetation in daytime and also seen flying at dusk. Whitish forewing marked with darker central transverse band. Flies May–August. Widespread and common in grassy areas. Larva feeds mainly on bedstraws.

FOXGLOVE PUG *Eupithecia pulchellata* Wingspan 18mm
Attractive little moth with colourful forewings. Widespread and often common in many parts of Ireland. Flies May–July and found on heaths, along woodland rides and on coasts in W and N. Larva feeds in Foxglove flowers.

THE MAGPIE *Abraxas grossulariata* Wingspan 38mm
Easily recognised by patterns of black spots and yellow on otherwise white wings. Flies July–August. Widespread and fairly common in Ireland. Favours woods, hedgerows and gardens. Larva feeds on various shrubs.

LILAC BEAUTY *Apeira syringaria* Wingspan 40mm
Resemblance to dead leaf enhanced by creased leading edge to forewing. Flies June–September. Widespread but local in Ireland. Favours wooded areas. Larva eats Honeysuckle and Privet.

SCORCHED WING *Plagodis dolabraria* Wingspan 23mm
Fairly common in Ireland. Flies May–June and favours wooded habitats. Larval foodplants include oak, birch and other deciduous trees. At rest, base of wings and tip of abdomen look scorched.

SCALLOPED OAK *Crocallis elinguaria* Length at rest 17mm
Colour of forewing rather variable but often buffish yellow with broad, transverse brown band containing single dark spot. Flies June–August. Widespread and fairly common in woodland. Larva feeds on most deciduous trees and shrubs.

CANARY-SHOULDERED THORN *Ennomos alniaria* Wingspan 35mm
Recognised by bright canary-yellow thorax; wings variable in colour but usually yellow-buff. Flies August–September and favours wooded areas. Larva feeds on birch, Hazel and other trees and shrubs. Widespread.

BRIMSTONE MOTH *Opisthographis luteolata* Wingspan 28mm
Recognised by bright yellow wings marked with chestnut blotches. Widespread and often common. Flies April–October in several broods in S and favours hedgerows, wooded areas and mature gardens.

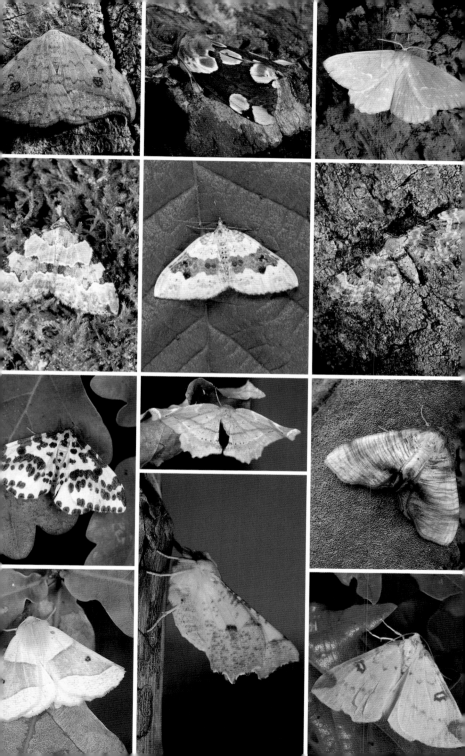

ORANGE MOTH *Angerona prunaria*   Wingspan 40mm
Attractive moth, male of which has orange-brown wings, those of female being yellowish. Forewings of both sexes marked with numerous short, transverse lines. Very local in S Ireland. Flies June–July and favours woodland and heaths. Larval foodplants include birches, Hawthorn and Ling.

SPECKLED YELLOW *Pseudopanthera macularia*   Wingspan 30mm
Wings have deep yellow ground colour and grey-brown blotches. Fairly common day-flying moth often disturbed from wayside vegetation. Flies May–June and locally common in S Ireland. Favours woodland rides, rough ground and hedgerows. Larval foodplants include Wood-sage.

SWALLOWTAILED MOTH *Ourapteryx sambucaria*   Wingspan 52mm
Attractive moth (B), easily recognised by pale yellow wings, angular tip to forewing and short tail streamer on hindwing. Flies June–July and widespread and locally common in Ireland. Found in woodland and gardens and along hedgerows. Comes to light. Foodplants of larva (A) include Ivy and Hawthorn.

WINTER MOTH *Operophtera brumata*   Wingspan of male 28mm
Flies October–February and often seen in car headlights on mild winter nights. Widespread and often extremely common along hedgerows and in woodland and gardens. Wingless female, sometimes coupled with male, can be found by searching twigs after dark by torchlight. Larva feeds on most deciduous trees and shrubs.

MOTTLED UMBER *Erannis defoliaria*   Wingspan of male 40mm
Forewings of male vary from pale to dark brown; pale central band, bordered by black line and containing black dot, usually visible. Female wingless. Flies October–December and comes to light. Widespread and fairly common. Favours woods, hedgerows and gardens. Larva feeds on wide range of deciduous trees and shrubs.

PEPPERED MOTH *Biston betularia*   Wingspan 48mm
Colour varies but usually one of two extremes: all-black melanic form and normal form with white ground colour well-marked with black which is camouflaged on bark. Flies May–August. Common and widespread in Ireland. Favours woods and gardens. Larva eats a wide range of plants.

OAK BEAUTY *Biston strataria*   Length at rest 23mm
Attractive moth with good camouflage on tree bark. Flies March–April. Widespread but rather local and scarce in Ireland. Favours wooded areas, hedgerows and gardens. Larval foodplants include deciduous trees such as oak, Hazel, Alder and elm. Male comes to light.

BRINDLED BEAUTY *Lycia hirtaria*   Wingspan 40mm
Colour rather variable but usually grey-brown; forewings also show black lines and stippling, with yellow-buff suffusion. Flies March–April and male comes to light. Widespread but scarce and local in Ireland. Favours wooded areas. Larva feeds on deciduous trees.

MOTTLED BEAUTY *Boarmia repandata*   Wingspan 38mm
Ground colour of wings usually pale grey-brown but sometimes darker. Wings always have fine black lines and stippling which produce superb camouflage on tree bark. Widespread and often common in Ireland. Flies June–July and found in woods and gardens. Larval diet includes birch, oak and Bramble.

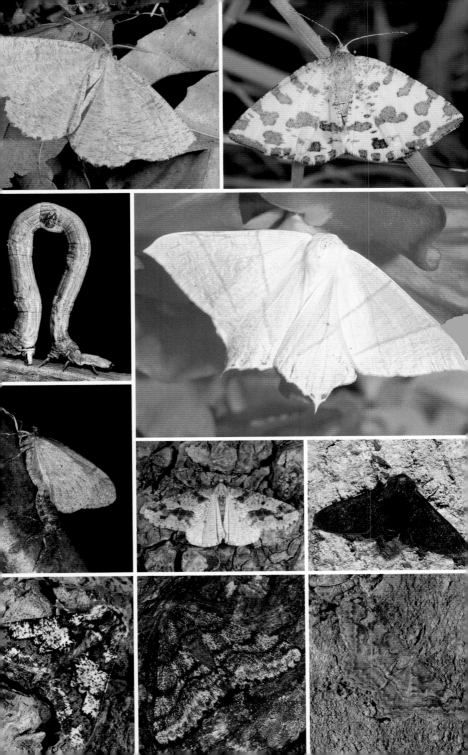

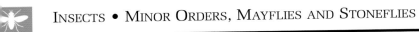

BRISTLETAIL   *Petrobius maritimus*   Body length 10mm
A curious little insect that is found on rocky shores above the high tide line and
in sea caves; widespread around the coasts of Ireland. The body is elongate and
it lacks wings. It has long antennae and three filaments at the tail end. Moves rapidly but in a curious scuttling manner. Feeds on detritus.

SPRINGTAIL   Order Collembola   Length 2–3mm
One of several common species, all of which are tiny, primitive insects that lack
wings. They are characterised by their ability to leap using a sprung projection on
the underside of the abdomen. Members of the Order are found in damp areas
such as leaf litter and compost heaps where they feed on detritus.

Ephemera danica   Body length 20mm
A familiar mayfly, widespread in Ireland. The orange-brown nymph has tapering,
snout-like projection and three tail appendages; it lives buried in the silt and sand
at the bottom of alkaline rivers and lakes. Like all mayflies, a winged sub-imago
emerges from the nymphal skin in the spring and shortly afterwards moults again
into the full adult stage, which has spots on the wing.

Ephemera vulgata   Body length 20mm
Superficially similar to *Ephemera danica* and much more scarce. Adult has a yellowish body but dark markings on upper surface of abdomen are usually triangular rather than oblong. Although, like all mayflies, the adult stage is short-lived,
the period of emergence extends May–August. The orange-brown nymph lives in
burrows in sand at the bottom of slow-flowing rivers.

Chloeon dipterum   Body length 5mm
A common and widespread mayfly in Ireland. The nymph can be found in a range
of standing water habitats including ponds, streams and canals; it has long, hairy
tail appendages and can swim well with a wriggling motion. The adult is seen in
spring and summer. It lacks hindwings and the forewings are clear but have a
beautiful sheen at some angles. The body colour is yellowish brown.

MAYFLY NYMPH   Order Ephemeroptera   Body length 8mm
Like all mayfly nymphs, this typical nymph shows the three tail appendages that
are characteristic of the group. Representative species can be found in all types of
fresh water from fast-flowing streams to the still waters of lakes and streams.
Some mayfly nymphs are capable of sustained swimming while others tire easily.
Pollution sensitive.

Perla bipunctata   Body length 16–24mm
The nymph of this stonefly shows the two tail appendages typical of the group. It
is found in stony rivers, mainly in the N and W. Nymphs are sometimes seen clinging to stones in the water and shed nymphal skins can be found among waterside
vegetation from May–July after adult has emerged. Adult's yellowish body is
shrouded by smoky wings at rest; two appendages project beyond wingtips.

Nemoura cinerea   Body length 6–9mm
A widespread and fairly common stonefly seen May–July. The adult is sometimes
disturbed from vegetation growing beside clean, fast-flowing streams and rivers.
It prefers to creep away from danger and has rather sluggish flight. The wings are
smoky-brown and, at rest, appear to be rolled lengthways around the body; the
tail appendages are very reduced and do not project beyond wings at rest.

Dinocras cephalotes   Body length 22mm
A large and robust stonefly, found in parts of the N and W. Nymph lives in fast-flowing stony, upland rivers and streams and adult is sometimes found among waterside vegetation from May–July. Body of adult is mostly dark brown and shows two
long tail appendages that project beyond smoky-grey wings when at rest.

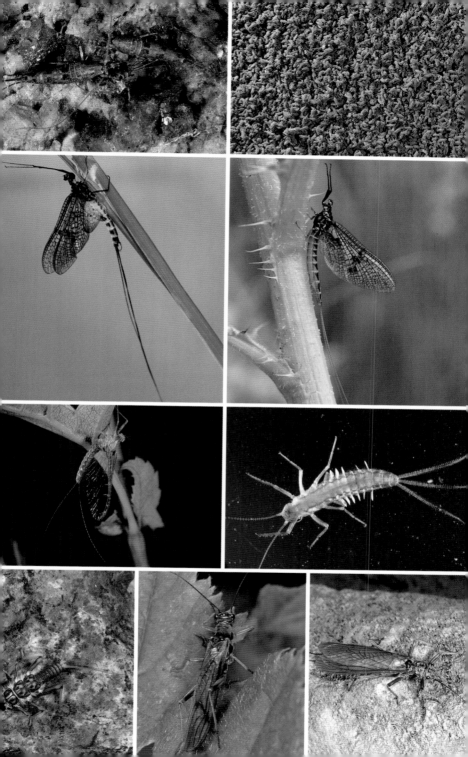

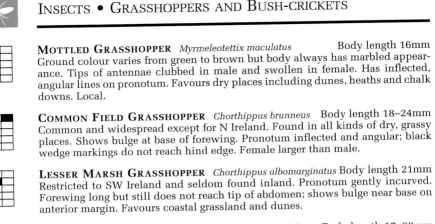

MOTTLED GRASSHOPPER *Myrmeleotettix maculatus*   Body length 16mm
Ground colour varies from green to brown but body always has marbled appearance. Tips of antennae clubbed in male and swollen in female. Has inflected, angular lines on pronotum. Favours dry places including dunes, heaths and chalk downs. Local.

COMMON FIELD GRASSHOPPER *Chorthippus brunneus*   Body length 18–24mm
Common and widespread except for N Ireland. Found in all kinds of dry, grassy places. Shows bulge at base of forewing. Pronotum inflected and angular; black wedge markings do not reach hind edge. Female larger than male.

LESSER MARSH GRASSHOPPER *Chorthippus albomarginatus* Body length 21mm
Restricted to SW Ireland and seldom found inland. Pronotum gently incurved. Forewing long but still does not reach tip of abdomen; shows bulge near base on anterior margin. Favours coastal grassland and dunes.

COMMON GREEN GRASSHOPPER *Omocestus viridulus*   Body length 17–20mm
Widespread and often common in Ireland. Favours all kinds of grassy places. Body colour usually pure green. Shows keel on top of head; pronotum distinctly incurved. Forewings do not have a bulge near base on anterior margin.

LARGE MARSH GRASSHOPPER *Stethophyma grossum*   Body length 28–32mm
Our largest grasshopper. Local and restricted to floating acid bogs in W Ireland where bog moss flourishes. Body and wings well marked with lime green, yellow and black. Hind legs marked with black and yellow bands.

SPECKLED BUSH-CRICKET *Leptophyes punctatissima*   Body length 14mm
Body green, speckled with black dots and rather compact, that of female bearing scimitar-shaped ovipositor. Legs long and spindly. Scarce and local in S. Favours hedges and scrub. Often on Bramble leaves.

OAK BUSH-CRICKET *Meconema thalassiniuim*   Body length 15mm
Slender green body, that of female having narrow, slightly upcurved ovipositor. Legs long and spindly. Most active after dark and attracted to lighted windows. Extremely local in SW Ireland. Favours woodland and gardens.

ROESEL'S BUSH-CRICKET *Metrioptera roeselii*   Body length 15–18mm
Recently recorded in Ireland for the first time. If recent expansion of range in England is a guide, the species could soon be widespread. Body marbled brown with pale margin to entire pronotum side-flap. Forewings reach halfway along abdomen. Favours damp meadows.

COMMON GROUNDHOPPER *Tetrix undulata*   Body length 10mm
Unobtrusive little insect, easily overlooked because of camouflaged appearance and small size. Colour variable but usually marbled brown. Wings shorter than pronotum which extends length of abdomen. Widespread but local in Ireland.

SLENDER GROUNDHOPPER *Tetrix subulata*   Total length 12–14mm
Similar to Common Groundhopper but pronotum is proportionally long, reaching to hind knees; wings are similarly long and insect is capable of flight. Colour variable but usually marbled brown. Associated with damp ground. Restricted to Galway.

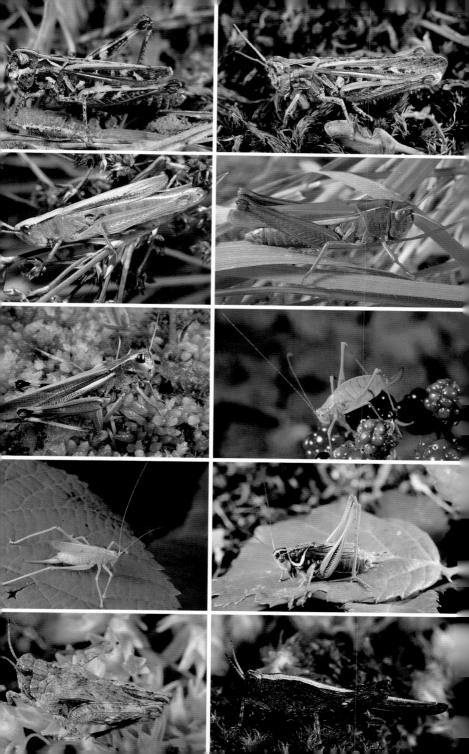

BROWN HAWKER *Aeshna grandis*　　　　　　　　Length 74mm
Easily recognised, even in flight, by brown body and bronze wings. At rest, blue spots on second and third segments of male's abdomen can be noticed; these are absent in female. Extremely local in Ireland. Found on well-vegetated ponds, lakes and canals. Patrols regular hunting territory around margins which is vigorously defended against intruders. Flies mainly July–September. Nymph mostly black and white.

BLACK-LINED SKIMMER *Orthetrum cancellatum*　　　Length 50mm
Mature male has blue eyes and black-tipped blue abdomen with orange-yellow spots on sides. Female and immature male yellow-brown with black lines on abdomen. Wings of both sexes clear even at base. Flies June–August. Skims low over water and frequently uses regular perch. Favours marshes, lakes and flooded gravel pits. Extremely local.

KEELED SKIMMER *Orthetrum coerulecens*　　　　Length 40–45mm
Mature male has blue eyes and narrow and keeled, powdery blue abdomen. Female and immature male have a uniformly yellowish brown body; wings often tinged yellow too. Flies June–August. Skims low over marshy ground near water. Local and restricted to pools in SW.

COMMON DARTER *Sympetrum striolatum*　　　　　Length 36mm
Widespread and generally common in Ireland. Mature male (A) has blood-red abdomen but in immature male and female this is orange-brown. Nymph (B) found among pondweeds and debris. Frequently rests on ground but also uses perches. Flies June–late autumn; often the latest-flying species of dragonfly.

RUDDY DARTER *Sympetrum sanguineum*　　　　　Length 35mm
Both sexes and all ages similar in size and colour to Common Darter. Male, however, is easily recognised by marked constriction towards front of abdomen. Locally common in SE Ireland. Favours ponds, marshes and lakes. Frequently perches with wings depressed slightly. Flies July and August.

DOWNY EMERALD *Cordulia aenea*　　　　　　　Length 48mm
Attractive dragonfly (A) with green head and thorax and bronze-green abdomen with metallic sheen. Thorax coated with hairs and base of wings yellowish. Front of abdomen constricted in male. Flies in June and July. Very scarce. Flies fast and low over water but perches high in overhanging tree or bush. Very alert. Nymph (B) found in ponds, lakes and canals.

FOUR-SPOTTED CHASER *Libellula quadrimaculata*　　Length 40–45mm
Well-marked dragonfly. Sexes alike. Adult has an orange-brown body, the margins of the abdominal segments scalloped yellow. Note the four wings spots – one centrally on the leading edge of each wing – and the dark and fulvous wing bases. Favours bogs and marshes. Widespread and common.

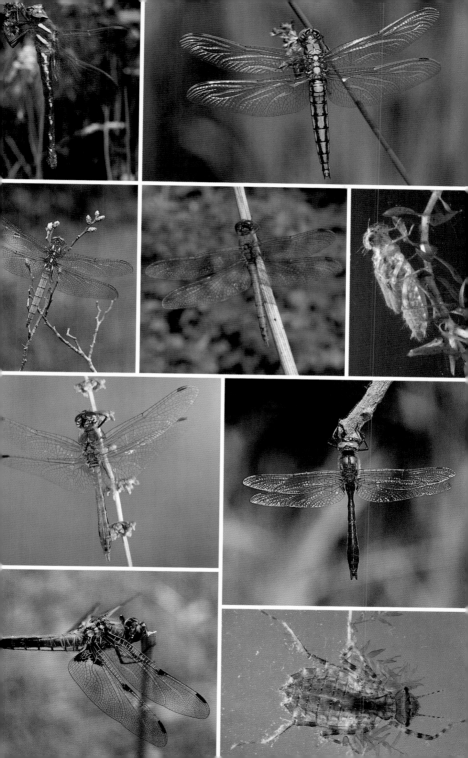

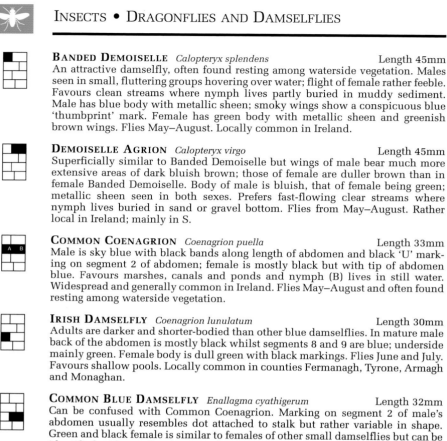

BANDED DEMOISELLE *Calopteryx splendens*　　　　Length 45mm
An attractive damselfly, often found resting among waterside vegetation. Males seen in small, fluttering groups hovering over water; flight of female rather feeble. Favours clean streams where nymph lives partly buried in muddy sediment. Male has blue body with metallic sheen; smoky wings show a conspicuous blue 'thumbprint' mark. Female has green body with metallic sheen and greenish brown wings. Flies May–August. Locally common in Ireland.

DEMOISELLE AGRION *Calopteryx virgo*　　　　Length 45mm
Superficially similar to Banded Demoiselle but wings of male bear much more extensive areas of dark bluish brown; those of female are duller brown than in female Banded Demoiselle. Body of male is bluish, that of female being green; metallic sheen seen in both sexes. Prefers fast-flowing clear streams where nymph lives buried in sand or gravel bottom. Flies from May–August. Rather local in Ireland; mainly in S.

COMMON COENAGRION *Coenagrion puella*　　　　Length 33mm
Male is sky blue with black bands along length of abdomen and black 'U' marking on segment 2 of abdomen; female is mostly black but with tip of abdomen blue. Favours marshes, canals and ponds and nymph (B) lives in still water. Widespread and generally common in Ireland. Flies May–August and often found resting among waterside vegetation.

IRISH DAMSELFLY *Coenagrion lunulatum*　　　　Length 30mm
Adults are darker and shorter-bodied than other blue damselflies. In mature male back of the abdomen is mostly black whilst segments 8 and 9 are blue; underside mainly green. Female body is dull green with black markings. Flies June and July. Favours shallow pools. Locally common in counties Fermanagh, Tyrone, Armagh and Monaghan.

COMMON BLUE DAMSELFLY *Enallagma cyathigerum*　　　　Length 32mm
Can be confused with Common Coenagrion. Marking on segment 2 of male's abdomen usually resembles dot attached to stalk but rather variable in shape. Green and black female is similar to females of other small damselflies but can be identified with certainty by ventral spine on segment 8 of abdomen. Widespread in Ireland and generally common. Favours well-vegetated lakes, ponds and canals and flies May–early September; often rests on emergent plants.

BLUE-TAILED DAMSELFLY *Ischnura elegans*　　　　Length 32mm
A common and widespread species in much of Ireland. Both sexes easily identified by mainly black body with segment 8 of abdomen sky blue. Favours ponds, lakes, canals and ditches; tolerant of slightly polluted waters. Flies May–August.

LARGE RED DAMSELFLY *Pyrrhosoma nymphula*　　　　Length 35mm
A distinctive, bright red damselfly; abdomen marked with black, more extensive on female than male. Common and widespread across much of Ireland. Found in a wide variety of freshwater habitats including ponds, lakes, streams, canals and bogs. Flight rather weak and frequently settles on waterside vegetation. Often the first damselfly seen in spring and flies May–August.

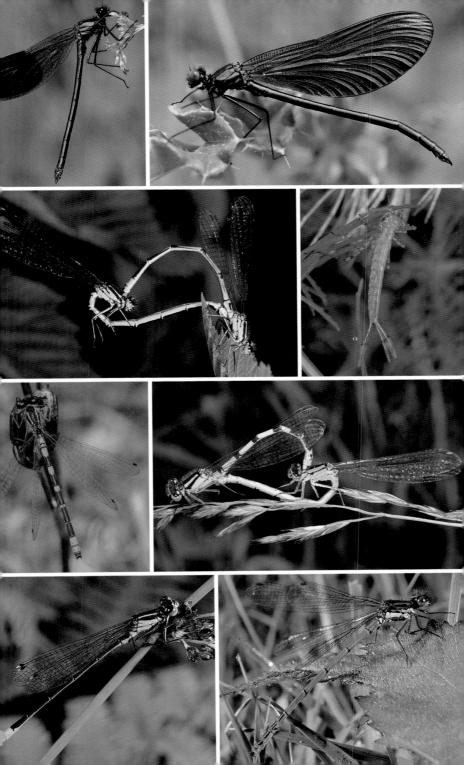

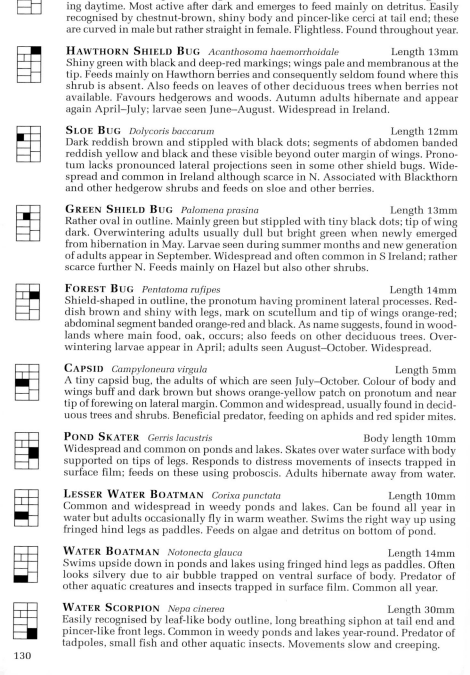

COMMON EARWIG *Forficula auricularia* Length 13mm
Common and widespread earwig. Found in leaf litter and under stones or logs during daytime. Most active after dark and emerges to feed mainly on detritus. Easily recognised by chestnut-brown, shiny body and pincer-like cerci at tail end; these are curved in male but rather straight in female. Flightless. Found throughout year.

HAWTHORN SHIELD BUG *Acanthosoma haemorrhoidale* Length 13mm
Shiny green with black and deep-red markings; wings pale and membranous at the tip. Feeds mainly on Hawthorn berries and consequently seldom found where this shrub is absent. Also feeds on leaves of other deciduous trees when berries not available. Favours hedgerows and woods. Autumn adults hibernate and appear again April–July; larvae seen June–August. Widespread in Ireland.

SLOE BUG *Dolycoris baccarum* Length 12mm
Dark reddish brown and stippled with black dots; segments of abdomen banded reddish yellow and black and these visible beyond outer margin of wings. Pronotum lacks pronounced lateral projections seen in some other shield bugs. Widespread and common in Ireland although scarce in N. Associated with Blackthorn and other hedgerow shrubs and feeds on sloe and other berries.

GREEN SHIELD BUG *Palomena prasina* Length 13mm
Rather oval in outline. Mainly green but stippled with tiny black dots; tip of wing dark. Overwintering adults usually dull but bright green when newly emerged from hibernation in May. Larvae seen during summer months and new generation of adults appear in September. Widespread and often common in S Ireland; rather scarce further N. Feeds mainly on Hazel but also other shrubs.

FOREST BUG *Pentatoma rufipes* Length 14mm
Shield-shaped in outline, the pronotum having prominent lateral processes. Reddish brown and shiny with legs, mark on scutellum and tip of wings orange-red; abdominal segment banded orange-red and black. As name suggests, found in woodlands where main food, oak, occurs; also feeds on other deciduous trees. Overwintering larvae appear in April; adults seen August–October. Widespread.

CAPSID *Campyloneura virgula* Length 5mm
A tiny capsid bug, the adults of which are seen July–October. Colour of body and wings buff and dark brown but shows orange-yellow patch on pronotum and near tip of forewing on lateral margin. Common and widespread, usually found in deciduous trees and shrubs. Beneficial predator, feeding on aphids and red spider mites.

POND SKATER *Gerris lacustris* Body length 10mm
Widespread and common on ponds and lakes. Skates over water surface with body supported on tips of legs. Responds to distress movements of insects trapped in surface film; feeds on these using proboscis. Adults hibernate away from water.

LESSER WATER BOATMAN *Corixa punctata* Length 10mm
Common and widespread in weedy ponds and lakes. Can be found all year in water but adults occasionally fly in warm weather. Swims the right way up using fringed hind legs as paddles. Feeds on algae and detritus on bottom of pond.

WATER BOATMAN *Notonecta glauca* Length 14mm
Swims upside down in ponds and lakes using fringed hind legs as paddles. Often looks silvery due to air bubble trapped on ventral surface of body. Predator of other aquatic creatures and insects trapped in surface film. Common all year.

WATER SCORPION *Nepa cinerea* Length 30mm
Easily recognised by leaf-like body outline, long breathing siphon at tail end and pincer-like front legs. Common in weedy ponds and lakes year-round. Predator of tadpoles, small fish and other aquatic insects. Movements slow and creeping.

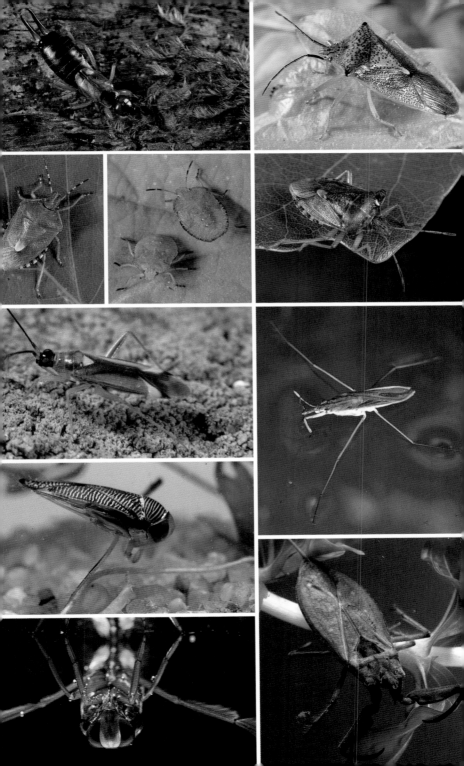

CUCKOO-SPIT FROGHOPPER *Philaenus spumarius*   Length 6mm
Adult is oval in outline; colour variable but usually marbled brown. Jumps well.
Nymph is green and, like adult, feeds on plant sap; creates frothy mass known as
'cuckoo-spit' in which it lives. Common and widespread from June–August.

RED AND BLACK LEAFHOPPER *Cercopis vulnerata*   Length 9mm
Distinctive, shiny red and black froghopper. Found resting on low vegetation and
jumps well to escape danger. Common and widespread in hedgerows, woodland
rides and meadows; seen from May–August. Feeds on plant sap. Nymphs found
on roots.

RHODODENDRON LEAFHOPPER *Graphocephala fennahi*   Length 9mm
Introduced from N America and associated with rhododendrons. Recognised
both by plant preference and by red forewing stripes on otherwise green body.

LEAFHOPPER *Ledra aurita*   Length 14mm
Despite size, this camouflaged leafhopper is easily overlooked. Favours oak wood-
land and feeds on lichen. Local. Brown, winged adult has thoracic projections.
Oval-shaped nymph is pale, squat and strangely flattened.

BLACKFLY *Aphis fabae*   Length 2mm
Widespread and at times extremely abundant. Eggs overwinter on Spindle. Wingless
females appear on beans in spring; huge colonies form by summer when winged
adults appear. Eaten by ladybirds but guarded and 'milked' for honeydew by ants.

ROSE APHID *Macrosiphum rosae*   Length 2mm
The familiar garden 'greenfly'. Can be either green or pink but has two black horn-
like projections towards end of abdomen. Widespread and often extremely abundant. Found in colonies on roses in spring but on other plants by summer.

ALDER FLY *Sialis lutaria*   Length 14mm
Adult (A) superficially Lacewing-like but has broad, brown wings with clearly
defined black veins forming a relatively simple network. Wings held in tent-like
manner at rest. A poor flier, often found resting on waterside vegetation
May–June. Aquatic larva (B) is predatory; its brown, tapering abdomen is fringed
with gills.

LACEWING *Chrysoperla carnea*   Length 15mm
Familiar insect of house and garden with transparent, well-veined wings. Found
among vegetation during summer months and attracted to lighted windows. In
autumn, often comes indoors to hibernate, turning from green to pink. Larva feeds
mainly on aphids and creates camouflaged home from their empty skins.

SCORPION FLY *Panorpa* sp.   Length 14mm
A strange-looking insect, the male of which has a scorpion-like, upturned
abdomen. Flight weak and at rest holds wings flat. Head has beak-like downward
projection used in feeding; scavenges dead animals, including contents of spiders' webs, and ripe fruit. Seen May–July in hedgerows and among Brambles.

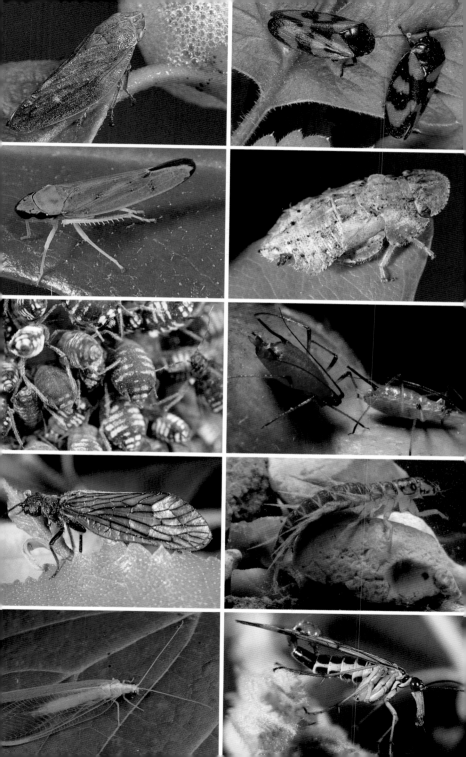

Agapetes fuscipes　　　　　　　　　　　　　　　　Length 9mm
A relatively small caddis fly, associated with fast-flowing streams with stony bottoms. Locally extemely common and larval cases, built from small stones, often cover larger pebbles. Adult has light brown, hairy wings; emerges in spring and masses often congregate on waterside vegetation.

Glyphotaelius pellucidus　　　　　　　　　　　　　Length 16mm
A widespread and often common caddis fly found in standing waters of ponds and lakes. The larva constructs a case from dead leaves and is difficult to detect in pond samples until occupant decides to move. Adult appears April–June and has marbled brown and white wings, the forewing having a notched outer margin.

Limnephilus sp.　　　　　　　　　　　　　Larval case length 18mm
A common caddis fly; widespread in a wide range of waterbodies from ponds to slow-flowing streams. Larval case constructed from stems and leaf stalks of water plants. Considering size of case, larva is fairly agile. Adults have mottled brown, rather narrow forewings.

Phryganea striata　　　　　　　　　　　　　　　Length 25mm
One of our largest caddis flies and a species that sometimes comes to light. Widespread and perhaps commonest in N and W regions. Wings are marbled brown and buff; female has broken black line on forewing. Larva builds case made from leaves, stems and other plant material, arranged spirally to form a cylinder.

Limnephilus elegans　　　　　　　　　　　　　　Length 12mm
A well-marked caddis fly with grey-brown, hairy wings bearing black lines on forewings. Like all caddis flies, at rest the antennae are held out in front of head. Rather cumbersome larval case constructed from plant material. Adult seen from May–July. Usually associated with upland pools and slow-flowing rivers.

Limnephilus marmoratus　　　　　　　　　　　　Length 13mm
Associated with well-vegetated upland lakes and locally common in suitable habitats. Adult has well-marked forewings and is seen resting among emergent vegetation from May–July. Larva constructs case from fragments of plant material; sometimes observed moving around in clear, shallow water.

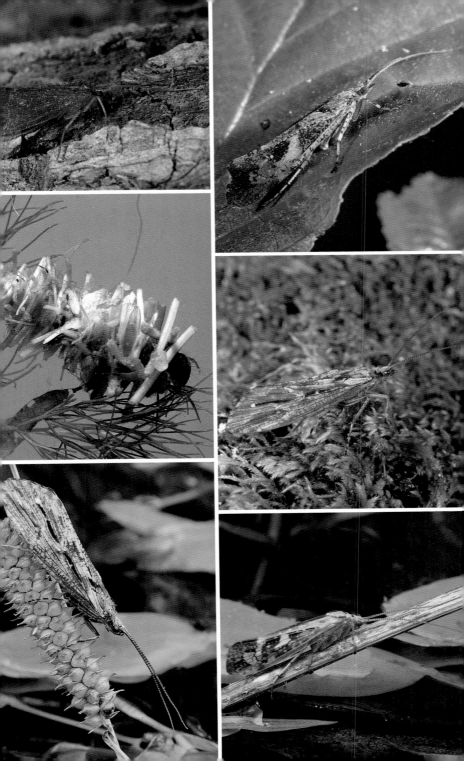

CRANEFLY *Tipula maxima*   Body length 30mm
A large and impressive crane-fly with wings conspicuously marked with patches of brown. Widespread and fairly common, adults seen in spring and summer. Found in damp woodland and beside wooded streams; leathery larva lives in watery margins.

 LEATHERJACKET *Tipula paludosa*   Body length 16mm
A familiar insect of garden lawns and grassland with weak flight and dangling legs. Adults most common August–October, especially after wet weather. Larva live in soil and eat roots and stems of plants; often known as 'Daddy-long-legs'.

 PHANTOM MIDGE *Chaoborus crystillinus*   Body length 16mm
Common, non-biting fly (A) associated with all sorts of standing freshwater. Male has plumed antennae and wings that do not reach tip of abdomen. Transparent aquatic larva (B) sometimes known as 'ghost worm'; feeds on small aquatic animals.

 MOSQUITO *Culex* sp.   Larval length 6mm
Adult (A) is familiar mosquito; female sucks blood while male feeds on nectar. Larval (B) and pupal stages found in all kinds of standing water including stagnant water-butts; easily disturbed from water surface and swim with wriggling motion.

 MIDGE *Chironomus plumosus*   Body length 10mm
A common, non-biting midge seen from spring to autumn. Males have wings shorter than abdomen and plumed antennae; form large swarms. Females have relatively longer wings and simple antennae. Aquatic larvae often known as 'bloodworms'.

 ST MARK'S FLY *Bibio marci*   Body length 11mm
Adult often appears around St Mark's Day (April 25th). Antennae are short and body is black and hairy. Rather sluggish when resting on vegetation. Male flies with dangling legs. Found in areas of short grass and larva lives in soils.

 HORSE FLY *Chrysops relictus*   Body length 10mm
An attractive horse-fly with patterned wings, yellow markings on abdomen and iridescent green eyes. Seen June–August and can inflict a painful bite. Associated with damp ground in woodland and on heaths; larva lives in wet soil.

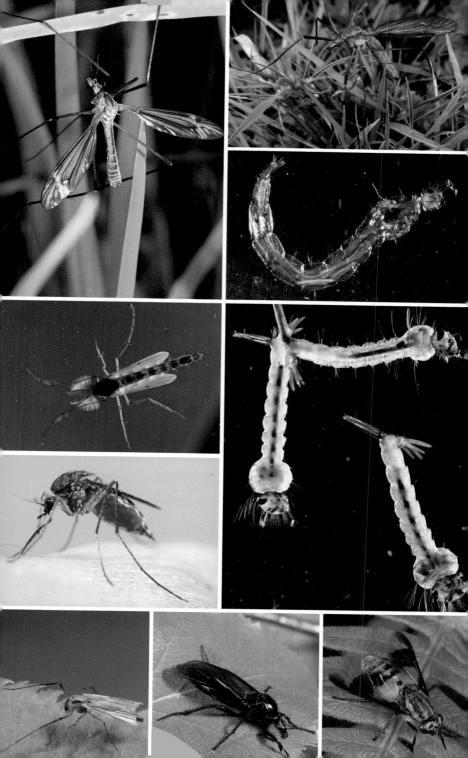

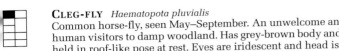

CLEG-FLY *Haematopota pluvialis*   Body Length 10mm
Common horse-fly, seen May–September. An unwelcome and attentive follower of human visitors to damp woodland. Has grey-brown body and mottled brown wings held in roof-like pose at rest. Eyes are iridescent and head is rather compressed.

Haematopota crassicornis   Body length 10mm
A common and widespread horse-fly, sometimes also called a 'cleg'. Seen in close-up, eyes are amazingly iridescent. Feeds on blood and inflicts a painful bite. Approaches victim silently and creeps over skin unfelt until ready to bite.

Tabanus bromius   Body length 14mm
Robust horse-fly. Abdominal segments show yellowish brown and black markings. Flies July–August and commonly found around cattle and ponies; can also inflict a painful bite on humans. Carnivorous larva lives in damp soil. Widespread.

BEE-FLY *Bombylius major*   Body length 10mm
Recognised at rest by hairy, bee-like body and long proboscis. In flight, even more bee-like and produces high-pitched hum. Flies April–May. Visits flowers to feed on nectar. Larva feeds on grubs of solitary bees. Widespread; mainly in S.

EMPID-FLY *Empis tesselata*   Body length 11mm
A small, dark empid or assassin fly, seen April–July. Visits flowers for nectar but also catches other flies; these are sometimes carried in flight and then sucked dry using long, downward-pointing proboscis. Abdomen strongly downcurved.

SNIPE-FLY *Rhagio scolopacea*   Body length 12mm
Common and widespread, seen May–July. Often sunbathes on vegetation but also sits head-down on tree trunks and will sometimes suddenly fly straight at observer. Adult feeds on nectar; larva is carnivorous and lives in leaf litter.

DRONE-FLY *Eristalis tenax*   Body length 12mm
Superficially very similar to Honey Bee drone but close inspection reveals relatively large eyes and body not 'waisted' between thorax and abdomen. Visits flowers to feed on nectar. 'Rat-tailed maggot' larva lives in stagnant water.

Helophilus pendulus   Body length 10mm
A common hover-fly often seen visiting garden flowers and wayside species such as Hogweed and Ragwort. Favours damp, wooded sites and male often hovers over water. Flies May–September. Frequently sunbathes. Larva lives in stagnant water.

Sericomyia silentis   Body length 16mm
A striking, wasp-like hover-fly, widespread in Ireland. Favours wet meadows, moors, heaths and damp woodland and frequently visits flowers to feed on nectar. Adult seen from May–August and larva lives in damp, peaty soil.

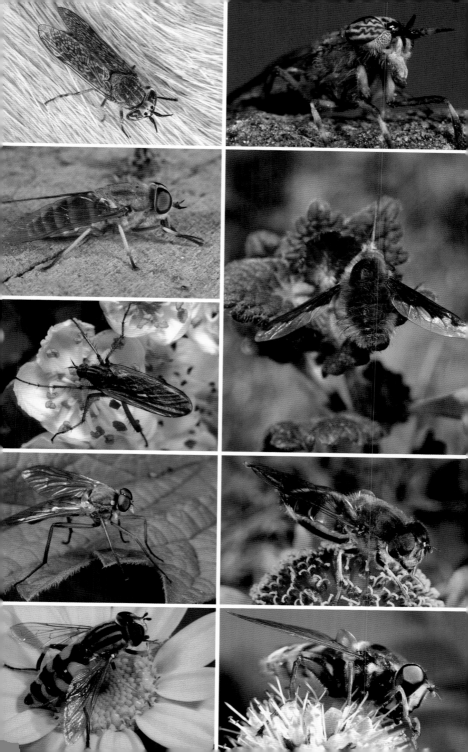

Syrphus ribesii   Body length 12mm
Extremely common hover-fly, widespread in Ireland. Found in gardens, hedgerows
and woodland rides and visits flowers to feed on nectar. Multiple-brooded, adults
seen April–October. Larva found on leaves and feeds on aphids.

Volucella bombylans   Body length 14mm
Extremely good bumble-bee mimic. Some individuals have white-tipped abdomen
while in others it is red. Frequent visitor to flowers in gardens, hedgerows and woods
and seen May–September. Larva scavenges in nests of bumble bees and wasps.

GREENBOTTLE *Lucilia caesar*   Body length 9mm
Has shiny green or bronzy-green body and red eyes. Common and widespread in
Ireland. Found in all sorts of habitats. Attracted to flowers, dung and carrion. Larvae found in rotting carcasses and sometimes attracted to open wounds.

FLESH-FLY *Sarcophaga carnaria*   Body length 15mm
Common and widespread. Adult has greyish body but with chequered markings
on abdomen; eyes red and feet proportionately large. Attracted to carrion and carcasses on which female gives birth to live young. Seldom ventures indoors.

COMMON HOUSE-FLY *Musca domestica*   Body length 8mm
Extremely common and widespread visitor to houses throughout Ireland. Has red
eyes and mostly dark body except for orange patches on abdomen. Sharp bend in
fourth long vein of wing. Attracted to rubbish where they lay their eggs.

LESSER HOUSE-FLY *Fannia canicularis*   Body length 5mm
Superficially similar to Common House-fly but smaller and fourth long vein of
wing straight, without sharp bend. Often found indoors; males fly repetitive circuits beneath ceiling lights and fixtures. Larvae in putrefying corpses and dung.

BLUEBOTTLE *Calliphora erythrocephala*   Body length 11mm
Extremely common visitor to homes. Found in most months but commonest in summer. Makes loud buzzing sound in flight. Female attracted to meat on which eggs are
laid and larvae feed. Adult has blue, shiny body and reddish eyes and jowls.

DUNG-FLY *Scatophaga stercoraria*   Body length 9mm
Swarms of furry, golden males collect on cowpats and seen March–October. Arrival
of female greeted with flurry of activity and mating pair subsequently seen. Adult
preys on other flies. Larvae develop inside cowpat. Widespread and common.

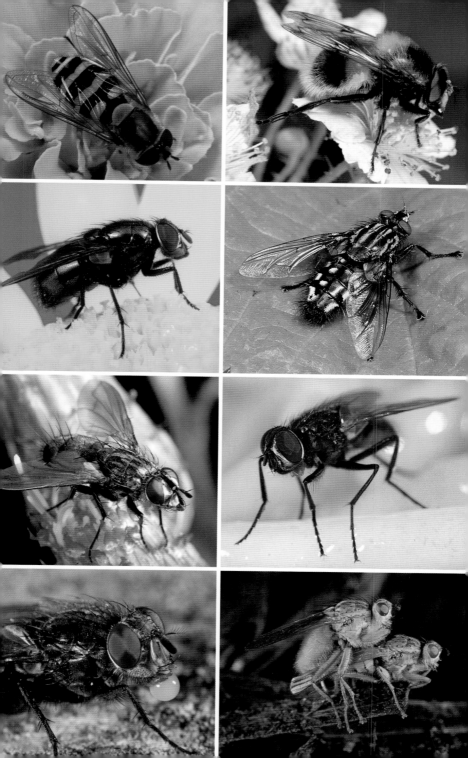

BIRCH SAWFLY *Cimbex femoratus* Length 21mm
Adult is large and impressive with yellow-tipped antennae and yellow on base of abdomen. Wings are smoky and dark-bordered. Flies May–June and makes buzzing sound in flight. Favours birch woods; larvae feed on birch leaves. Rather local.

GIANT WOOD WASP *Uroceras gigas* Body length 30mm
Also known as 'horntail', after female's long ovipositor; this is used to lay eggs in timber. Also recognised by black and yellow colours. Flies May–August. Widespread. Favours areas of pine forest; sometimes emerges from bought timber.

MARBLE GALL Diameter up to 20mm
Clusters of marble galls on oak are caused by larvae of tiny gall wasp *Andricus kollari*; green then brown when mature. Emergence holes seen from autumn onwards. Parthenogenetic females overwinter and then lay eggs on oak buds in spring.

KNOPPER GALL Length up to 28mm
Deeply ridged outgrowths on acorns of Pedunculate Oak caused by larvae of tiny gall wasp *Andricus quercuscalicis*. Subsequent generation develops in galls induced in ornamental Turkey Oak catkins. Cycle is then repeated in Pedunculate Oak.

OAK APPLE Diameter up to 25mm
Irregularly shaped buffish brown gall on oak caused by larva of gall wasp *Biorhiza pallida*. Adults emerge in June and July, each gall containing a single sex. Subsequent asexual generation develops in spherical galls on oak roots.

ROBIN'S PINCUSHION Diameter up to 25mm
Spherical, seemingly fibrous growths on dog rose caused by larvae of gall wasp *Diplolepis rosae* which live in hardened centre of gall. Widespread and rather common. Green at first but acquires a reddish tint with maturity in autumn.

CHERRY GALL Diameter up to 10mm
Attractive spherical galls on the underside of oak leaves caused by larvae of gall wasp *Diplolepis quercusfolii*. Individual galls often grade from bright red to green. Adults emerge in winter and subsequent generation found in oak buds.

SPANGLE GALL Diameter up to 4mm
Disc-like galls on underside of oak leaves caused by larvae of gall wasp *Neuroterus quercusbaccarum*. Found on ground after autumn leaf fall. Subsequent generation causes currant galls on oak flowers in spring. Common and widespread.

YELLOW OPHION *Ophion luteus* Length 20mm
Has yellowish or orange-yellow body and constantly twitching antennae. Common and widespread July–September. Female lacks an ovipositor but is still able to parasitise caterpillars of larger moths inside which its own larvae develop.

ICHNEUMON *Rhyssa persuasoria* Body length 35mm
Our largest ichneumon fly and an impressive insect. Associated with mature pine woods and flies July–August. Female uses long ovipositor to parasitise larvae of Giant Wood Wasp that are located deep in living timber. Locally common.

RUBY-TAILED WASP *Chrysis ignita* Length 11mm
Small but attractive insect with green, shiny head and thorax and ruby-red abdomen. Flies June–August. Female searches diligently on walls and banks for Mason Wasp nests which she enters, if owner is absent, to parasitise the larvae.

LEAF-CUTTER BEE *Megachile centuncularis* Length 13mm
Well-known for the neat, semi-circular holes which are cut from the leaf margins of garden roses (A) and other plants by female bees; these are used to create nest walls. Underside of abdomen is orange. Common and widespread in June and July.

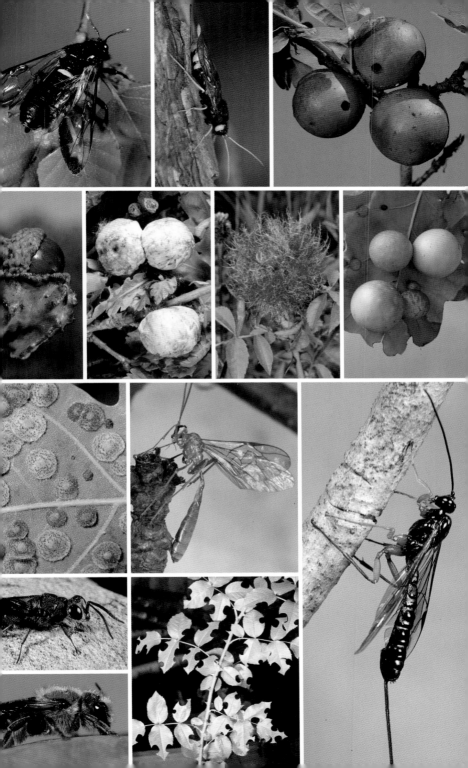

WOOD ANT *Formica rufa*   Length 10mm
Forms large colonies in woodland clearings, these easily recognised by sizeable mounds of dry plant stems and leaves. Reddish brown workers seen collecting caterpillars and other insects. Can spray formic acid from rear end if alarmed.

BLACK GARDEN ANT *Lasius niger*   Length 3mm
Widespread and common in a range of habitats but perhaps most familiar in gardens where nests are formed under paving stones and brickwork. Diet varied but 'milks' aphids for honeydew. Winged ants swarm in hot, humid weather.

RED ANT *Myrmica rubra*   Length 4mm
Favours garden soil and lawns. Yellowish red workers can deliver surprisingly painful sting. Active throughout year but winged ants swarm in late summer, often during hot, humid weather. Diet varied and includes many garden pests.

FIELD DIGGER WASP *Mellinus arvensis*   Length 12mm
Yellow and black colours recall those of true wasps but 'waisted' abdomen more pronounced. Excavates deep burrow in sandy soil. Breeding cells stocked with flies, immobilised by sting; these feed the developing young. Flies May–August.

SAND DIGGER WASP *Ammophila sabulosa*   Length 20mm
Favours sandy areas, particularly coasts; commonest in S. Often seen dragging immobilised caterpillar larger than itself back to burrow in which eggs are laid; burrow entrance plugged with soil. Has narrow 'waist'. Flies May–August.

GERMAN WASP *Vespula germanica*   Length 18mm
Has typical wasp colours and markings and, seen head on, face has three black dots. Common and widespread. Grey, papery nest built underground or sometimes in loft space. Beneficial since it collects large numbers of insects to feed its larvae.

COMMON WASP *Vespula vulgaris*   Length 17mm
Similar to German Wasp but, seen head on, face has black anchor mark. Common and widespread, active mainly June–September. Grey, almost spherical papery nest built underground or in buildings. Like other wasps, attracted to rotting fruit.

HONEY BEE *Apis mellifera*   Length 12mm
Widely kept in hives for honey. In wooded areas, wild colonies nest in holes in trees. Network of wax cells form comb in which honey is stored and young are raised. Female workers comprise bulk of colony, which is ruled by a single queen.

COMMON CARDER-BEE *Bombus pascuorum*   Length 13mm
A common and widespread species with buffish brown or reddish brown hairs on thorax and abdomen, the latter looking rather banded. Active from spring to autumn. Nests above ground, sometimes in old songbird nests or even nestboxes.

RED-TAILED BUMBLE BEE *Bombus lapidarius*   Length 23mm
A large and familiar species. Appears all-black except for hairs at tip of abdomen which are bright orange-red. After hibernation, female emerges in May and looks for burrow in which to build nest. Common and widespread except in N.

BUFF-TAILED BUMBLE BEE *Bombus terrestris*   Length 24mm
Common and widespread, except in N. After hibernation, female appears in April and visits flowers on sunny days. Builds nest in burrow. Recognised by broad, buffish yellow band at front of thorax and on abdomen; tip of abdomen buff.

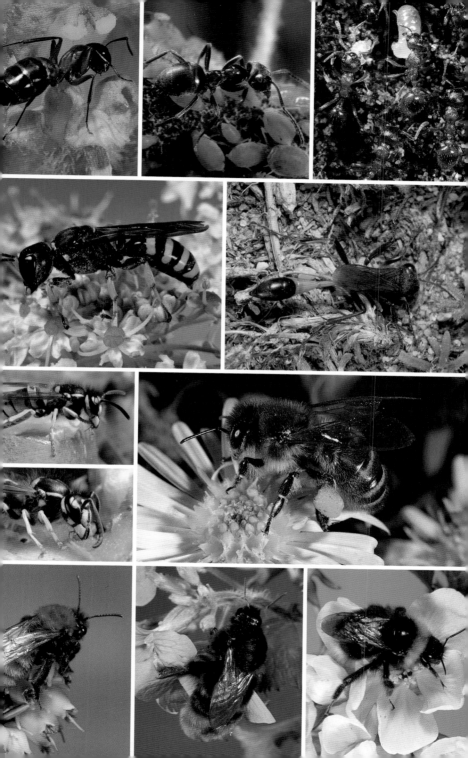

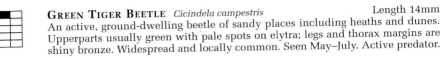

GREEN TIGER BEETLE *Cicindela campestris* Length 14mm
An active, ground-dwelling beetle of sandy places including heaths and dunes. Upperparts usually green with pale spots on elytra; legs and thorax margins are shiny bronze. Widespread and locally common. Seen May–July. Active predator.

GROUND BEETLE *Pterostichus madidus* Length 14mm
A common ground beetle, usually found under stones or logs in daytime; often in gardens. Shiny black in appearance, elytra with fine grooves; legs typically reddish. Predatory but also feeds on plant material including fruit. Flightless.

WATER BEETLE *Acilius sulcatus* Length 16mm
A local water beetle. Favours weedy ponds and canals. Swims well using fringed hind legs as paddles. Male has shiny, golden elytra that are finely marked; those of female are grooved. Active carnivore.

GREAT DIVING BEETLE *Dytiscus marginalis* Length 30mm
Large and impressive water beetle. Found in ponds and lakes. Widespread and generally common. Margins of elytra and thorax orange-brown. Male has smooth, shiny elytra; female's are grooved. Both adults and larvae are fierce predators.

SILVER WATER BEETLE *Hydrophilus piceus* Length 40mm
Our largest water beetle. Extremely local; favours weedy drainage ditches. Upper surface shiny black and underside silvery in water due to air film. Adult vegetarian but larva eats water snails.

BURYING BEETLE *Nicrophorus humator* Length 22mm
A large, all-black burying beetle sometimes found in the act of interring dead mouse or small bird. Female lays her eggs beside buried corpse which developing larvae use as source of food. Often covered in mites. Tips of antennae orange.

SEXTON BEETLE *Nicrophorus vespilloides* Length 16mm
A distinctive sexton beetle, recognised by orange-red markings on otherwise black elytra; has all-black antennae unlike other closely related species. Often found by turning over animal carcasses. Buries corpses of small mammals and birds on which eggs are laid and larvae feed. Attracted to light. Widespread.

DEVIL'S COACH-HORSE *Staphylinus olens* Length 24mm
An all-black, long-bodied beetle the abdominal segments of which are not covered by the elytra. If threatened, curls up abdomen and opens jaws. Shelters during daytime under stones and logs. Emerges after dark to feed on invertebrates. In autumn, may venture indoors. Common and widespread in hedgerows and gardens.

LESSER STAG BEETLE *Dorcus parallelipipedus* Length 28mm
Has all-black body and proportionately large and broad head and thorax. Rather local in S Ireland. Larva found in rotting wood and adults feed on sap of deciduous trees including Ash and willow. Adults seen May–September but commonest in spring.

RHINOCEROS BEETLE *Sinodendron cylindricum* Length 15mm
Male resembles a miniature Rhinoceros Beetle from the tropics, having a horn-like projection on head. Rather local but widespread; occurs in mature woodland, especially beech or oak. Adult sometimes found in or under rotting wood in which larva lives.

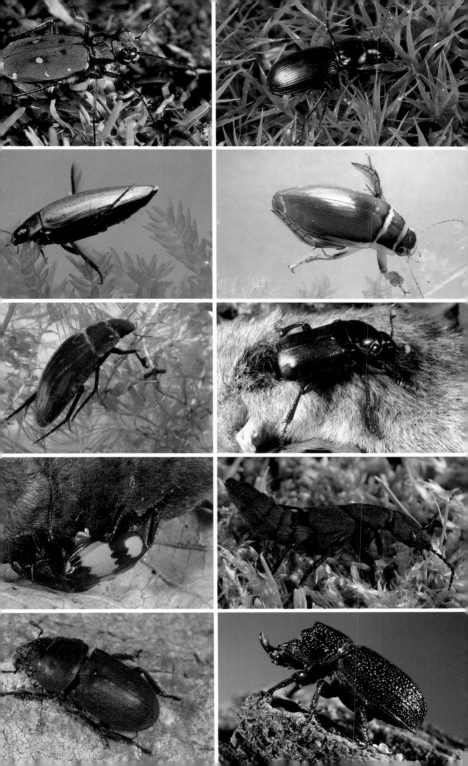

ROSE CHAFER *Cetonia aurata* Length 17mm
A large and attractive beetle. Colour usually shiny bronzy-green, the elytra flecked with white lines and marks. Elytra parallel-sided and rather flattened. Moves in a rather cumbersome manner among vegetation and often found in flowers, including roses. Widespread and locally common in Ireland. Active in sunny weather and seen May–September. Larva lives in rotting wood.

COCKCHAFER *Melolontha melolontha* Length 35mm
Adults (A) are seen in May and June, hence alternative name of 'may-bug'. Easily recognised by hairy, rufous-brown elytra and pointed-tipped abdomen. In many areas, common enough to form large swarms at dusk; these often fly around tree tops and consume large numbers of leaves. Larva (B) lives in soil and spends several years feeding on roots of grasses, herbaceous plants and trees; sometimes occurs at sufficient densities in lawns and cultivated land to cause visible damage.

BEE BEETLE *Trichius fasciatus* Length 14mm
An extremely hairy beetle with wasp- or bee-like black and orange-yellow markings on elytra; thorax and abdomen buffish brown. Adults seen from June–September and visit flowers including thistles and thyme. Mostly associated with upland areas. Seldom common.

SOLDIER BEETLE *Rhagonycha fulva* Length 11mm
A common soldier beetle. Body mostly orange-red except for tip of elytra which are dark. Very active in sunny weather and flies well. Frequently visits flowers, especially umbellifers, where it hunts for insect prey; often becomes dusted with pollen. Seen May–August; mating pairs are a common sight.

GLOW-WORM *Lampyris noctiluca* Length of female 14mm
Grub-like, wingless females (B) located after dark by greenish light emitted from underside of tip to abdomen; this serves to attract winged males. Females usually climb up grass stems and luminosity ceases temporarily if disturbed. Adults do not feed but larvae (A), which can also emit light, eat snails. Found in meadows and verges. Unconfirmed reports from Ireland and may have been overlooked.

CLICK BEETLE *Athous haemorrhoidalis* Length 14mm
Extremely common and widespread; generally associated with woodland, scrub and hedgerows. Body appears relatively narrow with reddish brown elytra and darker head and thorax; body cloaked in downy hairs. Best known for ability to hurl itself into air when placed on back, this process accompanied by a loud click. Adults seen May–June and often found on leaves of Hazel. Larvae in rotting wood.

CARDINAL BEETLE *Pyrochroa serraticornis* Length 14mm
An attractive cardinal beetle, so-called because of scarlet colour of head, thorax and abdomen. Adult seen May–July and often found under flaking bark or in rotting timber; in sunny weather also visits flowers to hunt for small insects. Carnivorous larva lives in rotting wood. Rather local in Ireland.

Oedemera nobilis Length 10mm
Distinctive little beetle. Body is shiny green and surprisingly slender. Elytra taper and splay towards tip of abdomen and do not completely cover wings. Male has distinctive swollen hind femora. Seen May–August. Fairly common. Favours grassy places and visits flowers to feed on pollen.

OIL BEETLE *Meloe proscarabeus* Length 26mm
An oil beetle, so-called because of pungent oil it produces when alarmed. Local and widespread in grassy places. Has shiny, bluish black body with small elytra that do not cover the swollen-looking abdomen. Adult seen April–June. After emerging from egg, young larva climbs flowers and attaches itself to passing solitary bee; then carried back to bee's nest inside which larva then develops.

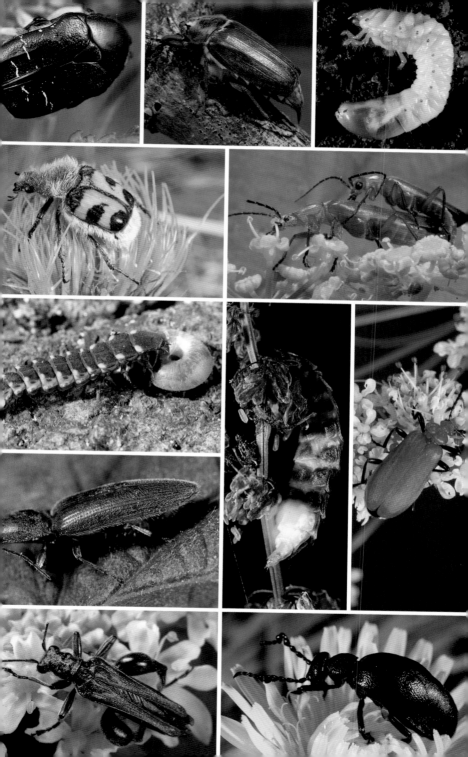

EYED LADYBIRD *Anatis ocellata*   Length 8mm
Widespread and locally common, usually associated with conifers. Elytra rich
orange-red and marked with black spots, these usually ringed paler producing an
eyed appearance. Adult seen during June and July and feeds mainly on aphids.

7-SPOT LADYBIRD *Coccinella 7-punctata*   Length 6mm
Familiar ladybird; widespread and often abundant. Elytra are reddish orange and, at
rest, show seven black spots; anterior spot embraces both elytra. Both adults and larvae feed on aphids. Adults hibernate and are active from March–October.

14-SPOT LADYBIRD *Propylea 14-punctata*   Length 5mm
Black and yellow markings rather variable, but suture between elytra always
black. Widespread and fairly common in Ireland. Found on a wide variety of wayside plants and shrubs. Active from April–September.

WASP BEETLE *Clytus arietus*   Length 16mm
Extremely wasp-like, both in terms of black and yellow appearance but also in its
behaviour. Flies well in sunny weather and often visits hedgerow and garden flowers. Seen May–July. Widespread and often common in Ireland.

LONGHORN BEETLE *Strangalia maculata*   Length 16mm
Has somewhat variable yellow markings on elytra and legs but is otherwise black.
Body elongate and elytra taper towards tail end. Frequently visits flowers to feed
on pollen and found among leaves of trees and shrubs. Active June–August.

LONGHORN BEETLE *Rhagium mordax*   Length 21mm
A well-marked and rather downy longhorn beetle. Widespread and fairly common in
mature woodlands, especially oak. Adults seen May–July. Sometimes seen foraging
among flowers or foliage; sometimes in rotting wood and stumps alongside larvae.

TORTOISE BEETLE *Cassida rubiginosa*   Length 7mm
An intriguing little beetle whose broad, flattened elytra and pronotum overlap body
by a considerable margin and provide camouflage and protection when clamped
down. Usually found on leaves of thistles and seen June–August. Fairly common.

POPLAR LEAF BEETLE *Chrysomela populi*   Length 10mm
Striking, rounded beetle with bright red elytra and black head, thorax and legs.
Superficially ladybird-like but elytra usually unmarked. Seen from April–August;
often associated with poplars and willows. Widespread and fairly common.

MINT LEAF BEETLE *Chrysolina menthastri*   Length 9mm
An extremely shiny, bronzy-green beetle which is usually found on mint leaves;
sometimes also on hemp-nettles. Body extremely rounded. Seen from May–August.
Favours damp, waterside meadows and hedgerows. Widespread and locally common.

BLOODY-NOSED BEETLE *Timarcha tenebricosa*   Length 20mm
A lumbering, flightless leaf beetle, often seen plodding across paths or through grass.
When disturbed, exudes drop of bright red, blood-like fluid from mouth. Wide-
spread and fairly common in Ireland and seen from April–June.

Phyllobius pomaceus   Length 9mm
A small weevil. The body is black but it is covered by greenish scales which are
easily rubbed off. Usually found on leaves of Common Nettle but also on other
wayside plants. Widespread and fairly common, seen mainly from April–August.

HAZEL WEEVIL *Curculio nucum*   Length 6mm
Widespread and locally common wherever larval foodplant, Hazel, occurs. Female
bores through husk of embryo nut to lay egg. Larva feeds on developing nut inside
case until it falls in autumn; pupates in ground. Adult seen April–June.

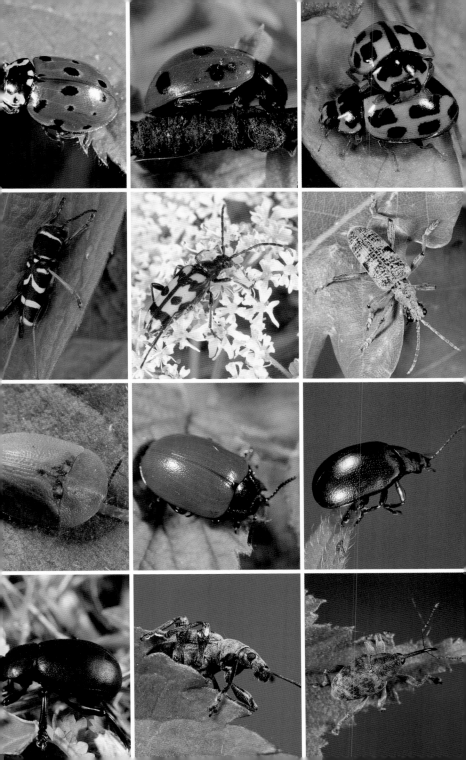

Spiders

Araniella curcurbitina   Body length up to 6mm
A small but attractive spider, the abdomen of which is lime green with yellow bands; the cephalothorax and legs are reddish brown. Spins a rather untidy orb-web among low wayside vegetation such as thistles and Brambles. Favours rough meadows, hedgerows and gardens. Widespread but commonest in S, May–September.

GARDEN SPIDER *Araneus diadematus*   Body length up to 12mm
Arguably our most familiar spider. Female considerably larger than male. Ground colour of body and legs rather variable but usually grey-brown or reddish brown. Abdomen has row of white dots down centre and transverse white streaks forming a distinct cross. Common in a wide range of habitats including gardens, hedgerows, rough meadows and woodland clearings. Spins a sophisticated web comprising radial and spiral silk threads. Widespread and seen as adult from July–October.

COMMON CROSS SPIDER *Araneus quadratus*   Body length up to 20mm
Superficially similar to Garden Spider but abdomen has four large white spots arranged almost in a square and a white anterior stripe. Abdomen colour varies from nut-brown to bright red; in mature females it can appear grotesquely swollen and almost spherical. Widespread and common in a wide range of habitats including gardens, scrub, hedgerows and meadows. Adults seen from July–October. Spins a large and sophisticated web. Female much larger than male.

WATER SPIDER *Argyroneta aquatica*   Body length up to 14mm
Our only truly aquatic spider. Very locally common in weedy lakes and ponds; also occasionally in slow-flowing streams. Looks silvery underwater due to film of air trapped around grey-brown abdomen; cephalothorax and legs reddish brown. Constructs domed, air-filled web among water plants in which it spends much of daytime; air periodically renewed by spider. Silk threads radiating from web alert occupant to passing prey. Adults can be found at most times of the year.

PURSE-WEB SPIDER *Atypus affinis*   Body length 12mm
An extraordinary spider that lives inside a subterranean silken tube. A small part of the tube lies on the soil surface like the finger of a glove. When an insect walks over the tube, the spider rushes to the source of the disturbance and, walking upside down, thrusts its long fangs through the silk, thus grabbing the prey; damage to the tube is repaired after the meal has been consumed. Favours dry, well-draining soil. Silken tubes, and hence presence, easily overlooked.

Amaurobius similis   Body length up to 12mm
A fairly common spider, especially in S. Usually found on walls, behind bark and on fences where it constructs a rather tangled web of bluish white silk leading back to a crevice. It is into this that the spider retreats for much of the time. Abdomen usually buffish with paired dark markings on dorsal surface and chevrons towards the rear end. Cephalothorax and legs usually orange-brown.

SWAMP SPIDER *Dolomedes fimbriatus*   Body length 25mm
Without doubt our most impressive spider. Body and legs chestnut-brown with yellow line around margins of cephalothorax and abdomen. Rather local. Restricted to damp heathland and typically found on or beside boggy pools. Sits with front legs touching water surface and attracted to vibrations caused by distress movements of insects trapped in surface film. Can skate with ease over surface but will also submerge if alarmed. Seen May–August.

Dysdera crocata   Body length 12mm
An attractive spider with reddish legs and cephalothorax and buffish brown abdomen. Fangs are huge relative to body size and are opposable; used to good effect when capturing woodlice. Hides under stones during daytime. Widespread and fairly common. Found in most habitats that support good numbers of woodlice.

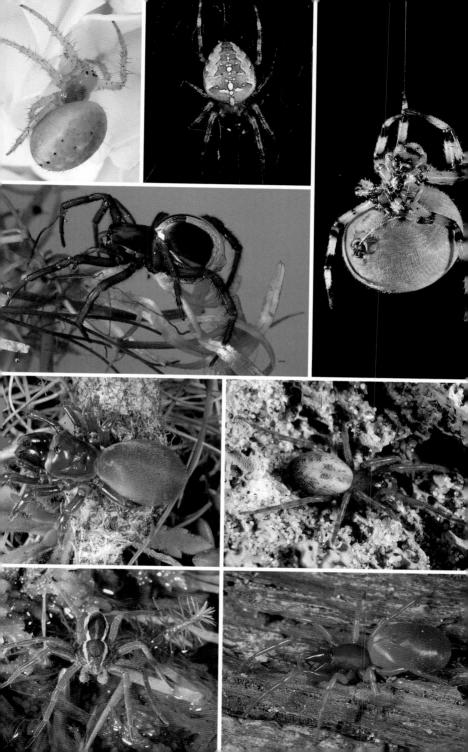

Pardosa lugubris　　　　　　　　　　　　　　　　　Body length 6mm
A common and widespread wolf spider found among leaf litter on woodland and forest floors. Adult has buffish brown band on carapace. Most active April–June when female can sometimes be seen carrying around egg sac attached to spinnerets at tip of abdomen. After the young hatch, they remain clinging to the mother's abdomen for several weeks. Actively hunts insect prey and does not spin a web.

Metellina merianae　　　　　　　　　　　　　　　　Body length 9mm
Sometimes referred to as a cave spider because of its preference for cave entrances, cellars and other dark, dank places; needs plenty of crevices into which it can retreat. Abdomen is marbled brown and black and shiny legs are marked with irregular bands of reddish brown and black. Widespread and fairly common in suitable habitats; often coastal. Seen mainly from May–July.

Misumena vatia　　　　　　　　　　　　　　Body length up to 10mm
A widespread and often common crab spider. Colour of female is variable and changeable but usually white, creamy yellow or pale green; sometimes has red lines on side of abdomen. Male much smaller than female and darker. Female usually found sitting on flowers that match her body colour such as Gorse or Ox-eye Daisy. Catches insects that land on flower to feed. Seen from May–August.

DADDY-LONG-LEGS SPIDER *Pholcus phalangioides*　　　Body length 8mm
A narrow-bodied, long-legged spider that is almost always associated with houses and buildings. Cannot survive in locations where temperature dips below 50°F and so commonest in homes with central heating. Can be found at most times of the year but most active during summer months. The spider is typically found hanging upside down from ceilings; spins a tangled, untidy web.

Pisaura mirabilis　　　　　　　　　　　　　　　　Body length 14mm
A common and widespread hunting spider that is found in hedgerows, woodland rides and grassland. Body colour buffish brown but shows a dark-bordered, yellow stripe on carapace. Actively hunts prey on ground without the aid of a web. Female sometimes seen carrying egg sac underneath body, secured by mouthparts. Builds a nursery tent just before eggs are due to hatch. Seen from May–July.

ZEBRA SPIDER *Salticus scenicus*　　　　　　　　Body length 7mm
An intriguing little jumping spider named after its black and white stripes; body rather hairy. Usually seen restlessly moving up sunny fences and walls. Spots potential prey using large eyes and then stalks to within leaping range. Will even jump up vertical surfaces. Seen from May–September. Occasionally ventures indoors in warm weather. Widespread, commonest in S.

HOUSE SPIDER *Tegenaria domestica*　　　　　　　Body length 10mm
A large, long-legged spider that is often found in and around houses. Body rather hairy and varies from pale to dark brown. Can look rather intimidating when trapped in bath or scurrying across floor. Spins untidy web in corner of room with tubular retreat. Female can survive for several years. Widespread.

Xysticus cristatus　　　　　　　　　　　　　　　　Body length 6mm
A common and widespread crab spider. Has pale stripes on thorax and patterns of pale and dark brown on abdomen forming series of overlapping triangles. Favours hedgerows and meadows and usually found waiting motionless with legs outstretched on bare stalk or flower for passing insect. Seen mostly from May–July.

Tetragnatha extensa　　　　　　　　　　　　　　　Body length 10mm
A long-legged spider, the abdomen of which is elongate and sausage-like. Legs and cephalothorax reddish brown and abdomen marbled yellow, brown and white. Found in damp meadows and hedgerows. When alarmed, typically aligns itself along plant stem with legs outstretched. Widespread, seen June–August.

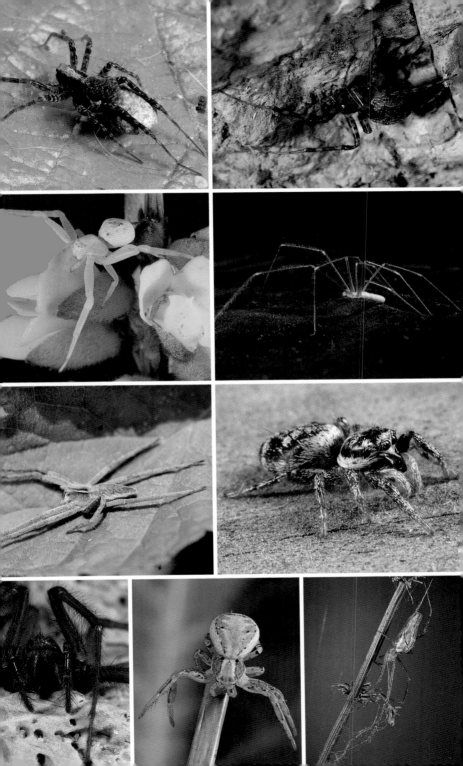

LARGE RED SLUG *Arion ater*   Length up to 12cm
Widespread and common throughout Ireland. Occurs in almost all terrestrial habitats. Body is uniform in colour but seen in two forms: orange-red form is commonest in S and in gardens while black form prevails in N and upland areas. When alarmed, contracts into an almost spherical ball and often rocks from side to side. Mucus colourless. Lays clusters of pale eggs under logs.

COMMON GARDEN SLUG *Arion distinctus*   Length up to 3cm
A comparatively small slug. Locally common in Ireland. Favours gardens and agricultural land and damages crops. Has yellowish orange sole and orange body mucus. Body usually striped and covered in tiny gold dots.

DUSKY SLUG *Arion subfuscus*   Length up to 7cm
Common in most parts of Ireland. Favours woodland and hedgerows but also found in gardens. Body pale brown but dark on dorsal surface and with single longitudinal dark stripe on each side. Often looks golden due to orange body mucus. Sole yellow but sole mucus colourless.

YELLOW SLUG *Limax flavus*   Length up to 10cm
A large, yellowish slug, the body of which is marbled and mottled with olive-brown. Tentacles blue and mantle with thumbprint-like pattern of concentric rings typical of all *Limax* species. Widespread and fairly common in Ireland but almost always associated with gardens and houses; ventures indoors after dark and into cellars. Feeds voraciously on seedlings and vegetables.

LEOPARD SLUG *Limax maximus*   Length up to 16cm
A large and well-marked slug. Ground colour of body usually pinkish grey but is covered with numerous dark blotches and spots. Has pronounced keel running along rear part of body to tail. Mucus sticky and colourless. Sole whitish. Widespread and common throughout most of Ireland. Favours woodland and gardens.

ASHY-GREY SLUG *Limax cinereoniger*   Length up to 25cm
Our largest slug when fully grown. Body colour ashy-grey but has pale yellowish keel along back from mantle to tail. Occurs locally in Ireland, mainly in S; restricted to mature and undisturbed woodland. Found under logs.

TREE SLUG *Limax marginatus*   Length up to 7cm
A rather pale and translucent-looking slug. Body colour pale greyish buff but marked with two dark lines on both sides of body from mantle to tail. As name suggests, climbs trees, usually in wet weather. Produces copious quantities of watery mucus when disturbed. Widespread in woodland in Ireland.

NETTED SLUG *Deroceras reticulatum*   Length up to 5cm
An extremely common slug of gardens and agricultural land; widespread throughout Ireland. Body colour variable but usually buffish brown with network of darker brown veins and blotches. Body often looks lumpy; keel is truncated at tail end. Produces large quantities of clear mucus when irritated.

SHELLED SLUG *Testacella scutulum*   Length up to 10cm
A strange slug with a fingernail-like shell covering the mantle at the rear end. A predator of earthworms and spends much of its life underground; easiest to find in garden compost heaps. Occurs locally in SE Ireland.

KERRY SLUG *Geomalacus maculosus*   Length 6–9cm
A well-marked slug. Body colour is dark greenish grey but note the numerous pale spots. Favours lichen- and moss-covered rocks and trees. Restricted to SW Ireland.

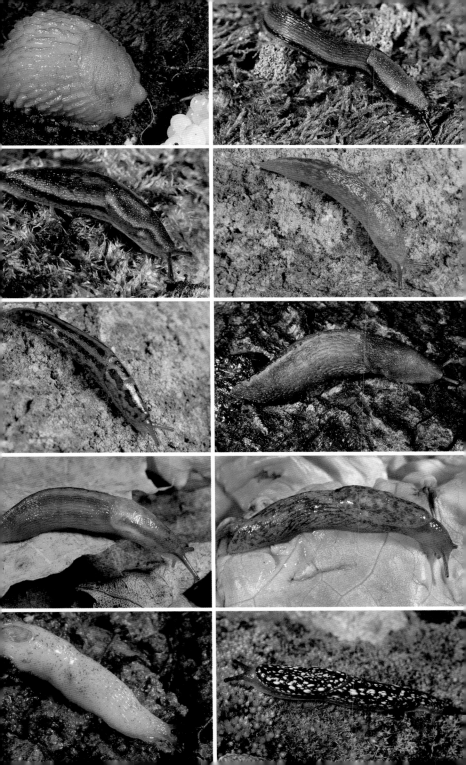

COPSE SNAIL *Arianta arbustorum* — Shell diameter 25mm
A rather local snail, restricted mainly to N. Restricted to damp lowland areas including hedgerows, meadows and woods. Shell almost spherical and usually orange-brown with a dark spiral band.

WHITE-LIPPED SNAIL *Cepaea hortensis* — Shell diameter 18mm
Shell colour extremely variable, ranging from uniform yellow to yellow with dark brown spiral bands; lip of shell almost always white. Local, commonest in SE. Favours wide range of habitats including woods and hedges.

BROWN-LIPPED SNAIL *Cepaea nemoralis* — Shell diameter 21mm
Shell colour variable and often similar to White-lipped Snail with which it may occur; shell lip almost always dark brown. Widespread and often common in much of Ireland. Favours woodland, hedgerows and dunes.

PLAITED DOOR SNAIL *Cochlodina laminata* — Shell length 16mm
Long, narrow shell is distinctive. Colour usually orange-brown but becomes worn with age. Favours damp, shady woodland and typically climbs trees in wet weather and at night. Extremely local in Ireland.

GARDEN SNAIL *Helix aspersa* — Shell diameter 40mm
A familiar garden resident but also found in woods and hedgerows. Common and widespread, especially in S. Shell marbled brown and black; often rather worn in older specimens.

CELLAR SNAIL *Oxychilus cellarius* — Shell diameter 12mm
Flattened, spiral shell is amber brown and rather translucent; body of snail is bluish grey. Widespread and generally common throughout Ireland. Favours gardens, woods and hedgerows.

GARLIC SNAIL *Oxychilus alliarius* — Shell diameter 6mm
Similar to, but smaller than, Cellar Snail with orange-brown, translucent shell; snail body blackish. Emits strong smell of garlic when handled. Widespread and often common throughout Ireland. Found in most terrestrial habitats.

AMBER SNAIL *Succinea putris* — Shell length 15mm
A delicate little snail with an orange-brown, translucent shell. Widespread in lowland wetland habitats throughout much of Ireland. Often observed climbing among leaves of waterside vegetation such as yellow iris.

STRAWBERRY SNAIL *Trichia striolata* — Shell diameter 12mm
Shell buffish brown in colour, rather flattened and shows growth ridges. Widespread and fairly common in Ireland. Favours lowland habitats including gardens, woodland and hedgerows.

ROUNDED SNAIL *Discus rotundatus* — Shell diameter 7mm
Shell rather flattened and has tightly-packed whorls; usually shows conspicuous ridges and is marked with bands. A widespread species throughout the whole of Ireland. Common in gardens; also in woods and stony places.

COMMON BULIN *Ena obscura* — Shell length 8mm
A snail of ancient and undisturbed woodland. Easily overlooked, especially when young since shell is often coated with mud. Very local in Ireland. Found in leaf litter. Climbs trees in wet weather.

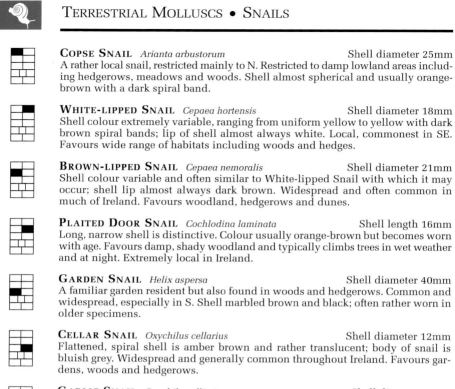

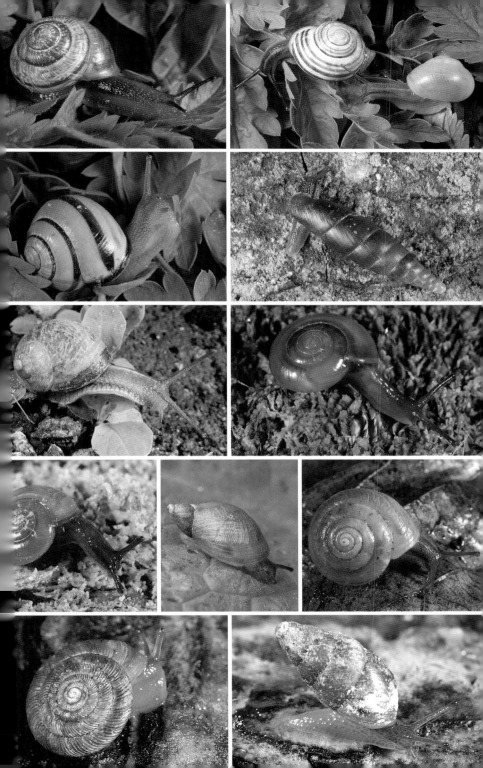

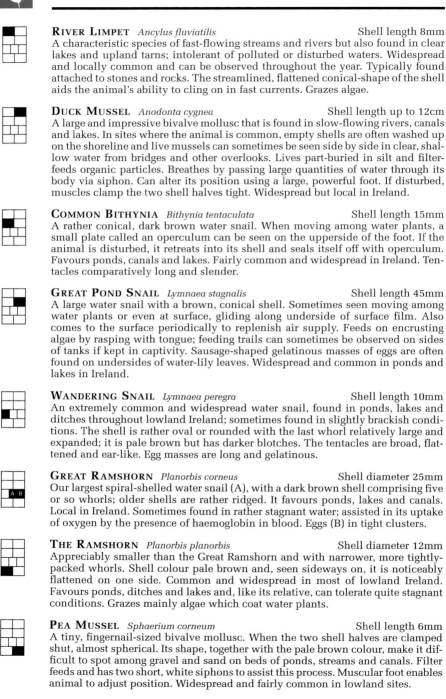

RIVER LIMPET *Ancylus fluviatilis*   Shell length 8mm
A characteristic species of fast-flowing streams and rivers but also found in clear lakes and upland tarns; intolerant of polluted or disturbed waters. Widespread and locally common and can be observed throughout the year. Typically found attached to stones and rocks. The streamlined, flattened conical-shape of the shell aids the animal's ability to cling on in fast currents. Grazes algae.

DUCK MUSSEL *Anodonta cygnea*   Shell length up to 12cm
A large and impressive bivalve mollusc that is found in slow-flowing rivers, canals and lakes. In sites where the animal is common, empty shells are often washed up on the shoreline and live mussels can sometimes be seen side by side in clear, shallow water from bridges and other overlooks. Lives part-buried in silt and filter-feeds organic particles. Breathes by passing large quantities of water through its body via siphon. Can alter its position using a large, powerful foot. If disturbed, muscles clamp the two shell halves tight. Widespread but local in Ireland.

COMMON BITHYNIA *Bithynia tentaculata*   Shell length 15mm
A rather conical, dark brown water snail. When moving among water plants, a small plate called an operculum can be seen on the upperside of the foot. If the animal is disturbed, it retreats into its shell and seals itself off with operculum. Favours ponds, canals and lakes. Fairly common and widespread in Ireland. Tentacles comparatively long and slender.

GREAT POND SNAIL *Lymnaea stagnalis*   Shell length 45mm
A large water snail with a brown, conical shell. Sometimes seen moving among water plants or even at surface, gliding along underside of surface film. Also comes to the surface periodically to replenish air supply. Feeds on encrusting algae by rasping with tongue; feeding trails can sometimes be observed on sides of tanks if kept in captivity. Sausage-shaped gelatinous masses of eggs are often found on undersides of water-lily leaves. Widespread and common in ponds and lakes in Ireland.

WANDERING SNAIL *Lymnaea peregra*   Shell length 10mm
An extremely common and widespread water snail, found in ponds, lakes and ditches throughout lowland Ireland; sometimes found in slightly brackish conditions. The shell is rather oval or rounded with the last whorl relatively large and expanded; it is pale brown but has darker blotches. The tentacles are broad, flattened and ear-like. Egg masses are long and gelatinous.

GREAT RAMSHORN *Planorbis corneus*   Shell diameter 25mm
Our largest spiral-shelled water snail (A), with a dark brown shell comprising five or so whorls; older shells are rather ridged. It favours ponds, lakes and canals. Local in Ireland. Sometimes found in rather stagnant water; assisted in its uptake of oxygen by the presence of haemoglobin in blood. Eggs (B) in tight clusters.

THE RAMSHORN *Planorbis planorbis*   Shell diameter 12mm
Appreciably smaller than the Great Ramshorn and with narrower, more tightly-packed whorls. Shell colour pale brown and, seen sideways on, it is noticeably flattened on one side. Common and widespread in most of lowland Ireland. Favours ponds, ditches and lakes and, like its relative, can tolerate quite stagnant conditions. Grazes mainly algae which coat water plants.

PEA MUSSEL *Sphaerium corneum*   Shell length 6mm
A tiny, fingernail-sized bivalve mollusc. When the two shell halves are clamped shut, almost spherical. Its shape, together with the pale brown colour, make it difficult to spot among gravel and sand on beds of ponds, streams and canals. Filter feeds and has two short, white siphons to assist this process. Muscular foot enables animal to adjust position. Widespread and fairly common in lowland sites.

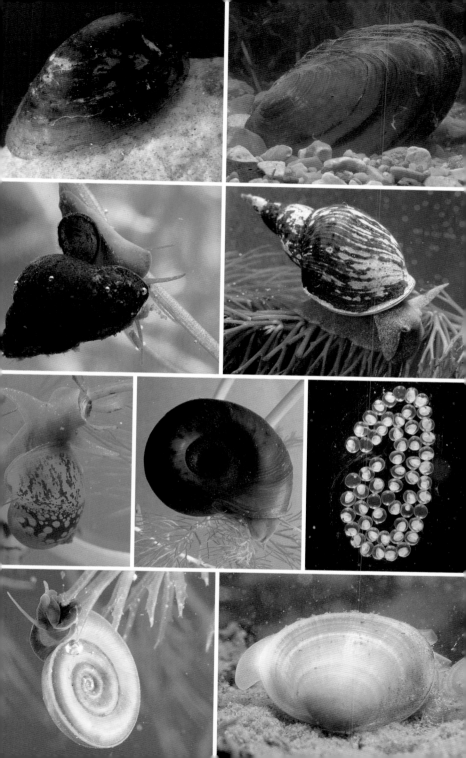

EDIBLE PERIWINKLE *Littorina littorea*   Shell length 25mm
Extremely common among seaweed on which it feeds. Found on rocky shores
from low- to high-tide levels. Shell is rather rounded but with a pointed, conical
apex and a thick lip. Usually dark brown in colour and bearing concentric ridges
and dark lines. Widespread on most suitable coasts around Ireland.

FLAT PERIWINKLE *Littorina littoralis*   Shell diameter 10mm
A rounded, almost spherical mollusc with a smooth, shiny shell. Colour extremely
variable but commonly bright yellow or reddish brown. Usually associated with
Egg Wrack and Bladder Wrack and could be mistaken for these species' air floats.
Often numerous at mid-tide level on rocky shores around Ireland.

PEPPERY FURROW SHELL *Scrobicularia plana*   Shell length up to 50mm
A common bivalve mollusc. Shell rather rounded in outline but thin when viewed
sideways on; marked with numerous, close-packed concentric growth ridges. Shell
colour pale grey-brown. Widespread and often common in sand and mud on shores
and estuaries around Ireland. Filter feeds using its long siphons.

LAVER SPIRE SHELL *Hydrobia ulvae*   Shell length 6mm
Widespread and often abundant on mud of estuaries around Ireland and sometimes
climbs Glasswort at low tide on sunny days. Found mostly between low- and high-
tide levels. Important source of food for many birds such as Shelduck. Shell is dark
brown and conical; apex appears blunt and usually rather worn.

TOOTHED TOPSHELL *Monodonta lineata*   Shell diameter 24mm
Shell is marked with close-packed concentric ridges and bears beautiful purple
zigzag patterns; older specimens are usually worn at the apex. Seen from below,
mouth of shell has sheen of mother-of-pearl and 'toothed' lip. Widespread and
common on rocky coasts of Ireland; favours mid-tide level.

COMMON OCTOPUS *Octopus vulgaris*   Length up to 50cm
An intriguing and advanced mollusc, occasionally found in rock pools at very
low tide off rocky coasts around Ireland. Easily recognised by bulbous, bag-like
body, large eyes and eight arms bearing powerful suckers. Active predator of
crabs and other invertebrates. Can change colour quickly and dramatically.

COMMON COWRIE *Trivia monacha*   Shell length 11mm
A small, bean-shaped mollusc whose shell is marked with pinkish purple lines
and has a slit-like opening on its lower side. In life, the animal's mottled mantle
edges envelop the margins of the shell. The foot is beautifully striped and, at the
head end, there is a conspicuous siphon. Widespread on the lower shore.

COMMON LIMPET *Patella vulgata*   Shell diameter up to 6cm
Commonest of several similar limpet species and found on exposed rocky shores
around Ireland; occurs between mid- and high-tide levels. Shell conical and ridged;
older specimens usually encrusted with barnacles and algae. Grazes algae when
covered by water; feeding trails usually visible at low tide.

SLIPPER LIMPET *Crepidula fornicata*   Shell length 30mm
Accidentally introduced from N America; populations seldom persist for long.
Shell ear-shaped and greyish. Sometimes found in large enough numbers for empty
shells to dominate debris on beaches. In life, attaches itself to mussels, oysters or
other Slipper Limpets. Favours sheltered coasts.

BLUE-RAYED LIMPET *Patina pellucida*   Shell length 15mm
A delicate little limpet. The brown, conical shell is marked with iridescent blue
lines which radiate from the apex; young specimens are brightest. In life, invariably found attached to fronds, stalks or holdfasts of kelp; usually found inside
excavated depression or cavity. Not normally visible until very low tide.

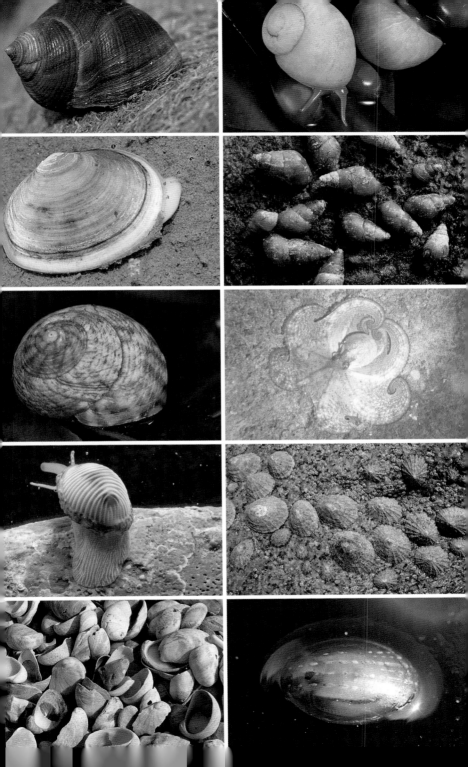

SEA-LEMON *Archidoris pseudargus*   Length up to 6cm
A shell-less mollusc. Mostly found in fairly deep waters but in summer moves to lower rocky shores to spawn. Body yellowish but with olive-brown blotches; skin texture rather warty. When undisturbed, looks rather sausage-like with two tentacles at head end and frilly gills at rear. Contracts body when alarmed.

Greilada elegans   Length up to 3cm
An attractive sea slug whose bright orange body colour and purple spots serve to indicate its unpleasant taste to potential predators. Intolerant of cold waters and restricted to SW Ireland. Mostly in fairly deep water but moves inshore in summer to spawn and sometimes trapped in rock pools at very low tide.

SEA-HARE *Aplysia punctata*   Length up to 12cm
A bizarre-looking mollusc whose body encloses its soft shell. Body often appears rather lumpy and is blotched grey and brown; has four tentacles at head end. Slow-moving creature, found among seaweeds in rock pools on very low tides. Ejects a purple dye if alarmed. Widespread around S and W coasts of Ireland.

COMMON COCKLE *Cardium edule*   Shell width up to 5cm
A common bivalve mollusc that is found buried in mud and sand in estuaries and on expansive beaches. Shell valves are identical; grey-buff outer surface scored with radiating ridges and inner surface shiny and white. Widespread and often common around suitable coasts of Ireland. Often grown commercially.

COMMON MUSSEL *Mytilus edulis*   Shell width up to 9cm
A common and familiar bivalve mollusc. Found both on exposed rocky shores and attached to stones or posts in estuary mouths. Both shell valves identical; dark grey-brown on outer surface but with mother-of-pearl coating on inside. Forms large groups, each attached to rocks by tough threads. Common and widespread.

COMMON OYSTER *Ostrea edulis*   Shell width up to 10cm
Formerly abundant and still fairly common bivalve mollusc in shallow water with gently shelving seabed. Lower shell valve is saucer-like and sits on sand or silt; upper valve is flattened. Outer surface of both valves rough and grey-brown; inner surface smooth with mother-of-pearl coating. Grown commercially.

POD RAZORSHELL *Ensis siliqua*   Shell length up to 18cm
An elongated bivalve mollusc, seen mostly when shell from dead animal is washed-up. In life, lives buried deep in sand around low-tide level on beaches; siphons reach surface of sand when immersed thus enabling animal to filter feed. Outer surface of shell valves olive-brown and flaky. Widespread and generally common.

COMMON WHELK *Buccinium undatum*   Shell length up to 8cm
Living animal sometimes found on sand or mud in shallow water at low tide. More usually encountered when shell of dead animal is washed-up on beach; empty shell often occupied by Hermit Crab. Shells of larger animals often coated with encrusting sponges and algae. Common and widespread around Irish coasts.

DOG WHELK *Nucella lapillus*   Shell length up to 3cm
Has a rather oval, pointed shell the colour of which is influenced by diet: this includes barnacles and mussels. Both creamy white and grey-brown forms are seen and banded individuals are not uncommon. Favours rocky shores wherever prey is common; sometimes seen beside egg masses that are secured to rocks. Widespread.

COMMON PIDDOCK *Pholas dactylus*   Shell length up to 12cm
An intriguing bivalve mollusc that bores into sandstone and other soft rocks. Shell is pale buffish brown and surprisingly fragile considering it is used to perform the boring process. In suitable substrates, often found at considerable densities on lower shore. Widespread and often common around coasts of SW Ireland.

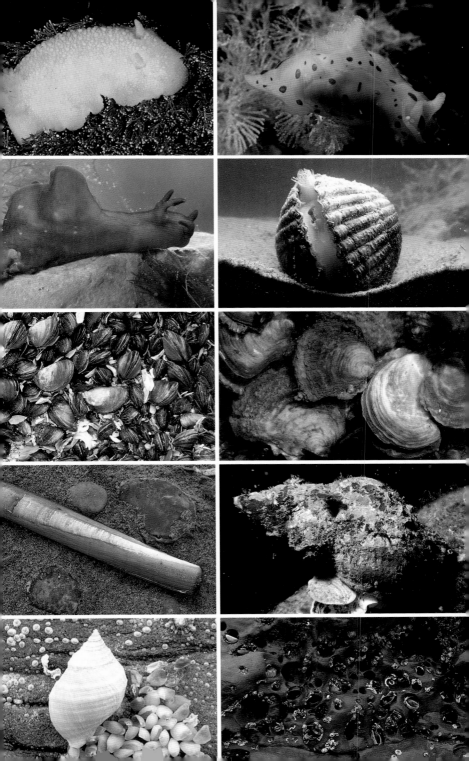

COMMON WOODLOUSE *Oniscus asellus* Length 14mm
A widespread and common woodlouse throughout most of Ireland. Often numerous in gardens but also found in woodland, and hedgerows on wasteground. Easily becomes desiccated and hides under stones and in crevices during daytime, especially during dry, hot weather. Forages for vegetable matter after dark.

PILL WOODLOUSE *Armadillidium vulgare* Length 11mm
An intriguing species, easily recognised by its ability to roll into a ball when disturbed. Body colour uniform slate-grey. Widespread and reasonably common. Usually found in mature woodland where it hides under logs and in rotting wood during daytime; also in hedgerows and rural gardens.

Porcellio scaber Length 10mm
An extremely common woodlouse that is widespread in most lowland parts of Ireland. Often numerous in gardens where it hides under stones and in compost heaps and crevices in walls. Also found in hedgerows, woodland and coastal dunes. Emerges after dark to feed on algae and other plant matter.

Trichoniscus pusillus Length 5mm
A small species of woodlouse. Body rather rounded in cross-section and elongate; usually pinkish purple in colour. Invariably found in damp locations and often common among leaves and debris that have collected in ditches or around the margins of woodland ponds. Widespread and fairly common but easily overlooked.

FRESHWATER LOUSE *Asellus aquaticus* Length 15mm
Widespread and often extremely common in ponds, lakes and slow-flowing streams. Rather woodlouse-like in appearance with flattened, segmented body but has very long antennae. Scuttles among water plants and scavenges organic matter from the sediment. In spring, female carries whitish eggs around with her in brood pouch.

FRESHWATER CRAYFISH *Astacus pallipes* Length up to 40mm
Formerly common and widespread but rather scarce and endangered today; numbers threatened by pollution and disturbance of favoured river and stream habitats and by competition from introduced N American species. Needs fast-flowing, well-oxygenated water and, during daytime, hides under stones and in holes in bank.

WATER-FLEA *Daphnia sp.* Length 1mm
Tiny crustacean which is present in phenomenal numbers in most bodies of still water at certain times of year. The body is almost transparent and internal organs can be seen through carapace. Swims through the water as if by hopping by beating second antennae. Body usually pinkish and has single dark compound eye.

FRESHWATER SHRIMP *Gammarus pulex* Length 11mm
Intolerant of polluted waters or ones with low oxygen content; favours fast-flowing streams and rivers but also found near inflows or outflows in stream-fed lakes. Body is laterally flattened and animal swims on its side. Often found under stones and around the bases of rooted water plants. Widespread and common.

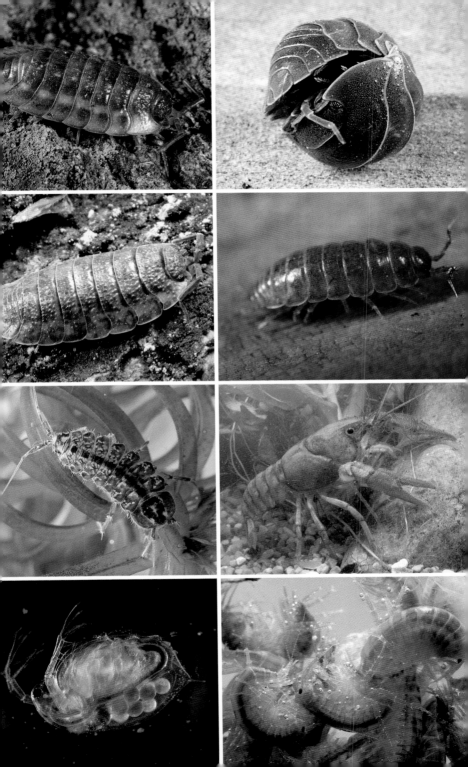

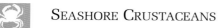

EDIBLE CRAB *Cancer pagurus*   Carapace width up to 15cm, often smaller
A familiar seashore animal, recognised by the 'piecrust' appearance to the margin of
the carapace and its pinkish orange colour; the tips of the broad pincers are black.
Widespread around the coasts of Ireland. Small specimens are found on the lower
shores of rocky coasts and are often encountered in rock pools and among seaweeds; larger individuals live further offshore. Has a mainly scavenging diet and
is attracted to decaying animals. Common throughout year.

SHORE CRAB *Carcinus maenas*   Carapace width up to 5cm
Generally the commonest crab found around the coasts of Ireland. Favours all kinds
of marine habitats from rocky shores to breakwaters on sandy beaches. Body colour
is rather variable but usually greenish or olive-brown. Characteristically has three
blunt teeth between the eyes. Found between mid- to low-tide levels on shoreline
and usually hides beneath seaweed or stones. Quite aggressive when cornered but
prefers to scuttle sideways away from danger.

MASKED CRAB *Corystes cassivellaunus*   Carapace length 4cm
A bizarre-looking and distinctive crab that lives on sandy beaches. Sometimes
found washed-up dead on shoreline but in life lives buried in sand, using its long
antennae to create passage for seawater to gills. Carapace much longer than it is
broad and pincer-bearing, front pair of legs are extremely long. Common on suitable beaches and fairly widespread around the coasts of Ireland.

HERMIT CRAB *Eupagurus bernhardus*   Body length up to 9cm
Body size difficult to determine since animal lives inside empty shell of periwinkle,
whelk or other mollusc; shell periodically exchanged for larger one as animal grows.
Body colour reddish brown and right-hand pincer larger than left; this serves to
block entrance to shell when crab retreats inside in alarm. Mainly scavenging diet.
Common on sheltered shores and often seen in rockpools.

SPIDER CRAB *Macropodia rostrata*   Carapace length 10mm
Has long, spider-like legs and a roughly triangular carapace. Outline of body usually
obscured, however, by covering of seaweeds and sponges; these afford the animal
excellent camouflage among the seaweeds where it is usually found. Occurs on the
lower shore and sometimes found in rockpools or among netted samples. Widespread and fairly common around Ireland but easily overlooked.

BROAD-CLAWED PORCELAIN CRAB *Porcellana platycheles* Carapace width 13mm
An extremely flattened crab with a rounded carapace and very broad pincers. Upper
surface sandy-brown in colour and rather hairy, especially so on walking legs and
front edge of pincers; hairs trap silt and add to the effect of the animal's camouflaged colour. The underside is white and porcelain-like. Found under stones where
silt and debris collect on sheltered rocky shores. Widespread and common around
coasts of Ireland.

VELVET SWIMMING CRAB *Macropipus puber*   Carapace width 7cm
A distinctive crab with beady red eyes and reddish joints along the legs; there are
8–10 teeth between the eyes. The upper surface of the carapace is rather hairy and
this collects silt, giving the animal a velvety appearance. Often easily told by its
behaviour: when cornered, becomes aggressive and will lift itself up and brandish
its pincers, which can deliver a painful nip. Tips of back legs are flattened to form
paddles. Widespread and often common on rocky shores.

COMMON LOBSTER *Homarus vulgaris*   Carapace length up to 40cm
Large specimens are found in deep water but smaller individuals are sometimes
discovered in rock pools at extreme low water. In life, body is blue and only turns
red when boiled. Usually found in crevices and small caves and defends itself using
powerful pincers. Has a scavenging diet. Widespread around Ireland.

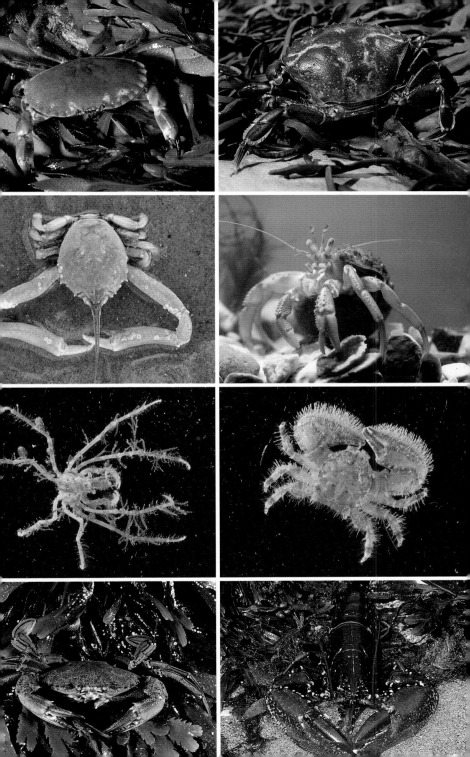

Chthalamus stellatus   Shell width up to 10mm
A typical barnacle and a locally abundant member of the rocky shore community. Forms encrusting communities between the upper and middle shores. Its range extends further up the shore in exposed areas compared to sheltered ones but it always occurs at a higher level on the shore than *Semibalanus balanoides*. Body of animal protected by volcano-like shell comprising six calcareous plates. The central opening is oval and, when exposed to air, this is sealed by four plates; the sutures to these meet at right angles to one another. When immersed by seawater, extends feathery thoracic appendages to catch food. Locally common in S.

ACORN BARNACLE *Semibalanus balanoides*   Shell width up to 12mm
A common barnacle on the lower shores of rocky coasts. Sometimes forms large, close-packed colonies, so dense that the true colour of the rock to which they are attached is completely obscured. Body protected by calcareous shell comprising six plates. Opening is diamond-shaped and sealed by four plates the sutures of which meet obliquely. Locally common in N.

Elminius modestus   Shell width up to 10mm
Introduced from Australia; occurs locally in SW Ireland. Shell comprises four greyish white, smooth plates. Favours the middle shore in sheltered waters where it attaches to stones; not averse to the influence of fresh water.

GOOSE BARNACLE *Lepas anatifera*   Shell length up to 4cm
An extraordinary animal. Normally pelagic but frequently washed-up on exposed beaches after onshore gales, mostly on W coasts. Typically found in sizeable groups attached to driftwood by 15cm long retractable stalk. Body of animal is protected by five translucent plates that are bluish white. Appearance of shell, and feathery appendages which often project, lead in the past to fanciful suggestion that goose barnacles were the embryonic stages of the Barnacle Goose.

COMMON PRAWN *Leander serratus*   Length up to 6cm
Common on rocky shores around coasts of SW Ireland. Often trapped in rock pools at low tide but difficult to spot until it moves because of near transparent body; closer inspection reveals an array of purplish brown dots and lines. Has very long antennae and toothed rostrum extending forward between the eyes. Diet mainly scavenging. Uses fan-like tail to swim backwards when alarmed.

COMMON SHRIMP *Crangon vulgaris*   Length up to 5cm
Found in shallow, sheltered waters including estuaries. Usually associated with sand and sometimes found in pools at low tide. Almost translucent body, stippled with dark dots, affords the animal superb camouflage when resting on sand or more especially when part-buried. Has long antennae but rostrum reduced to tiny tooth. Widespread around the coasts of Ireland and often abundant.

SAND-HOPPER *Talitris saltator*   Length up to 15mm
Very common and one of several rather similar species of crustaceans known as sand-hoppers. Found among rotting seaweed and under stones along the strandline, usually on sandy beaches. Easily seen by turning over piles of tideline debris when it escapes from danger by hopping and crawling under cover. Body is shiny and laterally compressed. Widespread around most coasts of Ireland.

SEA-SLATER *Ligia oceanica*   Length up to 25mm
A large relative of the woodlice, common under rocks in the splash zone and in sea walls. The body is greyish, segmented and flattened and carries two long antennae. Alert and rather fast-moving compared to its terrestrial relatives. Most active after dark when it scavenges for organic matter among the rocks and seaweed. Found in most suitable habitats on the coasts of Ireland.

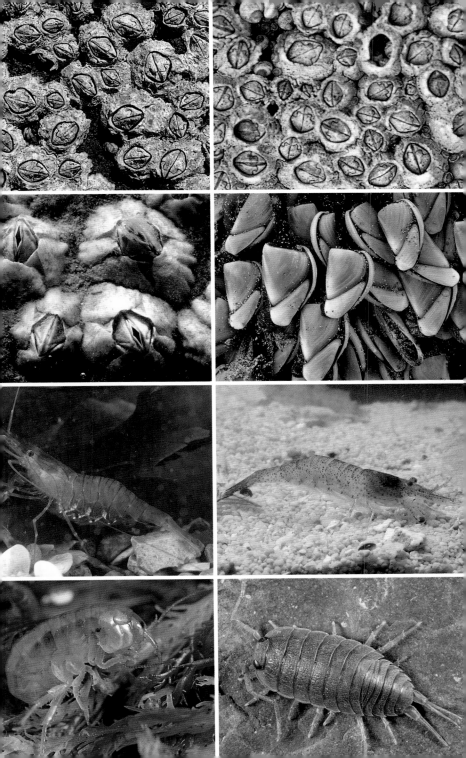

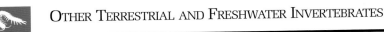

OTHER TERRESTRIAL AND FRESHWATER INVERTEBRATES

FLAT-BACKED MILLIPEDE *Polydesmus angustus*   Length 24mm
A widespread invertebrate found in organic-rich soils, compost heaps and under the bark of rotting wood. Body is rather flattened and centipede-like but the presence of two pairs of legs per segment identifies it as a millipede.

Cylindrosulus punctatus   Length 27mm
Widespread millipede in wooded areas and often found under the bark of rotting wood or among leaf litter. Body cylindrical in cross-section and pale reddish brown in colour. Feeds mainly on decaying plant matter but will also eat roots and bulbs.

PILL MILLIPEDE *Glomeris marginata*   Length 20mm
Armoured body is shiny chestnut-brown and superficially rather woodlouse-like in appearance. When disturbed, however, quickly rolls into a protective ball and reluctant to emerge again for some time. Locally common in mature woodland.

Haplophilus subterraneus   Length 35mm
A burrowing centipede, which is widespread and often common in garden soils and compost heaps. One pair of legs per segment typical of centipedes as a whole. An active predator of soil animals and is distinctly beneficial to the gardener.

Lithobius variegatus   Length 30mm
A common centipede and a familiar garden resident that also occurs in hedgerows and woods. Usually hides under stones during daytime and emerges after dark to hunt invertebrates. Body shiny, flattened and orange-brown. Widespread.

HARVESTMEN Order Opiliones   Body length up to 4mm
A common and widespread group of spider-like invertebrates with tiny bodies relative to the length of their spindly legs. Often found among wayside foliage, in bramble patches and grassland. Predatory and commonest in summer and autumn.

COMMON EARTHWORM *Lumbricus terrestris*   Length up to 8cm
An abundant and invaluable member of the soil community, important for its role in aeration and the incorporation of leaves and other organic matter. Comes to surface in wet weather and at night. Deposits conspicuous digested soil casts.

Lumbriculus sp.   Length 30mm
An often abundant group of annelid worms found in freshwater habitats. Resemble miniature earthworms and live in sediment and silt at the bottom of ponds and lakes. Transparent body reveals many of the internal organs. Feed on detritus.

FISH LEECH *Piscicola geometra*   Length 10mm
A fairly common external parasite of freshwater fish, particularly small species such as sticklebacks. Body long, narrow and sinuous with suckers at both ends. Often looks rather banded. Usually attaches to gills and other soft body parts.

Dugesia lugubris   Length up to 20mm
A common and widespread planarian worm found in slow-flowing streams and weedy ponds and lake. Body is grey-brown in colour with two pale spots at anterior end next to the eyes. Moves in a gliding manner. Predator of small invertebrates.

Hydra fusca   Length up to 5mm
Freshwater relative of sea anemones and jellyfish. Found in ponds, canals and lakes, usually attached to stems of water plants. If disturbed or removed from water, contracts into a blob and difficult to see. Buds new animals in summer.

FALSE SCORPIONS Order Pseudoscopiones   Length up to 3mm
A common but often overlooked group of soil animals with representative species found in gardens, woodlands and on the seashore. Body is rounded and tick-like. Pincers borne on long front legs. Predators of mites and other small animals.

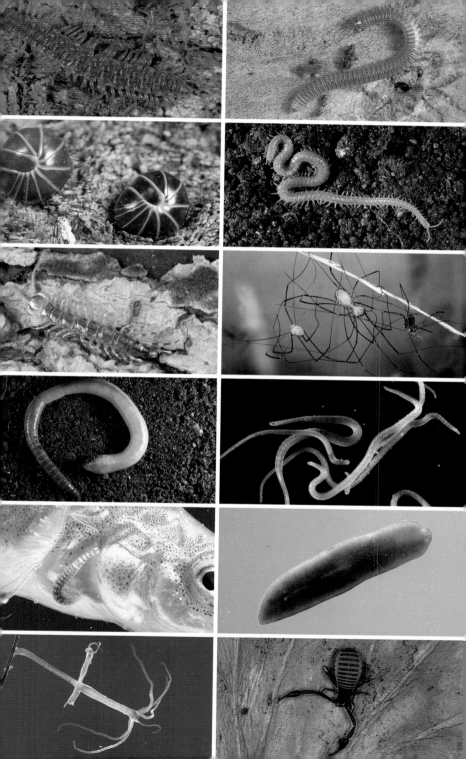

Chrysaora isosceles   Diameter up to 25cm
A mainly pelagic jellyfish but sometimes seen in inshore waters from piers or boats during summer months; occasionally washed ashore during gales. Umbrella-shaped body is marked with dark central spot and dark red radiating lines. Long tentacles suspended from lobed margin. Mainly off S and W Ireland.

COMMON JELLYFISH *Aurelia aurita*   Diameter up to 20cm
A pale, translucent jellyfish that is generally the commonest species around the coasts of Ireland; sometimes washed ashore in gales. Body colour pale yellowish brown but tinged with bluish purple as it pulsates through water. Underside of 'umbrella' has numerous short tentacles and four frilly mouth arms.

BEADLET ANEMONE *Actinia equina*   Height up to 5cm
Widespread and common on middle and lower shores of rocky coasts around Ireland. Attaches itself to rocks with sucker-like base. Colour variable but commonly seen as either red or green forms. Tentacles extended when immersed (A). When exposed to air or disturbed, retracts tentacles to become a jelly-like blob (B).

SNAKELOCKS ANEMONE *Anemonia sulcata*   Height up to 10cm
Rather squat and flattened sea anemone that is unable to retract its tentacles. Attached to rocks on middle and lower shores by sucker-like base. Body colour variable but commonly grey-brown or purplish green; tentacles same colour as body but often purple-tipped. Common on W and SW coasts of Ireland.

JEWEL ANEMONE *Corynactes viridis*   Height up to 2cm
More closely related to corals than to true sea anemones. Found in small colonies attached to rocks on lower shore around SW and W coasts of Ireland; often in gullies or crevices. Body colour usually pale buffish white but sometimes pale grey-green; tentacles tipped with iridescent pinkish purple.

Amphitrite johnstoni   Length up to 10cm, sometimes longer
A bizarre-looking marine annelid worm of sheltered muddy and sandy shores. The animal lives in a shallow burrow and this provides a degree of protection for its soft body; the burrow is often sited under, or close to, a stone. At the head end, there are numerous long tentacles and branched, blood-red gills.

LUGWORM *Arenicola marina*   Length up to 18cm
A burrowing marine annelid that is common in muddy estuaries and sandy beaches from the middle shore downwards. Presence often indicated by holes and casts which mark the entrances to its U-shaped burrow. Widespread around Irish coasts; often common. Important food for birds such as Curlew and godwits.

RAGWORM *Nereis diversicolor*   Length up to 10cm
An active, predatory annelid worm that is often abundant in estuaries and on sandy or muddy beaches. Widespread around the coasts of Ireland. Close examination reveals a toothed proboscis and jaws at the head end with tufts of hair-like chaetae on each of the 100 or so segments. Burrows freely.

Spirorbis borealis   Tube diameter up to 3mm
A curious little annelid worm that lives inside a spirally arranged, calcareous white tube. Small groups of these tubes can be observed on the fronds of various seaweeds such as Serrated Wrack; also found on rocks and mollusc shells on the lower shore. Common and widespread around the coasts of Ireland.

PEACOCK WORM *Sabella pavonia*   Height up to 20cm
An intriguing marine annelid worm that lives in tube constructed of sand and mud particles glued together by mucus. These tubes stand proud of the substrate in which they are embedded; found in large colonies on beaches at low tide. When immersed, radiating gills appear allowing the animal to filter feed and breathe.

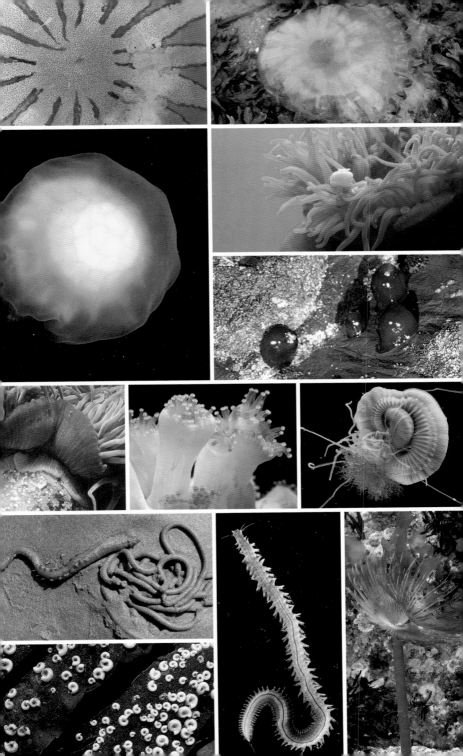

COMMON BRITTLE-STAR *Ophiothrix fragilis*   Disc diameter up to 15mm
Often found at low tide among seaweeds and under stones, especially where silt and sediment collect. Body comprises a central, flattened disc and five, narrow and radiating arms; the surfaces of both disc and arms are rather spiny. Colour rather variable but usually purplish brown but with paler bands visible along arms. As its name suggests, legs are brittle and easily broken. Widespread.

CUSHION-STAR *Asterina gibbosa*   Diameter up to 5cm
Identified by its distinctive shape and the five radiating arms projecting as short tips from the otherwise pentagonal outline. Upper surface is rather rough and usually blotched pinkish yellow and grey-brown; some specimens are greenish brown. Underside yellowish grey with numerous tube-feet. Widespread and often common off S and W Irish coasts. Found under rocks on lower shore.

COMMON STARFISH *Asterias rubens*   Diameter up to 40cm
A familiar seashore inhabitant, recognised by its five radiating arms. Upper surface is orange-red and covered with pale warts; the underside, which bears rows of tube-feet, is paler. A predator of bivalve molluscs such as mussels, oysters and scallops and so only common where prey species are numerous. Also scavenges at corpses of dead marine animals, sometimes in considerable numbers.

SPINY STARFISH *Marthasterias glacialis* Diameter up to 30cm, sometimes larger
Has rather slender arms that are usually olive-brown in colour and bear large and conspicuous pink spines; the radiating arms are often upturned at the tip. The underside is much paler. Sometimes occurs in comparatively deep water but can also be found in rock pools at low tide. Widespread but commonest off W and SW coasts of Ireland. Favours exposed and sheltered rocky shores.

COMMON SEA-URCHIN *Echinus esculentus*   Diameter up to 10cm
Common in deeper waters around the coasts of Ireland but also found in rockpools and among seaweeds at low tide; commonest off W and N coasts. Living animal is red and purplish brown; covered by spines and tube-feet. Dead animal loses spines to reveal rounded test which is reddish brown with radiating paler lines. A favourite food of Otters where their range is coastal.

HEART URCHIN *Echinocardium cordatum*   Length up to 8cm
A distinctive sea-urchin. Most familiar as the smooth, pale brown and potato-like *test* of the dead animal that is washed up on the tideline. In life, it is covered by a dense mat of fine spines, most of which are directed backwards. Burrows in sand and sometimes found near surface at low tide. Widespread and locally common around Ireland.

BREADCRUMB SPONGE *Halichondria panicea*   Thickness up to 2cm
An encrusting sponge that often forms large patches on rocky overhangs or in shady crevices from the middle shore downwards on rocky coasts. Colour rather variable but often bright orange, sometimes greenish brown. Spongy surface is pitted with crater-like openings through which seawater passes. Widespread.

DEAD MAN'S FINGERS *Alcyonium digitatum*   Length up to 15cm
Coral-like colonial animals that inhabit a branched, toughened skeleton. Colour rather variable but usually pale pink or yellowish white. When feeding, numerous tiny polyps emerge giving the surface a fuzzy appearance, fancifully resembling a decomposing hand. Widespread on rocky coasts from the lower shore downwards.

STAR ASCIDIAN *Botryllus schlosseri*   Star diameter up to 5mm
An encrusting, colonial animal that forms tough mats on shaded surfaces of rocks on the lower shore. Individual animals are arranged in a star-like fashion around a common opening. Colour rather variable but usually seen as white stars on a purplish brown background. Widespread; particularly common off W coasts.

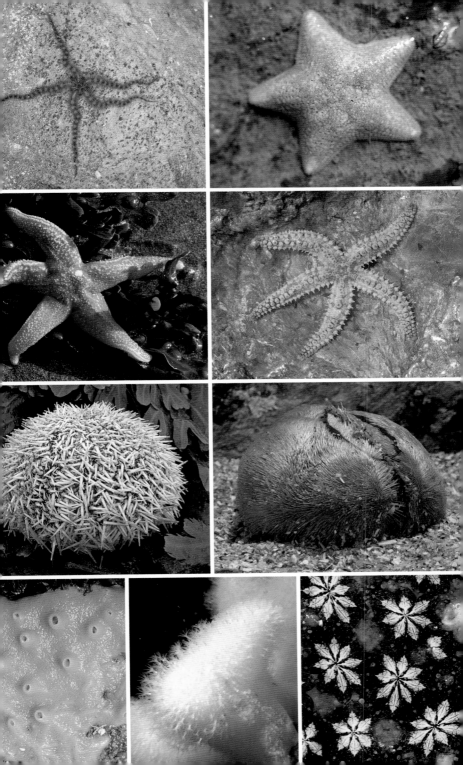

TREES AND SHRUBS

DOUGLAS-FIR *Pseudotsuga menziesii* Height up to 50m or more
Native to N America but widely planted. Crown conical and comprising whorls
of branches. Thick, corky bark becomes purplish brown and encrusted with algae
with age. Needles 2.5–3cm long, soft, dark green and pointed. Pendulous cones
are 5–10cm long, oval in outline and with 3-pronged, protruding bracts.

NORWAY SPRUCE *Picea abies* Height up to 60m
The most familiar 'Christmas Tree' species. Native to N Europe but widely grown.
Has distinctly curved branches, the lower ones drooping. Needles are 1.5–2.5cm
long, dark green and spreading; leave a peg on twig when they fall. Male cones
red; 15cm-long pendulous female cones are cigar-shaped and reddish brown.

SITKA SPRUCE *Picea sitchensis* Height up to 60m
Native to N America but widely planted. Evergreen foliage is blue-green. Needles
2–3cm long, flattened, stiff and pointed; radiate at first but pressed against shoot
with age. Pendulous, cigar-shaped cones are reddish brown when mature.

EUROPEAN LARCH *Larix decidua* Height up to 35m
Widely planted. In spring, needles are bright green but turn yellow in autumn
before they drop. Has grey-brown, cracking bark and pendulous twigs. The
1.5–2cm-long needles borne in tufts of 30–40. Mature ovoid cones 2–3cm long.

SCOTS PINE *Pinus sylvestris* Height up to 35mm
Widely planted. Mature tree domed and often rather lop-sided with bare lower
branches; young tree is more conical. Bluish green needles are paired and 3–7cm
long. Male cones are yellow; female cones are green when young but become
grey-brown when mature.

CORSICAN PINE *Pinus nigra* ssp. *laricio* Height up to 40m
A native of S Europe but often grown in plantations and coastal areas; favours
poor, light soils. Straggly and sparse foliage with soft, grey-green needles seen in
whorls and each up to 15cm long. The 6–8cm-long cones are borne in clusters.

WESTERN HEMLOCK-SPRUCE *Tsuga heterophylla* Height up to 65m
Native to N America but widely grown. Medium-sized specimens usually conical
in outline and with drooping leading shoot. Needles of variable length, usually
7–18mm; dark green above with two white bands below. Male cones reddish purple, those of female are reddish brown, ovoid and pendulous.

LAWSON CYPRESS *Chamaecyparis lawsoniana* Height up to 45m
A native of N America but widely planted as an ornamental or hedging species.
Mature tree is tall and conical but seldom allowed to reach this state and usually
heavily pruned. Shoots form flattened sprays that carry the scale-like leaves. Male
cones are dark red; female cones are blue-green and spherical.

LEYLAND CYPRESS × *Cupressocyparis leylandi* Height up to 35m
A hybrid cypress. Popular as a hedging plant in gardens. Usually heavily pruned
and seldom acquires tree-like proportions. Several colour forms exist but sprays
of foliage usually comprise dark green scale-like leaves. Female cones globular.

JUNIPER *Juniperus communis* Height up to 5m
Variable in size and shape, sometimes prostrate. Stiff, bluish green, needle-like
leaves arranged in whorls of three. Male and female flowers on separate plants.
Those of female green and oval, ripening to blue-black berries. Locally common.

YEW *Taxus baccata* Height up to 25m
Familiar evergreen tree, also used for hedging. Foliage comprises pointed and flattened dark green needles. Bark reddish and flaking. Male flowers yellow. Female
flowers on separate tree; green, maturing to bright red fruit. Locally common.

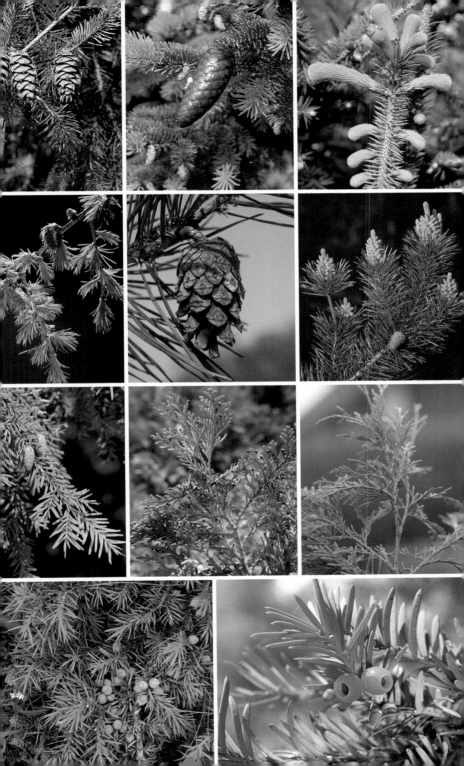

BAY WILLOW *Salix pentandra* Height up to 6m
A widespread shrub. Favours riversides and other wetland habitats. Leaves broad, glossy dark green and bay-like. Flowers May–June; male catkins are yellow and cylindrical, female green.

CRACK WILLOW *Salix fragilis* Height up to 25m
Usually has broad, rounded crown and leaning trunk although often pollarded. Twigs easily snap and trunk sometimes cracks open. Alternate leaves are 10–15cm long, narrow and dark glossy green above. Catkins appear April–May, with leaves.

WHITE WILLOW *Salix alba* Height up to 20m
Tree often appears silvery white due to colour of alternate leaves that are narrow, pointed and silky when young. Tree has upswept branches and trunk often leaning. Flowers April–May. Yellow male catkins are 4–5cm long and cylindrical.

WEEPING WILLOW *Salix × chrysocoma* Height up to 12m
Distinctive hybrid. Popular ornamental tree and often grown beside water. Long, trailing branches with long, yellow twigs. Leaves long and narrow. Male catkins yellow; on separate trees from females. Flowers April–May, when leaves appear.

GREY WILLOW *Salix cinerea* Height up to 10m
Fairly common in wet habitats; forms a broad crown in mature specimens. Broad, oval leaves and twigs softly hairy when young; leaves develop inrolled margins with age. Flowers March–April; 2–3cm-long male and female catkins on different trees.

SALLOW *Salix caprea* Height up to 10m
Forms a rounded shrub or small tree. Leaves are rounded-oval and are green and hairy above but greyish and woolly beneath. Flowers March–April, before leaves have appeared. Yellow male catkins on separate trees from green female catkins.

OSIER *Salix viminalis* Height up to 5m
Undisturbed shrub is highly branched; often pollarded and then produces numerous long, straight twigs that are reddish brown. Leaves narrow and tapering; green above but silvery below. Flowers February–April. Often seen along river margins.

WHITE POPLAR *Populus alba* Height up to 20m
Native to S Europe but widely grown as an ornamental tree. A spreading tree, the trunk often leaning. Leaves dark green above but white below making tree look silvery. Catkins appear February–March, male and female on different trees.

HYBRID BLACK POPLAR *Populus × canadensis* Height up to 30m
Hybrid species with greyish, furrowed bark and spreading branches. Alternate leaves are triangular to oval with toothed margins. Flowers March–April with 3–5cm-long male and female catkins on different trees. A popular timber tree.

ASPEN *Populus tremula* Height up to 20m
Easily distinguished in even dense woodland by its fluttering leaves that catch even the slightest breeze and reveal very pale undersides. Widespread, favouring damp areas. Flowers February–March, male and female catkins on separate trees.

SILVER BIRCH *Betula pendula* Height up to 30m
Common and widespread throughout Ireland. Silvery-grey bark cracks into rectangular plates with age and branches pendulous towards tips. 4cm-long oval to triangular leaves turn yellow in autumn. Catkins appear April–May.

DOWNY BIRCH *Betula pubescens* Height up to 25m
Common in damp areas and upland sites with high rainfall, especially in N and W. Young twigs downy and 5cm-long leaves have coarsely-toothed margins. Catkins appear February–April. Smooth, grey bark often covered with lichens and mosses.

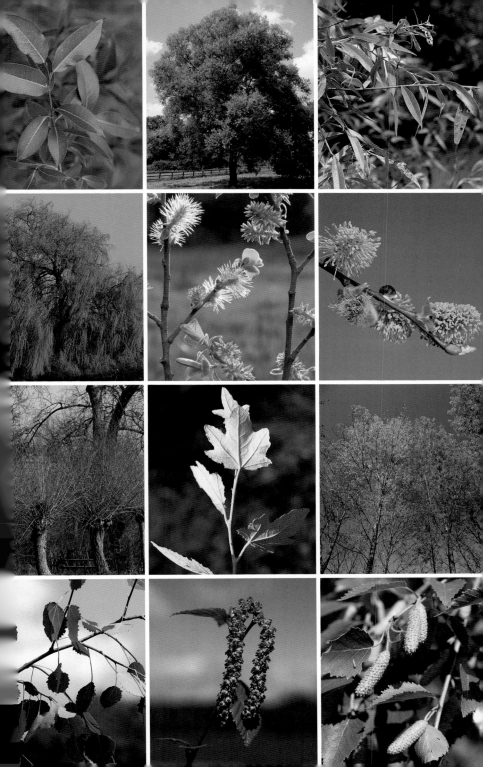

ALDER *Alnus glutinosa*   Height up to 20m
Common in damp habitats in most parts. Rounded leaves are bright green with
shallow teeth. Flowers appear before leaves, February–March; male catkins are
long and pendulous while those of female are ovoid and reddish. Cones brown.

BOG MYRTLE *Myrica gale*   Height up to 1m
Characteristic woody shrub of boggy habitats, usually on acid soils. Brown stems
bear aromatic, oval leaves which are grey-green. Orange, ovoid male catkins and
pendulous brown female catkins appear in April on separate plants, before leaves.

COMMON WALNUT *Juglans regia*   Height up to 30m
Widely planted tree with spreading crown. Grey bark becomes fissured with age.
Alternate leaves pinnately divided into 7–9 leaflets. Pendulous male catkins and
clustered female flowers appear May–June. Green fruit contains familiar walnut.

HAZEL *Corylus avellana*   Height up to 12m
Common and widespread small tree or shrub. Often coppiced. 8cm-long alternate
leaves are almost circular with double-toothed margins. Male catkins and tiny red
female flowers appear January–March, before leaves. Fruits ripen in autumn.

HORNBEAM *Carpinus betulus*   Height up to 30m
Mature tree is impressive with spreading crown and often twisted trunk. Bark
smooth and pale grey. 5–10cm-long oval leaves are pointed with sharply double-
toothed margins. Catkins appear April–May. The 3-lobed fruits carried in clusters.

BEECH *Fagus sylvatica*   Height up to 40m
Forms single-species stands, usually on calcareous soils. Mature trees large and
stately; dense canopy inhibits understorey plants. Leaf oval with wavy margin;
bright green in spring but golden in autumn. Paired nuts borne in spiky fruit.

PEDUNCULATE OAK *Quercus robur*   Height up to 45m
Typical tree of woodlands in lowland districts and S. Irregularly lobed, oblong
leaves borne on very short petioles but clustered acorns carried on long stalks.
Catkin-like flowers appear May–June.

SESSILE OAK *Quercus petraea*   Height up to 40m
The typical oak in W and N, and upland regions. Irregularly and shallowly lobed
oblong leaves are borne on short stalks and the clustered acorns are almost stalkless; the acorn cups have downy scales. Catkin-like flowers appear in May.

HORSE-CHESTNUT *Aesculus hippocastanum*   Height up to 35m
Well-known for its spreading habit, the pyramidal spikes of white flowers that
cover the tree in April and May, and for its seed, the familiar conker. Bright green
leaves divided into 5–7 oval leaflets. Introduced but widely planted.

SWEET CHESTNUT *Castanea sativa*   Height up to 12m
An introduced species but widely planted both for its timber and its spiny-cased
edible nuts. Bark fissured and spirally twisted around trunk. Shiny, dark green
leaves are narrow and oblong-oval with toothed margins. Catkins flower in July.

ENGLISH ELM *Ulmus procera*   Height up to 35m
Introduced and formerly fairly common. Mature trees killed by Dutch Elm disease
but shrub-sized specimens still found in hedgerows. Dark green oval leaves have
toothed margins and asymmetrical bases. Tufted red flowers seen February–March.

WYCH ELM *Ulmus glabra*   Height up to 40m
Mature tree has broad, spreading crown. Dark green oval leaves have 10–18 veins
and asymmetrical bases, one side overlapping the short leaf stalk. Clustered red flowers seen February–March. Still fairly common in N and W; fairly disease resistant.

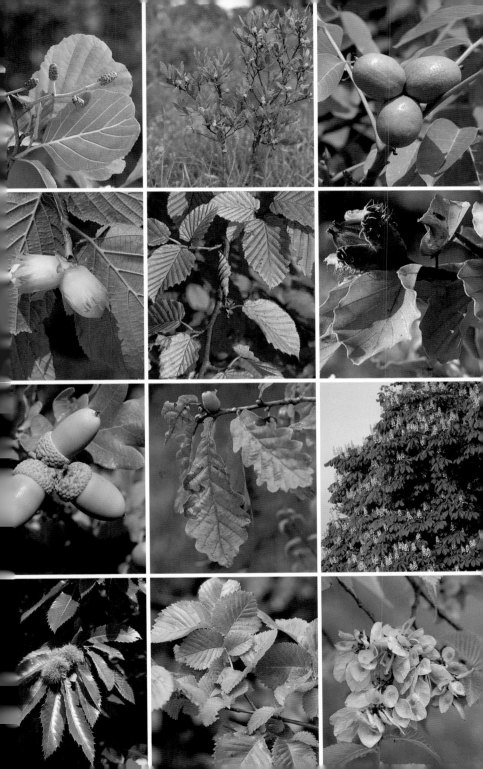

LONDON PLANE *Platanus × hispanica*   Height up to 35m
Tolerant of pollution and therefore widely planted along city streets. Grey bark flakes
to reveal patchwork of yellow-buff. The 5-lobed leaves have toothed margins. Flowers appear in June and comprise strings of spherical heads; ripen to brown fruits.

SYCAMORE *Acer pseudoplatanus*   Height up to 35m
Introduced but widely planted and now firmly established. The 5-lobed leaves
have toothed margins. Flowers appear in April and comprise hanging, yellowish
green clusters. Wings of paired fruits form angle of 90°. Tolerates salt-spray.

FIELD MAPLE *Acer campestre*   Height up to 25m
A common hedgerow shrub, sometimes forming a small tree. The 5-lobed leaves
are dark green but turn orange-yellow in autumn. Yellowish green flowers appear
in May, carried in upright spikes. Wings of paired fruits form an angle of 180°.

HOLLY *Ilex aquifolium*   Height up to 10m
Familiar Christmas decoration, common and widespread in woods and hedges.
Stiff, leathery leaves have spiny margins; dark green above but paler below. White,
4-petalled flowers appear May–July and clusters of red berries ripen in autumn.

ASH *Fraxinus excelsior*   Height up to 40m
Widespread and common. Tall with unkempt, rounded crown. Bark grey and
fairly smooth. Twigs bear large black buds before pinnate leaves appear, these
divided into 7–12 leaflets. Seeds winged.

ROWAN *Sorbus aucuparia*   Height up to 15m
Attractive, bushy tree sometimes known as Mountain Ash. Fairly common in
upland and waterlogged habitats; also planted as street tree. Leaves are pinnately
divided into 5–10 leaflets. White flowers appear in May; ripen to red berries in
August.

WHITEBEAM *Sorbus aria*   Height up to 25m
Tree looks silvery due to downy white undersides to leaves; upper surface of leaf
dark green. White flowers appear May–June and ripen to red, ovoid fruits by
autumn; avidly eaten by birds. Local and rather scarce in the wild; also grown
ornamentally.

WILD PEAR *Pyrus communis*   Height up to 20m
The ancestor of the cultivated pear. Local and rather scarce. Leaves are 5–8cm
long, oval and with finely-toothed margins. White, 5-petalled flowers appear in
April and ripen to form hard, greenish brown fruit.

CRAB APPLE *Malus sylvestris*   Height up to 10m
A familiar hedgerow and woodland tree or shrub. Alternate, finely-toothed leaves
are oval, deep green and slightly hairy. Pinkish white, 5-petalled flowers appear
in May and ripen to small, green apples by late summer.

WILD CHERRY *Prunus avium*   Height up to 30m
Recognised by its reddish brown bark that peels in horizontal bands. Alternate,
oval leaves have short-toothed margins. Clusters of 5-petalled, white flowers
appear in April–May and fruits ripen in summer, turning from green to dark red.

BLACKTHORN *Prunus spinosa*   Height up to 5m
Common, thorny hedgerow shrub that often forms dense thickets. Alternate, oval
leaves are 2–4cm long and have toothed margins. White, 5-petalled flowers (A)
appear March–April, before the leaves. Purplish fruits (sloes, B) have a powdery
bloom.

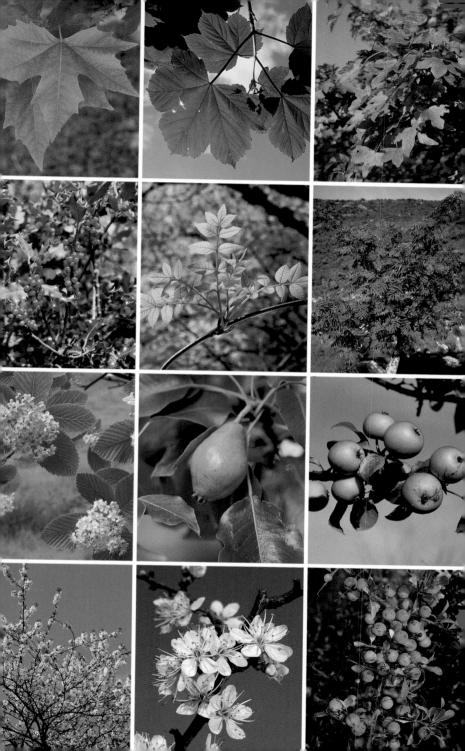

CHERRY LAUREL *Prunus laurocerasus*   Height up to 8m
A popular ornamental evergreen shrub whose leaves smell of almonds when bruised; they are glossy, elongate-oval and laurel-like in appearance. Spikes of white, 5-petalled flowers appear in April. The 2cm-long fruits ripen from red to black.

HAWTHORN *Crategus monogyna*   Height up to 15m
A common hedgerow shrub, forming dense, thorny thickets in many areas. Shiny, roughly oval leaves are divided into 3–7 pairs of lobes. The 5-petalled, white flowers appear May–June and ripen to form bright red clusters of berries.

SPINDLE-TREE *Euonymus europaeus*   Height up to 6m
Native shrub or small tree. Leaves are narrow-oval and pointed, with toothed margins; green in summer but turning reddish in autumn. Tiny greenish flowers appear May–June. Fruit is pink.

BUCKTHORN *Rhamnus catharticus*   Height up to 8m
Native to lowland areas, but rather scarce. Forms a thorny bush or small tree. Opposite leaves 3–6cm long, oval and finely toothed. Clusters of greenish yellow flowers appear in May and bunches of black berries are found in autumn.

ALDER-BUCKTHORN *Frangula alnus*   Height up to 5m
A rather open, thornless bush, native but local and rather scarce. Oval leaves have wavy margins; dark green, turning yellow in autumn. Pale green, 5-petalled flowers appear in May. Berries ripen from green to black.

GOOSEBERRY *Ribes uva-crispa*   Height up to 1m
Introduced and rather local. Spiny stems bear rounded and irregularly-toothed leaves. Small, yellowish flowers appear March–May. Green, hairy fruits eventually swell to form the familiar gooseberry.

SEA-BUCKTHORN *Hippophae rhamnoides*   Height up to 10m
Native to stabilised, coastal dunes, mainly in E; also planted ornamentally inland. Forms a dense shrub with thorny twigs and narrow, greyish leaves. Small, greenish female and male flowers grow on separate plants. Orange berries form on female bushes.

COMMON LIME *Tilia × vulgaris*   Height up to 45m
Widely planted ornamental hybrid. Mature trees often have a rather tall, narrow crown in proportion to width of the base. The 6–10cm-long heart-shaped leaves exude sap. Clustered flowers attached to a wing-like bract. Ovoid seed is hard-cased.

RHODODENDRON *Rhododendron ponticum*   Height up to 5m
A popular ornamental shrub but naturalised and invasive in some areas. Shiny and leathery evergreen leaves are elliptical and dark green. Clusters of stalked, pinkish red flowers appear May–June. Fruit capsule contains numerous flat seeds.

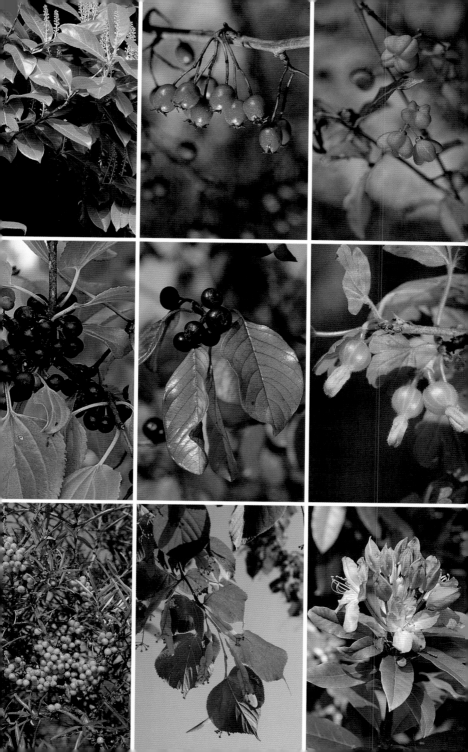

BUDDLEIA *Buddleia davidii*   Height up to 4m
Common garden shrub, also widely naturalised on wasteground and around coasts. Has long, narrow leaves which are darker above than below. Showy, often drooping spikes of purple flowers appear June–September. Very attractive to butterflies.

DOGWOOD *Cornus sanguinea*   Height up to 4m
A rather rare hedgerow shrub. Easily recognised, even in winter, by its red stems. The opposite, oval leaves have 3–5 veins and reddish stalks. Flat clusters of white flowers appear May–July. Ripen to black berries.

PRIVET *Ligustrum vulgare*   Height up to 10m
Fairly common hedgerow and wayside shrub. Shiny, oval leaves are sometimes evergreen. Twigs carry terminal spikes of scented, white flowers which are 4-petalled and appear May–June. Berries are black and ripen in autumn.

ELDER *Sambucus nigra*   Height up to 10m
Common shrub of hedgerows and waysides. Usually has outcurved main branches and corky bark. Unpleasant-smelling leaves divided into 5–7 leaflets. Flat-topped sprays of fragrant white flowers appear June–July. Berries black and luscious.

GUELDER-ROSE *Viburnum opulus*   Height up to 4m
Large shrub or small tree. Found in hedgerows and fairly common. Leaves are divided into five irregularly-toothed lobes. Flowers appear June–July in flat-topped heads, inner ones much smaller than outer ones. Berries are red.

HONEYSUCKLE *Lonicera periclymenum*   Height up to 5m
Common hedgerow and woodland climber that twines up other shrubs and trees. Leaves are grey-green, oval and opposite. Scented, trumpet-shaped flowers appear June–August; borne in whorled heads. Clusters of red berries ripen in autumn.

HOP *Humulus lupulus*   Height up to 6m
Twining hedgerow climber. Introduced to Ireland. Leaves divided into 3–5 coarse-toothed lobes. Male flowers seen in open clusters. Female flowers are green cone-like hops that ripen brown.

IVY *Hedera helix*   Height up to 20m
An evergreen, self-clinging climber which also carpets the ground. Glossy, dark green leaves are 3- or 5-lobed with paler veins. Heads of yellow-green flowers appear September–November; ripen to black berries. Widespread and very common.

STRAWBERRY TREE *Arbutus unedo*   Height up to 10m
Evergreen shrub or small tree. Leaves are broadly oval and shiny above. Flowers are whitish and bell- or urn-shaped; borne in pendant clusters. Develop and ripen into red berries. Flowers and fruit occur side by side. Locally common in SW.

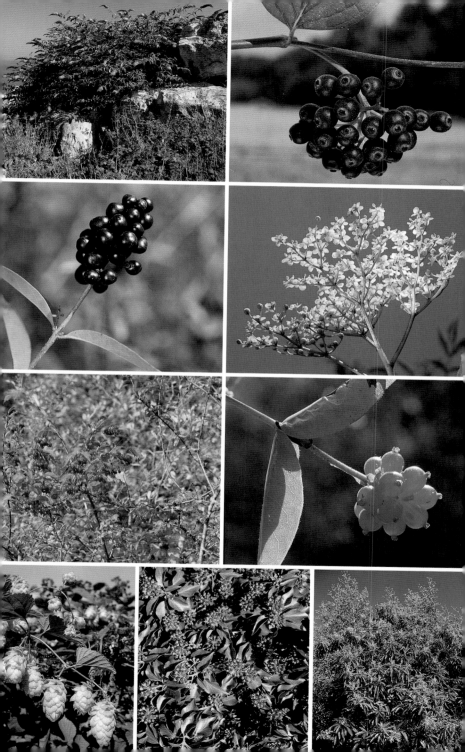

COMMON NETTLE *Urtica dioica* Height up to 1m
The familiar stinging nettle. Oval leaves are toothed and pointed-tipped; borne in opposite pairs and covered with sharp hairs. Flowers appear June–October in pendulous catkins; male and female on separate plants. Favours disturbed soils.

PELLITORY-OF-THE-WALL *Parietaria judaica* Height up to 7cm
Spreading, downy perennial found typically on walls and rocky ground. Oval, long-stalked leaves are borne on much-branched, red stems. Clusters of flowers appear June–October, at leaf bases. Widespread in Ireland.

FUCHSIA *Fuchsia magellanica* Height up to 1.5m
A popular alien garden plant but widely naturalised along hedgerows and around abandoned buildings. Leaves are oval and toothed. Flowers are distinctive and bell-shaped, comprising purple and pink elements.

KNOTGRASS *Polygonum aviculare* Often prostrate
Widespread and common much-branched annual of bare soil, paths and open ground generally. Oval, rather leathery leaves are alternate and have a silvery sheaf around leaf bases. Pale pink flowers appear June–October, arising in leaf axils.

BISTORT *Persicaria bistorta* Height up to 60cm
Medium-sized perennial of damp meadows, locally common only in the W. Leaves oval or arrow-shaped; borne on unbranched, upright stems. 30–40mm-long terminal cylindrical spikes of pink flowers appear June–August. Forms patches.

AMPHIBIOUS BISTORT *Persicaria amphibia* Height up to 40cm
Perennial seen both as a plant of pond margins and on dry land. Aquatic form has floating stems and oval leaves. Globular or cylindrical terminal spikes of pink flowers appear June–September on upright stems. Widespread and locally common.

WATER-PEPPER *Persicaria hydropiper* Height up to 70cm
Upright, branched annual, characteristic of damp, bare ground such as winter-wet ruts. Widespread and common except in N. Narrow oval leaves have peppery taste when chewed. Pale pink flowers borne in long spikes that often droop at tip.

REDSHANK *Persicaria maculosa* Height up to 60cm
Upright or sprawling annual that is widespread and common on disturbed ground. Narrow oval leaves typically show a dark, central mark. Reddish stems are much-branched. Pink flowers appear June–October and are borne in terminal spikes.

BLACK-BINDWEED *Fallopia convolvulus* Height up to 1m
A very common, clockwise-twining annual which both trails on ground and climbs among wayside plants. Arrow-shaped leaves are borne on angular stems. Clusters of dock-like greenish flowers appear July–October and arise from the leaf axils.

JAPANESE KNOTWEED *Fallopia japonica* Height up to 2m
Fast-growing, invasive perennial, quick to colonise roadsides, riverbanks and other wayside places. Large, triangular leaves are borne on red, zigzag stems. Loose spikes of white flowers arise from leaf bases and appear August–October.

CURLED DOCK *Rumex crispus* Height up to 1m
A common and widespread perennial of rough meadows and disturbed soils. Narrow leaves are 25cm long and have wavy edges. Oval, flattened flowers appear June–October; borne in dense, leafless spikes which do not spread away from stem.

COMMON SORREL *Rumex acetosa* Height up to 60cm
An often short, upright perennial. Common and widespread everywhere in all sorts of grassy habitats. Deep green leaves are arrow-shaped, narrow and taste vaguely of vinegar. Reddish flowers appear May–July and are carried in slender spikes.

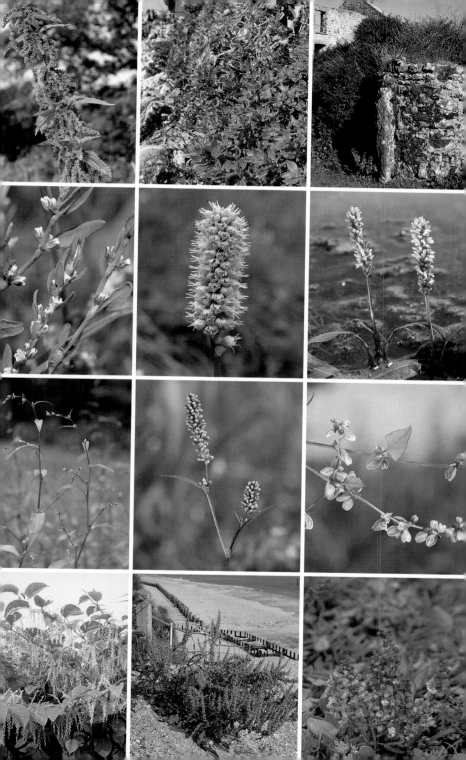

WILD FLOWERS

SHEEP'S SORREL *Rumex acetosella*   Height up to 25cm
Short, upright perennial of bare, well-drained acid soils. Common and widespread in suitable open habitats. Leaves are arrow-shaped but the basal lobes point forwards. Flowers appear May–August and are carried in slender, loose spikes.

GREAT WATER DOCK *Rumex hydrolapathum*   Height up to 1.5m
Large, branched perennial, associated with damp habitats such as ditches, river banks, canals and marshes. Widespread but local. Leaves large and oval. Dense flower spikes appear July–September.

BROAD-LEAVED DOCK *Rumex obtusifolius*   Height up to 1m
A widespread and often extremely common upright perennial of field margins and disturbed meadows. Leaves are large and broadly oval, heart-shaped at the base. Flowers appear June–October in loose spikes which are leafy at their bases.

WOOD DOCK *Rumex sanguineus*   Height up to 1m
Upright, straggly and branched perennial. Widespread and often common. Favours grassy woodland rides and shaded meadows. Easily identified when flowers (June–October), leaf veins and stems turn red.

SPRING BEAUTY *Claytonia perfoliata*   Height up to 30cm
Annual introduced from N America; locally naturalised. Basal leaves oval and stalked. Flowering stems with fused pair of perfoliate leaves. White, 5-petalled 5mm-diameter flowers appear April–July in loose spikes. Favours dry, sandy soil.

PINK PURSLANE *Claytonia sibirica*   Height up to 30cm
Introduced annual or perennial from N America; naturalised but rare in damp woods. Basal leaves oval and stalked. Flowering stems carry pair of unstalked leaves. Pink, 5-petalled flowers are 15–20mm across and appear April–July.

FAT HEN *Chenopodium album*   Height up to 1m
A very common and widespread plant of disturbed arable land and waste places. An upright annual. Green leaves look matt due to mealy coating; leaf shape varies from oval to diamond-shaped. Spikes of whitish flowers appear June–October.

RED GOOSEFOOT *Chenopodium rubrum*   Height up to 60cm
Variable upright annual. Rather scarce. Favours manure-rich soil. Leaves shiny, diamond-shaped and toothed. Leafy flower spikes appear July–October. Stems often turn red in old or parched specimens.

GOOD KING HENRY *Chenopodium bonus-henricus*   Height up to 50cm
Introduced, upright perennial. Widely established and often common on disturbed arable land. Lower leaves triangular; mealy when young but then green. Stems sometimes with red lines. Leafless flower spikes appear May–August.

BABINGTON'S ORACHE *Atriplex glabriuscula*   Prostrate and spreading
Entirely coastal but widespread around Ireland on stabilised shingle and bare ground. Has triangular or diamond-shaped leaves. Stems usually reddish and whole plant often turns red in autumn. Flower spikes appear July–September.

SEA BEET *Beta vulgaris* ssp. *maritima*   Height up to 1m
Sprawling perennial, forming clumps on cliffs, shingle beaches and other coastal habitats. Leaves glossy, dark green and leathery, with reddish stems; leaf shape varies from oval to triangular. Spikes of green flowers appear July–September.

SEA PURSLANE *Halimione portulacoides*   Height up to 1m
A spreading, often rather rounded perennial, all parts of which are mealy. Grey-green leaves are oval at the base but narrow further up stem. Yellowish flower spikes appear July–October. Grows on saltmarshes in Ireland.

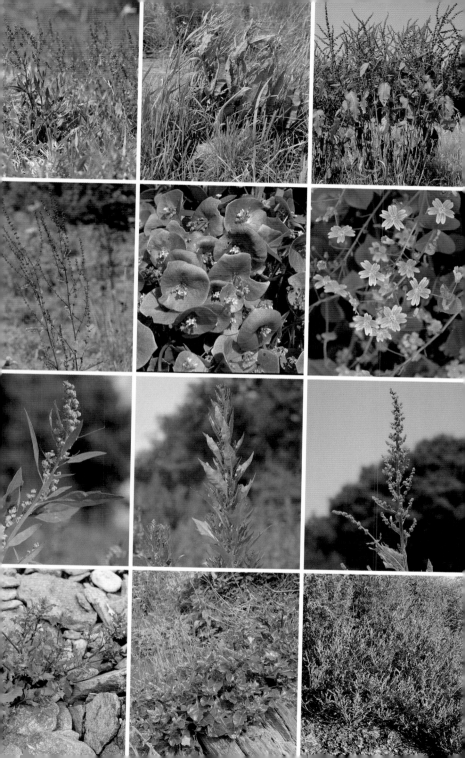

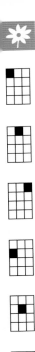

GLASSWORT *Salicornia europaea*   Height up to 30cm
A yellowish green, fleshy annual that fancifully resembles a miniature cactus. Usually much-branched and looks segmented. Tiny flowers appear August–September at stem junctions. A typical saltmarsh plant. Tolerates immersion in salt water.

ANNUAL SEA-BLITE *Suaeda maritima*   Height up to 50cm
Widespread annual of saltmarshes around the coasts of Ireland. Much-branched and forms small clumps that vary from yellowish green to reddish. Leaves are rather swollen and cylindrical. Tiny flowers appear August–October.

PRICKLY SALTWORT *Salsola kali*   Height up to 50cm
Spiky-looking, prickly annual, typical of sandy beaches around most of Ireland. Leaves are swollen, flattened-cylindrical and spiny-tipped. Tiny solitary flowers appear July–October at the leaf bases. Often rather prostrate.

THYME-LEAVED SANDWORT *Arenaria serpyllifolia*   Usually prostrate
Common in lowland areas of Ireland and favouring dry, bare soils. Slender, delicate stems bear oval leaves in opposite pairs. White, 5-petalled flowers are 5–7mm across; appear April–October. Green sepals longer than petals.

SPRING SANDWORT *Minuartia verna*   Height up to 10cm
An extremely local plant of bare limestone soils. Whorls of narrow, 3-veined leaves are carried on slender stems. White, 5-petalled flowers are 7–9mm across and appear May–September. Green sepals are shorter than petals.

SEA SANDWORT *Honkenya peploides*   Prostrate
Familiar coastal perennial found on stabilised shingle and sandy beaches. Often forms large mats which comprise creeping stems bearing opposite pairs of fleshy, oval leaves. The greenish white flowers are 6–8mm across and appear May–August.

GREATER STITCHWORT *Stellaria holostea*   Height up to 50cm
Widespread and common in open woodland and along rides and hedgerows. Leaves are narrow, fresh green and grass-like. Easily overlooked among foliage until white flowers appear April–June. These are 20–30mm across and have notched petals.

LESSER STITCHWORT *Stellaria graminea*   Height up to 50cm
Widespread and common in similar habitats to Greater Stitchwort; favours acid soils. Long, narrow and fresh green leaves found among grasses and other wayside plants. The white, 5-petalled flowers are 5–15mm across and appear May–August.

COMMON CHICKWEED *Stellaria media*   Height up to 30cm
Common annual of flowerbeds, vegetable patches and other areas of disturbed ground. Often prostrate and spreading. Leaves oval, fresh green and in opposite pairs; upper leaves unstalked. White flowers are 5–10mm across; seen all year.

COMMON MOUSE-EAR *Cerastium fontanum*   Height up to 30cm, often shorter
Hairy perennial, widespread and usually common in gardens and grassland, and on disturbed ground. Grey-green leaves borne in opposite pairs. Non-flowering and flowering shoots occur, the latter with white, 5-petalled flowers April–October.

STICKY MOUSE-EAR *Cerastium glomeratum*   Height up to 40cm
Stickily-hairy annual that is widespread and common on dry, bare ground. Leaves are pointed-oval and borne in opposite pairs. The white, 5-petalled flowers are 10–15mm across and are carried in clustered heads; they appear April–October.

CORN SPURREY *Spergula arvensis*   Height up to 30cm
A stickily-hairy annual that is a widespread and fairly common weed of arable land with sandy soils. Narrow leaves are borne in whorls along straggling stems. Flowers are 4–7mm across and comprise five whitish petals; they appear May–August.

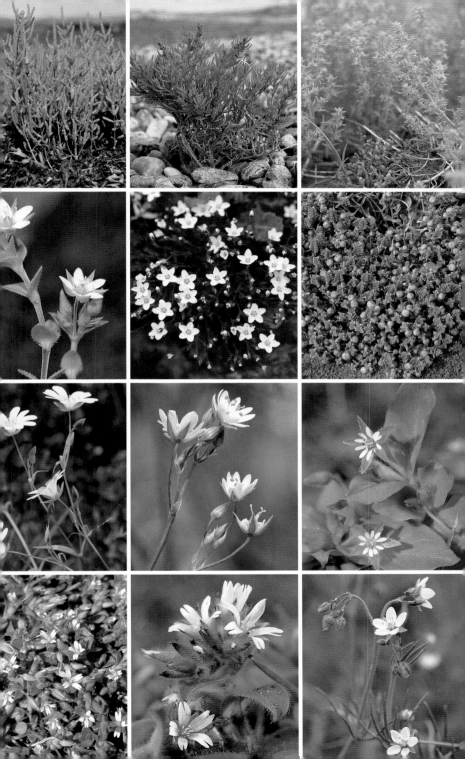

LESSER SEA-SPURREY *Spergularia marina*   Usually prostrate
Annual plant associated with grassy upper margins of saltmarshes; widespread and
locally common. Fleshy, narrow leaves are pointed and borne in opposite pairs on
trailing stems. Deep pink flowers appear June–September and are 6–8mm across.

ROCK SEA-SPURREY *Spergularia rupicola*   Height up to 20cm
A sticky perennial characteristic of rocky coastal habitats and found on cliffs, sea
walls and stone walls. Sometimes forms clumps comprising branched stems with
whorls of fleshy leaves. Pink flowers are 8–10mm across; appear June–September.

PROCUMBENT PEARLWORT *Sagina procumbens*   Prostrate
Creeping perennial of damp, bare ground; common in Ireland. Forms mats comprising central rosette with radiating shoots bearing narrow leaves. The green,
petal-less flowers are borne on side shoots and are seen May–September.

ANNUAL KNAWEL *Scleranthus annuus*   Height up to 10cm
Yellowish green annual. Locally common on dry, bare soil and arable land in
most of Ireland. Narrow, pointed leaves borne in opposite pairs along the stems.
Flowers comprise green, pointed sepals and no petals; appear May–August.

BLADDER CAMPION *Silene vulgaris*   Height up to 80cm
Grassland perennial favouring well-drained soil, often on chalk. Widespread but
common only in S. Upright stems bear opposite pairs of grey-green leaves. White
flowers appear May–September and comprise 5 petals and a swollen sepal tube.

SEA CAMPION *Silene maritima*   Height up to 20cm
A cushion-forming perennial. Confined to coastal habitats including shingle and
cliffs but widespread and locally abundant. Leaves grey-green and fleshy. White
flowers are 20–25mm across and have overlapping petals; appear June–August.

MOSS CAMPION *Silene acaulis*   Diameter up to 20cm
A cushion-forming perennial associated with uplands. Rare and restricted to N.
Leaves narrow and densely packed. Pink flowers appear June–August.

RED CAMPION *Silene dioica*   Height up to 1m
Hairy biennial or perennial. Local in Ireland. Hairy leaves are borne in opposite
pairs on upright stems. Pinkish red flowers are 20–25mm across and appear
March–October; they comprise five petals.

WHITE CAMPION *Silene alba*   Height up to 1m
Widespread and common hairy perennial which favours disturbed ground and
grassy habitats including hedgerows and verges. Oval leaves are borne in opposite pairs on stems. White, 5-petalled flowers appear May–October and are
25–30mm across.

RAGGED ROBIN *Lychnis flos-cuculi*   Height up to 65cm
Widespread and common perennial of damp meadows and marshes. The narrow,
grass-like leaves are rough, the upper ones in opposite pairs. The flowers comprise
5 pink petals each of which is divided into 4 lobes; they appear May–August.

STINKING HELLEBORE *Helleborus foetidus*   Height up to 75cm
A scarce, strong-smelling perennial, occasionally naturalised as a garden escape.
Leaves divided into toothed lobes; lower ones persist through winter. Green, bell-
shaped flowers are 15–30mm across and appear January–May.

GREEN HELLEBORE *Helleborus viridis*   Height up to 60cm
Scarce perennial, occasionally naturalised as a garden escape. Leaves divided
into bright green, elongate lobes; they are not evergreen. Green flowers have
pointed sepals but no petals; they appear February–April.

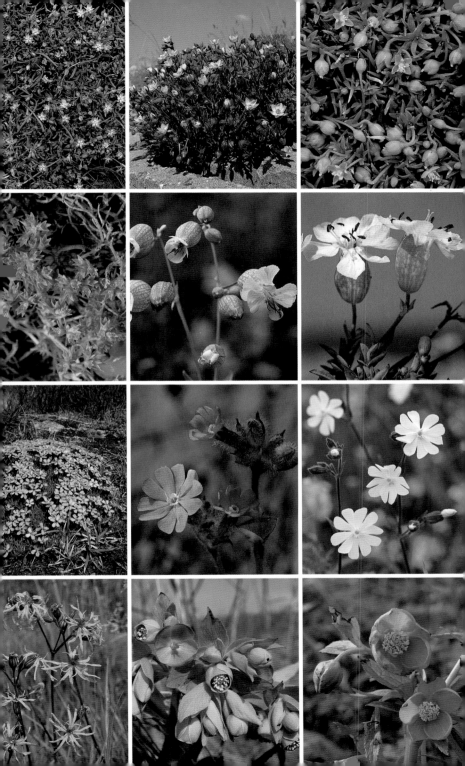

WILD FLOWERS

WINTER ACONITE *Eranthis hyemalis*   Height up to 10cm
An attractive perennial, introduced and naturalised locally. Upright stems carry
three spreading leaves, each divided into 3 lobes. Above these, flowers appear
January–April, these comprising 6 yellow sepals.

MARSH MARIGOLD *Caltha palustris*   Height up to 25cm
Familiar and widespread perennial of damp woodland, marshes and wet meadows.
Plant is borne on stout stems. Leaves kidney-shaped and shiny. Flowers comprise 5
yellow sepals but no petals; they are 20–50mm across and appear March–July.

GLOBEFLOWER *Trollius europaeus*   Height up to 60cm
Attractive perennial, absent from S but locally common in NW Ireland. Leaves
palmately divided into toothed lobes. Almost spherical flowers borne on long
stems; comprise 10–15 yellow sepals and appear May–August.

MEADOW BUTTERCUP *Ranunculus acris*   Height up to 1m
Widespread perennial of grassland habitats. Rounded leaves divided into 3–7
lobes; upper ones unstalked. The flowers appear April–October and are
18–25mm across; they comprise 5 shiny, yellow petals and have upright sepals.

CREEPING BUTTERCUP *Ranunculus repens*   Height up to 50cm, often shorter
Often unwelcome perennial of lawns and other grassy places. Long, rooting run-
ners assist its spread. Hairy leaves divided into 3 lobes, the middle lobe stalked.
Yellow flowers 20–30mm across with upright sepals; appear May–August.

BULBOUS BUTTERCUP *Ranunculus bulbosus*   Height up to 40cm
Widespread hairy perennial. Favours dry grassland including chalk downs.
Leaves divided into three lobes, each of which is stalked. The flowers are
20–30mm across and appear May–August. The sepals are folded back down stalk.

GREATER SPEARWORT *Ranunculus lingua*   Height up to 1m
Widespread but local perennial. Favours the shallow margins of ponds and lakes.
Plant has long runners and upright stems bearing narrow, 25cm long leaves which
are sometimes toothed. Flowers are 20–40mm across and appear June–September.

LESSER SPEARWORT *Ranunculus flammula*   Height up to 50cm
Upright or creeping perennial. Sometimes roots where leaf nodes touch ground.
Stem leaves are narrow and oval. Flowers are 5–15mm across and usually soli-
tary; appear June–October. Widespread on damp ground, often beside rivers.

CELERY-LEAVED BUTTERCUP *Ranunculus sceleratus*   Height up to 50cm
Fresh-green annual. Favours marshes and wet grazing meadows; often on trampled ground. Lower leaves are celery-like and divided into 3 lobes. The flowers,
5–10mm across, are borne in clusters; they appear May–September. Mainly in S.

LESSER CELANDINE *Ranunculus ficaria*   Height up to 25m
Common perennial of hedgerows, open woodland and bare ground, sometimes
forming clumps or patches. Leaves are heart-shaped, glossy and dark green. Flowers are 20–30mm across and appear March–May; open only in sunshine.

COMMON WATER-CROWFOOT *Ranunculus aquatilis*   Floating
Widespread and common annual or perennial found in both slow-flowing and still
waters. Has both thread-like submerged leaves and floating ones that are entire but
with toothed lobes. White flowers are 12–20mm across; appear April–August.

CHALK STREAM WATER-CROWFOOT *Ranunculus penicillatus*   Floating
Local annual or perennial of fast-flowing calcareous streams and rivers. Widespread
but local. Has lobed, rounded floating leaves and long, thread-like submerged ones
that collapse out of water. Flowers 15–25mm across; appear May–July.

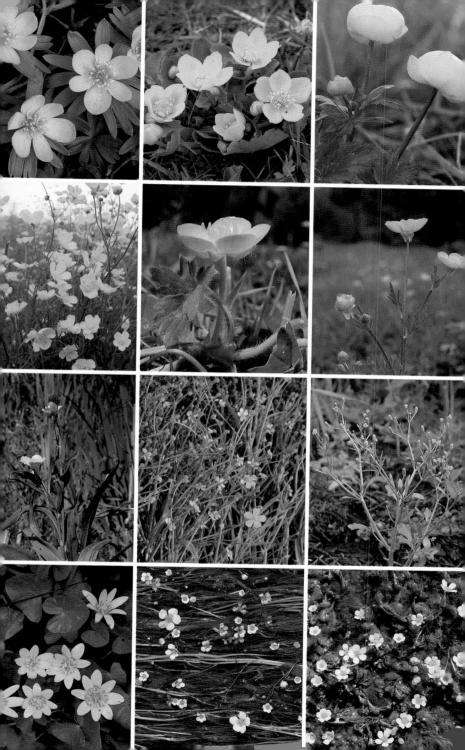

WILD FLOWERS

POND WATER-CROWFOOT *Ranunculus peltatus*   Floating
A widespread and common annual or perennial of ponds, lakes and other areas of still water. Has lobed but rounded floating leaves and short, rigid thread-like submerged ones. The flowers are white, 15–30mm across and appear May–August.

ROUND-LEAVED WATER-CROWFOOT *Ranunculus omiophyllus*   Floating
Creeping annual or biennial. Favours damp, muddy patches, often beside water seepages. Rather local and restricted mainly to S Ireland. Leaves lobed and rounded. Flowers 8–12mm across and appear May–August.

COMMON MEADOW-RUE *Thalictrum flavum*   Height up to 1m
Local plant of damp meadows, ditches and fens. Leaves are pinnately divided 2 or 3 times into toothed lobes. Flowers have yellow anthers and are borne in dense clusters June–August.

LESSER MEADOW-RUE *Thalictrum minus*   Height up to 1m, often shorter
Local plant of basic soils including rocky slopes or dunes. Leaves pinnately divided 3 or 4 times into toothed lobes. Yellow flowers are borne in open sprays not dense clusters, June–August.

COLUMBINE *Aquilega vulgaris*   Height up to 1m
A familiar garden perennial. Also native although local in many parts of Ireland. Grey-green leaves comprise three, 3-lobed leaflets. The nodding, purple flowers are 30–40mm long, the petals with hooked-tipped spurs; appear May–July.

WOOD ANEMONE *Anemone nemorosa*   Height up to 30cm
Widespread woodland perennial. Sometimes forms carpets. Long-stalked stem leaves are divided into 3 lobes, each being further divided. Solitary flowers comprise 5–10 white or pinkish sepals and appear March–May.

YELLOW WATER-LILY *Nuphar lutea*   Floating
Water plant with oval, floating leaves up to 40cm across. Widespread and locally common. Favours still or slow-flowing water and roots in mud in shallows. Flowers 50–60mm across, carried on stalks; appear June–September.

WHITE WATER-LILY *Nymphaea alba*   Floating
Water plant with round, floating leaves, 20–30cm across. Widespread and common on still or slow-flowing water. Flowers comprise 20–25 white or pinkish white petals. They are 15–20cm across and appear June–August; open only in sunshine.

COMMON FUMITORY *Fumaria officinalis*   Height up to 10cm
Spreading annual arable weed favouring well-drained soil. Leaves much-divided, the flat lobes all in one plane. Crimson-tipped pink flowers are 6–7mm long, spurred and 2 lipped; appear April–October. Widespread and fairly common.

CLIMBING CORYDALIS *Corydalis claviculata*   Height up to 70cm
Delicate, climbing annual of woodland and scrub on acid soils. Widespread but rather rare in Ireland. The much-divided leaves end in tendrils which assist climbing. Creamy white flowers are 5–6mm long and appear June–September.

COMMON POPPY *Papaver rhoeas*   Height up to 60cm
Hairy annual weed of arable land and disturbed ground. Widespread but local. Leaves are much-branched. Flowers 70–100mm across with 4 papery, scarlet petals; appear June–August. Note the ovoid seed capsule.

YELLOW HORNED-POPPY *Glaucium flavum*   Height up to 50cm
Blue-grey, clump-forming perennial of shingle beaches; locally common on suitable coasts. Leaves pinnately divided, clasping upper ones having shallow, toothed lobes. Flowers 60–90mm across; June–September. Seed pods long and curved.

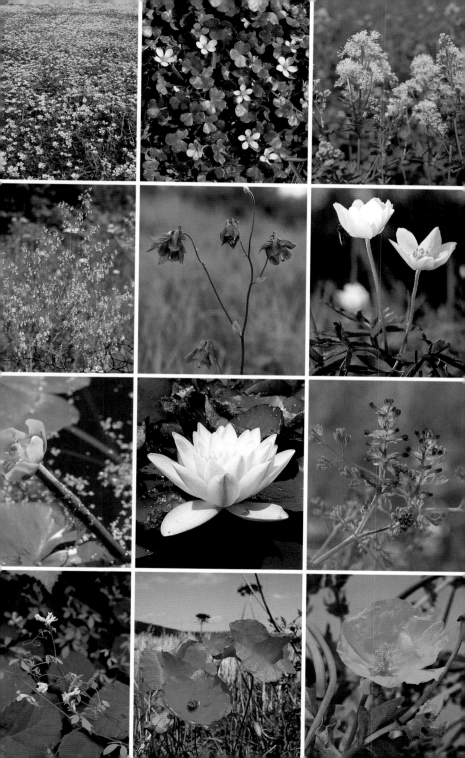

WELSH POPPY *Meconopsis cambrica* Height up to 50cm
Perennial of shady woods. Native to Ireland but also naturalised as a garden escape. Leaves pinnately divided and stalked. Flowers are 50–80mm across and comprise 4 overlapping, yellow petals; appear June–August.

GREATER CELANDINE *Chelidonium majus* Height up to 80cm
Tall, brittle-stemmed perennial with grey-green, pinnately divided leaves. Found in hedgerows and along woodland rides; native but also naturalised. Flowers 20–30mm across; comprise 4 non-overlapping petals, appearing April–October.

TREACLE MUSTARD *Erysimum cheiranthoides* Height up to 85cm
A wasteground and arable land annual; local and rather scarce. Shallowly-toothed, narrow leaves are borne on upright, angled stems. Topped with heads of yellow flowers, each one 6–10mm across, appearing June–September. Seed pods long and slender.

MARSH YELLOWCRESS *Rorippa palustris* Height up to 50cm
Widespread annual of damp, marshy hollows, sometimes growing in shallow water. Upright stems carry lobed leaves. Terminal heads of yellow flowers, each one 3mm across, appear June–October; sepals as long as petals. Seed pods 4–6mm long.

HEDGE MUSTARD *Sisymbrium officinale* Height up to 70cm
Tough upright annual or biennial of wasteground. Lower leaves deeply divided; stem leaves narrow. Unbranched upper part has cylindrical pods pressed close to stem and terminal head of small yellow flowers; appears May–October.

CHARLOCK *Sinapis arvensis* Height up to 1.5m
Widespread and common annual of arable land and wasteground. Dark green leaves are large and coarsely-toothed, the upper ones unstalked. Flowers appear April–October and are 15–20mm across. Seed pods are long, with a beaded appearance.

COMMON WINTER-CRESS *Barbarea vulgaris* Height up to 80cm
Upright, hairless perennial of damp ground. Widespread but commonest in the S. Leaves are dark green and shiny. Lower ones are divided, the end lobe large and oval; upper stem leaves entire. Flowers are 7–9mm across and appear May–August.

WATERCRESS *Rorippa nasturtium-aquaticum* Height up to 15cm
Usually creeping perennial of shallow streams and ditches. Pinnately divided leaves persist through winter. White flowers appear May–October and are 4–6mm across. Seed pod is 18mm long. Widespread and common.

HAIRY BITTERCRESS *Cardamine hirsuta* Height up to 30cm
Widespread and abundant annual; only slightly hairy. Forms a basal rosette of pinnately divided leaves, the lobes of which are rounded. Upright stem carries a few leaves and a head of white flowers, 2–3mm across. Flowers throughout year.

CUCKOO FLOWER OR LADY'S SMOCK *Cardamine pratensis* Height up to 50cm
Variable perennial of damp, grassy places. Has basal rosette of pinnately divided leaves; the lobes are rounded. Pale lilac or white flowers appear April–June and are 12–20mm across. Widespread and locally common.

WILD RADISH *Raphanus raphanistrum* ssp. *maritimus* Height up to 60cm
Robust, roughly hairy annual. Widespread on stabilised shingle, sand dunes and coastal grassland but commonest in S and W. Lower leaves pinnately divided but upper ones narrow and entire. Yellow flowers appear May–July. Seed pods beaded.

BLACK MUSTARD *Brassica nigra* Height up to 2m
Robust, greyish annual. Occasional and local, typically seen on sea cliffs and riverbanks. Leaves stalked, the lower ones pinnately lobed. Yellow flowers 12–15mm across; appear May–August. Pods pressed close to stem.

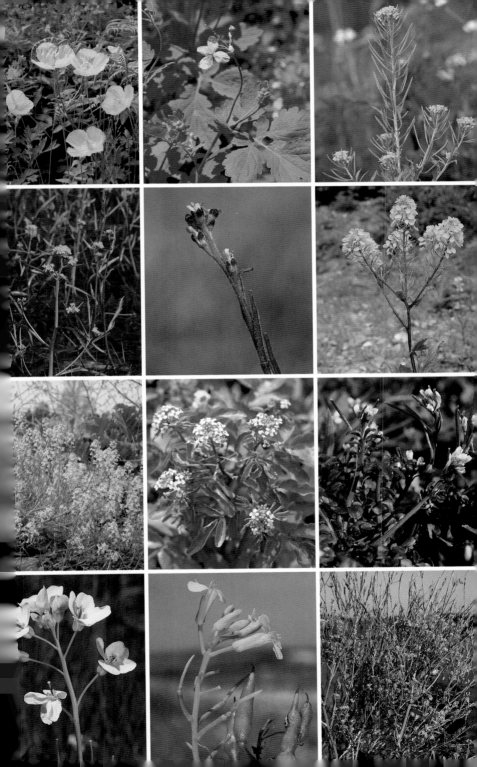

SWEET ALISON *Lobularia maritima*   Height up to 20cm
A hairy perennial, familiar as a garden plant but also occasionally naturalised as an escape. Leaves are narrow, entire and grey-green. Sweet-smelling white flowers appear June–October and are 5–6mm across. Small, oval seed pods on long stalks.

SHEPHERD'S-PURSE *Capsella bursa-pastoris*   Height up to 35cm
Widespread and often common annual of arable land, tracks and waysides. Leaves vary from lobed to entire; upper ones are toothed. Flowers are found all year; they are 2–3mm across and white. Seed pods are green and triangular in outline.

COMMON WHITLOWGRASS *Erophila verna*   Height up to 20cm
Common annual of dry, bare places. Narrow, toothed leaves form a basal rosette, from the centre of which arises leafless flowering stems. White flowers are 3–6mm across and comprise 4 deeply notched petals; appear March–May.

FIELD PENNY-CRESS *Thlaspi arvense*   Height up to 45cm
Common annual of arable land, with an unpleasant smell. Narrow, arrow-shaped leaves clasp the upright stem; no basal rosette. White flowers are 4–6mm across and appear May–September. Rounded seed pods have a terminal notch.

FIELD PEPPERWORT *Lepidium campestre*   Height up to 50cm
Widespread grey-green hairy annual, locally common on dry, bare soil, especially in the S. Basal leaves are oval and untoothed. Stem leaves are arrow-shaped and clasping. Flowers 2–3mm across; appear May–August. Seed pods oval and notched.

COMMON SCURVYGRASS *Cochleria officinalis*   Height up to 50cm
Locally common perennial of saltmarshes, coastal walls and cliffs. Has kidney-shaped basal leaves but arrow-shaped upper ones clasping the dark stem. White flowers are 8–10mm across; appear April–October. Seed pods round.

THALE CRESS *Arabidopsis thaliana*   Height up to 50cm
Scarce annual of dry, sandy soils, often on paths. Broadly-toothed, oval leaves form a basal rosette; upright flowering stems bear a few small leaves. White flowers are 3mm across; appear March–October. Pods cylindrical and long.

SWINE-CRESS *Coronopus squamatus*   Usually prostrate
Creeping annual or biennial. Rather scarce in Ireland. Leaves are pinnately divided and toothed, sometimes forming a dense mat on the ground. Compact clusters of 2–3mm diameter white flowers appear June–September.

LESSER SWINE-CRESS *Coronopus didymus*   Usually prostrate
Similar to Swine-Cress but flowers even smaller, sometimes completely lacking petals, and more finely divided leaves. A scarce annual or biennial that favours dry, disturbed soil and wasteground. Flowers June–October.

GARLIC MUSTARD *Alliaria petiolata*   Height up to 1m
A rather local wayside plant. Leaves are fresh green, heart-shaped and toothed. They are borne up the stem and smell of garlic when crushed. Clusters of white flowers appear April–June and are 6mm across.

SEA ROCKET *Cakile maritima*   Height up to 25cm
Straggling, fleshy annual found on sandy and shingle beaches. Widespread and locally common around coasts of Ireland. Leaves shiny and lobed. The flowers are pale lilac, 6–12mm across; appear June–September in dense clusters.

WELD *Reseda luteola*   Height up to 1.2m
Widespread but local biennial of disturbed base-rich ground. Has basal rosette of narrow leaves in first year only. Tall flower spike appears in second year with narrow stem leaves; yellowish, 4-petalled flowers appear June–August.

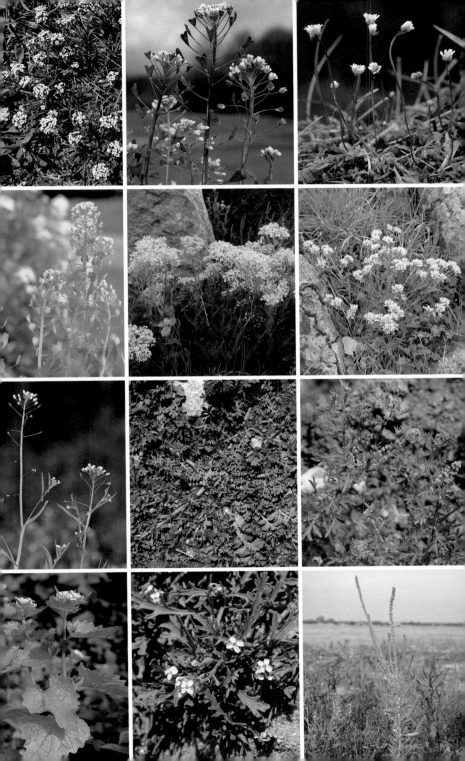

WILD MIGNONETTE *Reseda lutea*   Height up to 70cm
Biennial of disturbed base-rich ground; widespread and probably introduced. Similar to Weld but shorter and with pinnately divided leaves; yellow-green 6-petalled flowers carried in more compact spikes; appear June–August. Stem solid.

ROUND-LEAVED SUNDEW *Drosera rotundifolia*   Height up to 20cm
Widespread insectivorous plant of boggy heaths and moors. Rosette of reddish, rounded leaves are covered with long sticky hairs which trap insects; curl inwards to digest victims. Upright spike of white flowers appears June–August.

OBLONG-LEAVED SUNDEW *Drosera intermedia*   Height up to 20cm
Reddish leaves are narrow and oblong; these form a basal rosette. Upright spike of white flowers appears June–August and arises from below rosette. Widespread insectivorous perennial of wet heaths and moors. Locally common, mainly in W.

NAVELWORT *Umbilicus rupestris*   Flower spike up to 15cm tall
Distinctive perennial, widespread in Ireland. Leaves are rounded and fleshy, with a depressed centre above leaf stalk. Spikes of whitish flowers appear June–August. Grows on walls and stony banks, often in partial shade.

ROSEROOT *Rhodiola rosea*   Height up to 30cm
Characteristic plant of mountain ledges and sea cliffs. Locally common in Ireland. Robust stems bear succulent, overlapping oval leaves. Terminal, rounded clusters of yellow flowers appear May–July.

ORPINE *Sedum telephium*   Height up to 50cm
Perennial of shady woodland and scrub; naturalised in Ireland. The reddish stems carry green, fleshy leaves which are oval and irregularly toothed. Rounded terminal heads of reddish purple, 5-petalled flowers appear July–August.

ENGLISH STONECROP *Sedum anglicum*   Height up to 5cm
Widespread and locally common mat-forming perennial of rocky ground, shingle and old walls. Fleshy, 3–5mm long leaves are often tinged red; borne on wiry stems which are topped with white, 5-petalled, star-shaped flowers June–September.

BITING STONECROP *Sedum acre*   Height up to 10cm
Mat-forming perennial. Widespread and locally common on well-drained ground such as sand dunes. Crowded, fleshy leaves are pressed close to stem and taste hot. The bright yellow, star-shaped flowers appear May–July and are 10–12mm across.

GRASS-OF-PARNASSUS *Parnassia palustris*   Height up to 25cm
Perennial of peaty grassland, marshes and moors. Locally common in Ireland. Heart-shaped basal leaves are stalked. White, 5-petalled flowers are 15–30mm across and appear June–September; borne on stalks with clasping leaves.

MEADOW SAXIFRAGE *Saxifraga granulata*   Height up to 45cm
Attractive perennial of grassy meadows; local in E Ireland only. Leaves are kidney-shaped with blunt teeth; bulbils produced at leaf bases in autumn. Sprays of white, 5-petalled flowers appear April–June and are 20–30mm across.

STARRY SAXIFRAGE *Saxifraga stellaris*   Height up to 25cm
Streamside and damp-ground perennial found in uplands of Ireland. Oblong, toothed leaves form a basal rosette from which the flower stalk arises. Flowers comprise 5 white petals with red anthers; appear June–August.

MOSSY SAXIFRAGE *Saxifraga hypnoides*   Height up to 20cm
Upland perennial. Generally scarce in Ireland. Pointed 3-lobed leaves give plant a moss-like appearance. White flowers appear in small clusters May–July. Plant forms mats on rocks and bare ground.

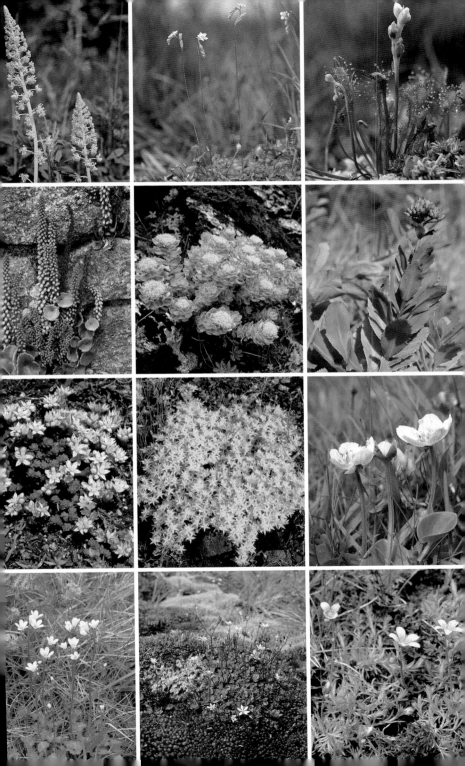

WILD FLOWERS

YELLOW SAXIFRAGE *Saxifraga aizoides*   Height up to 20cm
Colourful perennial of streamsides and damp ground in mountains; locally common in N Ireland. Plant forms clumps comprising masses of narrow, fleshy leaves. Yellow flowers appear June–September; 10–15mm across.

PURPLE SAXIFRAGE *Saxifraga oppositifolia*   Creeping
Mat-forming perennial found on mountain rocks. Local and scarce in NW Ireland. Plant comprises trailing stems bearing opposite pairs of small, dark green leaves. Purple flowers appear mainly March–April and are 10–15mm across.

OPPOSITE-LEAVED GOLDEN-SAXIFRAGE *Chrysosplenium oppositifolium*
Height up to 12cm
Patch-forming perennial of shady stream banks and damp woodland flushes. Locally common. Rounded, stalked leaves are carried in opposite pairs. Yellow flowers lack petals and appear March–July; they are 3–5mm across.

MEADOWSWEET *Filipendula ulmaria*   Height up to 1.25m
Striking perennial of damp meadows, marshes and stream margins. The dark green leaves comprise 3–5 pairs of oval leaflets with smaller leaflets between. Sprays of creamy flowers appear June–September, each 4–6mm across. Common throughout.

DROPWORT *Filipendula vulgaris*   Height up to 50cm
Restricted to calcareous grassland. Local in W Ireland. Leaves comprise 8–20 pairs of larger leaflets with smaller leaflets between. The creamy white flowers are borne in flat-topped sprays and appear May–August.

AGRIMONY *Agrimonia eupatoria*   Height up to 50cm
Widespread and common perennial of grassy places and roadsides. Best known for its upright spikes of yellow, 5-petalled flowers that appear June–August. Leaves comprise 3–6 pairs of oval, toothed leaflets with smaller leaflets between.

GREAT BURNET *Sanguisorba officinalis*   Height up to 1m
Local and declining perennial of damp grassland and riverbanks. Easily recognised when crimson, ovoid heads of flowers appear June–September. Pinnately divided leaves comprise 3–7 pairs of oval leaflets.

SALAD BURNET *Sanguisorba minor*   Height up to 35cm
Locally common perennial of base-rich grassland. The pinnate leaves comprise 4–12 pairs of rounded, toothed leaflets; basal leaves in a rosette. Rounded flower heads appear May–September; green with red styles.

LADY'S-MANTLE *Alchemilla vulgaris* agg.   Height up to 30cm
Grassland perennial, usually associated with upland areas. Easily recognised by palmately lobed leaves; leaf shape variation can be used to separate different species within this aggregate. Yellowish green flowers appear May–September.

PARSLEY-PIERT *Aphanes arvensis*   Creeping
Easily overlooked downy annual. Widespread and often common on dry, bare ground, often beside paths. Fan-shaped leaves are deeply divided into 3 lobes and are parsley-like. Clusters of tiny green, petal-less flowers appear April–October.

MOUNTAIN AVENS *Dryas octopetala*   Height up to 6cm
Locally common on basic soils in W Ireland. Dark green leaves are oblong and toothed. White flowers comprise 8 or more petals; appear June–July.

DOG-ROSE *Rosa canina*   Height up to 3m
Scrambling shrub of hedgerows and scrub whose long, arching stems bear curved thorns. Widespread in most parts although commonest in S. Leaves comprise 5–7 hairless oval leaflets. Pale pink flowers appear June–July. Red hips in autumn.

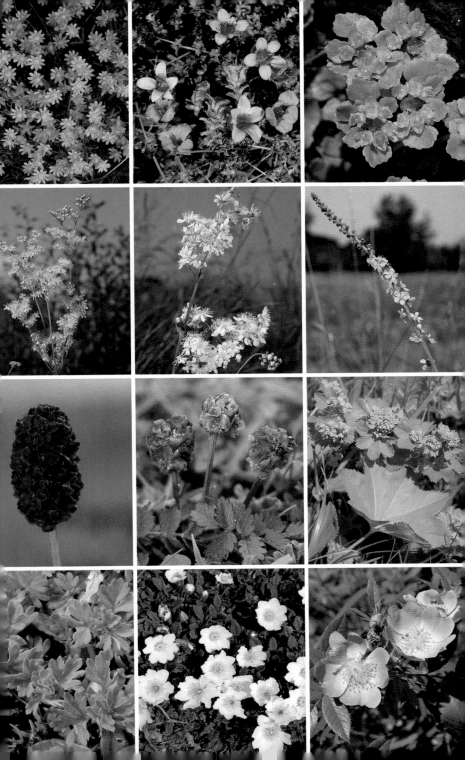

FIELD ROSE *Rosa arvensis*   Height up to 1m
Clump-forming hedgerow shrub whose trailing, purplish stems carry curved thorns. Widespread and common in Ireland. Leaves have 5–7 oval leaflets. White flowers appear July–August; 3–5cm across.

BURNET ROSE *Rosa pimpinellifolia*   Height up to 50cm
Clump-forming shrub of sand dunes, base-rich grassland and heaths. Stems armed with straight thorns and stiff bristles. Leaves comprise 7–11 oval leaflets. Creamy white flowers appear May–July; 3–5cm across. Ripe hips purplish black.

WILD STRAWBERRY *Fragaria vesca*   Height up to 30cm
Low perennial with long, rooting runners. Common and widespread on dry, grassy ground. Leaves comprise 3 oval leaflets, with undersides hairy. 5-petalled white flowers appear April–July and are 12–18mm across. Fruits are tiny strawberries.

BRAMBLE *Rubus fruticosus* agg.   Height up to 3m
Includes hundreds of microspecies of scrambling shrubs whose arching stems are armed with variably shaped prickles and which root when they touch the ground. White or pink flowers (A) appear May–August. Blackberries (B) mature in autumn. Widespread.

MARSH CINQUEFOIL *Potentilla palustris*   Height up to 40cm
Favours marshes and damp meadows. Widespread and locally common in Ireland. Greyish leaves divided into 3–5 toothed, oval leaflets. Star-shaped flowers comprise 5 reddish sepals and smaller purple petals; appear May–July.

TORMENTIL *Potentilla erecta*   Height up to 30cm
Widespread and abundant creeping perennial of grassy places, heaths and moors. Unstalked leaves are trifoliate but appear 5-lobed because of 2 large leaflet-like stipules at base. The 4-petalled flowers appear May–September; 7–11mm across.

CREEPING CINQUEFOIL *Potentilla reptans*   Creeping
Creeping perennial whose trailing stems root at the nodes. Leaves are 5–7 lobed and are borne on long stalks. The 5-petalled yellow flowers are 17–25mm across and appear June–August. Widespread and common on grassy places including verges.

SILVERWEED *Potentilla anserina*   Creeping
Creeping perennial of damp grassy places and bare ground. Widespread and common throughout. Leaves are divided into up to 12 pairs of silvery leaflets with tiny ones between them. Flowers are 5-petalled and 15–20mm across; appear May–August.

HERB BENNET *Geum urbanum*   Height up to 50cm
Widespread and common hairy perennial of shady hedgerows and woodland; also known as Wood Avens. Basal leaves are pinnate. Flowers soon droop and comprise 5 yellow petals; they are 8–15mm across. Fruits armed with hooked red styles.

WATER AVENS *Geum rivale*   Height up to 50cm
Perennial of damp meadows, mostly on base-rich soils. Widespread and locally common except in S. Basal leaves pinnate but stem leaves trifoliate. Bell-shaped, flowers comprise dark red sepals and pink petals; they appear May–September.

COMMON GORSE *Ulex europaeus*   Height up to 2m
Spiny, evergreen shrub. Common and widespread in Ireland, usually on acid soils on heaths. Leaves trifoliate when young. Spines are straight, 15–25mm long and grooved. The flowers appear mainly February–May and smell of coconut.

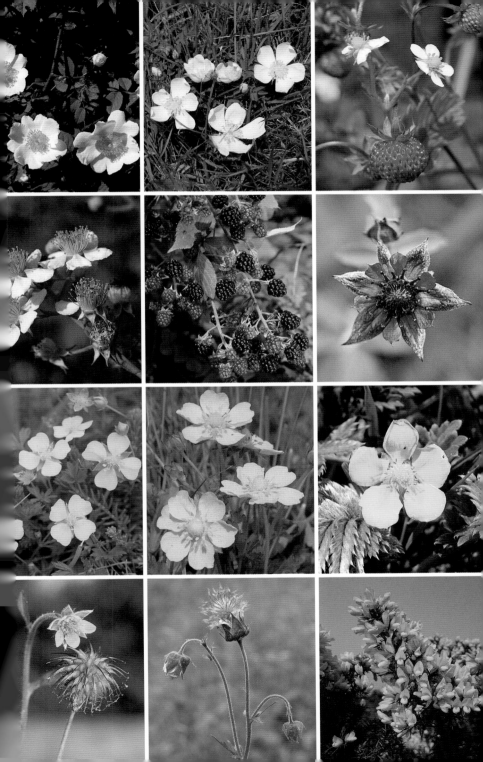

WESTERN GORSE *Ulex gallii*   Height up to 1.5m
Dense, spiny and evergreen shrub and similar to Common Gorse. Locally abundant, particularly in SW, sometimes covering entire slopes. Spines are 25mm long and almost smooth. Yellow flowers appear July–September.

BROOM *Cytisus scoparius*   Height up to 2m
Deciduous shrub with ridged, 5-angled green twigs. Common throughout on heaths and in hedgerows but favours acid soils. Leaves usually trifoliate. The flowers are 20mm long; appear April–June. Hairy black pods explode on dry, sunny days.

PURPLE MILK-VETCH *Astragalus danicus*   Height up to 30cm
Spreading perennial of dry calcareous grassland. Local and rare in W Ireland. Hairy, pinnate leaves comprise 6–12 pairs of oval leaflets. Clusters of purple flowers appear May–July, each flower 15–18mm long.

TUFTED VETCH *Vicia cracca*   Height up to 2m
Widespread and common scrambling perennial. Favours grassy places, hedgerows and scrub. Leaves comprise up to 12 pairs of narrow leaflets and end in a branched tendril. Spikes of bluish purple flowers, up to 4cm tall, appear June–August.

WOOD VETCH *Vicia sylvatica*   Height up to 1.5m
Straggling perennial of shady woods and steep, coastal slopes. Widespread but local. Leaves comprise 6–12 pairs of oblong leaflets ending in branched tendrils. Spikes of purple-veined white flowers appear June–August.

BUSH VETCH *Vicia sepium*   Height up to 1m
Scrambling perennial of rough, grassy places and scrub. Common and widespread throughout. Leaves comprise 5–9 pairs of leaflets ending in branched tendrils. Groups of 2–6 pale lilac flowers appear April–October; each flower 12–15mm long.

COMMON VETCH *Vicia sativa*   Height up to 75cm
Widespread and fairly common scrambling annual of grassy places and hedgerows. Leaves comprise 3–8 pairs of oval leaflets and end in tendrils. Groups of 1 or 2 pinkish purple flowers appear April–September. When mature, the pods are black.

SMOOTH TARE *Vicia tetrasperma*   Height up to 50cm
Easily overlooked scrambling annual of grassy places. Introduced and scattered in Ireland. Leaves comprise 2–5 pairs of narrow leaflets and end in tendrils. The 1 or 2 pinkish lilac flowers appear May–August. Pods smooth, usually with 4 seeds.

HAIRY TARE *Vicia hirsuta*   Height up to 60cm
Slender, scrambling annual of grassy places. Widespread but rather scarce in Ireland. Leaves comprise 4–10 pairs of leaflets and end in branched tendrils. The 1–9 pale lilac flowers appear May–August. Pods hairy and 2-seeded.

MEADOW VETCHLING *Lathyrus pratensis*   Height up to 50cm
Perennial with long, angled stems scrambling among and over vegetation. Common and widespread throughout, favouring grassy places. Leaves comprise single pair of narrow leaflets and have tendrils. Groups of 4–12 flowers appear May–August.

SEA PEA *Lathyrus japonicus*   Height up to 12cm
Spreading grey-green perennial with stems up to 1m long. Found exclusively on coastal shingle and sand; local and restricted to SW. Leaves with 2–5 pairs of oval leaflets. Groups of bluish purple flowers appear June–August.

REST-HARROW *Ononis repens*   Height up to 70cm
A robust, creeping perennial with hairy stems. Locally common throughout on base-rich soils. Stickily-hairy leaves usually trifoliate with oval leaflets. Clusters of pink flowers appear July–September; each flower is 10–15mm long.

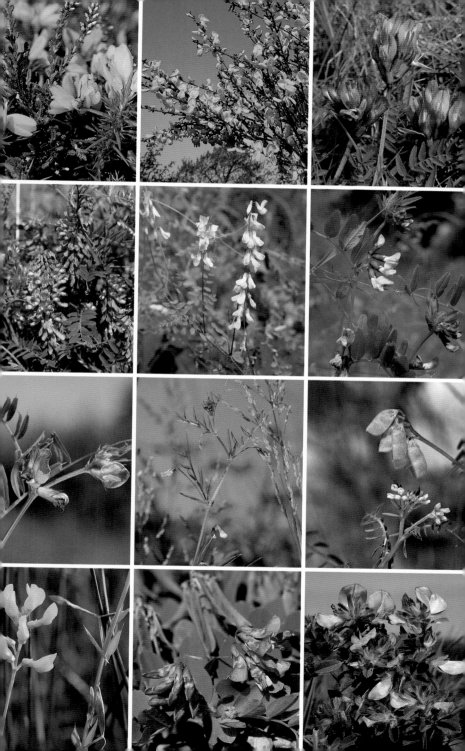

RIBBED MELILOT *Melilotus officinalis* Height up to 1.5m
Widespread biennial of grassy places. Scarce and introduced in Ireland. Leaves comprise 3 oblong leaflets. Yellow flowers borne in tall spikes and appear June–September. Ripe pods are brown.

KIDNEY VETCH *Anthyllis vulneraria* Height up to 30cm
Silky hairy perennial. Widespread and locally common in calcareous grassland and on coastal slopes. Leaves comprise pairs of narrow leaflets. Flowers are yellow, orange or red; borne in paired, kidney-shaped heads, 3cm across, May–September.

BIRDSFOOT TREFOIL *Lotus corniculatus* Usually creeping
Perennial with trailing stems. Widespread and common in grassy places. Leaves comprise 5 leaflets but appear trifoliate since lower pair sit at stalk base. Yellow or orange flowers appear May–September. Pods arranged like a bird's foot.

GREATER BIRDSFOOT TREFOIL *Lotus uliginosus* Height up to 50cm
Perennial of damp grassland and fens. Widespread and locally common throughout in suitable habitats. Grey-green, downy leaves comprise 5 leaflets but appear trifoliate. Heads of yellow flowers carried on long stalks; appear June–August.

LUCERNE *Medicago sativa* ssp. *sativa* Height up to 75cm
Downy perennial. Sometimes cultivated but also widely naturalised in grassy places. Leaves are trifoliate with narrow, toothed leaflets that broaden towards the tip. Spikes of purple flowers appear June–September; each flower is 7–8mm long.

BLACK MEDICK *Medicago lupulina* Height up to 20cm
Widespread and rather common downy annual of short grassland and waste places. Leaves are trifoliate, each leaflet bearing a point at the centre of its apex. Dense, rounded heads of yellow flowers appear April–October. Ripe pods black.

BIRD'S-FOOT *Ornithopus perpusillus* Height up to 30cm
An often trailing, downy annual of dry, sandy places. Local in E and S. Leaves comprise 5–13 pairs of leaflets. Red-veined, creamy flowers appear May–August. Ripe pods arranged like a bird's foot.

HOP TREFOIL *Trifolium campestre* Height up to 25cm
Widespread but local hairy annual of dry grassland. Leaves alternate and trefoil. Compact, rounded heads of yellow flowers appear May–October. The pale brown dead flower heads resemble tiny hops.

RED CLOVER *Trifolium pratense* Height up to 40cm
Familiar grassland perennial that is widespread and common throughout. Leaves trefoil, the oval leaflets each bearing a white crescent-shaped mark. Pinkish purple flowers borne in unstalked heads, 3cm across, and appear May–October.

WHITE CLOVER *Trifolium repens* Height up to 40cm
Common grassland perennial; widespread throughout. Leaves are trefoil, the rounded leaflets often bearing white marks. Flowers creamy white, becoming brown with age. Borne in rounded heads, 2cm across; appear May–October.

HARE'S-FOOT CLOVER *Trifolium arvense* Height up to 25cm
Annual of dry grassland, covered in soft hairs. Widespread and generally common. Trefoil leaves comprise narrow leaflets. The pale pink flowers are borne in oval or cylindrical heads, appearing June–September.

ROUGH CLOVER *Trifolium scabrum* Height up to 15cm
Downy annual of bare grassland, often on gravelly soils. Locally common in SE, but mainly coastal. Trefoil leaves have oval leaflets with obvious lateral veins. White flowers are borne in unstalked heads, May–July.

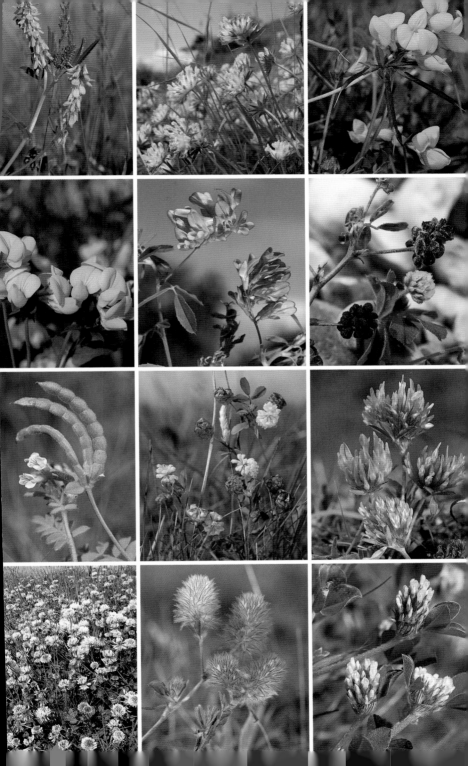

WOOD SORREL *Oxalis acetosella*   Height up to 10cm
Charming, creeping perennial. Widespread and locally common; an indicator of ancient woodlands and hedgerows. Trefoil leaves, which fold down at night, are borne on long stalks. Lilac-veined flowers carried on stalks; appear April–June.

FAIRY FLAX *Linum catharticum*   Height up to 12cm
Delicate annual, also known as Purging Flax. Found in both wet and dry grassland often on calcareous soil. Slender stems carry opposite pairs of narrow, 1-veined leaves. Loose, terminal clusters of small white flowers appear May–September.

COMMON STORK'S-BILL *Erodium cicutarium*   Height up to 25cm
Stickily-hairy annual of bare, grassy places. Widespread and locally common, especially around coasts. Leaves finely divided and feathery. Pink flowers appear May–August; petals easily lost. Fruit is long and beak-like.

MEADOW CRANE'S-BILL *Geranium pratense*   Height up to 75cm
Perennial of roadside verges and meadows, mostly on base-rich soils. Extremely local. Lower leaves deeply divided into 5–7 lobes. Bluish violet flowers 3–5cm across; appear June–August.

WOOD CRANE'S-BILL *Geranium sylvaticum*   Height up to 60cm
Showy perennial of upland meadows and open woodlands, usually found on base-rich soils. Local in N. Leaves deeply cut into 5–7 lobes. Reddish purple flowers are 20–30mm across; appear June–August.

BLOODY CRANE'S-BILL *Geranium sanguineum*   Height up to 25cm
Spreading or clump-forming perennial found on calcareous grassland and limestone pavements. Locally common in central and W Ireland. Leaves deeply cut into 5–7 lobes. The reddish purple flowers appear June–August.

HERB ROBERT *Geranium robertianum*   Height up to 30cm
Straggling, hairy annual of shady hedgerows, rocky banks and woodlands. Common and widespread throughout. Hairy leaves deeply cut into three or five lobes. Loose clusters of pink flowers appear April–October; each flower is 12–15mm across.

DOVE'S-FOOT CRANE'S-BILL *Geranium molle*   Height up to 20cm
Spreading, very hairy annual of dry, grassy places including roadside verges. Common and widespread, especially in the S. Leaves hairy and rounded but margins cut into 5–7 lobes. Pairs of pink flowers, 5–10mm across, appear April–August.

CUT-LEAVED CRANE'S-BILL *Geranium dissectum*   Height up to 45cm
Hairy annual that is widespread and common throughout, favouring disturbed ground and cultivated soils. Leaves are deeply dissected into very narrow lobes. Pinkish flowers, 8–10mm across, appear May–September; petals sometimes notched.

SHINING CRANE'S-BILL *Geranium lucidum*   Height up to 30cm
Almost hairless annual of shady banks and rocky slopes, mostly on limestone. Widespread but local. Shiny leaves are green, sometimes tinged red; they are rounded but with margins cut into 5–7 lobes. Pink flowers appear April–August.

SEA SPURGE *Euphorbia paralias*   Height up to 60cm
Sand-dune plant, widespread and locally common around the coasts of Ireland. Upright stems carry close-packed, grey-green, fleshy leaves. Yellowish flowers, which lack petals and sepals, appear June–October.

SUN SPURGE *Euphorbia helioscopia*   Height up to 50cm
Widespread and common hairless annual found on disturbed ground and cultivated soils. Unbranched, upright stems carry an array of spoon-shaped leaves, broadest near the tip. Yellow flowers, lacking petals and sepals, appear May–November.

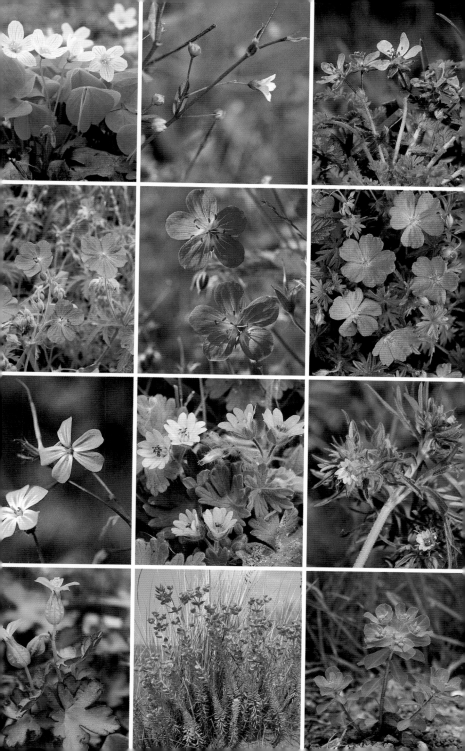

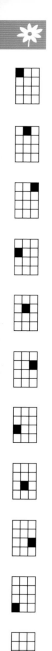

PETTY SPURGE *Euphorbia peplus*   Height up to 30cm
Upright, hairless annual that is common and widespread on cultivated ground and arable land. Branched stems carry oval, blunt-tipped and stalked leaves. These are topped by umbels of greenish flowers, comprising oval bracts, April–October.

IRISH SPURGE *Euphorbia hyberna*   Height up to 55cm
Attractive tufted perennial restricted to shady wooded slopes in SW Ireland. Upright stems carry stalkless, tapering leaves and are topped by striking yellowish flowers which lack petals and sepals; these appear May–July.

COMMON MILKWORT *Polygala vulgaris*   Height up to 30cm
Trailing or upright perennial. Common and widespread in grassland on all but the most acid of soils. Leaves are alternate, narrow and pointed. The flowers may be blue, pink or white; borne in loose, terminal clusters and seen May–September.

HIMALAYAN BALSAM *Impatiens balsamifera*   Height up to 2m
Introduced from Himalayas but widely naturalised along riverbanks and on damp wasteground. Upright, reddish stems carry leaves in whorls of 3 or opposite pairs. Pink-purple flowers, 30–40mm long, appear July–October. Seeds explosive.

MUSK MALLOW *Malva moschata*   Height up to 75cm
Perennial of dry, grassy places. Local in Ireland. Leaves rounded and 3-lobed at base but increasingly dissected up the stem. Pale pink flowers, 30–60mm across, are seen July–August.

COMMON MALLOW *Malva sylvestris*   Height up to 1.5m
Upright or spreading perennial of grassy verges and disturbed ground. Leaves are rounded at base but 5-lobed on stem. Purple-veined pink flowers, 25–40mm across, appear June–October. Widespread in S, but scarce elsewhere.

TREE MALLOW *Lavatera arborea*   Height up to 3m
Imposing woody biennial which favours rocky ground near the coast, often near seabird colonies. Locally common on coasts of S and W Ireland. The leaves are 5–7 lobed. Dark-veined pinkish purple flowers appear June–September.

MARSH MALLOW *Althaea officinalis*   Height up to 2m
Attractive downy perennial of coastal wetlands, often found on upper reaches of saltmarshes. Locally common in SW Ireland. The leaves are triangular and slightly lobed. The pale pink flowers appear August–September.

TUTSAN *Hypericum androsaemum*   Height up to 80cm
Upright, semi-evergreen shrub. Locally common in shady woods and hedgerows. Oval leaves are borne in opposite pairs. Yellow flowers, 15–25mm across, appear June–August. Berries ripen red to black.

PERFORATE ST JOHN'S-WORT *Hypericum perforatum*   Height up to 80cm
Upright perennial, found in grassland, scrub and open woodland; usually on calcareous soils. Widespread but commonest in the S. The 2-lined stems carry paired unstalked, narrow leaves with translucent dots. Flowers appear June–September.

SLENDER ST JOHN'S-WORT *Hypericum pulchrum*   Height up to 80cm
Upright perennial of dry, grassy places and heaths, mostly on acid soils. Common and widespread throughout. Paired, oval leaves have translucent dots. Flowers comprise 5 yellow petals with black dots along their margins; seen July–August.

MARSH ST JOHN'S-WORT *Hypericum elodes*   Height up to 20cm
Creeping, hairy perennial of peaty ground and marshes on acid soils. Rather local and confined mainly to W Ireland. The rounded, grey-green leaves clasp the stem slightly. Yellow flowers, 15mm across, appear June–August.

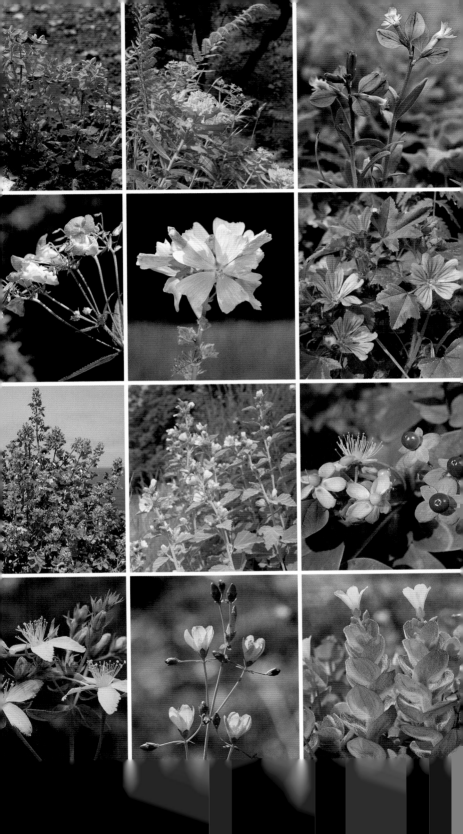

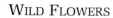

TRAILING ST JOHN'S-WORT *Hypericum humifusum*   Creepin
Hairless perennial favouring bare ground on heaths and moors with acid soil.
Widespread but commonest in W Ireland. The leaves have translucent dots an
are borne in pairs on trailing stems. Flowers appear June–September.

SWEET VIOLET *Viola odorata*   Height up to 15cr
Perennial herb of woods and hedgerows, mostly on calcareous soils. Widesprea
and locally common. Long-stalked leaves rounded in spring; larger and hear
shaped in summer. Violet or white flowers appear February–May.

COMMON DOG-VIOLET *Viola riviniana*   Height up to 12cr
Familiar perennial herb of woodland rides and grassland. Widespread and local
common throughout. Long-stalked leaves are heart-shaped. Bluish violet flower
have a blunt, pale spur and are 15–25mm across; they appear mainly March–Ma

MARSH VIOLET *Viola palustris*   Height up to 10cr
Perennial of bogs and acid wetlands. Local but widespread. Long-stalked leave
are round or kidney-shaped. Dark-veined, pale lilac flowers are 10–15mm acros
with a short spur; appear April–June.

WILD PANSY *Viola tricolor*   Height up to 12cr
Widespread and common annual or perennial of grassy areas. Subspecies *tricolo*
has yellow and violet flowers and grows inland while subspecies *curtisii* wit
yellow flowers is mainly coastal. Flowers 10–25mm across; appear April–Octobe

MOUNTAIN PANSY *Viola lutea*   Height up to 30cr
Perennial of upland calcareous grassland. Locally common in central and S
Ireland. Leaves lanceolate with palmate stipules at leaf bases. Flowers ar
15–30mm across and vary from yellow to yellow and violet; appear May–August

FIELD PANSY *Viola arvensis*   Height up to 15cr
Widespread and fairly common annual of arable land and cultivated groun
generally. Has deeply toothed stipules. Flowers are 10–15mm across and cream
white with orange flush on lower petal; appear April–October.

ROSEBAY WILLOWHERB *Epilobium angustifolium*   Height up to 1.5r
Familiar perennial of wasteground, cleared woodland and riverbanks. Widesprea
and common throughout. Lanceolate leaves arranged spirally up stem. Pinkish
purple flowers, 2–3cm across, appear July–September. Pods contain cottony seeds

GREAT WILLOWHERB *Epilobium hirsutum*   Height up to 2r
Imposing perennial of damp habitats such as fens and riverbanks. Widesprea
and common throughout. Unstalked hairy leaves borne on hairy stems; topped by
pinkish purple flowers, 25mm across, with pale centres; July–August.

MARSH WILLOWHERB *Epilobium palustre*   Height up to 50cm
Slender perennial of damp habitats, particularly on acid soils. Widespread and
locally common throughout. Rounded stems carry opposite pairs of narrow leaves.
Pale pink flower is 4–7mm across and has club-shaped stigma; seen July–August.

AMERICAN WILLOWHERB *Epilobium ciliatum*   Height up to 50cm
Introduced perennial from N America which is spreading. Hairy stems bear opposite pairs of oval leaves. Pink flower has notched petals and club-shaped stigma;
seen June–August.

ENCHANTER'S-NIGHTSHADE *Circaea lutetiana*   Height up to 65cm
Delicate perennial of shady woodlands. Widespread and generally common.
Upright stems are sometimes slightly hairy and carry opposite pairs of oval,
pointed leaves. White flowers borne in loose spikes above leaves, June–August.

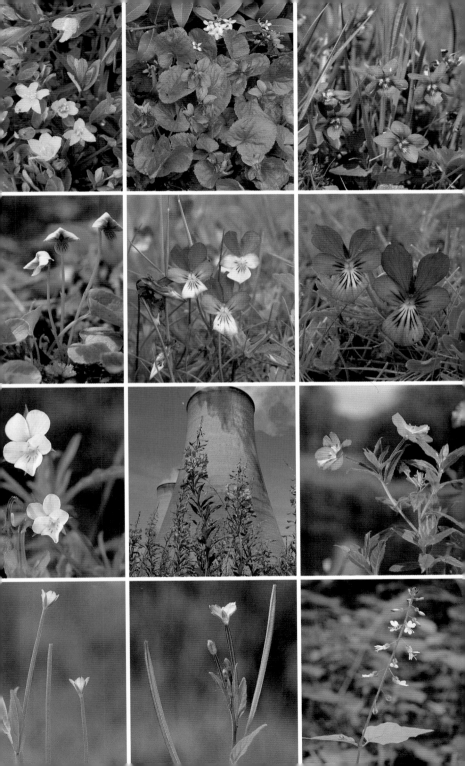

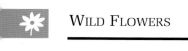

COMMON EVENING-PRIMROSE *Oenothera biennis* Height up to 1.25m
Downy biennial, introduced from N America but now established locally in many parts on dry ground including sand dunes and railway sidings. Lanceolate leaves have red veins. Flowers, 4–5cm across, comprise 4 petals; seen June–September.

PURPLE-LOOSESTRIFE *Lythrum salicaria* Height up to 1.5m
Downy perennial of damp habitats such as riverbanks and fens. Widespread and common. Upright stems carry opposites pairs of narrow, unstalked leaves. Reddish purple, 6-petalled flowers borne in tall spikes, June–August.

MARSH PENNYWORT *Hydrocotyle vulgaris* Creeping
An atypical umbellifer, best known for its round, dimpled leaves found among low vegetation on damp, mostly acid, ground. Widespread and locally common. Tiny pinkish flowers are hidden by leaves; appear June–August.

SANICLE *Sanicula europaea* Height up to 50cm
Slender, hairless perennial of deciduous woodland, mostly on neutral or basic soils. Widespread and locally common. Basal leaves have 5–7 lobes. Small umbels of pinkish flowers borne on reddish stems, May–August.

SEA-HOLLY *Eryngium maritimum* Height up to 60cm
Distinctive perennial of coastal shingle and sand. Widespread around the coasts of Ireland. Grey-green leaves are spiny and holly-like. Globular umbels of blue flowers appear July–September.

ALEXANDERS *Smyrnium oleraceum* Height up to 1.25m
Distinctive biennial, introduced but now established on wasteground and verges. Widespread and locally common near coasts in Ireland. Leaves 3 times divided into dark green, shiny lobes. Yellowish flowers seen March–June.

COW PARSLEY *Anthriscus sylvestris* Height up to 1m
Downy perennial herb. Widespread and common throughout on roadside verges and along lanes. Upright, hollow and ridged stems carry 2 or 3 times pinnately divided leaves. Umbels of white flowers lack lower bracts and appear April–June.

HEDGE-PARSLEY *Torilis japonica* Height up to 1m
Familiar white hedgerow umbellifer which flowers July–August, after the similar Cow Parsley has finished. Solid, hairy stems carry leaves which are 2 or 3 times pinnately divided. Umbels have upper and lower bracts. Widespread and common.

PIGNUT *Conopodium majus* Height up to 25cm
Delicate perennial, locally common in open woodland and grassland, mainly on dry acid soils. Finely divided basal leaves soon wither. Stem leaves divided into narrow lobes. Small umbels, 3–6cm across, of white flowers appear April–June.

SWEET CICELY *Myrrhis odorata* Height up to 1.5m
Upright perennial which smells of aniseed when bruised. Introduced and locally naturalised in NE. Fern-like leaves are 2 or 3 times pinnately divided. Umbels of white flowers with unequal petals appear May–June.

HOGWEED *Heracleum sphondylium* Height up to 2m
Robust perennial of open, grassy places including roadside verges. Common and widespread throughout. Broad, hairy and pinnate leaves borne on hollow, hairy stems. Large umbels of off-white flowers with unequal petals seen May–August.

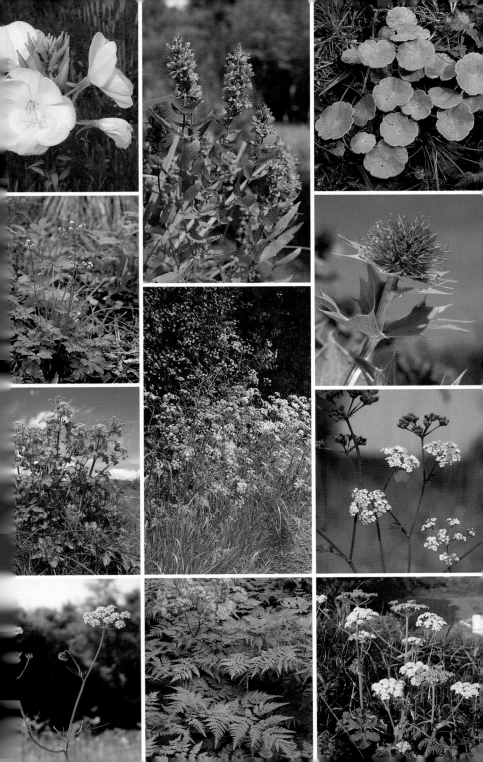

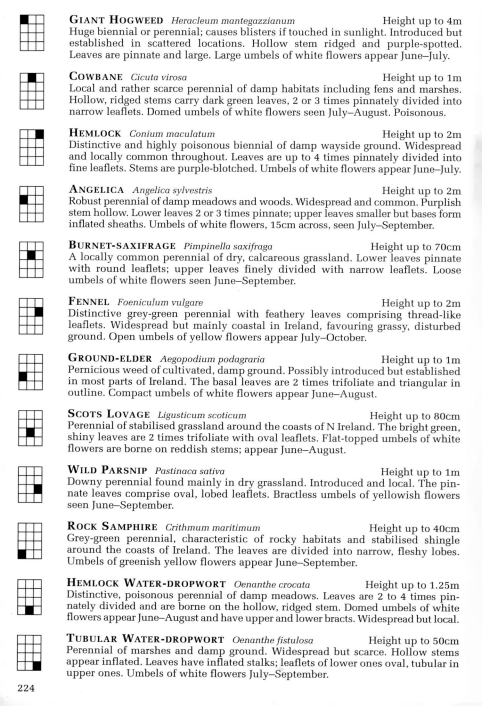

GIANT HOGWEED *Heracleum mantegazzianum* Height up to 4m
Huge biennial or perennial; causes blisters if touched in sunlight. Introduced but established in scattered locations. Hollow stem ridged and purple-spotted. Leaves are pinnate and large. Large umbels of white flowers appear June–July.

COWBANE *Cicuta virosa* Height up to 1m
Local and rather scarce perennial of damp habitats including fens and marshes. Hollow, ridged stems carry dark green leaves, 2 or 3 times pinnately divided into narrow leaflets. Domed umbels of white flowers seen July–August. Poisonous.

HEMLOCK *Conium maculatum* Height up to 2m
Distinctive and highly poisonous biennial of damp wayside ground. Widespread and locally common throughout. Leaves are up to 4 times pinnately divided into fine leaflets. Stems are purple-blotched. Umbels of white flowers appear June–July.

ANGELICA *Angelica sylvestris* Height up to 2m
Robust perennial of damp meadows and woods. Widespread and common. Purplish stem hollow. Lower leaves 2 or 3 times pinnate; upper leaves smaller but bases form inflated sheaths. Umbels of white flowers, 15cm across, seen July–September.

BURNET-SAXIFRAGE *Pimpinella saxifraga* Height up to 70cm
A locally common perennial of dry, calcareous grassland. Lower leaves pinnate with round leaflets; upper leaves finely divided with narrow leaflets. Loose umbels of white flowers seen June–September.

FENNEL *Foeniculum vulgare* Height up to 2m
Distinctive grey-green perennial with feathery leaves comprising thread-like leaflets. Widespread but mainly coastal in Ireland, favouring grassy, disturbed ground. Open umbels of yellow flowers appear July–October.

GROUND-ELDER *Aegopodium podagraria* Height up to 1m
Pernicious weed of cultivated, damp ground. Possibly introduced but established in most parts of Ireland. The basal leaves are 2 times trifoliate and triangular in outline. Compact umbels of white flowers appear June–August.

SCOTS LOVAGE *Ligusticum scoticum* Height up to 80cm
Perennial of stabilised grassland around the coasts of N Ireland. The bright green, shiny leaves are 2 times trifoliate with oval leaflets. Flat-topped umbels of white flowers are borne on reddish stems; appear June–August.

WILD PARSNIP *Pastinaca sativa* Height up to 1m
Downy perennial found mainly in dry grassland. Introduced and local. The pinnate leaves comprise oval, lobed leaflets. Bractless umbels of yellowish flowers seen June–September.

ROCK SAMPHIRE *Crithmum maritimum* Height up to 40cm
Grey-green perennial, characteristic of rocky habitats and stabilised shingle around the coasts of Ireland. The leaves are divided into narrow, fleshy lobes. Umbels of greenish yellow flowers appear June–September.

HEMLOCK WATER-DROPWORT *Oenanthe crocata* Height up to 1.25m
Distinctive, poisonous perennial of damp meadows. Leaves are 2 to 4 times pinnately divided and are borne on the hollow, ridged stem. Domed umbels of white flowers appear June–August and have upper and lower bracts. Widespread but local.

TUBULAR WATER-DROPWORT *Oenanthe fistulosa* Height up to 50cm
Perennial of marshes and damp ground. Widespread but scarce. Hollow stems appear inflated. Leaves have inflated stalks; leaflets of lower ones oval, tubular in upper ones. Umbels of white flowers July–September.

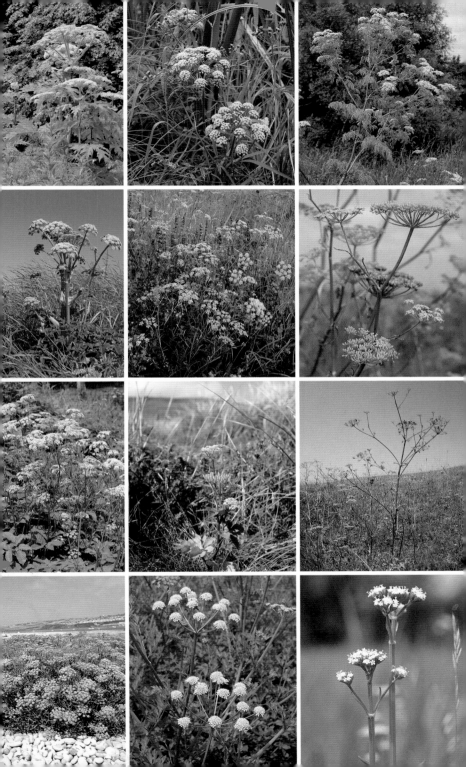

FOOL'S PARSLEY *Aethusa cynapium* Height up to 50cm
Delicate annual found in gardens and other areas of disturbed ground. Leaves 2 times pinnate and triangular in outline. Umbels of white flowers have long upper bracts; appear June–August.

WILD CARROT *Daucus carota* Height up to 75cm
Widespread, hairy perennial of rough grassland. Commonest around coasts. Leaves are 2 or 3 times pinnate with narrow leaflets. Dense umbels are pinkish in bud but white in flower, central flower red; June–September. Umbels concave in fruit.

WILD CELERY *Apium graveolens* Height up to 1m
Biennial smelling strongly of celery. Favours rough, often saline, grassland and distribution mainly coastal. Leaves 1 or 2 times pinnate. Umbels of greenish white flowers are 4–6cm across; appear June–August.

FOOL'S WATER-CRESS *Apium nodiflorum* Height up to 20cm
Creeping perennial of ditches and wet hollows. Widespread and fairly common. Shiny leaves comprise oval, toothed leaflets and are rather similar to Water-cress. Loose umbels of white flowers appear July–August.

PRIMROSE *Primula vulgaris* Height up to 20cm
Familiar perennial of woods, hedgerows and shady meadows. Widespread and common throughout. Oval, tapering leaves, up to 12cm long, form a rosette. The solitary flowers, 2–3cm across, are borne on long, hairy stalks; appear February–May.

COWSLIP *Primula veris* Height up to 25cm
Locally common perennial of unimproved grassland, often on calcareous soils. Wrinkled, hairy leaves form a basal rosette. Heads of 10–30 orange-yellow, bell-shaped flowers borne on stalks, April–May.

YELLOW LOOSESTRIFE *Lysimachia vulgaris* Height up to 1m
Softly hairy perennial of damp ground, often beside rivers and in fens. Widespread but local. The upright stems carry narrow, ovate leaves in whorls of 3 or 4. Clusters of yellow flowers appear July–August.

CREEPING JENNY *Lysimachia nummularia* Creeping
Low, hairless perennial of damp grassy ground. Local and possibly a naturalised garden escape. The rounded or heart-shaped leaves are carried in opposite pairs. Bell-shaped yellow flowers, 15–25mm across, borne on stalks, June–August.

YELLOW PIMPERNEL *Lysimachia nemorum* Creeping
Evergreen, hairless perennial, similar to Creeping Jenny but more delicate. The oval or heart-shaped leaves are carried in opposite pairs along creeping stems. Yellow, star-like flowers, 10–15mm across, borne on slender stalks, May–August.

SEA MILKWORT *Glaux maritima* Height up to 10cm
Generally a creeping perennial, found on upper reaches of saltmarshes and on sea walls. Locally common around most coasts. Trailing stems carry opposite pairs of succulent leaves. Flowers comprise 5 pink sepals; these appear May–September.

WATER VIOLET *Hottonia palustris* Aquatic
Delicate perennial of still or slow-flowing water. Naturalised and very local in NE. Has feathery floating and submerged leaves, divided into narrow lobes. Lilac flowers, 20–25mm across, on emergent stems, May–June.

SCARLET PIMPERNEL *Anagallis arvensis* Prostrate
Hairless annual of cultivated ground. Widespread and generally common. Opposite pairs of unstalked, oval leaves borne on trailing stems. Flowers on slender stalks, May–September. Usually red but sometimes blue.

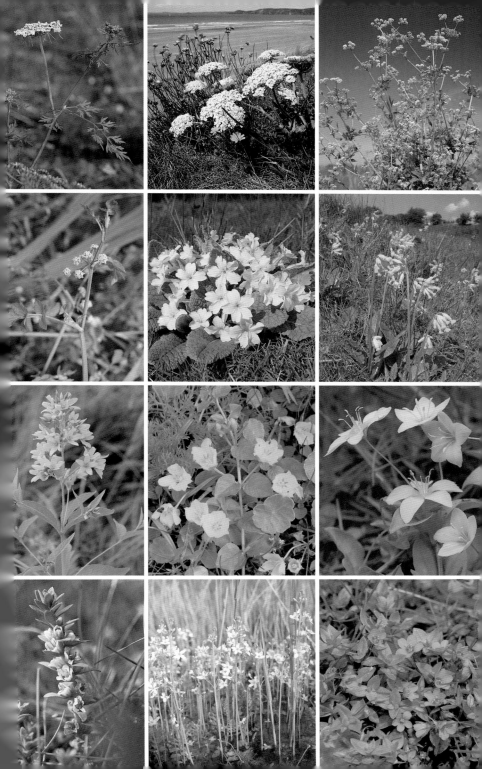

BOG PIMPERNEL *Anagallis tenella*   Creeping
Delicate perennial of damp ground, such as bogs and dune-slacks, mostly on acid soils. Trailing stems carry opposite pairs of short-stalked, rounded leaves. The pink, funnel-shaped flowers are borne on slender, upright stalks, June–August.

LING *Calluna vulgaris*   Height up to 50cm
Dense undershrub, characteristic of acids soils on heaths and moors; also known as Heather. Widespread and locally abundant. The short, narrow leaves are borne in 4 rows along stems. The small pink flowers, 4–5mm long, appear July–October.

BELL HEATHER *Erica cinerea*   Height up to 50cm
Hairless undershrub of dry acid soils on heaths and moors. Widespread and locally common. Narrow leaves are borne in whorls of 3 up wiry stems. Bell-shaped, purplish red flowers, 5–6mm long, in groups along stems, June–September.

MACKAY'S HEATH *Erica mackaiana*   Height up to 60cm
Clump-forming undershrub in peat bogs. Leaves are arranged in whorls of 4. Flowers are pinkish purple, 5–7mm long, and borne in terminal clusters, August–September. Confined to W Mayo, W Donegal and W Galway.

IRISH HEATH *Erica erigena*   Height up to 2m
Impressive shrub, found on the drying margins of bogs. Leaves are arranged in whorls of four. Flowers are pinkish purple, 5–7mm long, and borne in long, terminal spikes, March–June. Confined to W Mayo and W Galway.

CROSS-LEAVED HEATH *Erica tetralix*   Height up to 30cm
Downy, grey-green undershrub. Favours damp, acid soils; typical of boggy-margins on heaths and moors. Widespread and locally common. Narrow leaves in whorls of 4 along stems. Pink flowers, 6–7mm long, borne in terminal clusters, June–October.

BILBERRY *Vaccinium myrtillus*   Height up to 75cm
Deciduous shrub of heaths, moors and open woodland on acid soils. Widespread but fairly common. Bright green, oval leaves borne on green, 3-angled stems. Greenish pink flowers April–June; ripen to edible purplish fruits in autumn.

COWBERRY *Vaccinium vitis-idaea*   Height up to 20cm
Small, evergreen shrub found on acid soils in woods and on moors. Local and rather scarce in Ireland. Leaves are leathery, dark green and oval. Pink, bell-shaped flowers, 5–6mm long, appear May–July; red berries ripen in autumn.

CRANBERRY *Vaccinium oxycoccos*   Height up to 12cm
Creeping, evergreen shrub of bogs. Widespread but locally common only in E Ireland. Trailing stems carry small, dark green leaves with inrolled margins. Flowers with pink, reflexed petals and protruding stamens, May–July. Fruit red.

CROWBERRY *Empetrum nigrum*   Height up to 10cm
Mat-forming, heather-like shrub found on upland moors; locally common. Reddish stems carry narrow, dark green leaves with inrolled margins. The pink, 6-petalled flowers appear April–June. The black berries ripen in late summer.

COMMON WINTERGREEN *Pyrola minor*   Height up to 20cm
An evergreen perennial of woods and moors, often on calcareous soils. Locally common in N Ireland. Oval, toothed and stalked leaves form a rosette. White, rounded flowers, 5–6mm across, seen June–August.

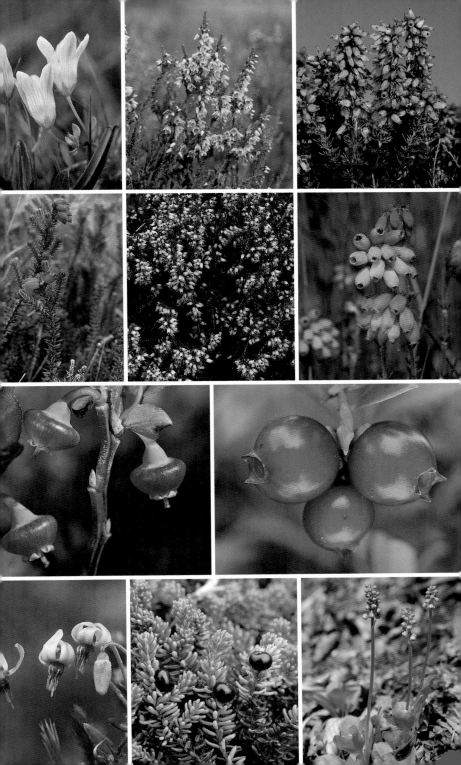

THRIFT *Armeria maritima* Height up to 20cm
Cushion-forming, coastal perennial, often carpeting cliff slopes. Widespread and locally common. Leaves dark green, long and narrow. Dense, globular heads of pink flowers are borne on stalks, 10–20cm long, and appear mainly April–July.

LAX-FLOWERED SEA-LAVENDER *Limonium humile* Height up to 30cm
Locally common perennial of saltmarshes around S and E coasts. Leaves are stalked and narrowly spoon-shaped. Pinkish lilac flowers borne in open, branched and spreading sprays, July–September.

BOGBEAN *Menyanthes trifoliata* Height up to 15cm
Aquatic perennial found in shallow water as well as damp peaty soil in marshes and bogs. Widespread and locally common. Emergent leaves trifoliate and resemble broad bean. Clusters of star-shaped, pinkish white, fringed flowers, March–June.

FRINGED WATER-LILY *Nymphoides peltata* Floating
Aquatic perennial, occasionally naturalised as a garden escape; found in still or slow-flowing water. Leaves are floating, rounded or kidney-shaped and 3–8cm across. Flowers, 30–35mm across, comprise 5 fringed petals; appear June–September.

LESSER PERIWINKLE *Vinca minor* Height up to 20cm
Trailing perennial of woods and hedgerows. Occasionally naturalised. Evergreen leaves are leathery and oval. The 5-lobed flowers are bluish violet and 25–30mm across; appear February–May.

COMMON CENTAURY *Centaurium erythraea* Height up to 25cm
Upright annual of dry, grassy places. Widespread and common throughout. Has basal rosette of oval leaves and opposite pairs of leaves on stems. Clusters of pink, 5-petalled flowers appear June–September.

YELLOW-WORT *Blackstonia perfoliata* Height up to 30cm
Upright, grey-green annual of short, calcareous grassland. Locally common in central and W Ireland. Leaves form basal rosette; appear up stem in opposite pairs, fused at base around stem. Flowers 6–8 petalled, June–October.

SPRING GENTIAN *Gentiana verna* Height up to 7cm
Scarce perennial of limestone grassland in the Burren in W Ireland. Oval leaves form a basal rosette and are borne in opposite pairs up the stem. Solitary, bright blue flowers, 1–2cm long, with 5 lobes, appear May–June.

AUTUMN GENTIAN *Gentianella amarella* Height up to 25cm
Biennial of dry, mostly calcareous grassland and dunes. Widespread and locally common. Leaves form a basal rosette in first year; wither before flowering stem appears in second year. Clusters of 4- or 5-lobed purplish flowers, appear July–October.

FIELD GENTIAN *Gentianella campestris* Height up to 10cm
Biennial, similar to Autumn Gentian but flowers are bluish and comprise 4 lobes. Favours grassland on neutral or acid soils. Local in NW Ireland. Clusters of flowers seen July–October.

HEDGE BINDWEED *Calystegia sepium* Climbing, up to 2–3m
Perennial, twining around other plants to assist its progress. Favours hedgerows and woodland margins. Widespread and fairly common. Leaves arrow-shaped and up to 12cm long. Flowers white, 3–4cm across, June–September.

FIELD BINDWEED *Convolvulus arvensis* Creeping or climbing, up to 2–3m
Widespread and very common perennial of disturbed ground. Twists around other plants to assist its progress. Long-stalked, 2–5cm long leaves are arrow-shaped. The white-striped pink flowers are 15–30mm across and appear June–September.

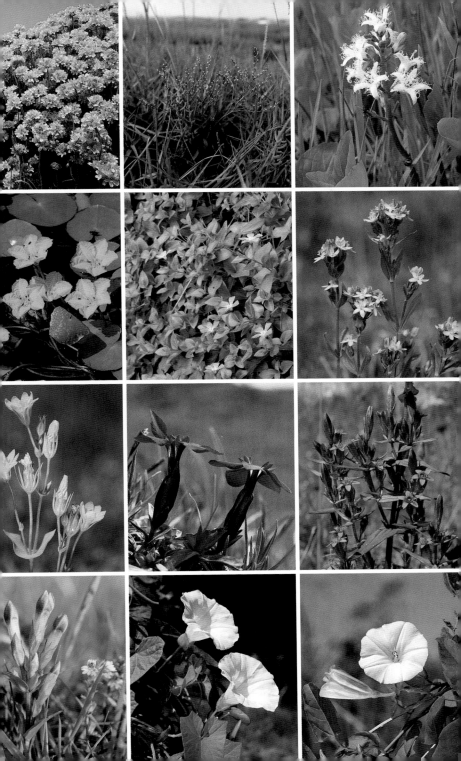

SEA BINDWEED *Calystegia soldanella*   Creeping
Perennial of coastal sand dunes. Widespread and locally common on most suitable coasts. Long-stalked leaves are kidney-shaped. White-striped pink flowers, 4–5cm across, appear June–August.

COMMON DODDER *Cuscuta epithymum*   Climbing
Parasitic, leafless plant which lacks chlorophyll and gains its nutrition from host plants, which include ling, clovers and other herbaceous plants. Clusters, 7–10mm across, of pink flowers are borne on red, twining stems, July–September.

FIELD MADDER *Sherardia arvensis*   Creeping
Hairy annual of arable land and disturbed ground. Widespread; rather common in the S but becoming scarce further N. Narrow, oval leaves in whorls of 4–6 along stems. Heads of pinkish flowers, each one 3–5mm across, appear May–September.

SQUINANCYWORT *Asperula cynanchica*   Height up to 15cm
Usually prostrate perennial of dry grassland, mainly on calcareous soil. Locally common only in W. The 4-angled stems carry narrow leaves in whorls of 4. Dense clusters of pink, 4-petalled flowers, 3–4mm across, appear June–September.

WOODRUFF *Galium odoratum*   Height up to 25cm
Upright, hairless perennial of shady woodlands, mostly on basic soils; smells of hay. Locally common and widespread. Square stems carry lanceolate leaves in whorls of 6–8; leaf margins with prickles. Clusters of 4-lobed flowers May–June.

LADY'S BEDSTRAW *Galium verum*   Height up to 30cm
Branched perennial of dry grassland. Widespread and common. The 4-angled stems carry narrow leaves with rolled margins in whorls of 8–12 and blacken when dry. Clusters of yellow flowers appear June–September.

HEDGE-BEDSTRAW *Galium mollugo*   Scrambling, up to 1.5m
Widespread and fairly common perennial. Favours hedges and scrub. Stems smooth and square; oval leaves, with single vein and pointed tips, borne in whorls of 6–8. Clusters of 4-lobed flowers appear June–September.

COMMON CLEAVERS *Galium aparine*   Height up to 1.5m
Sprawling annual of disturbed ground. Widespread and common. Backward-pointing prickles secure plant in its scrambling progress through vegetation. Leaves in whorls of 6–8. Tiny white flowers May–September. Fruits with hooked bristles.

COMMON MARSH-BEDSTRAW *Galium palustre*   Height up to 60cm
Rather delicate, straggling plant of damp, grassy ground. Widespread and common throughout. The narrow leaves are borne in whorls of 4–6 and are not spine-tipped. Open clusters of white flowers, each 3–4mm across, appear June–August.

CROSSWORT *Cruciata laevipes*   Height up to 50cm
Attractive perennial of grassy woodland rides, hedgerows and verges, mainly on calcareous soils. Introduced and local in Ireland. Oval, hairy leaves borne in distinct whorls of 4. Clusters of yellow flowers appear April–June.

BORAGE *Borago officinalis*   Height up to 30cm
Widely cultivated in gardens and sometimes found naturalised as an escape, often on disturbed ground. Entire plant is bristly. Lower leaves are stalked; upper ones clasp the stem. The 5-petalled flowers, 20–25mm across, appear April–September.

BUGLOSS *Anchusa arvensis*   Height up to 50cm
Roughly hairy annual of disturbed, often sandy, soil. Widespread and locally common, mainly in N. Narrow leaves have wavy margins; lower ones stalked, upper ones clasping stem. Sprays of blue flowers, 5–6mm across, appear May–September.

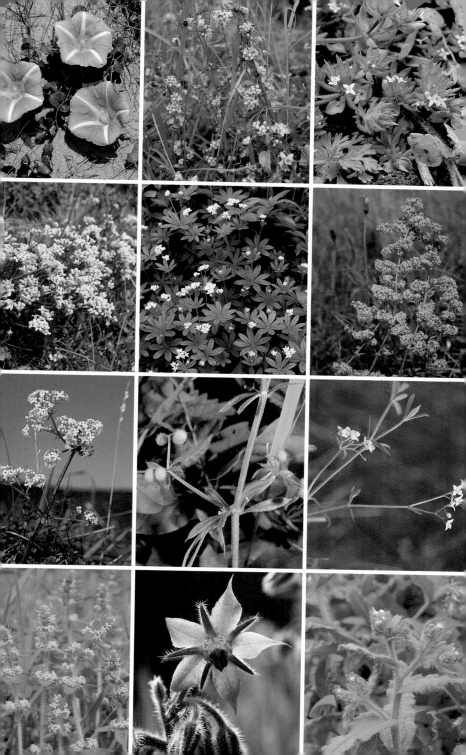

WILD FLOWERS

OYSTERPLANT *Mertensia maritima*   Prostrate
Trailing perennial of coastal shingle. Rare in N. Oval, fleshy, blue-green leaves
borne on reddish stems. Leafy, long-stalked clusters of flowers appear June–August;
pink, turning blue-purple.

RUSSIAN COMFREY *Symphytum × uplandicum*   Height up to 1m
Fertile hybrid, now widely naturalised and often common in hedgerows, grassland
and verges. Stems slightly winged. Oval leaves softly hairy, upper ones forming
wings down stem. Blue-purple flowers are borne in curved clusters, May–August.

COMMON COMFREY *Symphytum officinalis*   Height up to 1m
Hairy perennial of damp ground, often found beside rivers. Widespread but generally rather rare. Stems prominently winged. Oval leaves hairy, upper ones
clasping stem. Curved clusters of pink-purple or cream flowers appear May–June.

HOUND'S-TONGUE *Cynoglossum officinale*   Height up to 75cm
Downy biennial smelling strongly of mice. Favours dry, grassy places, often near
the coast; locally common in E only. Narrow, hairy leaves are stalked near the
base of the plant. Clusters of maroon, 5-lobed flowers appear June–August.

COMMON GROMWELL *Lithospermum officinale*   Height up to 50cm
Downy perennial of woodland margins and rides, usually on calcareous soils.
Generally scarce and local. Leaves narrow and alternate. Clusters of white, 5-
petalled flowers, appear June–July.

EARLY FORGET-ME-NOT *Myosotis ramossissima*   Height up to 12cm
Downy annual of arable fields, bare grassy places and open woodland. Wide-
spread and common in most parts. Leaves ovate, basal ones forming a rosette.
Clustered spikes of blue, 5-lobed flowers, 5mm across, April–October.

WATER FORGET-ME-NOT *Myosotis scorpioides*   Height up to 12cm
Creeping perennial with upright flowering shoots. Found in watery habitats on
neutral and basic soils. Common and widespread throughout. Leaves narrow and
oblong. Curved clusters of sky-blue flowers, each 10mm across, June–September.

GREEN ALKANET *Pentaglottis sempervirens*   Height up to 75cm
Roughly hairy perennial of hedgerows and roadside verges. Widely naturalised as
a garden escape. Leaves large, oval and pointed; basal ones stalked. Clusters of
bright blue flowers, 2–3mm across, appear April–July.

VIPER'S-BUGLOSS *Echium vulgare*   Height up to 80cm
Roughly hairy biennial of dry grassland, mainly on sandy or calcareous soils.
Leaves are narrow and pointed; basal leaves stalked. Dense spikes of bright blue
funnel-shaped flowers, 15–20mm long, appear May–September. Commonest in E.

BUGLE *Ajuga reptans*   Height up 20cm
Familiar perennial of woodland rides and verges. Widespread and often common.
The leafy, creeping runners root at intervals and bear ovate, stalked leaves. The
pale blue flowers, 15mm long, appear on upright flowering stems April–June.

GREATER SKULLCAP *Scutellaria galericulata*   Height up to 40cm
Often hairy perennial of damp ground in marshes and river banks. Widespread
but generally scarce. Stems square and leaves oval, stalked and toothed. Blue-
violet flowers, 6–10mm long, borne on upright, leafy stems June–September.

WOOD SAGE *Teucrium scorodonia*   Height up to 40cm
Downy perennial of acid soils along woodland rides, heaths and coastal cliffs.
Widespread and locally common throughout. Leaves heart-shaped and stalked. The
paired, yellowish flowers are borne in leafless spikes; appear June–September.

234

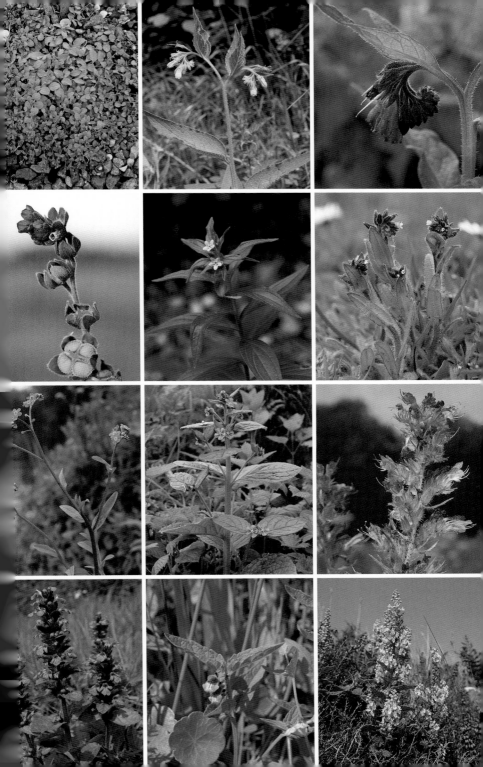

SELFHEAL *Prunella vulgaris*   Height up to 20cm
Creeping, downy perennial of short grassland and woodland rides on calcareous or neutral soils. Widespread and common throughout. Leaves are paired and oval. The blue-violet flowers are borne in dense clusters, on leafy stems, June–October.

GROUND-IVY *Glechoma hederacea*   Height up to 15cm
Softly hairy, strong-smelling perennial with creeping stems that root at regular intervals. Found in woodland, hedgerows and grassland; widespread and common. Leaves kidney-shaped and stalked. Violet flowers in whorls of 2–4, March–June.

WHITE DEAD-NETTLE *Lamium album*   Height up to 40cm
Downy-stemmed perennial of verges and disturbed ground. Widespread and common throughout. Heart-shaped leaves are nettle-like but lack stinging hairs. White flowers, 20–25mm long, borne in whorls and appear March–November.

RED DEAD-NETTLE *Lamium purpureum*   Height up to 30cm
Branched, downy annual of disturbed ground and cultivated soil. Widespread and common throughout. Leaves are heart-shaped, toothed and stalked. Purplish pink flowers, 10–17mm long, are borne in whorls on upright stems, March–October.

HENBIT DEAD-NETTLE *Lamium amplexicaule*   Height up to 20cm
An often trailing annual of cultivated soil and disturbed ground. Widespread but commonest in the S. Similar to Red Dead-nettle but leaves are unstalked, rounded and clasp stem in pairs. The pinkish purple flowers appear March–November.

COMMON HEMP-NETTLE *Galeopsis tetrahit*   Height up to 50cm
Hairy-stemmed annual of arable land and disturbed ground. Widespread and common throughout. Leaves are ovate, stalked and toothed. Stems are swollen at leaf nodes. Pinkish flowers are borne in whorls, July–September. Sepal tubes persist.

LARGE-FLOWERED HEMP-NETTLE *Galeopsis speciosa*   Height up to 50cm
Bristly-hairy annual of arable land, found mostly on peaty soils. Local in central and S Ireland. Leaves are ovate, stalked and toothed and stems are swollen at leaf nodes. Large yellowish flowers have purple on lower lip; July–September.

YELLOW ARCHANGEL *Lamiastrum galeobdolon*   Height up to 45cm
Hairy perennial of woodland rides and hedgerows, mostly on basic soils. Local in E Ireland. Nettle-like leaves are toothed and oval. Yellow flowers borne in whorls up flowering stems, May–June.

BLACK HOREHOUND *Ballota nigra*   Height up to 50cm
Unpleasant-smelling, hairy perennial of disturbed ground and roadside verges. Local and possibly introduced. Ovate or heart-shaped leaves are stalked. Whorls of pink-purple flowers, June–September.

BETONY *Stachys officinalis*   Height up to 50cm
Perennial of grassland and open woods on sandy or chalky soil. Local in Ireland. Lower leaves heart-shaped and stalked; narrower up stem. Dense spikes of reddish purple flowers appear June–September.

HEDGE WOUNDWORT *Stachys sylvatica*   Height up to 75cm
Roughly hairy perennial with unpleasant smell. Found in hedgerows and widespread and often common. Heart-shaped leaves are toothed and long-stalked. Spikes of flowers appear June–October; reddish purple with white markings on lower lip.

MARSH WOUNDWORT *Stachys palustris*   Height up to 1m
Non-smelling perennial of damp ground. Widespread and locally common throughout. Leaves are narrow-oblong and mostly unstalked. Pinkish purple flowers with white markings are borne in spikes, June–September.

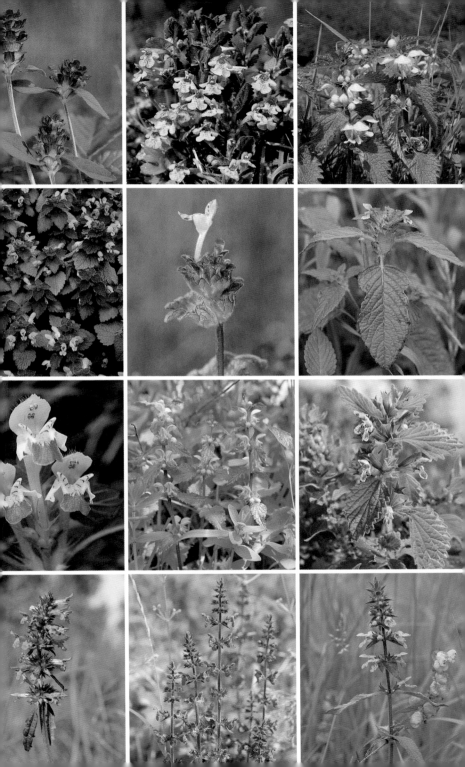

WATER MINT *Mentha aquatica*   Height up to 50cm
Strongly mint-scented perennial of damp ground, sometimes even growing in water. Oval, toothed leaves borne on reddish, hairy stems. Lilac-pink flowers carried in dense terminal heads 2cm long and appear July–October. Popular with insects.

CORN MINT *Mentha arvensis*   Height up to 30cm
Mint-scented perennial of damp arable land, paths and disturbed ground. Common and widespread throughout. Toothed, oval leaves are short-stalked. Lilac flowers borne in dense whorls at intervals along stem, not terminally, May–October.

SPEARMINT *Mentha spicata*   Height up to 75cm
Popular, strongly-scented garden mint but also occasionally naturalised as an escape on damp ground. Leaves are narrow-ovate, toothed and unstalked. The pale lilac flowers are borne in whorls forming long, terminal spikes; appear July–October.

PENNYROYAL *Mentha pulegium*   Height up to 30cm
Often creeping perennial of damp hollows on grazed, grassy heaths. Very local and mainly coastal. Leaves oval and toothed. Pink-lilac flowers in separated whorls without distinct terminal spike; appear August–October.

GIPSYWORT *Lycopus europaeus*   Height up to 75cm
Hairy perennial of damp ground such as ditches and pond margins. Scattered and local in Ireland. Leaves deeply cut into lobes or pinnately divided. Whorls of whitish flowers appear July–September.

MARJORAM *Origanum vulgare*   Height up to 50cm
Hairy perennial of dry grassland on calcareous soil. Widespread but local. Oval, pointed leaves are borne in pairs on reddish stems. Dense, terminal clusters of pink-purple flowers, July–September.

THYME *Thymus polytrichus*   Height up to 5cm
Aromatic, creeping and often mat-forming perennial of dry grassland and heaths. Widespread and common throughout. Ovate, short-stalked leaves borne in pairs along stems. Dense terminal heads of pink-purple flowers appear June–September.

BITTERSWEET OR WOODY NIGHTSHADE *Solanum dulcamara* Height up to 1.5m
Scrambling perennial. Found in hedgerows and on shingle beaches; widespread but scarce. Oval leaves have narrow basal leaflets or lobes. Purple flowers with yellow stamens, May–September. Berries red and poisonous.

HENBANE *Hyoscyamus niger*   Height up to 75cm
Branched, stickily-hairy and strong-smelling plant of disturbed ground, often near the sea. Local and scattered in Ireland. Leaves oval and pointed. Dark-veined yellow flowers, 2–3cm across; appear June–August.

GREAT MULLEIN *Verbascum thapsus*   Height up to 2m
Robust perennial covered in white, woolly hairs. Fairly common on dry, grassy ground. Leaves form rosette in first year. Tall, leafy stalks in second year; flowers, 2–3cm across, in terminal spikes, June–August.

WATER FIGWORT *Scrophularia auriculata*   Height up to 70cm
Upright perennial of damp woods and water margins. Has characteristic 4-winged stems. Widespread and common throughout. Leaves blunt-tipped with rounded teeth. Maroon and green, 2-lipped flowers appear June–September.

COMMON FIGWORT *Scrophularia nodosa*   Height up to 70cm
Upright perennial of damp woodlands and verges. Widespread and common. Stems are square in cross section but not winged. Leaves are oval and pointed with sharp teeth. Maroon and green flowers appear June–September.

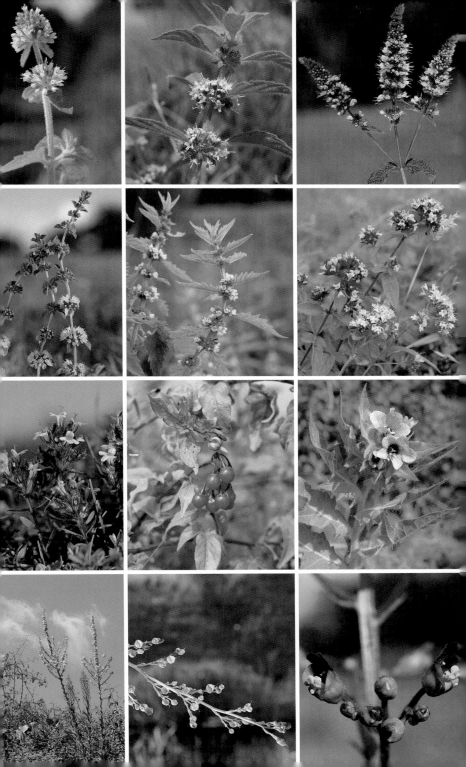

COMMON TOADFLAX *Linaria vulgaris* Height up to 75cm
Grey-green perennial of hedgerows and grassland. Local in Ireland. Upright, often branched stems bear very narrow leaves. Long-spurred, orange-centred yellow flowers, 15–25mm long, seen June–October in tall clusters.

PALE TOADFLAX *Linaria repens* Height up to 75cm
Greyish perennial found in dry, often bare places in grassland. Possibly native; rather local in E only. Several upright flowering shoots, bearing narrow leaves, arise from rhizome. Dark-veined, lilac flowers June–September.

IVY-LEAVED TOADFLAX *Cymbalaria muralis* Trailing
Perennial of rocks and walls. Originally a garden plant but widely naturalised throughout. The long-stalked, ivy-shaped leaves are 5-lobed and are borne on long reddish stems. Yellow-centred lilac flowers, 8–10mm long, April–November.

THYME-LEAVED SPEEDWELL *Veronica serpyllifolia* Height up to 20cm
Mostly creeping perennial of grassy places and cultivated ground. Widespread and common throughout. Thyme-like leaves are small and oval. Flowers, 5–6mm across and blue, are borne on upright stalks in loose spikes; appear April–October.

GERMANDER SPEEDWELL *Veronica chamaedrys* Height up to 20cm
Grassland perennial. Widespread and common throughout. Oval leaves are toothed and hairy. Prostrate stems root at nodes. Upright stems with two lines of hairs. The white-centred, blue flowers are 10–12mm across and appear April–June.

BLUE WATER-SPEEDWELL *Veronica anagallis-aquatica* Height up to 25cm
Hairless perennial of water margins and marshy ground. Widespread and locally common. Upright stems carry oval and pointed leaves. Pairs of pale blue flowers, arising from leaf axils, are borne in spikes June–August.

HEATH SPEEDWELL *Veronica officinalis* Height up to 10cm
Mat-forming perennial of grassland and woodland rides. Widespread and generally common throughout. Prostrate stems root at nodes and are hairy all round. The pale bluish lilac flowers, 6–8mm across, are borne in upright spikes May–August.

COMMON FIELD-SPEEDWELL *Veronica persica* Prostrate
Sprawling, hairy annual of arable land and cultivated soils. Probably not native but widespread and common throughout. Pairs of pale green, toothed oval leaves are borne on reddish stems. Solitary blue flowers, 8–12mm across, seen all year.

BROOKLIME *Veronica beccabunga* Height up to 30cm
Hairless perennial of shallow water and damp soil. Widespread and locally common throughout. Oval, fleshy leaves have short stalks. Stems creeping, then upright. Blue flowers, 7–8mm across, are borne in pairs from leaf axils, May–September.

MONKEYFLOWER *Mimulus guttatus* Height up to 50cm
Perennial of damp ground, often beside streams and rivers. Introduced from N America but now widely naturalised in many parts. Oval leaves in opposite pairs. Showy, yellow flowers, 25–45mm across, have red spots in throat; June–September.

FOXGLOVE *Digitalis purpurea* Height up to 1.5m
Tall, greyish biennial or perennial of woods, moors and sea cliffs. Downy, oval leaves, 20–30cm long, form rosette in first year. In second year, tall spikes arise bearing succession of pink-purple, tubular flowers, 4–5cm long, June–September.

RED BARTSIA *Odontites verna* Height up to 40cm
Straggly, branched downy annual of disturbed ground, tracks and verges. Common and widespread throughout. Narrow, toothed leaves borne in opposite pairs. Pink-purple flowers, 8–10mm long, in spikes June–September. Plant often tinged red.

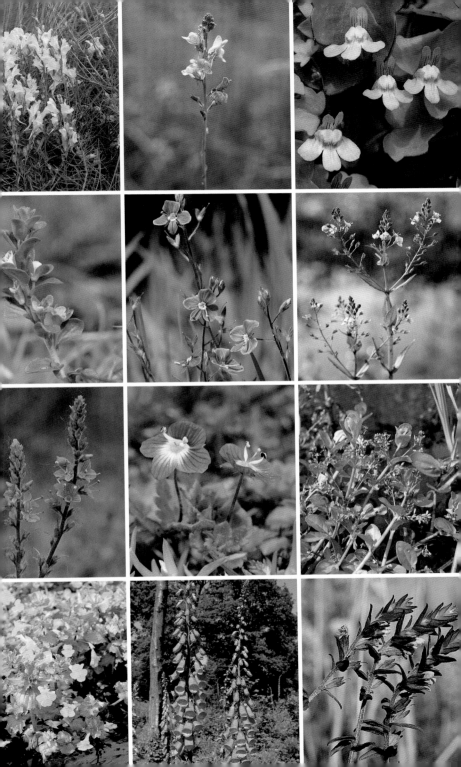

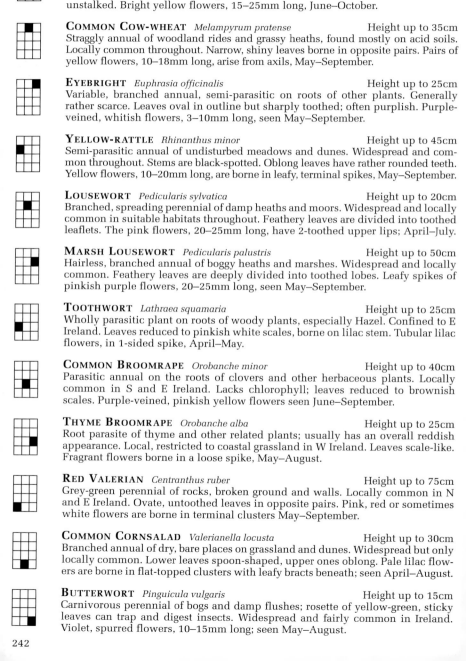

YELLOW BARTSIA *Parentucellia viscosa*   Height up to 40cm
Stickily-hairy, unbranched annual of damp, grassy places, mostly near the sea and often in dune-slacks. Very local in W Ireland. Leaves are lanceolate and unstalked. Bright yellow flowers, 15–25mm long, June–October.

COMMON COW-WHEAT *Melampyrum pratense*   Height up to 35cm
Straggly annual of woodland rides and grassy heaths, found mostly on acid soils. Locally common throughout. Narrow, shiny leaves borne in opposite pairs. Pairs of yellow flowers, 10–18mm long, arise from axils, May–September.

EYEBRIGHT *Euphrasia officinalis*   Height up to 25cm
Variable, branched annual, semi-parasitic on roots of other plants. Generally rather scarce. Leaves oval in outline but sharply toothed; often purplish. Purple-veined, whitish flowers, 3–10mm long, seen May–September.

YELLOW-RATTLE *Rhinanthus minor*   Height up to 45cm
Semi-parasitic annual of undisturbed meadows and dunes. Widespread and common throughout. Stems are black-spotted. Oblong leaves have rather rounded teeth. Yellow flowers, 10–20mm long, are borne in leafy, terminal spikes, May–September.

LOUSEWORT *Pedicularis sylvatica*   Height up to 20cm
Branched, spreading perennial of damp heaths and moors. Widespread and locally common in suitable habitats throughout. Feathery leaves are divided into toothed leaflets. The pink flowers, 20–25mm long, have 2-toothed upper lips; April–July.

MARSH LOUSEWORT *Pedicularis palustris*   Height up to 50cm
Hairless, branched annual of boggy heaths and marshes. Widespread and locally common. Feathery leaves are deeply divided into toothed lobes. Leafy spikes of pinkish purple flowers, 20–25mm long, seen May–September.

TOOTHWORT *Lathraea squamaria*   Height up to 25cm
Wholly parasitic plant on roots of woody plants, especially Hazel. Confined to E Ireland. Leaves reduced to pinkish white scales, borne on lilac stem. Tubular lilac flowers, in 1-sided spike, April–May.

COMMON BROOMRAPE *Orobanche minor*   Height up to 40cm
Parasitic annual on the roots of clovers and other herbaceous plants. Locally common in S and E Ireland. Lacks chlorophyll; leaves reduced to brownish scales. Purple-veined, pinkish yellow flowers seen June–September.

THYME BROOMRAPE *Orobanche alba*   Height up to 25cm
Root parasite of thyme and other related plants; usually has an overall reddish appearance. Local, restricted to coastal grassland in W Ireland. Leaves scale-like. Fragrant flowers borne in a loose spike, May–August.

RED VALERIAN *Centranthus ruber*   Height up to 75cm
Grey-green perennial of rocks, broken ground and walls. Locally common in N and E Ireland. Ovate, untoothed leaves in opposite pairs. Pink, red or sometimes white flowers are borne in terminal clusters May–September.

COMMON CORNSALAD *Valerianella locusta*   Height up to 30cm
Branched annual of dry, bare places on grassland and dunes. Widespread but only locally common. Lower leaves spoon-shaped, upper ones oblong. Pale lilac flowers are borne in flat-topped clusters with leafy bracts beneath; seen April–August.

BUTTERWORT *Pinguicula vulgaris*   Height up to 15cm
Carnivorous perennial of bogs and damp flushes; rosette of yellow-green, sticky leaves can trap and digest insects. Widespread and fairly common in Ireland. Violet, spurred flowers, 10–15mm long; seen May–August.

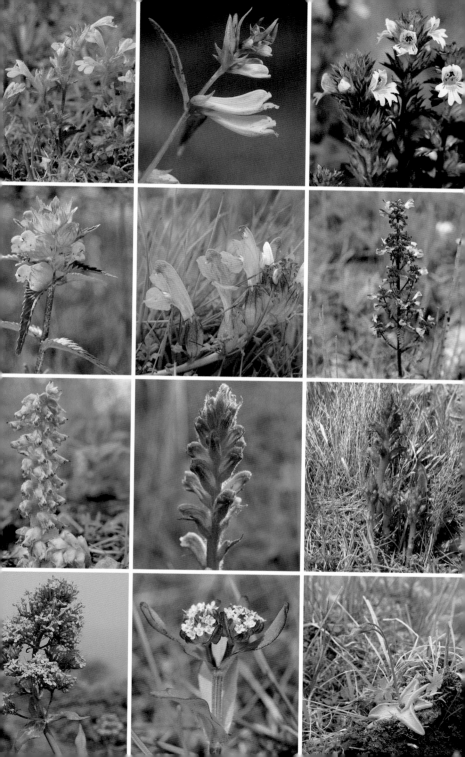

GREATER PLANTAIN *Plantago major*   Height up to 20cm
Persistent perennial of lawns and disturbed grassy places. Widespread and common throughout. Broad, oval leaves, up to 25cm long, have 3–9 veins and form a basal rosette. The flowers are borne in long, stalked spikes and appear June–October.

BUCK'S-HORN PLANTAIN *Plantago coronopus*   Height up to 15cm
Downy, grey-green perennial of disturbed ground and rocky sites, mainly near the sea. Widespread and common around coasts of Ireland. The deeply cut, pinnately divided leaves form a rosette. Stalked flower heads seen May–October.

SEA PLANTAIN *Plantago maritima*   Height up to 15cm
Characteristic coastal plant that is tolerant of salt spray and occasional immersion. Widespread and common around shores of Ireland. Strap-like leaves form a rosette. Flower heads borne on long stalks, June–September.

RIBWORT PLANTAIN *Plantago lanceolata*   Height up to 15cm
Perennial of disturbed grassland, cultivated ground and tracks. Widespread and common throughout. Leaves lanceolate and up to 20cm long; form a spreading basal rosette. Compact, ovoid flower heads borne on furrowed stalks, April–October.

SHOREWEED *Littorella uniflora*   Creeping
Hairless aquatic perennial, often found growing on the drying margins of ponds and lakes. Widespread and locally common. Narrow, fleshy leaves form a basal rosette. Tiny flowers, with minute petals, appear June–August.

SEA ARROWGRASS *Triglochin maritima*   Height up to 50cm
Plantain-like tufted perennial of saltmarshes. Widespread and common throughout. Leaves are long, narrow and unveined. The flowers are 3-petalled, 2–3mm across and borne in a long, narrow spike which itself is long-stalked; May–September.

FIELD SCABIOUS *Knautia arvensis*   Height up to 75cm
Robust, hairy biennial or perennial of dry grassland. Widespread and common. Spoon-shaped, lobed basal leaves form rosette; those on stem are less divided. Bluish violet flower heads, 3–4cm across, seen June–October.

DEVIL'S-BIT SCABIOUS *Succisa pratensis*   Height up to 75cm
Perennial of damp grassland, woodland rides and marshes. Widespread and common throughout. Basal leaves are spoon-shaped; those on stem are narrow. Blue-purple flowers are borne in rounded heads, 15–25mm across, and appear June–October.

TEASEL *Dipsacus fullonum*   Height up to 2m
Biennial of damp grassland on heavy soils. Rather scarce. Produces rosette of spine-coated leaves in first year. In second year, conical heads of purple flowers are borne on tall, angled and spined stems, July–August. Dead heads persist.

SHEEP'S-BIT *Jasione montana*   Height up to 30cm
Spreading biennial of dry, grassy places on acid soils, commonest near the sea. Widespread but local. Wavy-edged, hairy basal leaves form rosette; stem leaves narrow. Blue flowers are borne in rounded heads, 30–35mm across, May–September.

HAREBELL *Campanula rotundifolia*   Height up to 40cm
Attractive, delicate perennial of dry, grassy places, on both calcareous and acid soils. Widespread and mostly common. Rounded basal leaves soon wither; stem leaves narrow. Clusters of nodding blue flowers, 15mm long, seen July–October.

IVY-LEAVED BELLFLOWER *Wahlenbergia hederacea*   Creeping
Trailing perennial of damp, shady ground on moors and heaths. Local in S and SE Ireland. Ivy-shaped leaves carried on long stems. Pale blue flowers, 5–10mm long, borne on long stalks, appear July–August.

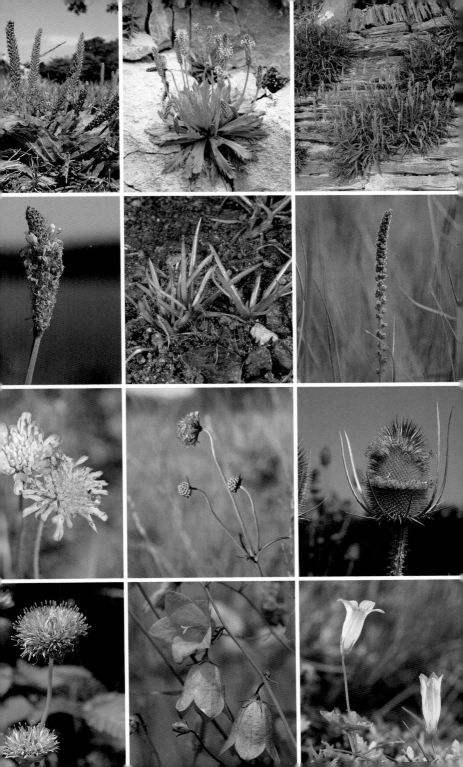

WATER LOBELIA *Lobelia dortmanna* Aquatic
Perennial of clear, acid waters of upland lakes with gravelly bottoms. Locally common in N and SW Ireland. Narrow, fleshy leaves form basal rosette on lake bed. Lilac flowers borne on emergent stalks, June–August.

HEMP AGRIMONY *Eupatorium cannabinum* Height up to 1.5m
Tall perennial of damp grassland and marshes. Widespread and locally common in Ireland. Trifoliate leaves borne in opposite pairs up stem. Heads of dull pink flowers form terminal inflorescences July–September.

GOLDENROD *Solidago virgaurea* Height up to 75cm
Variable perennial found in woods and grassland, and among rocks. Widespread and locally common. Stalked basal leaves are spoon-shaped; stem leaves are narrower and unstalked. Flower heads, 5–10mm across, in branched spikes, June–September.

CANADIAN GOLDENROD *Solidago canadensis* Height up to 1m
Familiar garden perennial that occurs as a naturalised escape, mostly in damp wayside places. Leaves are oval, toothed and 3-veined. Flower heads are borne on crowded, arching, 1-sided sprays in branching clusters, July–October.

DAISY *Bellis perennis* Height up to 10cm
Familiar perennial of lawns and short grass. Widespread and common throughout. Spoon-shaped leaves form prostrate rosettes from which flower stalks arise, each bearing single flower heads, 15–25mm across; yellow disc and white ray florets.

SCENTLESS MAYWEED *Matricaria perforata* Height up to 75cm
Scentless, hairless perennial of disturbed ground and cultivated soil. Common and widespread throughout. Leaves are much-divided and feathery. Clusters of long-stalked, daisy-like flower heads, 2–4cm across, appear April–October.

PINEAPPLE MAYWEED *Chamomilla suaveolens* Height up to 12cm
Bright green perennial of disturbed ground, paths and tracks; smells strongly of pineapple when crushed. Leaves are finely divided and feathery. Rounded-oval flower heads comprise yellowish green disc florets only and appear May–November.

SEA ASTER *Aster tripolium* Height up to 75cm
Salt-tolerant perennial of saltmarshes and cliffs. Locally common around coasts of Ireland. Leaves are fleshy and narrow. Clusters of flowers, 1–2cm across, comprising yellow disc and blue ray florets, appear July–September.

BLUE FLEABANE *Erigeron acer* Height up to 30cm
Annual or biennial of dry, grassy places. Generally rather scarce. Stems reddish and hairy. Basal leaves stalked and spoon-shaped; stem leaves narrow, unstalked. Flower heads, 12–18mm across, in clusters June–August.

MARSH CUDWEED *Gnaphalium uliginosum* Height up to 20cm
Grey-green, woolly, branched annual of damp, disturbed ground. Widespread except in central Ireland. Leaves narrow and up to 4cm long. Flowers comprise yellow disc florets and brown bracts; shrouded by leaves and seen July–October.

COMMON CUDWEED *Filago vulgaris* Height up to 25cm
Upright, woolly annual of dry, often sandy, grassland. Generally rather local and scattered. Usually branched near tip. Leaves narrow. Rounded clusters of 20–35 flower heads are seen July–August.

SMALL CUDWEED *Filago minima* Height up to 20cm
Slender, woolly annual of grassy heaths on sandy, acid soils. Generally rather local and scattered. Leaves lanceolate and 10mm long. Clusters of conical or ovoid flower heads, 3–4mm long, appear July–September.

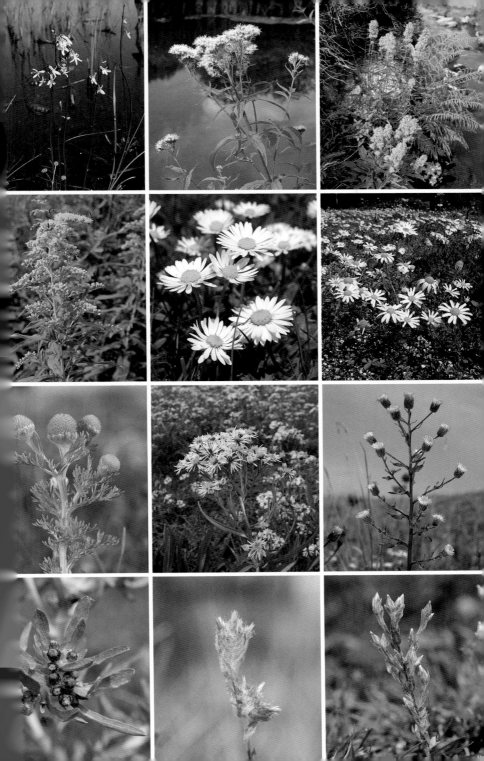

GOLDEN SAMPHIRE *Inula crithmoides*   Height up to 75cm
Tufted perennial of saltmarshes, shingle and sea cliffs. Widespread and locally common around coasts of Ireland. Upright stems with bright green, narrow, fleshy leaves. Flower heads, 15–30mm across, in clusters, July–September.

FLEABANE *Pulicaria dysenterica*   Height up to 50cm
Woolly perennial of damp meadows and ditches, mostly on heavy soils. Widespread and fairly common in Ireland. Basal leaves soon wither; stem leaves heart-shaped and clasping. Flower heads, 15–30mm across, appear July–September.

YARROW *Achillea millefolium*   Height up to 50cm
Strong-smelling wayside perennial. Widespread and common throughout. Dark green leaves finely divided and feathery. Flat-topped clusters of flower heads, 4–6cm across, comprise yellowish disc and pinkish white ray florets; June–November.

SNEEZEWORT *Achillea ptarmica*   Height up to 60cm
Upright, downy perennial of damp ground in woods and meadows. Locally common throughout. Leaves narrow and finely toothed. Open clusters of flower heads, 1–2cm across and comprising yellowish disc and white ray florets, seen July–September.

CORN MARIGOLD *Chrysanthemum segetum*   Height up to 50cm
Hairless annual of cultivated ground, mostly on acid, sandy soils. Widespread and locally common although much reduced in range and abundance. Leaves narrow and deeply lobed. Bright yellow flowers, 3–6cm across, appear June–October.

TANSY *Tanacetum vulgare*   Height up to 75cm
Aromatic, downy perennial of waysides. Widespread and common throughout. Pinnately divided leaves have deeply cut lobes. Yellow flower, 7–12mm across, form flat-topped clusters up to 12cm in diameter; July–October.

FEVERFEW *Tanacetum parthenium*   Height up to 50cm
Aromatic, downy perennial of disturbed ground and walls. Introduced but widely naturalised in many places. Yellowish leaves are pinnately divided. Daisy-like flowers, 1–2cm across, comprise yellow disc and white ray florets; July–August.

OX-EYE DAISY *Leucanthemum vulgare*   Height up to 60cm
Perennial of dry, grassy meadows and disturbed ground. Widespread and common throughout. Spoon-shaped, toothed basal leaves form a rosette; smaller stem leaves are pinnately lobed. Solitary flowers, 3–5cm across, May–September.

BUTTERBUR *Petasites hybridus*   Height up to 50cm
Perennial of damp ground, often beside rivers. Widespread and locally common. Robust flowering spikes appear March–May, before leaves, with pink-red flower heads. Heart-shaped leaves, up to 1m across, appear in summer.

WINTER HELIOTROPE *Petasites fragrans*   Height up to 20cm
Spreading perennial of damp or shady hedgerows. Introduced but naturalised as a garden escape in many areas. Rounded leaves, 20cm across, are present all year. Flowering stems appear December–March with fragrant, pink-lilac flower heads.

MUGWORT *Artemisia vulgaris*   Height up to 1.25m
Aromatic perennial of roadside verges and wasteground. Widespread and common throughout. Stems reddish. Pinnate leaves dark green above but silvery-downy below. Small, reddish flower heads are borne in branched spikes July–September.

WORMWOOD *Artemisia absinthium*   Height up to 80cm
Highly aromatic perennial of disturbed coastal grassland and wayside places. Very local, mainly in coastal districts. Pinnate leaves are silvery-hairy on both surfaces. Yellowish flower heads are slightly nodding; seen July–September.

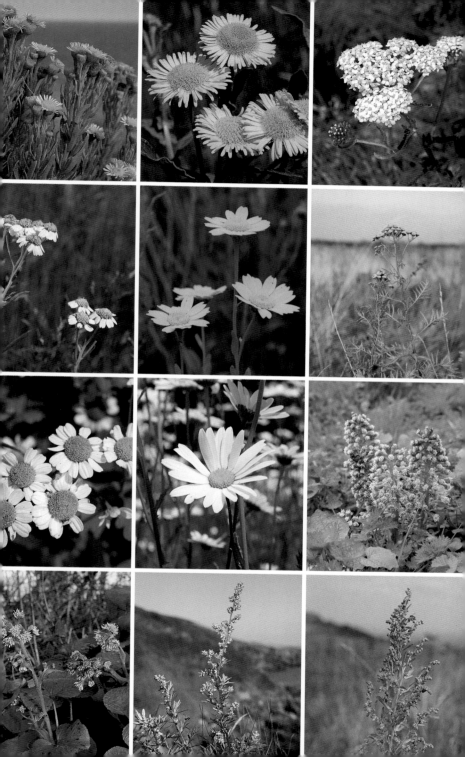

SEA WORMWOOD *Artemisia maritima*   Height up to 65cm
Aromatic perennial of saltmarshes and sea walls. Local in W and E Ireland. Stems woody, downy-white. Pinnate leaves downy on both sides. Yellow flower heads in leafy spikes August–October.

COLT'S-FOOT *Tussilago farfara*   Height up to 15cm
Creeping perennial of bare, often disturbed, ground. Widespread and common in most parts. Yellow flowers appear February–April, before the leaves; they are borne on scaly stems. Leaves are rounded or heart-shaped and 10–20cm across.

RAGWORT *Senecio jacobaea*   Height up to 1m
Poisonous biennial or perennial of grazed grassland and verges. Widespread and common throughout. Leaves are pinnately divided with a blunt end lobe. Flat-topped clusters of yellow flower heads, 15–25mm across, appear June–November.

GROUNDSEL *Senecio vulgaris*   Height up to 40cm
Annual weed of disturbed ground. Widespread and very common throughout. Leaves are pinnately-lobed; lower ones stalked, upper ones clasping stem. Open clusters of small, rayless flower heads can be found almost all year.

OXFORD RAGWORT *Senecio squalidus*   Height up to 50cm
Branched annual or perennial of wasteground, verges and railway tracks. Occasionally naturalised. Leaves are pinnately lobed and end in a pointed lobe. Open clusters of bright yellow flower heads, each 15–20mm across, appear April–November.

GREATER BURDOCK *Arctium lappa*   Height up to 1m
Branched biennial of woodland, scrub and verges. Scattered and local in Ireland. Leaves large, downy and heart-shaped. Egg-shaped flower heads, 3–4cm across, are borne in open clusters, July–September.

CARLINE THISTLE *Carlina vulgaris*   Height up to 60cm
Spiny biennial of dry, calcareous grassland. Locally common throughout. Oblong leaves have wavy margins and spiny lobes. Brown, rayless flower heads surrounded by golden bracts; July–September. Dead flower heads persist.

MUSK THISTLE *Carduus nutans*   Height up to 1m
Upright biennial of dry grassland. Rare, restricted to W Ireland. Winged stems spiny and cottony. Leaves are pinnately lobed and spiny. Rayless, nodding flower heads, 3–5cm across, appear June–August, fringed by spiny bracts.

SLENDER THISTLE *Carduus tenuiflorus*   Height up to 1m
Biennial of dry, grassy places, mostly near the sea. Locally common in SW and NE. Stems are winged and spiny to the top. Spiny leaves are cottony below. Clusters of pinkish flower heads, 8–10mm across, June–August.

SPEAR THISTLE *Cirsium vulgare*   Height up to 1m
Biennial of disturbed ground. Widespread and common. Pinnately lobed leaves are spiny. Stems are cottony, winged and spiny between leaves. Flower heads, 2–4cm across, comprise purple florets topping ball of spiny bracts, seen July–September.

MELANCHOLY THISTLE *Cirsium helenoides*   Height up to 1m
Unbranched perennial of damp meadows. Local and scarce; NW only. Stems are cottony, spineless and unwinged. Oval, toothed leaves are barely spiny, green above but white below. Flower heads, 3–5cm across, June–August.

MEADOW THISTLE *Cirsium dissectum*   Height up to 75cm
Perennial of damp meadows. Locally common in Ireland. Stem is unwinged, downy and ridged. Oval, toothed leaves are green and hairy above and white cottony below. Flower heads, 20–25mm across, appear June–July.

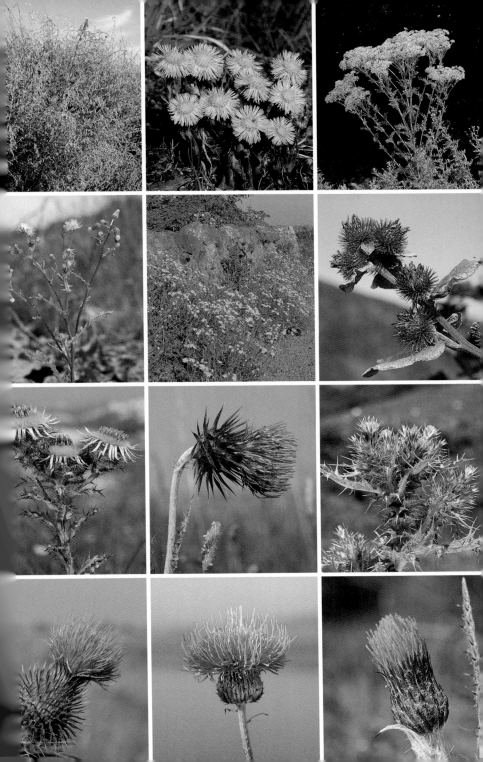

CREEPING THISTLE *Cirsium arvense*   Height up to 1m
Creeping perennial with upright, unwinged stems. Widespread and very common on disturbed ground and in grassland. Leaves are pinnately-lobed and spiny. The pinkish lilac flower heads, 10–15mm across, appear in clusters June–September.

MARSH THISTLE *Cirsium palustre*   Height up to 1.5m
Branched biennial of damp grassland. Widespread and common throughout. Stems are spiny-winged and cottony. Leaves are pinnately-lobed and spiny. Leafy clusters of reddish purple flower heads, each 10–15mm across, appear July–September.

COMMON KNAPWEED *Centaurea nigra*   Height up to 1m
Hairy perennial of grassy places. Widespread and common. Grooved stems branch towards the top. Leaves narrow, slightly lobed near base of plant. Flower heads 2–4cm across and with brown bracts and purple florets, appear June–September.

GREATER KNAPWEED *Centaurea scabiosa*   Height up to 1m
Downy perennial of dry grassland, mostly on calcareous soils. Locally common, mainly in S. Oblong leaves are deeply pinnately lobed. Flower heads, 3–5cm across, have enlarged outer florets; seen June–September.

CHICORY *Cichorium intybus*   Height up to 1m
Branched perennial of bare, grassy places and verges, often on calcareous soils. Introduced and local. Lower leaves stalked and lobed, upper ones narrow and clasping. Sky-blue flower heads, 3–4cm across, appear June–September.

GOAT'S-BEARD *Tragopogon pratensis*   Height up to 60cm
Perennial of grassy places. Local and scattered. Leaves narrow, clasping or sheathing at base. Flower heads, 3–4cm across, are fringed by bracts and close on dull days and by midday; seen May–August. Fruit is a large white 'clock'.

SMOOTH SOWTHISTLE *Sonchus oleraceus*   Height up to 1m
Annual of disturbed and cultivated ground. Widespread and common in lowlands. Broken stems exude milky sap. Pinnate leaves have toothed margins and pointed basal lobes. Pale yellow flower heads, 20–25mm across, in clusters May–October.

PERENNIAL SOWTHISTLE *Sonchus arvensis*   Height up to 2m
Perennial of damp, grassy places and disturbed ground. Widespread and common throughout. Grey-green leaves have rounded lobes and bases, and clasp the stem. Yellow flower heads, 4–5cm across, appear in branched clusters, July–September.

DANDELION *Taraxacum officinale*   Height up to 35cm
Perennial complex of numerous 'micro-species'. Lobed, spoon-shaped leaves form a basal rosette. Flower heads, 3–6cm across, borne on hollow stems yielding milky sap if broken; appear March–October. Fruits form familiar white 'clock'.

MOUSE-EAR HAWKWEED *Hieraceum pilosella*   Height up to 25cm
Common spreading perennial of grassy places. Spoon-shaped leaves are green and hairy above, white downy below; form a basal rosette. Solitary flower heads, 2–3cm across, are pale yellow with red stripes below; seen May–October.

BRISTLY OXTONGUE *Picris echioides*   Height up to 80cm
Branched, bristly-stemmed perennial of dry, disturbed ground. Local, restricted to coastal SE. Narrow, clasping leaves covered with swollen-based bristles and pale spots. Pale yellow flower heads, 20–25mm across, in clusters, June–October.

HAWKWEED OXTONGUE *Picris hieracioides*   Height up to 70cm
Bristly-stemmed perennial of rough grassland, often near coasts. Scarce in SE Ireland. Resembles Bristly Oxtongue but narrower, toothed leaves have bristles without swollen bases. Flower heads are 20–25mm across; appear June–October.

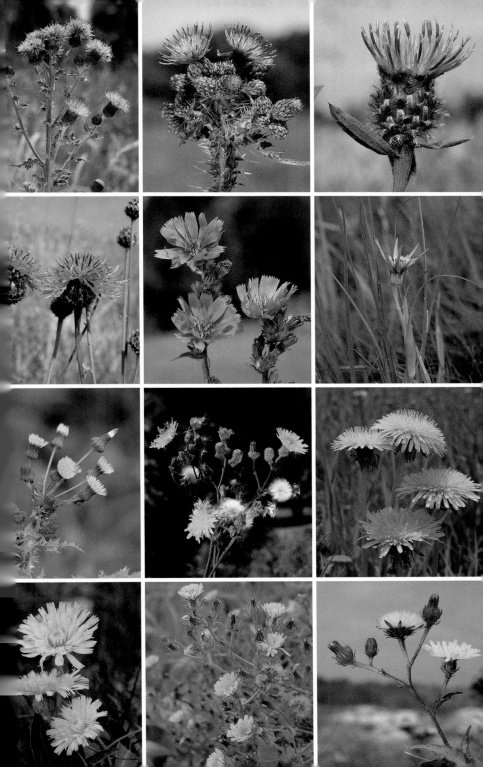

ROUGH HAWKBIT *Leontodon hispidus* Height up to 35cm
Roughly-hairy perennial of dry grassland, mostly on calcareous soils. Locally common. Hairy, wavy-lobed leaves form basal rosette. Leafless, unbranched stalk arises with single flower head, 25–40mm across; appears June–October.

COMMON CATSEAR *Hypochoeris radicata* Height up to 50cm
Perennial of dry grassland. Widespread and common throughout. Lanceolate, hairy leaves with lobed edges form a basal rosette. Flower heads, 25–30mm across, are borne on branched stalks that have a few purple-tipped bracts; seen June–September.

SMOOTH HAWK'S-BEARD *Crepis capillaris* Height up to 1m
Hairless annual or biennial of dry grassy places. Common in lowlands throughout. Lower, lobed leaves form a basal rosette; stem leaves arrow-shaped and clasping. Flower heads, 15–25mm across, borne in branched clusters and appear May–July.

COMMON WATER-PLANTAIN *Alisma plantago-aquatica* Height up to 1m
Aquatic perennial of margins and shallows of ponds and lakes. Locally common. Oval, long-stalked leaves have parallel veins. Pale lilac flowers, 1cm across, borne in branched whorls, June–September.

ARROWHEAD *Sagittaria sagittifolia* Height up to 80cm
Aquatic perennial of still and slow-flowing water. Local and scarce in Ireland. Arrow-shaped emergent leaves, oval floating leaves and narrow submerged ones. 3-petalled flowers, 2cm across, appear July–August.

BOG ASPHODEL *Narthecium ossifragum* Height up to 20cm
Tufted perennial of boggy heaths and moors. Locally common on suitable peaty soils. Narrow, iris-like leaves borne in a flattened fan. Spikes of flowers appear June–August; turns orange in fruit.

RAMSONS *Allium ursinum* Height up to 35cm
Bulbous perennial that smells strongly of garlic. Sometimes forms extensive carpets in damp woods, mainly on calcareous soils. Rather local and scarce. The leaves are ovate and all basal. The leafless flower stems carry clusters of up to 20 white flowers, April–May.

BLUEBELL *Hyacinthoides non-scripta* Height up to 50cm
Familiar bulbous perennial, often carpeting whole woodland floors if management regime suits its requirements; also found on coastal cliffs. Widespread and locally common, least so in E. Leaves narrow and all basal. Bell-shaped flowers in 1-sided spikes, appear April–June.

SPRING SQUILL *Scilla verna* Height up to 5cm
Compact perennial of dry grassland near the sea. Locally common on coasts of E Ireland. Produces 4–6 wiry, curly leaves in spring. Flowers appear subsequently on short stalk, April–June. They are lilac-blue and 10–15mm across.

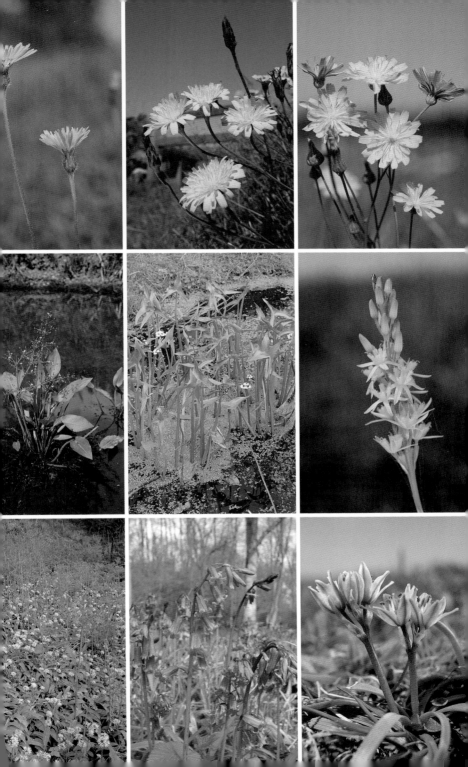

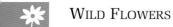

THREE-CORNERED GARLIC *Allium triquetrum*　　　　　　Height up to 45cm
A perennial that, as its name suggests, smells strongly of garlic. Three-cornered Garlic has three narrow leaves and an upright, three-angled stem that bears white, bell-shaped flowers in a drooping umbel. Flowers can be found throughout spring, typically March–May. This southern European species is alien to the region but, through introductions, it has become naturalised in scattered colonies.

BLUE-EYED GRASS *Sisyrinchium bermudiana*　　　　　Height up to 50cm
A perennial with narrow, grass-like leaves that all arise from the base. The flowers are blue and 15–20mm across; they are borne in terminal clusters, and appear July–August. Blue-eyed Grass is restricted to W Ireland and although there is controversy as to its exact status in the region it is probably native.

MONTBRETIA *Crocosmia × crocosmiiflora*　　　　　　Height up to 60cm
A familiar plant of cultivation, Montbretia's status is also that of an introduced perennial and it is now widely naturalised as a garden escape. The leaves are iris-like but narrow, arising from base and giving rise to sizeable clumps. The flowers are orange and are borne in a terminal spike, appearing July–September. Widespread and often invasive.

SNOWDROP *Galanthus nivalis*　　　　　　　　　　　Height up to 25cm
A familiar spring flower in gardens, the Snowdrop is also occasionally naturalised in woodland, generally where it has been deliberately introduced. The leaves are narrow, grey-green and all basal. An upright stem carries a single, drooping white flower, 15–25cm long, and this appears January–March.

YELLOW IRIS *Iris pseudacorus*　　　　　　　　　　　Height up to 1m
A familiar and robust perennial of pond margins, marshes and riverbanks. The Yellow Iris is widespread and common throughout the region. The grey-green leaves are sword-shaped and often wrinkled. Clusters of 2–3 yellow flowers, each up to 10cm across, appear May–August. The plant forms dense tussock-like stands and, if the conditions suit it, it can spread to form sizeable stands, often growing to the exclusion of other species.

LORDS-AND-LADIES *Arum maculatum*　　　　　　　Height up to 50cm
A familiar perennial of woods and hedgerows. Lords-and-Ladies, or Cuckoo-pint as it is also known, is locally common in S Ireland; it is rather scarce further N in the region. The leaves are arrow-shaped and shiny, and are sometimes purple-spotted. The unusual flowers comprise a purple, rod-like spadix, which is shrouded by a cowl-like spathe; April–May. Spikes of bright red berries appear later in the season and are quickly consumed by birds.

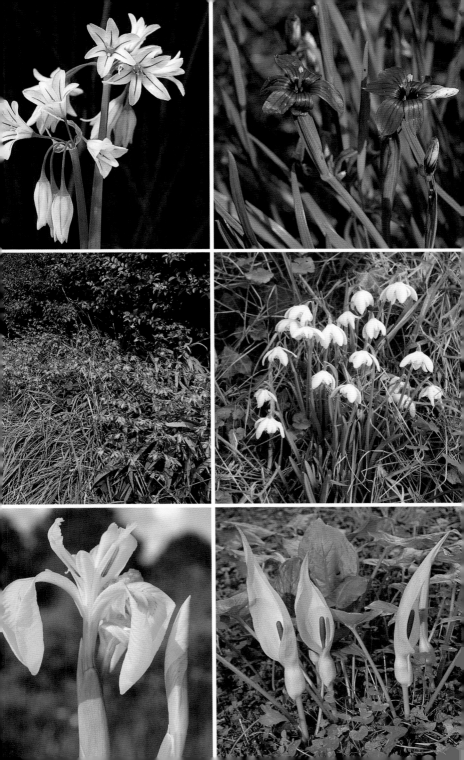

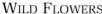

BEE ORCHID *Ophrys apifera*   Height up to 30cm
Locally common in dry grassland in central S Ireland; scarce or absent elsewhere.
Leaves form a basal rosette and two sheathing leaves appear up stem. Flowers,
12mm across, comprise pink sepals, green upper petals; expanded, furry lower
petal maroon with pale yellow markings giving it a fanciful resemblance to a
bumblebee. Borne in spikes, June–July.

FLY ORCHID *Ophrys insectifera*   Height up to 40cm
Intriguing, rather slender plant of dry grassland, open woodland and scrub on calcareous soils. Rare in Ireland, mainly in W. Oval, glossy leaves appear as a basal
rosette and up stem. The superficially insect-like flowers comprise greenish
sepals and thin, brown and antennae-like upper petals; lower petal is elongated
with two side lobes and is maroon with a blue patch. Flowers borne in open
spikes, May–June.

EARLY-PURPLE ORCHID *Orchis mascula*   Height up to 40cm
Widespread and locally common orchid of woodland, scrub and grassland, doing
especially well on neutral or base-rich soils. Rosettes of glossy, dark green leaves
with dark spots, appear from January onwards from which the flower stalk arises
later in spring. The pinkish purple flowers are borne in tall spikes, April–June;
the lower lip is 3-lobed, 8–12mm long, and there is a long spur.

FROG ORCHID *Coeloglossum viride*   Height up to 20cm
An often rather short and compact orchid of base-rich grassland, sometimes in
upland areas. Widespread and very locally common throughout. Broad, oval leaves
form a basal rosette and narrower leaves partially sheathe the lower part of the stem.
The sepals and upper petals form a green hood and the lip is 6–8mm long and yellow-brown. The flowers are borne in an open spike and appear June–August.

PYRAMIDAL ORCHID *Anacamptis pyramidalis*   Height up to 30cm
Attractive orchid of dry grassland, usually on calcareous soils, and stabilised
sand dunes. Locally common in parts of Ireland. The leaves are grey-green, lanceolate and usually carried upright, partially sheathing the flower stem. The flowers are deep pink with a 3-lobed lip and a long spur; borne in dense, conical or
domed flower heads, June–August.

FRAGRANT ORCHID *Gymnadenia conopsea*   Height up to 40cm
Robust orchid found on both dry and damp grassland, mostly on base-rich soils.
Locally common in many parts. Short leaves are found at the base of the plant and
a few, very narrow leaves are borne up the stem. The highly fragrant flowers are
usually pink although plants can vary from purple to almost white; the lip is 3-
lobed and there is a long spur. They are produced in tall spikes, up to 15cm long,
and appear June–July.

TWAYBLADE *Listera ovata*   Height up to 50cm
Distinctive orchid of woodlands and grasslands on a wide range of soil types, it
is widespread and generally rather common. A pair of broad, oval basal leaves
appear well before the flowering stem, from March onwards. The yellowish green
flowers are borne in a loose spike, May–July; the lower lip is deeply forked.

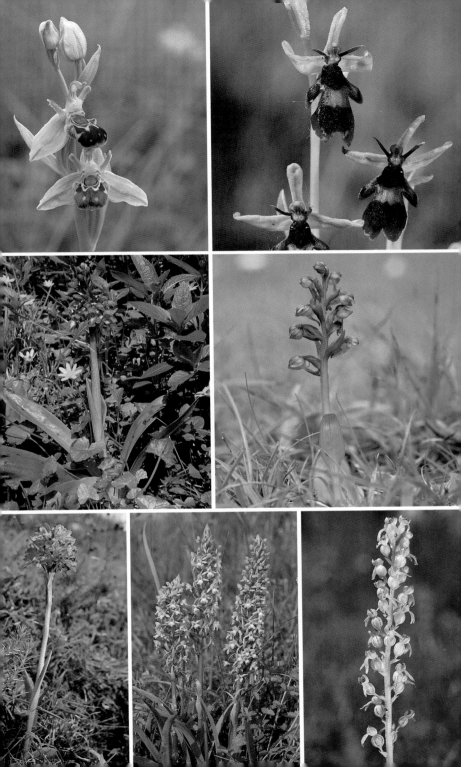

NORTHERN MARSH-ORCHID *Dactylorhiza purpurella*   Height up to 50cm
Widespread and locally common orchid of meadows, marshes and damp ground
generally. Leaves are fresh green and often unspotted. The flowers are typically
reddish purple, marked with darker streaks and spot, especially on the lip, which
is broad and diamond-shaped; June-July.

NARROW-LEAVED MARSH-ORCHID *Dactylorhiza traunsteineri* Height up to 40cm
A rather delicate marsh-orchid found locally in base-rich marshes. Leaves are
narrow, keeled and typically unspotted. Flowers are pinkish purple, the rather
pale, three-lobed and reflexed lip marked with darker spots; borne in lax spikes,
May-June. Rather local in Ireland.

COMMON SPOTTED-ORCHID *Dactylorhiza fuchsii*   Height up to 60cm
Robust and familiar orchid of grassland, woodland rides and roadside verges,
mostly on base-rich or neutral soils. The green, glossy leaves are indeed dark-
spotted and appear as a rosette long before the flower stalk is produced; narrower
leaves sheathe the lower part of the stalk. The flowers range from pale pink to
pink-purple but are marked with darker streaks and spots on the lip that has 3
even-sized lobes and is 1cm across; in tall spikes, June–August.

HEATH SPOTTED-ORCHID *Dactylorhiza maculata*   Height up to 50cm
Superficially rather similar to Common Spotted-orchid but restricted to damp,
mostly acid soils on heaths and moors. The leaves are lanceolate and dark-
spotted, those at the base of the plant being largest and broadest; narrower leaves
sheathe the lower part of the stalk. The flowers are usually very pale, sometimes
almost white, but have darker streaks and spots; the lower lip is broad and
3-lobed but, unlike Common Spotted-orchid, the central lobe is smaller than
the outer two. Flowers are borne in rather open, domed spikes, May–August.
Widespread and often common.

EARLY MARSH-ORCHID *Dactylorhiza incarnata*   Height up to 60cm
Orchid of damp meadows, often on base-rich soils but sometimes also acid conditions. The leaves are unmarked, yellowish green and narrow-lanceolate. Flowers are usually flesh-pink but can range from almost white to purple. The 3-lobed
flower lip is strongly reflexed along the mid-line. Flowers borne in open spikes,
May–June. Widespread but local.

GREATER BUTTERFLY-ORCHID *Platanthera chlorantha*   Height up to 50cm
Found in undisturbed woodland, scrub and grassland, mostly on base-rich soils.
Locally common throughout. Has a single pair of large, oval leaves at base of plant
and a few small stem leaves. Greenish white flowers have long, narrow lip, long
spur and pollen sacs forming an inverted V; in open spikes, June–July.

LESSER BUTTERFLY-ORCHID *Platanthera bifolia*   Height up to 40cm
Favours undisturbed grassland, moors and woodland. Locally common throughout. Has a single pair of broad, oval leaves at base and smaller, scale-like leaves
up stem. Flowers are greenish white with a long, narrow lip, a long spur and
pollen sacs that are parallel; borne in rather open spikes and appear May–July.

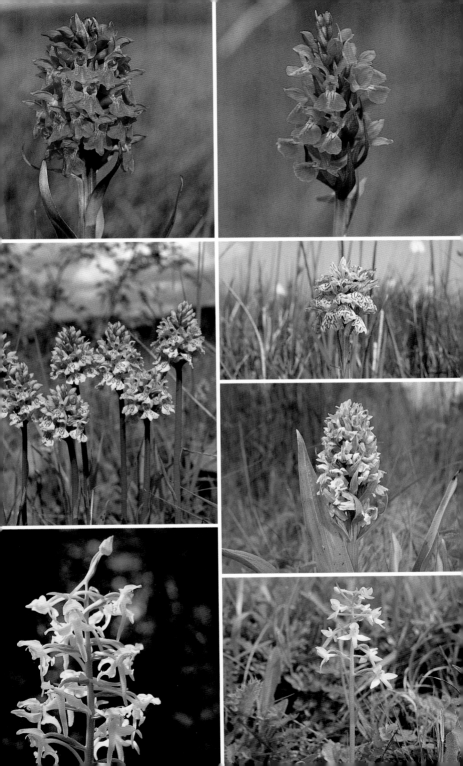

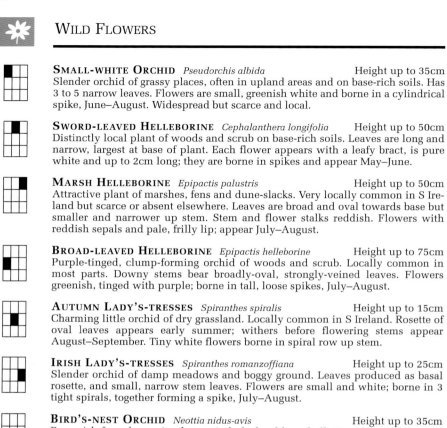

SMALL-WHITE ORCHID *Pseudorchis albida*   Height up to 35cm
Slender orchid of grassy places, often in upland areas and on base-rich soils. Has 3 to 5 narrow leaves. Flowers are small, greenish white and borne in a cylindrical spike, June–August. Widespread but scarce and local.

SWORD-LEAVED HELLEBORINE *Cephalanthera longifolia*   Height up to 50cm
Distinctly local plant of woods and scrub on base-rich soils. Leaves are long and narrow, largest at base of plant. Each flower appears with a leafy bract, is pure white and up to 2cm long; they are borne in spikes and appear May–June.

MARSH HELLEBORINE *Epipactis palustris*   Height up to 50cm
Attractive plant of marshes, fens and dune-slacks. Very locally common in S Ireland but scarce or absent elsewhere. Leaves are broad and oval towards base but smaller and narrower up stem. Stem and flower stalks reddish. Flowers with reddish sepals and pale, frilly lip; appear July–August.

BROAD-LEAVED HELLEBORINE *Epipactis helleborine*   Height up to 75cm
Purple-tinged, clump-forming orchid of woods and scrub. Locally common in most parts. Downy stems bear broadly-oval, strongly-veined leaves. Flowers greenish, tinged with purple; borne in tall, loose spikes, July–August.

AUTUMN LADY'S-TRESSES *Spiranthes spiralis*   Height up to 15cm
Charming little orchid of dry grassland. Locally common in S Ireland. Rosette of oval leaves appears early summer; withers before flowering stems appear August–September. Tiny white flowers borne in spiral row up stem.

IRISH LADY'S-TRESSES *Spiranthes romanzoffiana*   Height up to 25cm
Slender orchid of damp meadows and boggy ground. Leaves produced as basal rosette, and small, narrow stem leaves. Flowers are small and white; borne in 3 tight spirals, together forming a spike, July–August.

BIRD'S-NEST ORCHID *Neottia nidus-avis*   Height up to 35cm
Brownish fungal parasite that entirely lacks chlorophyll. Found in undisturbed woodland, often under beech. Widespread but rather scarce. Flowers, with hood and 2-lobed lip, appear May–July.

BOG-ORCHID *Hammarbya paludosa*   Height up to 8cm
Delicate, yellowish green orchid found among bog moss in floating bogs. Rare and restricted to SE Ireland. Small, oval leaves at base. Yellowish flowers appear July–September.

DENSE-FLOWERED ORCHID *Neotinea maculata*   Height up to 30cm
Compact orchid of base-rich grassland. Local and scarce; a Burren speciality. Leaves are fresh green and partly sheath the stem. Flowers are pinkish or whitish and comprise a hood and a three-lobed lip; borne in dense spikes, April–May.

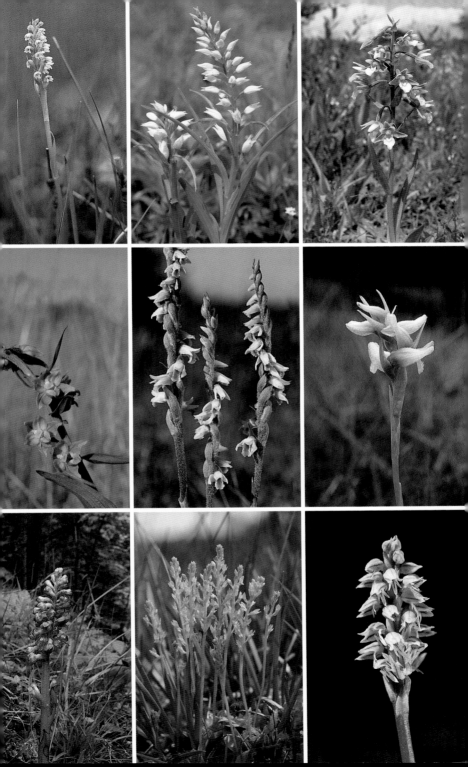

WATER MILFOIL *Myriophyllum aquaticum*   Aquatic
Introduced freshwater plant. Scattered colonies in lowland areas, favouring still waters of lakes, drainage ditches and canals. Submerged stems carry whorls of feathery, 4-times pinnately divided leaves. Emergent flower stalks with tiny flowers, June–July.

CANADIAN PONDWEED *Elodea canadensis*   Aquatic
Freshwater plant, introduced from N America but now naturalised in ponds and lakes throughout. Submerged, rather brittle stems carry narrow, back-curved, unstalked leaves in whorls of three. The flowers are tiny and seldom seen.

MARE'S-TAIL *Hippuris vulgaris*   Aquatic
Widespread freshwater plant favouring ponds and lakes but avoiding acid waters. Submerged part of plant produces upright, emergent stems which carry very narrow leaves in whorls of 6–12; appearance somewhat horsetail-like. Flowers are minute.

PIPEWORT *Eriocaulon aquaticum*   Aquatic
Slender aquatic plant. Tufts of submerged narrow leaves are borne at intervals along stem. Flowers are produced in dense, button-like heads that are borne on stems that rise 30cm or more above water's surface. Local in W Ireland only.

GREATER BLADDERWORT *Utricularia vulgaris*   Aquatic
Intriguing freshwater plant, widespread but local in Ireland. Long submerged stems with finely divided leaves and small, flask-shaped bladders that trap tiny invertebrates. Yellow flowers borne on emergent stems, July–August.

COMMON DUCKWEED *Lemna minor*   Aquatic
Floating, perennial freshwater plant that often forms a carpet over the surface of suitable ponds and lakes. Widespread and locally common throughout. Leaf-like thallus, up to 5mm across, has a single, dangling root. Multiplies by division.

BROAD-LEAVED PONDWEED *Potamogeton natans*   Aquatic
Freshwater plant that is widespread and often common in still or slow-flowing waters throughout. Floating leaves are dark green, broadly-oval, 10–12cm long and borne on long stems. Emergent, plantain-like flower spikes, May–September.

BOG PONDWEED *Potamogeton polygonifolius*   Aquatic
Widespread and locally common freshwater plant, favouring boggy pools and acid waters. Has both floating and submerged, oval leaves; sometimes forms dense carpet over surface of suitable habitats. Emergent flower spikes May–October.

WATER HORSETAIL *Equisetum fluviatile*   Height up to 1m
Grows in marshes and margins of ponds and lakes. Widespread and locally common in Ireland. Tall, unbranched stems jointed and thin with whorls of narrow, jointed branches. Spores in cone-like structures at ends of some stems.

COMMON HORSETAIL *Equisetum arvense*   Height up to 75cm
The commonest horsetail, forming spreading patches in dry, grassy places and on wasteground. Produces sterile shoots with ridged stems; these carry whorls of unbranched branches. Fertile stems appear in early spring and ripen in May.

WOOD HORSETAIL *Equisetum sylvaticum*   Height up to 50cm
Elegant horsetail of shady woodland and moors. Widespread but commonest in N. Sterile stems resemble the growing tips of conifers, carrying whorls of slender branches which are themselves branched. Fertile stems ripen in May.

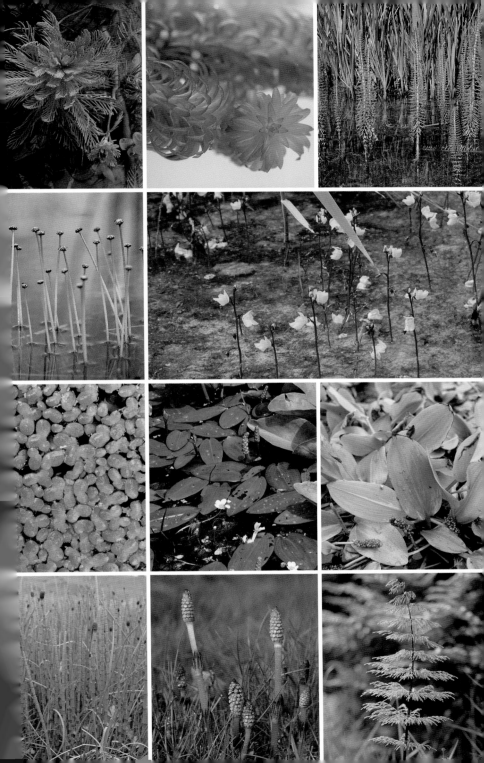

TOAD RUSH *Juncus bufonis*   Height up to 40cm
Tufted annual of damp, bare ground including wheel ruts along tracks and the
margins of ponds. Widespread and locally common throughout. Narrow leaves
arise at the base of the plant. The flowers are borne in branched clusters, May–July.

HARD RUSH *Juncus inflexus*   Height up to 1m
Perennial of damp ground. Widespread and locally common. Grey-green stems
are leafless and ridged. The brown flowers are borne in a loose cluster, May–July,
and this is topped by a narrow, pointed bract.

COMPACT RUSH *Juncus conglomeratus*   Height up to 1m
Perennial of damp, often grazed, grassland, mostly on acid soils. Widespread but
scarce in Ireland. Ridged stems bear brown flowers in rounded clusters,
May–July, topped by long bract appearing as a continuation of stem.

SALTMARSH RUSH *Juncus gerardii*   Height up to 50cm
Characteristic rush of saltmarshes around the coasts of Ireland, often covering
extensive areas. The dark green leaves arise at the base of the plant and on the
stems. Flowers in a loose cluster flanked by shortish bracts.

SOFT RUSH *Juncus effusus*   Height up to 1.5m
Tall perennial of overgrazed grassland, mostly on acid soils. Widespread and
locally common throughout. Stems green and smooth-looking. Pale brown
flowers are borne in a loose, rounded cluster topped by a narrow bract; May–July.

FIELD WOODRUSH *Luzula campestris*   Height up to 25cm
Tufted perennial with grass-like leaves that are fringed with long white hairs.
Widespread but local in short grassland, especially on base-rich soil. Rounded,
yellow-brown flower heads are borne in clusters and appear April–May.

GREAT WOOD-RUSH *Luzula sylvatica*   Height up to 75cm
Tufted, clump-forming perennial found in damp woodlands. Widespread and
generally common in Ireland. Grass-like leaves are fringed with long white hairs.
Reddish brown flowers are borne in branched clusters, April–June.

COMMON SPIKE-RUSH *Eleocharis palustris*   Height up to 50cm
Creeping perennial of marshes and pond margins. Widespread but generally
scarce. Green, leafless stems arise in tufts and are topped by brown, egg-shaped
spikelets that contain the flowers, May–July. Fruits are yellow-brown.

SEA CLUB-RUSH *Scirpus maritimus*   Height up to 1.25m
Creeping perennial found growing at the margins of brackish water near the sea.
The stems are rough and triangular in cross-section and are topped by clusters of
brown spikelets, flanked by leaf-like bracts. Leaves are rough and keeled.

FLOATING CLUB-RUSH *Scirpus fluitans*   Aquatic
Widespread but scarce in still or slow-flowing, usually acid, water. The narrow
stems and leaves form rather tangled, floating and submerged mats. Pale, stalked
and egg-shaped spikelets are borne on long, emergent stalks, May–July.

BLACK BOG-RUSH *Schoenus nigricans*   Height up to 50cm
Tufted perennial of bogs, dune-slacks and marshes, usually on base-rich soils.
Widespread, commonest in W. Long, green leaves arise at base of stems which
carry flower heads comprising black spikelets flanked by long bract.

WHITE BEAK-SEDGE *Rhynchospora alba*   Height up to 40cm
Tufted perennial of bogs and wet heaths on acid soils. Commonest in W Ireland.
Pale green leaves arise at base of plant and on stems. Flowers comprise clusters
of pale brown spikelets, June–September.

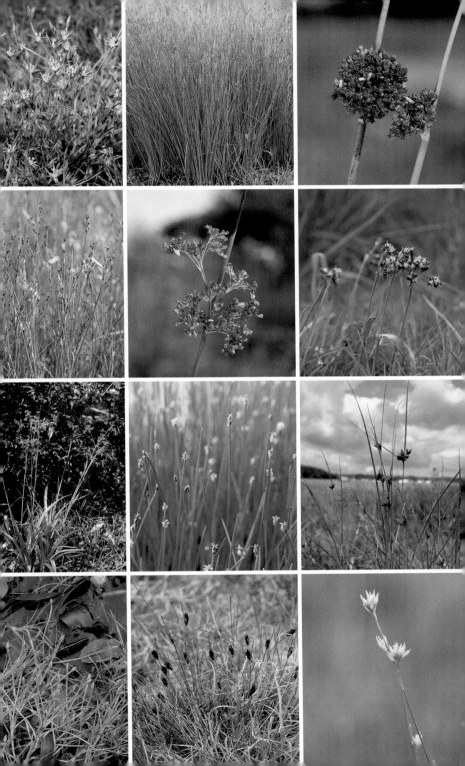

GRASSES, RUSHES AND SEDGES

LESSER POND SEDGE *Carex acutiformis*   Height up to 1.5m
Creeping, tuft-forming sedge that forms extensive carpets in marshes and around the margins of ponds. Widespread but scarce in lowland areas. Leaves long, blue-grey and rough. Flowers comprise 2–3 male spikes above 3–4 female spikes.

SAND SEDGE *Carex arenaria*   Height up to 35cm
Creeping perennial of sand dunes and locally common on many coasts. Progress of underground stems detected by aerial shoots that appear in straight lines. The leaves are wiry and the inflorescence comprises pale brown spikes, May–July.

COMMON YELLOW SEDGE *Carex demissa*   Height up to 40cm
Tufted plant of damp ground, usually on acid soils. Widespread but commonest in the N and W. Leaves narrow, curved and longer than the stems. The inflorescence comprises a terminal, stalked male spike above small clusters of female spikes.

GLAUCOUS SEDGE *Carex flacca*   Height up to 50cm
Common grassland sedge, often on base-rich soils. Widespread and locally common throughout. Leaves are pale green and stiff. 3-sided stems carry inflorescence which comprises 1–3 brown male spikes above 2–5 female spikes in April–May.

COMMON SEDGE *Carex nigra*   Height up to 50cm
Creeping sedge of damp grassland and marshes. Generally common. Long, narrow leaves appear in tufts. 3-sided stems are rough and taller than leaves. The inflorescence has 1–2 thin male spikes and 1–4 female spikes with black glumes.

FALSE FOX SEDGE *Carex otrubae*   Height up to 80cm
Tufted sedge of damp ground. Widespread but generally scarce. Leaves are stiff, upright and 5–10mm wide. Robust stems are rough and 3-sided. Inflorescence comprises a dense head of greenish brown spikes and a long bract.

TUSSOCK SEDGE *Carex paniculata*   Height up to 1m
Distinctive plant of marshes and fens, easily recognised throughout the year by the large tussocks that it forms. Widespread but rather scarce. The leaves are long and narrow and the inflorescence comprises pale brown spikes.

PENDULOUS SEDGE *Carex pendula*   Height up to 1.5m
Clump-forming sedge of damp woodlands on heavy soils. Widespread but rather scarce. Leaves long, yellowish and up to 2cm wide. Tall, 3-sided and often arched stems carry 1–2 male spikes above 4–5 long, drooping female spikes.

WOOD SEDGE *Carex sylvatica*   Height up to 50cm
Tufted sedge of damp woodlands. Widespread but generally scarce. Leaves are pale green, 3–6mm across and often appear rather drooping. The inflorescence comprises one terminal male spike and 3–5 slender, long-stalked female spikes.

PILL SEDGE *Carex pilulifera*   Height up to 25cm
Tufted sedge of heaths and dry grassland on acid soils. Widespread but local. Leaves yellowish green, narrow and wiry. Flower head with one male spike above cluster of egg-shaped female spikes with a long lower bract.

SAW OR GREAT FEN SEDGE *Cladium mariscus*   Height up to 2.5m
Imposing plant that sometimes forms dense stands in fens and around the margins of lakes. Locally common only in parts of NW Ireland. Leaves long, saw-edged; often bent at an angle. Flower head with clusters of brown spikelets.

COMMON REED *Phragmites communis*   Height up to 2m
Familiar perennial of damp ground, marshes and freshwater margins which often forms vast stands. Common throughout. Robust stems carry broad leaves and large, terminal clusters of flowers. Plants turn brown and persist through the winter.

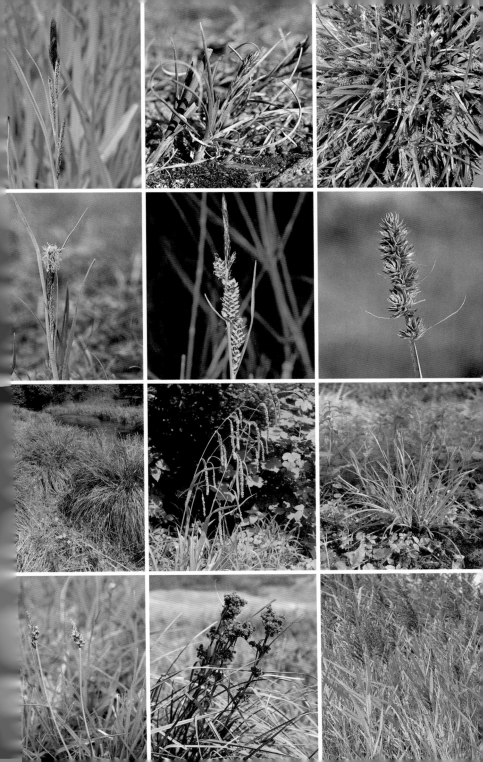

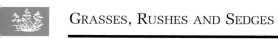

BRANCHED BUR-REED *Sparganium erectum* Height up to 1m
Sedge-like perennial found in still and slow-flowing fresh water. Locally common throughout. The bright green, linear leaves are keeled and triangular in cross-section. The spherical flower heads are borne in branched spikes, June–August.

GREAT REEDMACE *Typha latifolia* Height up to 2m
Impressive sedge-like plant of freshwater margins. Widespread and common. The leaves are grey-green, long and up to 2cm wide. Flower spikes comprise a brown, sausage-like array of female flowers and a narrow spire of males; seen June–August.

COMMON COTTONGRASS *Eriophorum angustifolium* Height up to 75cm
Distinctive perennial when in fruit. Favours very boggy ground with peaty, acid soils and locally common throughout. The leaves are dark green and narrow. The inflorescence comprises drooping, stalked spikelets. Fruits have cottony hairs.

HARE'S-TAIL COTTONGRASS *Eriophorum vaginatum* Height up to 50cm
Tussock-forming perennial of moors and heaths on acid, peaty soil. Widespread and locally common in N and W Ireland. Leaves very narrow. Upright, stalked flower spike emerges from inflated sheath. Fruits with cottony hairs.

PURPLE MOOR-GRASS *Molinia caerulea* Height up to 80cm
Tussock-forming perennial, usually associated with damp ground on acid heaths and moors. Widespread and locally common. The leaves are grey-green and 3–5mm wide. Purplish green flowers are borne in long, narrow spikes, July–September.

COMMON BENT *Agrostis gigantea* Height up to 1.5m
Widespread perennial of wasteground, verges and arable fields. Rather scarce and local. Leaves dark green, up to 6mm across with long ligules. Numerous 1-flowered, purplish brown spikelets borne in branching clusters, July–August.

CREEPING BENT *Agrostis stolonifera* Height up to 1m
Creeping perennial whose stems run along ground before becoming upright. Found on grassland and in waste places; widespread and common. Leaves have pointed ligules. Purplish 1-flowered spikelets appear June–August.

MARRAM GRASS *Ammophila arenaria* Height up to 1m
Familiar and widespread perennial of coastal dunes. Colonises and stabilises shifting sands by means of its underground stems. Leaves are tough, grey-green and rolled. Dense flower spikes, comprise 1-flowered spikelets; seen July–August.

SWEET VERNAL GRASS *Anthoxanthum odoratum* Height up to 50cm
Widespread and common perennial of grassland throughout the region; aromatic when dried. Leaves are flat and relatively broad. The inflorescence comprises a relatively dense, spike-like cluster of spikelets which flower April–July.

FALSE OAT-GRASS *Arrhenatherum elatius* Height up to 1.5m
Tall perennial of disturbed grassland, roadside verges and waysides generally. Widespread and very common throughout, except in uplands. Leaves are broad and long with a blunt ligule. The inflorescence is open and comprises numerous 2-flowered spikelets, one floral element of which has a long awn; May–September.

WILD OAT *Avena fatua* Height up to 1m
Distinctive annual weed of arable crops and also found growing on wasteground. Widespread and fairly common throughout. The leaves are dark green, broad and flat. The inflorescence is an open array of stalked, dangling spikelets each of which is shrouded by the glumes and has a long awn; flowers June–August.

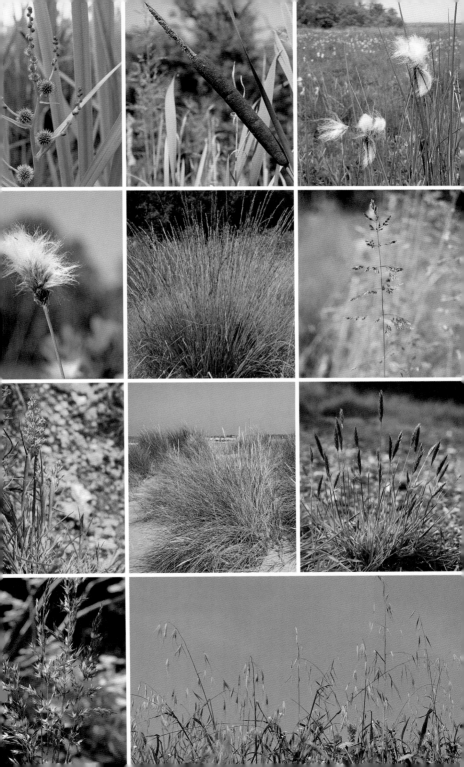

QUAKING GRASS *Briza media*   Height up to 40cm
Distinctive plant when in flower. Favours grassland, often on base-rich soils;
local and rather scarce. The pale green leaves form loose tufts. Narrow, wiry stalks
carry the inflorescence of flowers, June–September; this comprises dangling
spikelets that resemble miniature flattened hops or cones.

TUFTED HAIR-GRASS *Deschampsia cespitosa*   Height up to 1.5m
Tufted, clump-forming perennial of damp grassland, woodland rides and marshes.
Widespread and locally common throughout. The leaves are dark green, wiry and
narrow with rough edges. The inflorescences are borne on tall stems, June–July,
and comprise spreading clusters of 2-flowered, silvery-purple spikelets.

COCKSFOOT GRASS *Dactylis glomerata*   Height up to 1m
Tufted, tussock-forming perennial of grassland and woodland rides. Widespread
and often extremely common in most parts. Leaves rough with slightly inrolled
margins. Easiest to identify in flower, May–July: inflorescence has purplish,
rounded-stalked flower heads that spread and fancifully resemble a bird's foot.

WAVY HAIR-GRASS *Deschampsia flexuosa*   Height up to 1m
Tufted perennial of dry ground on heaths and moorland, usually on acid
soils. Widespread but rather scarce in Ireland. Leaves are inrolled and hair-like.
Inflorescence has open clusters of purplish spikelets, June–July.

SEA LYME GRASS *Elymus arenarius*   Height up to 1.5m
Blue-grey perennial of sand dunes and sandy beaches. Widespread but local near
coasts. Leaves up to 15mm across; margins are inrolled. Grey-green spikelets in
tall spikes, June–August.

RED FESCUE *Festuca rubra*   Height up to 50cm
Clump-forming grass found in grassy places throughout the region and often very
common. Dark green leaves are narrow, wiry and stiff. Inflorescence comprises
spikelets that are 7–10mm long and are usually reddish; flowers May–July.

VIVIPAROUS FESCUE *Festuca vivipara*   Height up to 40cm
Tufted plant of grassy places on moors and mountains. Widespread but local. The
leaves are thread-like and green. Instead of having flowers, stems produce tiny
plantlets that develop leaves and fall off to colonise new ground.

FLOATING SWEET-GRASS *Glyceria fluitans*   Floating
Aquatic grass of still and slow-flowing fresh water in lowland regions. Locally
common throughout. Broad, green leaves usually seen floating on water's surface.
Emergent inflorescence comprises an open array of narrow spikelets, May–August.

REED SWEET-GRASS *Glyceria maxima*   Height up to 2m
Impressive plant of shallow water and marshy ground; often forms large patches.
Widespread but local. Bright green leaves are long and 2cm across. Inflorescence
is large and much-branched with narrow spikelets; appears June–August.

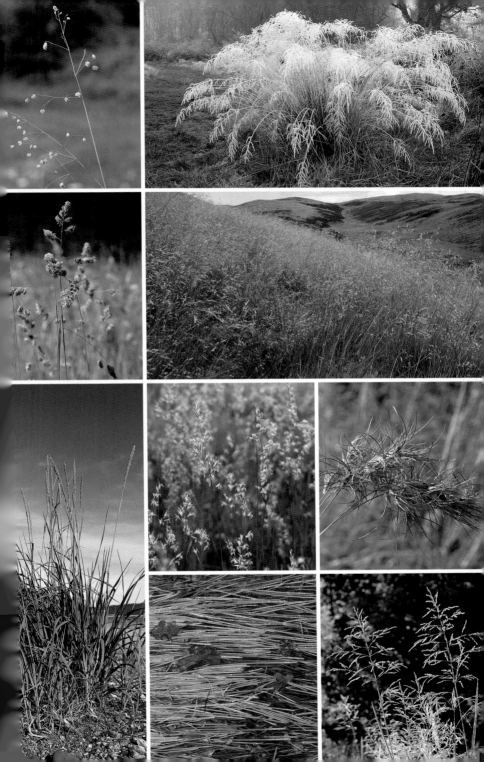

YORKSHIRE FOG *Holcus lanatus*   Height up to 1m
A tufted perennial that is grey-green and downy both on its leaves and stems. Widespread throughout the region and generally very common, favouring meadows, woodland rides and wasteground. Flower head tightly packed at first but then spreads; comprises reddish-tipped, grey-green, 2-flowered spikelets; May–August.

CREEPING SOFT-GRASS *Holcus mollis*   Height up to 60cm
Superficially rather similar to Yorkshire Fog but more slender and has stems which are hairy only at the pale joints. Found along woodland rides and on bare ground and heaths, usually on acid soils. Widespread and common in most parts. Flower head is purplish green and compact at first but spreads; appears June–August.

SAND CAT'S-TAIL *Phleum arenarium*   Height up to 30cm
A distinctive tufted annual grass of stabilised sand and shingle. Rather scarce and found very locally around the coasts of Ireland. The leaves are grey-green and flat. The inflorescence, which is borne on a long, straight and narrow stem, is a dense head of purplish or green spikelets; flowers May–June.

LESSER CAT'S-TAIL *Phleum bertelonii*   Height up to 60cm
Similar to Timothy and considered by some authorities to be a subspecies of this grass. Favours bare, grassy places, often on calcareous soils. Widespread and locally common except in the far N. The leaves are flat and grey-green. The inflorescence is a cylindrical head of spikelets, 6–8cm long; flowers June–July.

TIMOTHY GRASS *Phleum pratense*   Height up to 1.5m
Extremely common tufted perennial of meadows, agricultural land and waysides generally. Found throughout the region and often cultivated as a fodder plant. Leaves are grey-green and flat. Inflorescence 15–20cm long, dense and cylindrical; borne on a tall, slender stem and flowering June–August.

WOOD MELICK *Melica uniflora*   Height up to 50cm
A rather delicate, creeping perennial of dry, shady woodland, often on chalk and under beech. Widespread and locally common. The leaves are pale green and rather lax. The inflorescence is loose and open with brown spikelets along the side branches; flowers May–July.

ANNUAL MEADOW-GRASS *Poa annua*   Height up to 25cm
Extremely common annual or short-lived perennial grass found in bare grassland and on disturbed ground. Widespread throughout the region. The leaves are pale green, blunt-tipped and often wrinkled. Inflorescence is triangular in outline and comprises branches with oval spikelets at their tips; flowers all year.

BLUE MOOR GRASS *Sesleria albicans*   Height up to 45cm
A distinctive blue-green, tufted perennial found on dry grassland on limestone soils, sometimes forming large patches. Locally common only in W Ireland. Leaves are rather narrow. The inflorescence comprises a tightly-packed, ovoid head of blue-green spikelets which flower April–June.

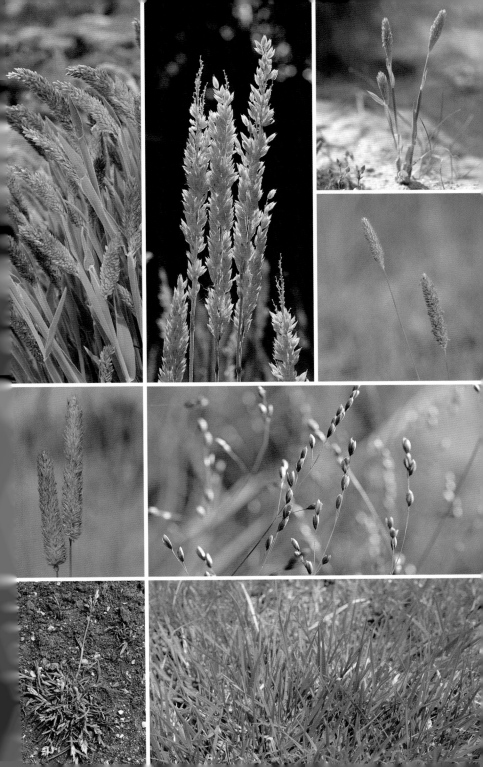

BRACKEN *Pteridium aquilinum*   Height up to 2m or more
The commonest fern in the region; carpets woodland floors and covers hillsides. Favours dry, acid soils. Compact, curled-tipped fronds appear in spring. Mature fronds are green and 3-times pinnate. Spore cases borne around leaf margins.

BRITTLE BLADDER FERN *Cystopteris fragilis*   Frond length up to 40cm
A delicate fern that grows in tufts arising from crevices in rocks and stone walls, mostly on limestone. Local and scattered. The leaves are 2–3-times pinnate and appear April–October. Spore cases are rounded.

BROAD BUCKLER FERN *Dryopteris dilitata*   Frond length up to 1m
Robust fern, widespread and common in Ireland, favouring damp woods, heaths and mountain slopes, usually on acid soils. Fronds are dark green and 3-times pinnately divided, the stalks with dark-centred scales; April–November.

HAY-SCENTED FERN *Dryopteris aemula*   Frond length up to 50cm
Locally common only in W Ireland. Favours W-facing slopes and damp valleys. Fresh green fronds smell of hay when crushed; remain green through winter; 3-times pinnately divided with pale brown scales on stalk.

MALE-FERN *Dryopteris filix-mas*   Frond length up to 1.25m
Large, clump-forming fern of woods and banks. Common and widespread throughout. Fronds remain green through winter; broadly oval in outline, 2-times pinnately divided and with pale brown scales on stalk. Spore cases round, August–October.

SCALY MALE-FERN *Dryopteris affinis*   Frond length up to 1m
Locally common in Ireland. Favours shady woods, usually on acid soils. The yellow-green fronds do not overwinter. Stalks have orange-brown scales; margins of smaller frond lobes look as though cut neatly with scissors.

MAIDENHAIR FERN *Adiantum capillus-veneris*   Frond length up to 15cm
Charming and distinctive fern of sheltered sea cliffs, mostly on limestone. Scarce in W Ireland. Fronds are 2–3-times pinnately divided into fan-shaped lobes that are borne on slender, black stalks; these have scales at the base.

ROYAL FERN *Osmunda regalis*   Frond length up to 3m
Large and impressive fern, found in damp shady places. Fronds are 2-times pinnate and form a large clump; central fronds are covered in spores and turn brown, resembling flower spikes. Widespread in Ireland, commonest in W.

HARD FERN *Blechnum spicant*   Frond length up to 60cm
Distinctive fern of woods and shady heaths on acid soils that is locally common throughout. Bright green, sterile, overwintering fronds are 1-pinnate and form spreading clumps. Fertile fronds are borne upright and have very narrow lobes.

HART'S-TONGUE FERN *Phyllitis scolopendrium*   Frond length up to 60cm
Evergreen fern of damp, shady woods and banks. Fairly widespread and common in Ireland. Fresh green, undivided fronds are strap-like and form clumps. Dark brown spore cases are borne in rows on underside of fronds.

LADY FERN *Athyrium filix-femina*   Frond length up to 1.5m
Large but rather delicate fern, forming large clumps in damp woods and on banks and hillsides. Widespread and fairly common throughout. Fronds are pale green and 2-times pinnately divided. The spore cases are curved and ripen in autumn.

PARSLEY FERN *Cryptogramma crispa*   Frond length up to 25cm
Parsley-like fern which grows among rocks on mountain slopes, mostly on acid rocks. Local and scarce in NE. Pale green fronds form clustered tufts; stalks have basal scales.

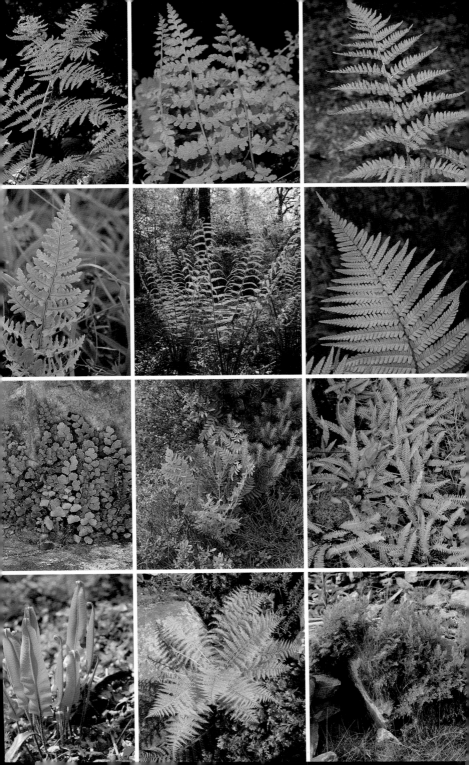

POLYPODY FERN *Polypodium vulgare*   Frond length up to 50cm
Characteristic fern of damp, shady gorges and banks in woods and valleys, mostly on acid soils. Widespread and common in Ireland. The dark green, leathery fronds are 1-pinnate on slender stalks. Appear in May and overwinter.

RUSTY-BACK FERN *Ceterach officinarum*   Frond length up to 20cm
Distinctive fern of stone walls and rocks. Widespread and generally common in Ireland. The dark green fronds are pinnately divided into rounded lobes and form tufted clumps; underside covered in rusty-brown scales.

MAIDENHAIR SPLEENWORT *Asplenium trichomanes*   Frond length up to 20cm
Attractive little fern of rocky places and stone walls. Evergreen fronds comprise oval pinnae borne either side of a blackish midrib. Widespread and generally common.

WALL-RUE *Asplenium ruta-muraria*   Frond length up to 12cm
Delicate little fern found growing on stone walls and rocks, often in areas of limestone. Widespread and common in Ireland. Evergreen fronds dull green and 2-times pinnately divided into oval lobes with spores beneath.

ADDER'S-TONGUE FERN *Ophioglossum vulgatum*
                                    Height up to 20cm, often shorter
Intriguing fern found growing in damp, undisturbed grassland and dune-slacks. Widespread but local and seldom common. Frond is bright green, oval and borne upright on a short stalk. Spores are borne terminally on a tall fertile spike.

MOONWORT *Botrychium lunaria*   Height up to 20cm
Unusual fern of grassy moors, mountain slopes and undisturbed meadows. Widespread but seldom common. The single stalk bears a solitary frond, pinnately divided into 3–9 rounded lobes. Spores are borne on a divided, fertile spike.

STAG'S-HORN CLUBMOSS *Lycopodium clavatum*   Height up to 10cm
Creeping evergreen with long, trailing stems; these and the branched, fancifully antler-like, upright stems cloaked in pointed, scale-like leaves. Cones borne on long stalks. Local and scarce on moors and mountains.

FIR CLUBMOSS *Huperzia selago*   Height up to 10cm
Tufted, upright clubmoss with stems cloaked in green, needle-like leaves giving it more than a passing resemblance to a young conifer. Spore cases borne on stem. Favours dry, grassy moors and upland slopes. Rather scarce.

Dicranella heteromalla   Height up to 3cm
A widespread and often extremely common moss found on bare ground on tracks and along woodland rides; favours neutral to acid soils. The leaves are narrow, slightly curved and pointed. The ripe capsule is brown and held at an angle.

LAWN MOSS *Caligeron cuspidatum*   Height up to 4cm
Widespread and common moss of both dry grassland and in damp ground such as lawns. Typically appears yellow-green and has pointed tips to the shoots. Leaves, pressed together when young, can give it a rather bedraggled appearance.

CATHERINE'S MOSS *Atrichium undulatum*   Height up to 5cm
Common and widespread moss of woodlands, found on most soil types except chalk. The long, narrow leaves are dark green and have wavy, toothed-edged margins. The curved, brown spore capsules are borne on long stalks and are held at an angle.

Eurhynchium praelongum   Spreading
An extremely common moss of shady woodlands in most parts; often found growing at the base of tree trunks or on ancient banks. Forms tangled, spreading mats with much-branched stems. Yellowish leaves larger on main stems than near tips.

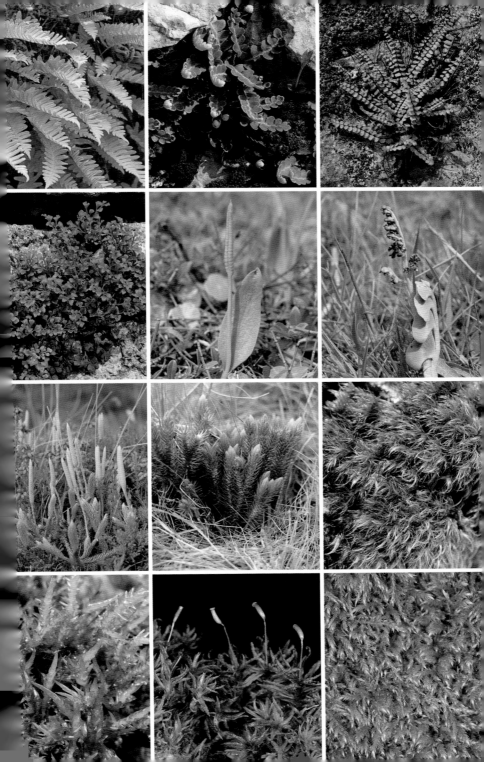

Brachythecium rutabulum   Height up to 4cm
Extremely common lawn moss on damp ground but also found growing in woodland and on banks. Branching stems are covered with shiny, oval, pointed leaves; usually dark green but can be tinged yellow. Capsule curved and long-stalked.

Bryum capillare   Height up to 3cm
A common and widespread moss that forms compact and distinctive cushions on roofs and walls. The oval leaves are tipped with a fine point. The elongate-ovoid spore capsules are long-stalked and drooping; green ripening to brown.

Fissidens taxifolius   Height up to 2cm
A moss of damp, shady places. Forms straggly masses. The stems carry oval, pointed-tipped leaves which are usually more-or-less in one plane, creating a yew-like appearance. Narrow spore capsules are borne on stalks arising near plant base.

Grimmia pulvinata   Height up to 3cm
Common and widespread, especially in limestone areas. Forms compact cushions. The leaves are narrow and grey green; the greyish, pointed tips can sometimes give whole cushion a silvery appearance, especially in dry weather.

Homalothecium sericeum   Height up to 2cm
A common and widespread moss. The stems are much-branched and mat-forming, covered with narrow, finely-tipped leaves which have a rather glossy appearance. In dry weather, the plant stems curl and turn brown.

Hypnum cupressiforme   Spreading
Common and widespread. Forms flattened clusters or mats at the base of tree trunks, but also occurs on walls and boulders. The stems are covered with overlapping, curved leaves that are oval and pointed. The spore capsule is borne on a short stalk.

Leucobryum glaucum   Height up to 4cm
Distinctive moss of damp woodland and moors. It often forms large cushions on the ground. Leaves are narrow and grey-green but become almost white in dry weather. Larger specimens of cushions may become eroded towards the centre.

Polytrichum commune   Height up to 20cm
Upright moss of moorland and acid woodland. Needle-like leaves are pointed and held almost at right-angles to the stems, giving a rather clubmoss-like appearance. Box-shaped spore capsules are brown when ripe and held on tall, slender stems.

WOOLLY HAIR MOSS *Racomitrum lanuginosum*   Height up to 2cm
Locally dominant moss of mountain tops. Where not trampled, it is a spreading plant that sometimes forms deep carpets. Long, branched stems are covered with narrow, grey-green leaves that are tipped with a white, hair-like point.

SPHAGNUM MOSS *Sphagnum sp.*   Height up to 5cm
Collection of difficult to distinguish species of bog mosses, most of which favour wet, peaty ground. It can sometimes be picked out at a distance by the fresh green colour of its leaves. The leaf tips become recurved when dry.

Thuidium tamariscinum   Spreading
Fresh green fronds are 3-times pinnately divided, in one plane, creating a fern-like appearance. Main stems are dark. Typically found in woodlands, where it grows beside fallen branches and among leaf-litter; widespread and common in most parts.

Tortula muralis   Height up to 1cm
Widespread and common moss of old brick walls. Forms low, spreading, cushions. Oval, rounded-tipped leaves end in a fine point. Spore capsules are narrow and held upright, borne on long, slender stalks; they are yellow when young but ripen brown.

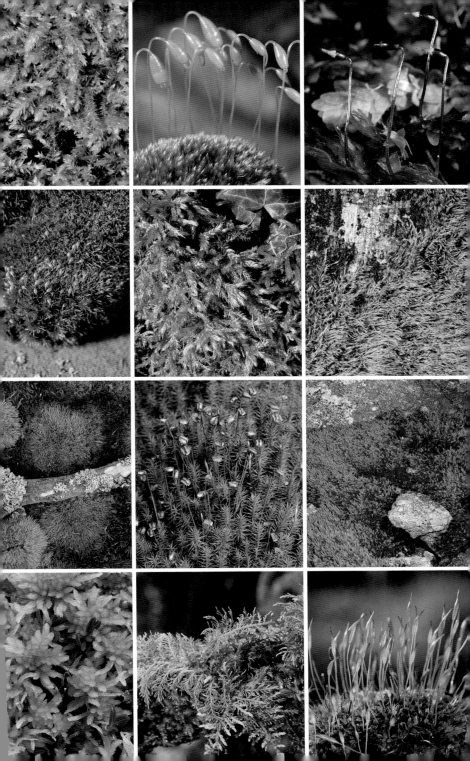

Lophocolea heterophylla   Spreading
A superficially moss-like liverwort that is found growing on the bark of living trees
and fallen branches. Widespread and common in deciduous woodland habitats
throughout. Stems branching and trailing, up to 2cm long. Leaves in two forms, the
smaller leaves being almost hidden by larger, toothed-tipped, overlapping ones.

Anthoceros laevis   Spreading
A common and widespread liverwort of damp ground, often found on shady banks
beside woodland streams and ditches. The plant comprises a broad and flattened
thallus with lobed margins; it is often divided with the lobes overlapping one
another and the surface is minutely pitted. Attached by rootlets to the ground.

Conocephalus conicum   Spreading
A large, carpeting liverwort which is widespread and common on damp rocks
and stones, often in or beside woodland streams and rivers. The plant comprises
a broad or narrow fleshy thallus that is dark green, sometimes up to 15cm long;
lobes often overlap. On close inspection, thallus surface marked with pale dots.

Marchantia polymorpha   Spreading
A common and widespread liverwort found typically on the shady banks of
streams and rivers but also frequently found growing on well-watered compost of
potted garden-centre plants. It comprises a divided, dark green thallus, the lobes
of which often overlap one another. Surface bears shallow cups and umbrella-
shaped reproductive structures: female stalked and rayed and male toadstool-like.

Metzgeria furcata   Spreading
A common and widespread liverwort, found growing on tree trunks, rocks and
walls in shady places throughout the region. The plant comprises a long, narrow
thallus that is barely 2mm wide. It is only one cell thick except for the midrib,
which is thickened, giving it a superficial resemblance to a miniature seaweed.

Plagiochila asplenioides   Spreading
A delicate, leafy liverwort which is found growing on damp, shady banks; it is
widespread and fairly common. Oval, overlapping leaves are borne in two rows on
a thickened stem; plant resembles a miniature version of Maidenhair Spleenwort.

Pellia epiphylla   Spreading
Familiar, patch-forming liverwort of damp, shady banks, often beside streams.
Common and widespread. The broad, flattened and branched thallus has a thick-
ened midrib. Round, black and shiny capsules, on green stalks, appear in spring.

Caloplaca marina   Encrusting
Bright orange lichen forming irregular patches up to 5cm across on rocks around
high-water mark on the seashore. Tolerant of salt spray and brief immersion in
seawater. Widespread around coasts of Ireland.

TREE LUNGWORT *Lobaria pulmonaria*   Spreading
Large, lobed lichen of woodlands in areas of high rainfall and low pollution. Grows
attached to the bark of trees and forms spreading sheets, pitted with depressions.

Cladonia impexa   Spreading
A common lichen of heaths and moors. Comprises a tangled network of hollow,
branched stems that sometimes form dense, thick cushions or mats where not
trampled. These are found growing in amongst the stems of plants such as Ling.

Cladonia floerkeana   Spreading
Familiar lichen of bare peaty ground on heaths and moors. Widespread and locally
common. Forms an encrusting patch of greyish white scales from which granular,
scale-encrusted stalks arise, topped with bright red, spore-producing bodies.

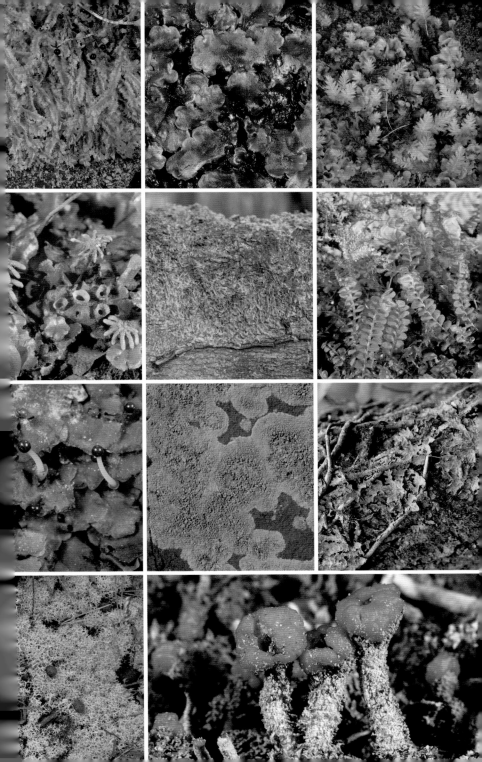

Graphis scripta   Up to 15mm across
A distinctive, encrusting lichen found on the bark of deciduous trees including hazel and ash. It forms an irregularly rounded patch that is blue-grey or green-grey in colour. Over the surface of this are spore-producing structures in the form of black lines and scribbles that, on close inspection, are slit-like.

Hypogymnia physodes   Up to 25mm across
A common lichen in most parts of Ireland. Often found growing on twigs and branches but also on rocks and walls. Although much-branched, forms an encrusting, irregularly rounded patch, smooth and grey on the upper surface.

BLACK SHIELDS LICHEN *Lecanora atra*   Spreading
A patch-forming lichen that is found encrusting boulders and rocks on the seashore, at and just above the high-tide mark; not surprisingly, it is tolerant of salt spray. Also grows on walls inland. The surface is knobbly and grey while the spore-producing structures are rounded and black with pale grey margins.

CRAB-EYE LICHEN *Ochrolechia parella*   Spreading
Encrusting, patch-forming lichen found on walls and rocks. Surface is greyish with a pale margin. Clusters of raised, rounded and flat-topped spore-producing structures give rise to its common English name.

Parmelia caperata   Spreading
An encrusting lichen which is found growing on the bark of mature trees. Widespread and fairly common. Patches are grey-green and comprise rounded, often overlapping lobes; surface has brown, flat-topped, spore-producing discs.

Placynthium nigrum   Spreading
An encrusting, patch-forming lichen that is found growing on limestone as well as on weathered concrete. The surface is black and granular, and often faintly cracked in places. This species' colour and irregular shape give it a passing resemblance to a splash of black paint. It is widespread and locally common.

SEA IVORY *Ramalina siliquosa*   Tufts up to 3cm long
A tufted and branched lichen which is found on coastal rocks and stone walls. It grows well above the high-tide mark but is still very tolerant of salt spray. Widespread around most coasts but particularly abundant in W. The branches are flattened and grey, and bear disc-like spore-producing bodies.

MAP LICHEN *Rhizocarpon geographicum*   Spreading
An aptly named, encrusting lichen found on rocks in uplands and mountains. The surface is yellowish and etched with black spore-producing bodies. When two neighbouring colonies meet, the boundaries between them are defined by their black margins, creating a map-like appearance. The effect is further enhanced if map lichen colonies adjoin lichen species whose surfaces are a different colour.

YELLOW SCALES LICHEN *Xanthoria parietina*   Spreading
Arguably the most familiar and certainly most colourful coastal lichen, which forms bright orange-yellow patches on rocks, walls and brickwork near the sea. The surface of the encrustation comprises leafy, narrow scales that are rather wrinkled. Yellow Scales is widespread around coasts of Ireland.

Verrucaria maura   Spreading
An encrusting lichen that is found growing on rocks and stabilised shingle around the coasts of Ireland. It is often found just above the barnacle zone and is tolerant of periodic immersion in seawater as well as salt spray. The surface is sooty black and covered with a delicate network of cracks. As a sad indictment of modern times, this species is sometimes mistaken for oil.

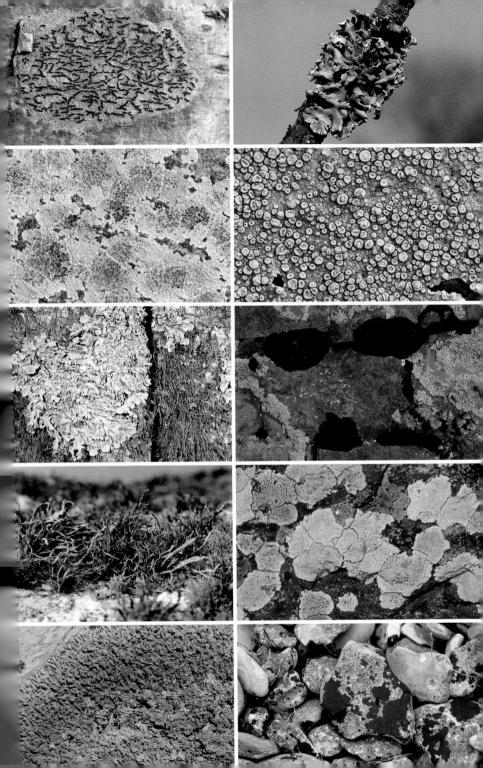

EGG WRACK *Ascophyllum nodosum* Length up to 1.5m
Found on sheltered rocky shores where it grows between the upper- and middle-shore levels. Widespread around the coasts of Ireland and is sometimes abundant in suitable habitats. The long, greenish stems, are tough, leathery and flat. Air bladders are found at regular intervals along the stems, which also branch repeatedly. The yellowish green reproductive bodies resemble sultanas.

GUTWEED *Enteromorpha intestinalis* Length up to 75cm or more
An aptly-named seaweed found in sheltered estuaries, brackish lagoons and rock pools on the upper shore. The fronds are membranous and green, and comprise long tubes that soon become inflated; these are occasionally constricted along their length, adding to their already gut-like appearance. Sometimes attached to the substrate by a holdfast but often detached and then forming floating masses.

SERRATED WRACK *Fucus serratus* Length up to 65cm
Common and widespread seaweed around the coasts of Ireland, which grows attached to rocks on the lower middle shore. Fronds are greenish brown and flattened, but with a distinct midrib; they branch regularly along their length and have margins that are diagnostically toothed or serrated. Air bladders are absent. The reproductive bodies are found in pitted, swollen tips to the fronds.

SPIRAL WRACK *Fucus spiralis* Length up to 35cm
A familiar seaweed found growing attached to rocks on the upper shore. Common and widespread around the coasts of Ireland but absent from the most exposed shores. The frond branches regularly along its length and is typically twisted in a spiral fashion towards the tip; the margin is not serrated and the species lacks air bladders. Rounded reproductive bodies are found at frond tips.

BLADDER WRACK *Fucus vesiculosus* Length up to 1m
A tough seaweed that is found growing, attached to rocks, on the middle shore. It is widespread and common around the coasts of Ireland although often absent from the most exposed sites. The frond is olive- or greenish brown and branches regularly. Air bladders are found in groups of two or three along the seaweed's length and spongy reproductive bodies occur at the tips of the fronds.

THONGWEED *Himanthalia elongata* Length up to 2m
A distinctive seaweed that starts life as a short button-shaped structure found growing from the holdfast attached to rocks on the lower shore. Later in the season, a long, slightly flattened and strap-like frond develops, this being forked only towards the tapering tip; the frond colour is olive-green. Thongweed is widespread and common on Irish coasts.

KELP *Laminaria digitata* Length up to 1m
An impressive seaweed that often forms dense beds on the lower shore with only the floating fronds, and not the stipe, exposed at most low tides. It is olive-brown and comprises a branched and tough holdfast, home to small marine animals, a robust, flexible stipe, and a broad blade, divided into strap-like fronds.

CHANNELED WRACK *Pelvetia canaliculata* Length up to 15cm
A distinctive seaweed that forms a zone on the upper shore around rocky coasts. Fronds are olive-brown and much branched. Inrolled margins help conserve water when seaweed is exposed to air for long periods at neap tides. The species lacks air bladders; reproductive bodies at frond tips. Widespread and mostly common.

SEA LETTUCE *Ulva lactuca* Length up to 40cm
Delicate green and membranous seaweed that is found growing attached to rocks on sheltered shores; often thrives in rockpools on upper and middle shores, even if detached from substrate. The seaweed's precise shape can be difficult to determine because of its often-tattered appearance. Tolerates brackish water.

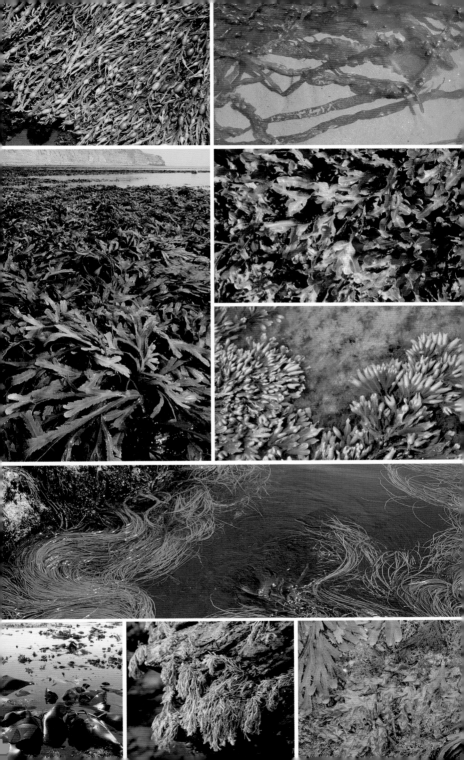

ORANGE PEEL *Aleuria aurantia*   Up to 8cm across
Extremely distinctive fungus that comprises a wavy-edge, saucer-shaped disc.
Upper surface is bright orange and smooth while the lower surface is greyish orange
and rather powdery. Grows on bare ground, September–November. Widespread.

WHITE HELVELLA *Helvella crispa*   Height up to 15cm
Unusual-looking fungus with a strangely convoluted and distorted cap resembling
melted plastic. Cap is creamy white and is usually slightly paler than the stem
which is greyish white and deeply furrowed. Found on rides and verges in autumn.

CANDLE SNUFF *Xylaria hypoxylon*   Height up to 5cm
Widespread and common fungus in deciduous woodlands. Flattened, antler-shaped
stems arise from dead wood; they start off white but gradually blacken as they
mature. Usually found in clusters on stumps. Can be found throughout the year.

KING ALFRED'S CAKES *Daldinia concentrica*   Up to 5cm across
Forms hard, knobbly balls on the bark of dead and dying branches of deciduous
trees, particularly on Ash. Surface is usually shiny black and the fungus is
brittle. Concentric rings revealed in cross-section. Widespread. Found all year.

ORANGE-SPOT FUNGUS *Nectria cinnabarina*   Up to 2mm across
Tiny but distinctive fungus that forms clusters of orange-pink inflated cushions
and cinnabar-red lumps on the dead and dying twigs and branches of deciduous
trees. It is widespread and often very common; can be found throughout the year.

BIRCH POLYPORE *Piptoporus betulinus*   Up to 20cm across
Familiar bracket fungus that is found exclusively on the trunks of birch trees. The
fungus is semi-circular and up to 4cm thick. The upper surface is buffish brown
while the underside is white with tiny pores. Widespread. Found all year.

MANY-ZONED POLYPORE *Coriolus versicolor*   Up to 7cm across
Extremely common bracket fungus that grows on dead stumps and fallen branches
of deciduous trees, often in tiers. Each bracket is semi-circular; upper surface is
zoned with concentric rings of different colours. Widespread. Found all year.

CHANTERELLE *Cantharellus cibarius*   Height up to 10cm
Well-known autumn fungus. Edible and delicious, smelling of apricots. The cap is
bright yellow and rounded at first but becoming funnel-shaped with age. Gill-like
ribs run down stem, which is short and tapering. Locally common in woodland.

BLUSHING BRACKET *Daedaleopsis confragosa*   Up to 18cm across
Widespread and common bracket fungus on dead branches of willow, Sallow and
birch. Upper surface is concentrically zoned with brown and buff. Underside has
white pores that bruise reddish and darken with age. Found September–November.

DRYAD'S SADDLE *Polyporus squamosus*   Up to 50cm across
Imposing and often massive polypore fungus that forms tiered brackets on Ash,
elms and other deciduous trees. Appears June–September. Upper surface is creamy
buff, covered in dark brown scales. Lower surface creamy white with large pores.

HAIRY STEREUM *Stereum hirsutum*   Up to 4cm across
Forms irregular tiers of rubbery but tough brackets that have wavy margins and
are about 1mm thick. Although variable, lower surface colour is usually orange-
yellow; upper surface greyish and hairy. Widespread on dead wood. All year.

Crepidotus variabilis   Up to 3cm across
Widespread and fairly common woodland fungus that forms kidney-shaped brackets on fallen twigs and other debris from deciduous trees. The upper surface is pale
cream and downy while the lower surface has pale gills which become pink-buff.

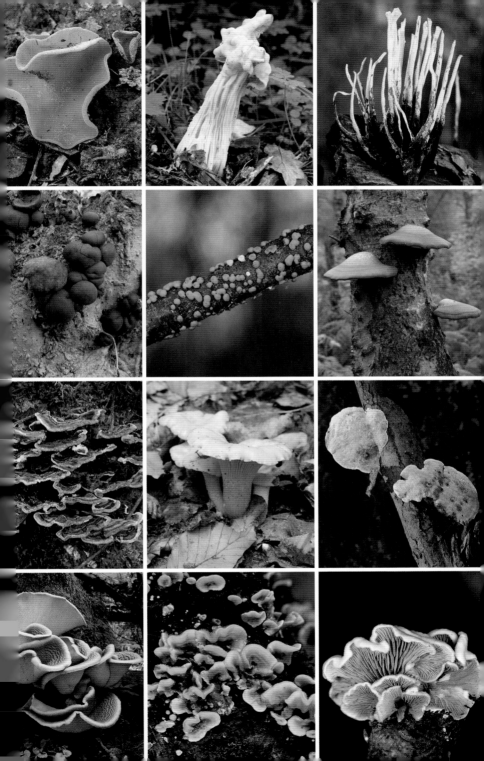

OYSTER FUNGUS *Pleurotus ostreatus*　　　　　　　　Up to 13cm across
Edible and delicious fungus that forms tiers of brackets on the trunks of Beech
and other deciduous trees. The upper surface is greyish buff and smooth while
the lower surface has whitish gills. Widespread and locally common in autumn.

HONEY FUNGUS *Armillaria mellea*　　　　　　　　　Height up to 15cm
Widespread and common woodland fungus found on tree stumps; also parasitises
living trees, sometimes killing them. Cap brown and slightly scaly; domed but
expands and flattens with age. Gills pale buff. Stem has a ring. Appears autumn.

WOOD BLEWITS *Lepista nuda*　　　　　　　　　　　Height up to 8cm
Edible fungus found in deciduous woodlands and hedgerows. The cap is smooth
and buffish lilac; conical at first but expands and flattens irregularly with age.
The gills are lilac-purple and the stem is streaked lilac. Widespread in autumn.

CLOUDED AGARIC *Clitocybe nebularis*　　　　　　　Height up to 12cm
Widespread and common fungus of deciduous woodland; appears October–November. Cap is blue-grey, usually paler towards the edges, rounded at first but flattens
with age. The gills are creamy and decurrent and the stem expands towards base.

DECEIVER *Laccaria laccata*　　　　　　　　　　　　Height up to 8cm
Variable fungus found among leaf litter in deciduous and coniferous woodlands,
July–October. Widespread and common. Cap usually orange-brown and irregularly
rounded. Gills pinkish buff and stem twisted, fibrous and concolorous with cap.

AMETHYST DECEIVER *Laccaria amethystea*　　　　　Height up to 9cm
Attractive fungus of deciduous woodland leaf litter that is wholly lilac or purple. Widespread and locally common. Cap domed at first; expands and flattens
irregularly with age. Gills widely spaced. Twisted stem has white basal hairs.

BUTTER CAP *Collybia butyracea*　　　　　　　　　Height up to 8cm
Most easily identified by cap's greasy, buttery texture. Widespread and common
in both deciduous and coniferous woodland. Gills and flesh are whitish. Tough
stem is pale brown, tapers upwards and is bulbous at the base. Appears autumn.

FAIRY-RING CHAMPIGNON *Marasmius oreades*　　　Height up to 10cm
Typical ring-forming fungus, these being found on lawns and grassland. Cap is
usually pale buffish tan but is sometimes stained darker. Gills white and widely
spaced and flesh is white. Stem concolorous with cap. Widespread in autumn.

PORCELAIN FUNGUS *Oudemansiella mucida*　　　　Up to 7cm across
Distinctive fungus that is white, slimy and translucent. Found growing on dying
and fallen branches of deciduous trees, mainly Beech; attached by slender stem
of variable length. Gills are widely spaced. Widespread, September–November.

FLY AGARIC *Amanita muscaria*　　　　　　　　　Height up to 20cm
A familiar toadstool. Widespread and common, always associated with birches and
found on heaths and in mixed woodland. Red cap is covered with white flecks. Gills
white and stem white with a ring. Occurs in troops, August–November. Poisonous.

FALSE DEATH CAP *Amanita citrina*　　　　　　　　Height up to 8cm
Widespread and fairly common fungus of deciduous woodland, often under
Beech. Cap is whitish or yellowish but often bears tatty remains of veil. Gills white
and flesh white, smelling of raw potatoes. Stem has ring and is swollen at base.

TAWNY GRISETTE *Amanita fulva*　　　　　　　　　Height up to 12cm
Distinctive autumn fungus that is found growing in deciduous woodlands, often
under oaks. Tawny brown cap is sometimes marked with radial streaks around
the margin. Gills and flesh white. Stem, which has no ring, is tall. Widespread.

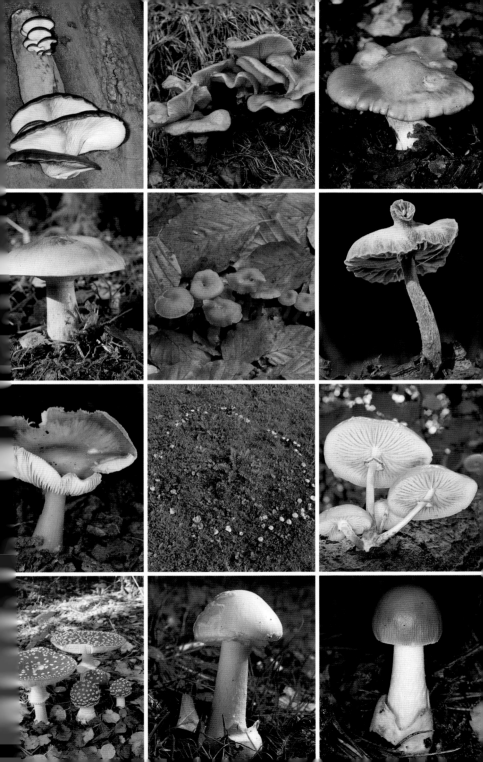

DEATH CAP *Amanita phalloides*   Height up to 10cm
Highly poisonous fungus. Appears September–November in deciduous woods, mainly under Beech or oaks. Has a sickly sweet smell. Cap is tinged green. Gills and flesh white. White stem has a ring; base surrounded by sac-like volva. Widespread.

THE BLUSHER *Amanita rubescens*   Height up to 15cm
Widespread and common fungus of deciduous woodland, which appears August–October. Cap is pale buffish brown and covered with pinkish grey fragments of veil. Gills white. Stem has a ring and usually flushes pinkish buff.

Volvariella speciosa   Height up to 12cm
Superficially mushroom-like species. Locally abundant on manure-enriched fields and other fertile sites, July–September. Cap is sticky when wet; domed at first but flattens with age. Gills are pink and stem has a swollen base. Widespread.

PARASOL MUSHROOM *Lepiota procera*   Height up to 30cm
Large and familiar fungus, found in grassy places July–October. Cap is pale buff and marked with brown scales; egg-shaped when young but flattens with age. Gills white and stem brown with scale-like patterns. Edible and good. Widespread.

Lepiota mastoidea   Height up to 25cm
Similar to closely related Parasol Mushroom but stem is cleaner-looking. Widespread but rather scarce, found in grassy woodland rides and field edges. Pale cap is marked with brown scales, densest at centre. Gills white. Appears in autumn.

WOOD MUSHROOM *Agaricus silvicola*   Height up to 10cm
Edible and delicious mushroom found in both deciduous and coniferous woodland, September–November. Smells of aniseed. Cap smooth and white but bruises yellow. Gills and flesh are pinkish. Stem has ring and bulbous base. Locally common.

FIELD MUSHROOM *Agaricus campestris*   Height up to 8cm
Familiar mushroom of pastures and grassland generally, appearing July–October. Cap is pale buffish brown and gills pink at first but darken brown. Flesh smells mushroomy. Stem has a ring that is easily lost. Widespread and locally common.

SHAGGY INK CAP *Coprinus comatus*   Height up to 30cm
Distinctive fungus, seen in troops on roadside verges and other grassy places, August–October. At first, cap egg-shaped and whitish with shaggy fibres; shrouds stem. Expands with age and, together with gills, blackens and liquefies. Common.

SULPHUR TUFT *Hypholoma fasciculare*   Height up to 8cm
Extremely common and widespread fungus, often found growing in large clumps on the dead stumps and fallen branches of deciduous trees. Appears June–November. Cap sulphur-yellow, darker in centre. Gills and flesh yellow. Stem often curved.

Panaeolus sphinctrinus   Height up to 10cm
Locally common fungus found growing on dung or manure-enriched ground. Appears almost throughout the year. Cap is conical and grey-brown but pale buff when dry; margin fringed with veil 'teeth'. Stem slender and brown.

CEP *Boletus edulis*   Height up to 25cm
Edible and delicious fungus, found in deciduous woodland, usually under oaks or Beech, August–November. Cap is brown and often dimpled and lobed. Pores are white at first, becoming creamy or yellow. Stem is fat and bulbous. Widespread.

RED-CRACKED BOLETE *Boletus chrysenteron*   Height up to 10cm
Distinctive fungus of deciduous woodland, widespread and locally common August–November. The cap is buffish brown at first but soon cracks, especially around the margins, to reveal red flesh. Pores buffish yellow. Stem flushed red.

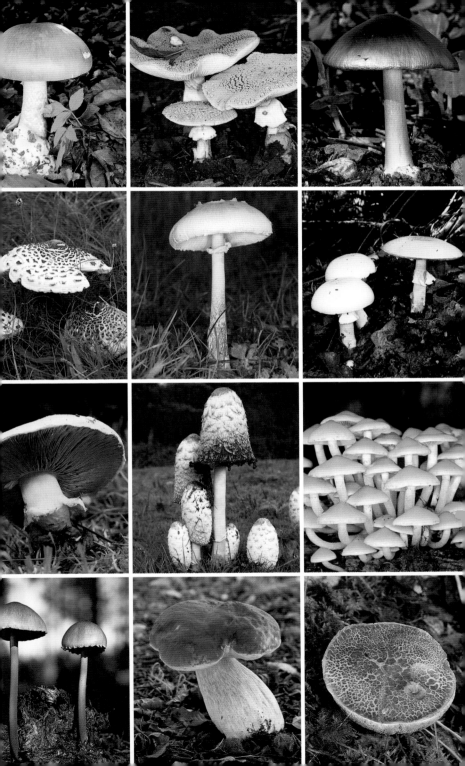

BAY BOLETE *Boletus badius* Height up to 15cm
Widespread and fairly common fungus of both deciduous and coniferous woodland. Appears September–November. Cap colour ranges from tan to buff. Pores are yellow but bruise bluish green. White flesh flushes blue when cut. Stem often tapers.

ORANGE BIRCH BOLETE *Leccinum versipelle* Height up to 25cm
Impressive fungus, almost always associated with birches and seen August–November. Cap is orange-brown and domed; margin sometimes overlaps pores which are greyish white. Flesh white but blackens when cut. Stem white with dark scales.

Suillus variegatus Height up to 12cm
Widespread and locally common fungus, restricted to conifer woodlands; appears September–November. Cap is brown and domed at first but flattens irregularly with age; slightly scaly but slimy when wet. Pores dark brown. Stem yellowish.

COMMON YELLOW RUSSULA *Russula ochroleuca* Height up to 10cm
Colourful and very common fungus, found mostly in deciduous woods. Cap is uniformly ochre-yellow; domed at first but flattening with age. Gills and flesh are white. Stem white and straight. Appears September–November.

BRIGHT YELLOW RUSSULA *Russula claroflava* Height up to 9cm
Common fungus in deciduous woods, mostly associated with birches. Cap is bright yellow and smooth but margins sometimes grooved. Gills and stem are off-white; flesh is white. Widespread, appearing August–November.

BLACKISH-PURPLE RUSSULA *Russula atropurpurea* Height up to 9cm
Widespread and common fungus of deciduous woodland, found mostly under oaks or Beech. Cap colour usually grades from almost black in centre to reddish purple around edge. Gills off-white; stem and flesh white. Appears September–November.

SICKENER *Russula emetica* Height up to 8cm
Colourful fungus of conifer woodlands, which, as its name suggests, is poisonous. Widespread and locally common, appearing September–November. Cap is bright red; domed at first but flattened later. Gills creamy white; stem and flesh white.

STINKING RUSSULA *Russula foetans* Height up to 14cm
Widespread and common fungus, found in conifer and deciduous woodland, August–November. Cap is dirty yellow and extremely slimy and sticky when young. Often has debris stuck to cap. Creamy gills often blotched; stem stout. Rancid smell.

ROSE RUSSULA *Russula rosea* Height up to 7cm
An attractive fungus found growing in deciduous woodland, appearing September–November. Cap is pale rose-pink, the margins lined in older specimens. The gills are creamy white. Flesh and stem are whitish. Widespread and generally common.

CHARCOAL BURNER *Russula cyanoxantha* Height up to 9cm
A rather variable fungus whose cap is usually greyish lilac but often blotched with black and reddish purple. It grows in deciduous woodland and is widespread and common, July–November. Gills are white and feel slightly greasy. Stem white.

BROWN ROLL-RIM *Paxillus involutus* Height up to 12cm
Widespread fungus of deciduous woods, usually associated with birches. Cap colour is tan to dirty brown; flattened then funnel-shaped but with margin inrolled. Gills brown and decurrent down brown stem. Appears September–November.

BLACKENING WAX-CAP *Hygrocybe nigrescens* Height up to 5cm
Widespread and common grassland fungus that appears August–October. Cap conical when young; becomes rounded with age, retaining pointed apex. Cap colour changes from orange-red to black with age. The gills and stem are yellowish orange.

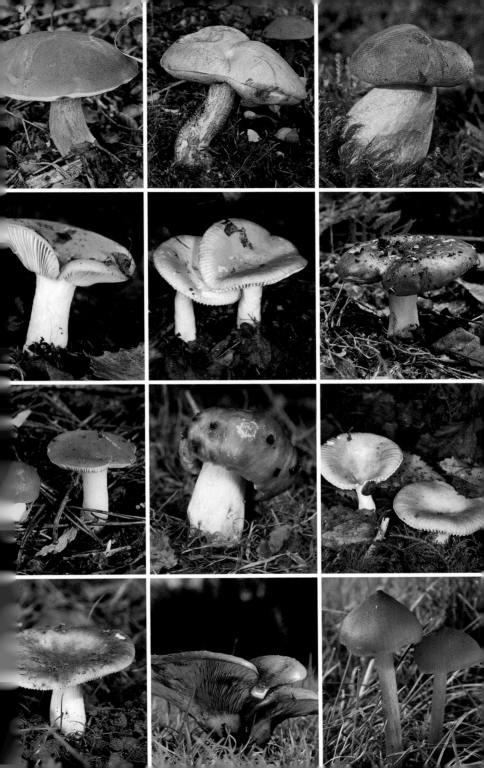

WOOLLY MILK-CAP *Lactarius torminosus* Height up to 8cm
Orange cap is marked with darker concentric rings and covered with a peach-coloured coat of woolly fibres. Widespread and common in deciduous woods, mostly under birches. Gills white. Yields white milk. Widespread and common in autumn.

Lactarius pyrogalus Height up to 6cm
Widespread and often common under Hazel, especially where this is managed for coppice. The cap is buffish brown, rounded at first but funnel-shaped with age. Gills yellowish and stem pale brown. Milk white and acrid. Appears in autumn.

STINKHORN *Phallus impudicus* Height up to 15cm
Unmistakable fungus of deciduous woodland; appears May–November. Seen initially as soft, white ball, 5–6cm across, from which phallus-like fruit body emerges. Stalk's oval tip coated with stinking, spore-containing mucus; attracts flies.

COMMON PUFFBALL *Lycoperdon perlatum* Height up to 7cm
Distinctive, club-shaped fruit bodies are found in clusters growing on dead and part-buried decaying wood, September–November. Fruit body is off-white with dark spines when young; mature specimens brown and wrinkled. Widespread and common.

COMMON EARTH-STAR *Geastrum triplex* Up to 10cm across
Extraordinary-looking fungus, found in woodlands September–November. Initially, fruit body resembles an onion. Outer layer splits into 4–7 segments which fold back eventually lifting central orb off ground. Spores expelled via pore. Local.

WITCHES' BUTTER *Exidia glandulosa* Up to 4cm across
The fruit bodies comprise black, gelatinous blobs that appear in brain-like clusters on the twigs and branches of deciduous trees, especially oaks. The fungus is widespread and generally common, and can be found throughout the year.

YELLOW BRAIN FUNGUS *Tremella mesenterica* Up to 8cm across
Often very distinctive, appearing as it does in winter, usually December–March. Fruit bodies are bright orange-yellow and jelly-like, forming convoluted, brain-like masses on dead twigs of deciduous trees. Widespread and generally common.

EAR FUNGUS *Hirneola auricula-judae* Up to 5cm across
Bizarre fungus with a strangely ear-like appearance. Found in clusters or tiers on dead branches of deciduous trees and shrubs, especially Elder. Fruit body is reddish brown, translucent with wrinkles resembling veins. Widespread in winter.

Ramaria stricta Height up to 7cm
Stiffly upright, highly branched fungus, found locally in deciduous and conifer woodland throughout; warm buff but often paler at tips of branches. It grows on rotting stumps and part-buried, decaying timber; appears September–November.

YELLOW STAGSHORN FUNGUS *Calocera viscosa* Height up to 7cm
Distinctive fungus. Bright yellow and much-branched, the result fancifully like antlers; its colour darkens with age. Widespread and fairly common in conifer woodlands. Grows on dead stumps and part-buried fallen timber, October–November.

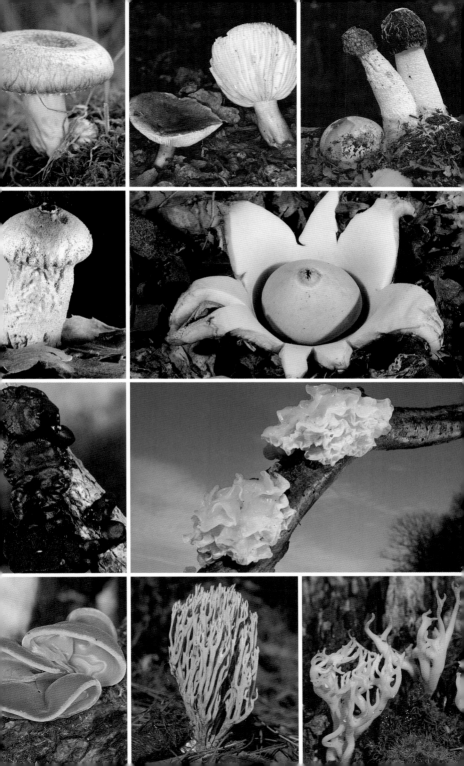

GLOSSARY

ABDOMEN: hind section of an insect's body; usually appears segmented

ANNELID: a type of worm (see Plant and Animal Groups)

ANNUAL: a plant that lives for a single growing season

ANTENNAE: slender, paired sensory organs on the head of an insect

ANTHER: pollen-containing structure in a flower, located on the end of the male reproductive structure, the stamen

ARBOREAL: tree-dwelling

AWN: bristle found in flowers of many grasses

AXIL: angle where upper surface of a leaf meets the stem on a plant

BALEEN: fibrous plates in the mouths of certain whale species; used for filtering food from water

BERRY: fleshy fruit containing several seeds

BIENNIAL: a plant that takes two years to complete its life cycle

BIVALVE: mollusc whose shell comprises two halves

BRACT: a small leaf- or scale-like structure beneath a flower

BULB: fleshy, underground structure found in certain plants and comprising leaf bases and next years bud

BULBIL: small, bulb-like structure

CAP: structure seen in fungi under which spore-bearing structures, usually gills or pores, are suspended

CAPSULE: structure within which seeds are formed in flowering plants and spores develop in mosses and liverworts

CARAPACE: hard, upper surface of a crustacean's shell

CARPAL: area on a bird's wing corresponding to the 'wrist' joint

CATERPILLAR: larval stage of butterfly or moth

CATKIN: flowering structure of certain trees and shrubs

CEPHALOTHORAX: fused head and thorax found in spiders

CERCI: paired appendages at hind end of an insect's body

CHLOROPHYLL: green pigment found in plant tissue and essential for photosynthesis

COMPOUND EYE: eye structure typical of insects and some other invertebrates comprising numerous cells and lenses, not a single lens

CONE: structure bearing reproductive elements of conifers

CONIFER: tree which bears its reproductive structures in cones

DECIDUOUS: woody plant which sheds its leaves in winter

DISC FLORETS: small flowers found at centre of inflorescence of members of daisy family

DORSAL: upper surface

DIURNAL: active during daylight

ELYTRA: hardened forewings of a beetle

EVERGREEN: plant which retains its leaves throughout the year

FERAL: having returned to the wild

FLORET: small flower

FROND: leaf-like structure found in some lower plants

FRUIT: seeds together with their surrounding tissues

GALL: plant growth induced by another organism, often a gall wasp

GLUME: stiffened bract found on a grass flower

HAEMOGLOBIN: red pigment in blood which absorbs oxygen

HOLDFAST: root-like structure which anchors seaweeds to rocks

HYBRID: offspring from different parent species

INFLORESCENCE: combination of a flower, its bracts and flowering stems

INSECTIVORE: an organism which feeds on insects

JUVENILE: newly fledged bird which has not yet acquired adult plumage

LANCEOLATE: lance-shaped

LARVA: soft-bodied, pre-adult stage in the life-cycle of certain insect species

LEAFLET: small, separate segment of a leaf

LEK: communal display area used by certain bird species

LIGULE: membranous leaf sheath found in grasses

MELANIC: showing dark pigmentation

MIGRANT: bird which spends the summer and winter in different areas

MOULT: process seen in birds during which old feathers are lost and replaced by new ones

MUCUS: slimy, viscous fluid secretion

NEEDLE: narrow leaves found in conifers

NOCTURNAL: active after dark

NODE: part of stem at which leaves arise

NUT: dry and often hard fruit containing a single seed

NYMPH: pre-adult stage in certain insects, notably bugs, which has some characters in common with its adult stage

OPERCULUM: plate found in some molluscs and used to seal off entrance to shell

OVATE: roughly oval in outline

OVIPOSITOR: egg-laying structure found at the tail-end of some female insects

OVOID: egg-shaped

PALMATE: leaf divided into lobes which fancifully resembles a hand

PALPS: sensory appendages found around the mouth in insects and crustaceans

PARASITE: organism which lives on or in another organism, relying on it entirely for its nutrition

PASSAGE MIGRANT: bird species seen mostly on migration and which does not necessarily breed in Ireland

PERENNIAL: plant which lives for more than two years

PETAL: often colourful inner row of structures surrounding reproductive part of a flower

PINNATE: leaf divided into more than three leaflets, these being arranged in pairs on either side of stem

PLANARIAN: a flatworm (see section on Plant and Animal groups)

POLLEN: minute grains produced by anthers and containing male sex cells

PRONOTUM: hardened dorsal plate covering the thorax of an insect

PUPA: stage in an insect's life-cycle between the larva and adult; also called the chrysalis

RAY FLORETS: small flowers found on the outer fringe of the inflorescence in flowers of the daisy family

RHIZOME: underground stem

ROSETTE: radiating arrangement of leaves

RUNNER: creeping stem which occurs above ground and may root at nodes or tip

SEPAL: outer row of structures surrounding the reproductive part of a flower

SOLE: underside of the foot in molluscs

SPADIX: upright spike of florets, found in arums

SPATHE: large bract surrounding spadix in arums

SPECIES: unit of classification defining animals or plants which are able to breed with one another and produce viable offspring

SPECULUM: species-specific patch of colour seen on ducks' wings

SPIKE: simple, branched inflorescence

SPIKELET: inflorescence arrangement in grasses and sedges etc

SPORE: tiny reproductive body that disperses and gives rise to a new organism

STAMEN: male reproductive structure of a flower

STIGMA: receptive tip of female part of flower, the style

STIPULE: leaf-like or scale-like structure at base of leaf stalk

STYLE: female reproductive structure of a flower

SUBSPECIES: sub-division of a species, members of which are able to breed with other subspecies but seldom do so because of geographical isolation

TENDRIL: slender, modified leaf or stem structure which assists climbing in some plants

THALLUS: unspecialised vegetative body of a lower plant

THORAX: middle section of an insect's body

TRAGUS: pointed inner ear outgrowth found in some bat species

TRIFOLIATE: leaf divided into three sections

UMBEL: umbrella-like inflorescence

VENTRAL: lower surface

FURTHER READING

NATURAL HISTORY

Michael Viney, *Ireland, a Smithsonian Natural History*. The Blackstaff Press, 2003.

David Cabot, *Ireland, a Natural History*. Collins, 1999.

MAMMALS

James Fairley, *A Basket of Weasels*. Published privately, 2001.

Tom Hayden and Rory Harrington, *Exploring Irish Mammals*. The Heritage Service, 2000.

David MacDonald and Priscilla Barrett, *Collins Field Guide to Mammals of Britain and Europe*. Collins, 1993.

BIRDS

David Cabot, *Irish Birds*. Collins, 2004.

Haken Delin and Lars Svensson, *Photographic Guide to the Birds of Britain and Europe*. Hamlyn, 1988.

Hermann Heinzel, Richard Fitter and John Parslow, *Pocket Guide Birds of Britain and Europe with North Africa and the Middle East*. Collins, 2001.

Peter Lack, *The Atlas of Wintering Birds in Britain and Ireland*. T & AD Poyser.

Paul Sterry, *Field Guide to the Birds of Britain and Europe*. The Crowood Press, 1994.

Paul Sterry and Jim Flegg, *A Photographic Guide to the Birds of Britain and Europe*. New Holland, 1995.

Lars Svensson and Peter Grant, *Collins Bird Guide*. Collins, 2000.

David Wingfield Gibbons, James Reid and Robert Chapman, *The New Atlas of Breeding Birds in Britain and Ireland: 1988–1991*. T & AD Poyser, 1993.

OTHER VERTEBRATES

Nicholas Arnold and Denys Ovenden, *Field Guide to the Reptiles and Amphibians of Britain and Europe*. Collins, 2002.

Peter Maitland and Keith Linsell, *The Hamlyn Guide to Freshwater Fishes of Britain and Europe*. Hamlyn, 1977.

Peter J. Miller, *Pocket Guide Fish of Britain and Europe*. Collins, 2001.

BUTTERFLIES AND MOTHS

Bernard Skinner and David Wilson, *Colour Identification Guide to Moths of the British Isles*. Viking, 1984.

Paul Sterry, *A Photographic Guide to the Butterflies of Britain and Europe*. New Holland, 1995.

Tom Tolman and Richard Lewington, *Collins Field Guide Butterflies of Britain and Europe*. Collins, 2004.

Paul Waring, Martin Townsend and Richard Lewington, *Field Guide to the Moths of Great Britain and Ireland*. British Wildlife Publishing, 2003.

OTHER INVERTEBRATES

J. D'Aguilar, J-L. Dommanget and R. Prechac, *Field Guide to Dragonflies of Britain, Europe and North Africa*. Collins, 1986.

Michael Chinery, *Field Guide to the Insects of Britain and Northern Europe*. Collins, 1993.

Heiko Bellman, *A Field Guide to the Grasshoppers and Crickets of Britain and Northern Europe*. Collins, 1988.

M.P. Kerney, R.A.D. Cameron and G. Riley, *Field Guide to the Land Snails of Britain and North-west Europe*. Collins, 1979.

Michael Tweedie and John Wilkinson, *Handguide to the Butterflies and Moths of Britain and Ireland*. Collins, 1980.

THE SEASHORE

Peter Hayward, Tony Nelson-Smith and Chris Shields, *Collins Pocket Guide to the Seashore of Britain and Europe*. Collins, 2001.

TREES

Andrew Cleave, *Field Guide to the Trees of Britain, Europe and North America*. The Crowood Press, 1994.

David Hickie and Mike O'Toole, *Native Trees & Forests of Ireland*. Gill and MacMillan, 2002.

Owen Johnson and David More, *Collins Tree Guide*. Collins, 2004.

Jonathan Pilcher and Valerie Hall, *Flora Hibernica*. The Collins Press, 2001.

Paul Sterry and Bob Press, *A Photographic Guide to the Trees of Britain and Europe*. New Holland, 1995.

Alan Mitchell, *Collins Field Guide Trees of Britain and Northern Europe*. Collins, 2001.

WILD FLOWERS

Richard Fitter, Alistair Fitter and Marjorie Blamey, *Pocket Guide Wild Flowers of Britain and Northern Europe*. Collins, 2001.

Bob Gibbons and Peter Brough, *The Hamlyn Photographic Guide to the Wild Flowers of Britain and Northern Europe*. Hamlyn, 1992.

Paul Sterry and Bob Press, *A Photographic Guide to the Wild Flowers of Britain and Europe*. New Holland, 1995.

LOWER PLANTS

Hans Martin Jahns, *Photoguide to the Ferns, Mosses and Lichens of Britain and Northern and Central Europe*. Collins, 1996.

FUNGI

R. Courtecuisse and B. Duhem, *Field Guide to Mushrooms and Toadstools of Britain and Europe*. Collins, 1995.

Paul Sterry, *A Photographic Guide to the Mushrooms of Britain and Europe*. New Holland, 1995.

The Collins **New Naturalist** series has titles which cover most aspects of British natural history.

NATURAL HISTORY SOCIETIES

Irish Wildlife Trust. Tel: (01)6604530. www.iwt.ie
BirdWatch Ireland. Tel: (01)2804322. www.birdwatchireland.ie
Irish Bat Group. Tel: (021)7339247. www.batdetective.com. batline@eircom.net
Irish Whale and Dolphin Group. Department of Zoology, University College, Cork

PICTURE CREDITS

The copyright for the photographs in this book belong to the individual photographers. All have been taken by Paul Sterry with the exception of:

Nature Photographers:
S. C. Bisserot: 25(a, b, c, d, e, g), 97i, 111b, 139c, 143(i, j, l), 145(i, j, k), 161d, 165c, 175(b, f)
Frank B. Blackburn: 49h, 97f, 73a, 91d, 143g, 179d, 249i
Mark Bolton: 67g
T. D. Bonsall: 123e, 143f
Idris Bowen: 255e
Nicholas Phelps Brown: 111i, 123(c, f), 137(a, b, c, d, e), 139 (b, e), 151c, 167g, 173(f, k)
Brinsley Burbidge: 179b, 181e, 199(i, k), 203g, 205d, 209l, 225a, 231e, 233l, 269(a), 277(k)
Robin Bush: 107(b, l), 109f, 195d, 199f, 203(c, f), 205g, 207(e, k), 227g, 235(g, h), 249e, 253g, 263f, 265d, 277g
N. A. Callow: 129f, 131f, 133f, 139f, 141(a, e, g), 145(a, b, c, d, h), 149(e, j), 151(d, g), 153a, 155a, 271k
Kevin Carlson: 45e, 49(d, e), 55a, 77a, 79g, 81f
Colin Carver: 23(c, g), 27e, 79f, 81(e, h), 87e
Bob Chapman: 229e, 247a
Hugh Clark: 47a, 123b, 129e, 139a, 143b, 157j, 229d
Andrew Cleave: 163(c, i), 165(d, f, i, j), 169(c, h), 171b, 175(a, e, i), 177(b, c, d), 179(a, g, i), 181(a, b, c, d, g, h, i, k), 183(c, e, f, h, i, k, l), 185(f, h), 187(a, i), 189e, 191j, 193(e, j), 195c, 199i, 201(b, c), 203h, 205(e, h), 207f, 209i, 211f, 221d, 223(d, j), 225g, 227j, 229(g, l), 231b, 233h, 235k, 239j, 241(b, j), 245f, 247(c, d), 263b, 265(j, k), 267(a, b, d, g, h, j, k), 269(b, c, d, h, j, k, l), 271(f, g, h, i, j), 273(f, h), 275(g, h), 277(i, j), 279(a, b, g,

h), 281 (i), 283(h, i, j), 285(c, d, e, f, j), 287(b, e, f, i)
Ron Croucher: 87f
Andrew Davies: 185a
David Elias: 193f, 273(d, g), 275c
Geoff du Feu: 129c, 133e, 137(f, g), 139h, 141(c, f), 143m, 151k, 233e
Chris Gomersall: 113f
Jean Hall: 257a, 265(a, g)
Michael J. Hammett: 97(d, f, g), 101(d, e, g, h), 103a, 123g, 135(e, f), 165a, 175l, 177(a, f)
James Hyett: 223a
E. A. Janes: 23(a, d), 29a, 47f, 51d, 67a, 123i, 141d, 179j, 197i, 201g, 231d, 233a, 249j, 265e, 281g, 289f, 291a
Hugh Miles: 23f, 97h, 99(b, e)
Lee Morgan: 265c
C. Mylne: 31h
Owen Newman: 21a, 23h 25f, 33h, 237d
Philip Newman: 47j, 49(b, i, j), 81g, 83e
David Osborn: 29(b, c), 45f, 191k, 203d
Charles Palmar: 97e
W. S. Paton: 21f, 23e, 49(c, f, k)
Jim Russell: 185g, 257f
Tony Schilling: 181c, 201d
Don Smith: 163f, 165h, 175c, 177h
J. Sutherland: 261b
E. K. Thompson: 33a
Roger Tidman: 47(b, k), 53e, 59a, 67b, 69e, 73(c, d), 81(a, c), 87h, 225c
Jeff Watson: 263a, 269(e, i)
Andrew Weston: 221c
Wolmuth and Muller: 47i

Other photographers and agencies:
Graeme Cresswell: 31d
FLPA: 31(c, e, f, g)
Natural Image: 257b
NHPA: 5, 7, 15, 17, 18, 19, 23b, 29i, 35c, 99i, 129e, 157j, 229d
Brent Stephenson: 35d

INDEX

Abramis brama 98
Abraxas grossulariata 118
Abrostola triplasia 116
Acanthosoma
   haemorrhoidale 130
Accipiter gentilis 46
   nisus 46
Acer campestre 184
   pseudoplatanus 184
Achillea millefolium 248
   ptarmica 248
Acilius sulcatus 146
Aconite, Winter 198
Acrocephalus
   schoenobaenus 80
   scirpaceus 80
Acronicta leporina 114
   megacephala 114
   psi 114
Actinia equina 174
Actitis hypoleucos 56
Adiantum capillus-veneris
   276
Admiral, Red 104
Aegithalos caudatus 86
Aegopodium podagraria
   224
Aesculus hippocastanum
   182
Aeshna grandis 126
Aethusa cynapium 226
Agapetes fuscipes 134
Agaric, Clouded 290
Agaric, Fly 290
Agaricus campestris 292
   silvicola 292
Agrimonia eupatoria 208
Agrimony 208
   Hemp 246
Agrion, Demoiselle 128
Agrostis gigantea 270
   stolonifera 270
   exclamationis 114
Ajuga reptans 234
Alauda arvensis 76
Alca torda 68
Alcedo atthis 74
Alchemilla vulgaris agg.
   208
Alcyonium digitatum 176
Alder 182
Alder-buckthorn 186
Aleuria aurantia 288

Alexanders 222
Alisma plantago-aquatica
   254
Alison, Sweet 204
Alkanet, Green 234
Alle alle 68
Alliaria petiolata 204
Allium triquetrum 256
   ursinum 254
Alnus glutinosa 182
Althaea officinalis 218
Amanita citrina 290
   fulva 290
   muscaria 290
   phalloides 292
   rubescens 292
Amaurobius similis 152
Ammophila arenaria 270
   sabulosa 144
Amphitrite johnstoni 174
Anacamptis pyramidalis
   258
Anagallis arvensis 226
   tenella 228
Anas acuta 42
   clypeata 40
   crecca 40
   penelope 40
   platyrhynchos 40
   querquedula 42
   strepera 40
Anatis ocellata 150
Anchusa arvensis 232
Ancylus fluviatilis 160
Anemone nemorosa 200
Anemone, Beadlet 174
   Jewel 174
   Snakelocks 174
   Wood 200
Anemonia sulcata 174
Angelica 224
Angelica sylvestris 224
Angerona prunaria 120
Angle Shades 116
Anguilla anguilla 96
Anguis fragilis 94
Anodonta cygnea 160
Anser albifrons 38
   anser 38
   brachyrhynchus 38
   fabilis 38
Ant, Black Garden 144
   Red 144
   Wood 144
Anthoceros laevis 282
Anthocharis cardamines
   104
Anthoxanthum odoratum
   270

Anthriscus sylvestris 222
Anthus petrosus 76
   pratensis 76
Anthyllis vulneraria 214
Apeira syringaria 118
Aphanes arvensis 208
Aphantopus hyperantus
   106
Aphid, Rose 132
Aphis fabae 132
Apis mellifera 144
Apium graveolens 226
   nodiflorum 226
Aplysia punctata 164
Apodemus sylvaticus 20
Apple, Crab 184
Apus apus 74
Aquila chrysaetos 46
Arabidopsis thaliana 204
Araneus diadematus 152
   quadratus 152
Araniella curcurbitina 152
Arbutus unedo 188
Archangel, Yellow 236
Archidoris pseudargus 164
Arctia caja 112
Arctium lappa 250
Ardea cinerea 34
Arenaria interpres 58
   serpyllifolia 194
Arenicola marina 174
Argynnis aglaja 106
   paphia 106
Argyroneta aquatica 152
Arianta arbustorum 158
Arion ater 156
   distinctus 156
   subfuscus 156
Armadillidium vulgare
   166
Armeria maritima 230
Armillaria mellea 290
Arrhenatherum elatius 270
Arrowgrass, Sea 244
Arrowhead 254
Artemisia absinthium 248
   maritima 250
   vulgaris 248
Arum maculatum 256
Ascidian, Star 176
Ascophyllum nodosum
   286
Asellus aquaticus 166
Ash 184
Asio flammeus 72
   otus 72
Aspen 180
Asperula cynanchica 232
Asphodel, Bog 254

Asplenium ruta-muraria 278
  trichomanes 278
Astacus pallipes 166
Aster tripolium 246
Aster, Sea 246
Asterias rubens 176
Asterina gibbosa 176
Astragalus danicus 212
Athous haemorrhoidalis 148
Athyrium filix-femina 276
Atrichium undulatum 278
Atriplex glabriuscula 192
Atypus affinis 152
Auk, Little 68
Aurelia aurita 174
Autographa gamma 116
  pulchrina 116
Avena fatua 270
Avens, Mountain 208
Avens, Water 210
Avocet 52
Aythya ferina 42
  fuligula 42
  marila 42

Badger 22
Balaenoptera acutorostrata 28
  physalus 28
Ballota nigra 236
Balsam, Himalayan 218
Barbarea vulgaris 202
Barnacle, Acorn 170
  Goose 170
Bartsia, Red 240
  Yellow 242
Bass 100
Bat, Brown Long-eared 24
  Daubenton's 24
  Leisler's 24
  Lesser Horseshoe 24
  Natterer's 24
  Pipistrelle 24
  Soprano Pipistrelle 24
  Whiskered 24
Beak-sedge, White 266
Beautiful Golden Y 116
Beauty, Brindled 120
  Lilac 118
  Mottled 120
  Oak 120
Bedstraw, Lady's 232
Bee, Buff-tailed Bumble 144
  Honey 144
  Leaf-cutter 142
  Red-tailed Bumble 144

Bee-fly 138
Beech 182
Beet, Sea 192
Beetle, Bee 148
  Bloody-nosed 150
  Burying 146
  Cardinal 148
  Click 148
  Great Diving 146
  Green Tiger 146
  Ground 146
  Lesser Stag 146
  Longhorn 150
  Mint Leaf 150
  Oil 148
  Poplar Leaf 150
  Rhinoceros 146
  Sexton 146
  Silver Water 146
  Soldier 148
  Tortoise 150
  Wasp 150
  Water 146
Bellflower, Ivy-leaved 244
Bellis perennis 246
Bent, Common 270
  Creeping 270
Beta vulgaris ssp. *maritima* 192
Betony 236
Betula pendula 180
  pubescens 180
Bibio marci 136
Bilberry 228
Bindweed, Field 230
  Hedge 230
  Sea 232
Birch, Downy 180
  Silver 180
Bird's-foot 214
Biston betularia 120
  straria 120
Bistort 190
  Amphibious 190
Bithynia tentaculata 160
Bithynia, Common 160
Bittercress, Hairy 202
Bittern 36
Bittersweet 238
Black-bindweed 190
Blackbird 84
Blackcap 82
Blackfly 132
Blackstonia perfoliata 230
Blackthorn 184
  Greater 264
Blechnum spicant 276
Blennius pholis 102

Blenny, Common 102
Blewits, Wood 290
Blue, Common 108
  Holly 108
  Small 108
Bluebell 254
Bluebottle 140
Blusher, The 292
Boarmia repandata 120
Bog-orchid 262
Bog-rush, Black 266
Bogbean 230
Bolete, Bay 294
  Orange Birch 294
  Red-cracked 292
Boletus badius 294
  chrysenteron 292
  edulis 292
Boloria euphrosyne 104
Bombus lapidarius 144
  pascuorum 144
  terrestris 144
Bombycilla garrulus 78
Bombylius major 138
Borage 232
Borago officinalis 232
Botaurus stellaris 36
Botrychium lunaria 278
Botryllus schlosseri 176
Brachythecium rutabulum 280
Bracken 276
Bracket, Blushing 288
Bramble 210
Brambling 88
Branta bernicla 38
  canadensis 38
  leucopsis 38
Brassica nigra 202
Bream, Common 98
Brimstone 104
Bristletail 122
Brittle-star, Common 176
Briza media 272
Brooklime 240
Broom 212
Broomrape, Common 242
Broomrape, Thyme 242
Brown, Meadow 106
  Wall 106
Brown-line Bright-eye 114
Bryum capillare 280
Buccinium undatum 164
Bucephala clangula 44
Buckthorn 186
Buddleia 188
Buddleia davidii 188
Buff-tip 110
Bufo calamita 94

Bug, Forest 130
  Sloe 130
Bugle 234
Bugloss 232
Bulin, Common 158
Bullfinch 88
Bunting, Reed 86
  Snow 86
Bur-reed, Branched 270
Burdock, Greater 250
Burnet, Five-spot 108
  Great 208
    Salad 208
Burnet-saxifrage 224
Burnished Brass 116
Bush-cricket, Oak 124
  Roesel's 124
  Speckled 124
Buteo buteo 46
Butter Cap 290
Butterbur 248
Buttercup, Bulbous 198
  Celery-leaved 198
  Creeping 198
  Meadow 198
Butterfish 102
Butterfly-orchid, Greater 260
  Lesser 260
Butterwort 242
Buzzard 46

Cakile maritima 204
Calidris alba 54
  alpina 54
  canutus 54
  ferruginea 54
  maritima 54
  melanotos 56
  pusilla 54
Caligeron cuspidatum 278
Calliphora erythrocephala 140
Callistege mi 116
Calliteara pudibunda 112
Callophrys rubi 108
Calluna vulgaris 228
Calocera viscosa 296
Caloplaca marina 282
Calopteryx splendens 128
  virgo 128
Caltha palustris 198
Calystegia sepium 230
  soldanella 232
Campanula rotundifolia 244
Campion, Bladder 196
  Moss 196
  Red 196

  Sea 196
  White 196
Campyloneura virgula 130
Cancer pagurus 168
Candle Snuff 288
Cantharellus cibarius 288
Capra hircus 26
Caprimulgus europaeus 72
Capsella bursa-pastoris 204
Capsid 130
Carcinus maenas 168
Cardamine hirsuta 202
  pratensis 202
Carder-bee, Common 144
Cardium edule 164
Carduelis cabaret 90
  cannabina 90
  carduelis 88
  chloris 88
  flavirostris 90
  spinus 88
Carduus nutans 250
  tenuiflorus 250
Carex acutiformis 268
  arenaria 268
  demissa 268
  flacca 268
  nigra 268
  otrubae 268
  paniculata 268
  pendula 268
  pilulifera 268
  sylvatica 268
Carlina vulgaris 250
Carp 96
Carpet, Green 118
  Silver Ground 118
Carpinus betulus 182
Carrot, Wild 226
Cassida rubiginosa 150
Castanea sativa 182
Cat's-tail, Lesser 274
  Sand 274
Catharacta skua 64
Catocala nupta 116
Catsear, Common 254
Celandine, Greater 202
  Lesser 198
Celastrina argiolus 108
Celery, Wild 226
Centaurea nigra 252
  scabiosa 252
Centaurium erythraea 230
Centaury, Common 230
Centranthus ruber 242
Cep 292
Cepaea hortensis 158
  nemoralis 158

Cephalanthera longifolia 262
Cepphus grylle 68
Ceramica pisi 114
Cerastium fontanum 194
  glomeratum 194
Cercopis vulnerata 132
Certhia familiaris 86
Cerura vinula 110
Cervus elaphus 26
  nippon 26
Ceterach officinarum 278
Cetonia aurata 148
Chafer, Rose 148
Chaffinch 88
Chamaecyparis lawsoniana 178
Chamomilla suaveolens 246
Champignon, Fairy-ring 290
Chanterelle 288
Chaoborus crystillinus 136
Charadrius hiaticula 52
Charcoal Burner 294
Charlock 202
Charr, Arctic 96
Chaser, Four-spotted 126
Chelidonium majus 202
Chelon labrosus 100
Chenopodium album 192
  bonus-henricus 192
  rubrum 192
Cherry, Wild 184
Chestnut, Sweet 182
Chickweed, Common 194
Chicory 252
Chiffchaff 80
Chironomus plumosus 136
Chlidonias niger 66
Chloeon dipterum 122
Chorthippus albomarginatus 124
  brunneus 124
Chough 92
Chrysanthemum segetum 248
Chrysaora isosceles 174
Chrysis ignita 142
Chrysolina menthastri 150
Chrysomela populi 150
Chrysoperla carnea 132
Chrysops relictus 136
Chrysosplenium oppositifolium 208
Chthalamus stellatus 170
Cicely, Sweet 222
Cichorium intybus 252
Cicindela campestris 146

Cicuta virosa 224
Ciliata mustela 100
Cimbex femoratus 142
Cinclus cinclus 78
Cinnabar, The 112
Cinquefoil, Creeping 210
  Marsh 210
Circaea lutetiana 220
Circus aeruginosus 48
  cyaneus 48
  pygargus 48
Cirsium arvense 252
  dissectum 250
  helenoides 250
  palustre 252
  vulgare 250
Cladium mariscus 268
Cladonia floerkeana 282
  impexa 282
Clangula hyemalis 44
Claytonia perfoliata 192
  sibirica 192
Cleavers, Common 232
Cleg-fly 138
Clethrionomys glareolus 20
Clitocybe nebularis 290
Clover, Hare's-foot 214
  Red 214
  Rough 214
  White 214
Club-rush, Floating 266
  Sea 266
Clubmoss, Fir 278
  Stag's-horn 278
Clytus arietus 150
Coccinella 7-punctata 150
Cochleria officinalis 204
Cochlodina laminata 158
Cockchafer 148
Cockle, Common 164
Coeloglossum viride 258
Coenagrion lunulatum 128
  puella 128
Coenagrion, Common 128
Coenonympha pamphilus 106
  tullia 106
Colias crocea 104
Collembola 122
Collybia butyracea 290
Colocasia coryli 116
Colostygia pectinataria 118
Colt's-foot 250
Columba livia 70
  oenas 70
  palumbus 70
Columbine 200

Comfrey, Common 234
  Russian 234
Conger conger 100
Conium maculatum 224
Conocephalus conicum 282
Conopodium majus 222
Convolvulus arvensis 230
Coot 50
Copper, Small 108
Coprinus comatus 292
Cordulia aenea 126
Coriolus versicolor 288
Corixa punctata 130
Cormorant 34
Corncrake 50
Cornsalad, Common 242
Cornus sanguinea 188
Coronopus didymus 204
  squamatus 204
Corvus corax 92
  corone ssp. cornix 92
  frugilegus 92
  monedula 92
Corydalis claviculata 200
Corydalis, Climbing 200
Corylus avellana 182
Corynactes viridis 174
Corystes cassivellaunus 168
Cottongrass, Common 270
  Hare's-tail 270
Cow-wheat, Common 242
Cowbane 224
Cowberry 228
Cowrie, Common 162
Cowslip 226
Crab, Broad-clawed
  Porcelain 168
  Edible 168
  Hermit 168
  Masked 168
  Shore 168
  Spider 168
  Velvet Swimming 168
Cranberry 228
Crane's-bill, Bloody 216
  Cut-leaved 216
  Dove's-foot 216
  Meadow 216
  Shining 216
  Wood 216
Cranefly 136
Crangon vulgaris 170
Crategus monogyna 186
Crayfish, Freshwater 166
Crenilabrus melops 100
Crepidotus variabilis 288
Crepidula fornicata 162
Crepis capillaris 254

Cress, Thale 204
Crex crex 50
Crithmum maritimum 224
Crocallis elinguaria 118
Crocosmia × crocosmiiflora 256
Crossbill, Common 90
Crosswort 232
Crow, Hooded 92
Crowberry 228
Cruciata laevipes 232
Cryptogramma crispa 276
Cuckoo 70
Cuckoo Flower 202
Cucullia umbratica 114
Cuculus canorus 70
Cudweed, Common 246
  Marsh 246
  Small 246
Culex sp. 136
Cupido minimus 108
× Cupressocyparis leylandi 178
Curculio nucum 150
Curlew 58
Cuscuta epithymum 232
Cushion-star 176
Cyclopterus lumpus 102
Cygnus columbarius 36
  cygnus 36
  olor 36
Cylindrosulus punctatus 172
Cymbalaria muralis 240
Cynoglossum officinale 234
Cypress, Lawson 178
  Leyland 178
Cyprinus carpio 96
Cystopteris fragilis 276
Cytisus scoparius 212

Dactylis glomerata 272
Dactylorhiza fuchsii 260
  incarnata 260
  maculata 260
  purpurella 260
  traunsteineri 260
Daedaleopsis confragosa 288
Dagger, Grey 114
Daisy 246
Daisy, Ox-eye 248
Daldinia concentrica 288
Dama dama 26
Damselfly, Blue-tailed 128
  Common Blue 128
  Irish 128
  Large Red 128

Dandelion 252
Daphnia sp. 166
Darter, Common 126
Ruddy 126
Daucus carota 226
Dead Man's Fingers 176
Dead-nettle, Henbit 236
Red 236
White 236
Death Cap 292
False 290
Deceiver 290
Amethyst 290
Deer, Fallow 26
Red 26
Sika 26
Delichon urbica 74
Delphinus delphis 30
Demoiselle, Banded 128
Deroceras reticulatum 156
Deschampsia cespitosa 272
flexuosa 272
Devil's Coach-horse 146
Diachrisia chrysitis 116
Diaphora mendica 112
Dicentrachus labrus 100
Dicranella heteromalla 278
Dielephila elpenor 110
Digitalis purpurea 240
Dinocras cephalotes 122
Dipper 78
Dipsacus fullonum 244
Discus rotundatus 158
Diver, Black-throated 32
Great Northern 32
Red-throated 32
Dock, Broad-leaved 192
Curled 190
Great Water 192
Wood 192
Dodder, Common 232
Dog-rose 208
Dog-violet, Common 220
Dogfish, Lesser Spotted 100
Dogwood 188
Dolomedes fimbriatus 152
Dolphin, Atlantic White-sided 30
Bottle-nosed 30
Common 30
Northern Bottlenose 30
Risso's 30
Striped 30
Dolycoris baccarum 130
Dorcus parallelipipedus 146

Douglas-fir 178
Dove, Collared 70
Rock 70
Stock 70
Drepana falcataria 118
Drone-fly 138
Dropwort 208
Drosera intermedia 206
rotundifolia 206
Dryad's Saddle 288
Dryas octopetala 208
Dryopteris aemula 276
affinis 276
dilitata 276
filix-mas 276
Duck, Long-tailed 44
Ruddy 44
Tufted 42
Duckweed, Common 264
Dugesia lugubris 172
Dung-fly 140
Dunlin 54
Dunnock 78
Dysdera crocata 152
Dytiscus marginalis 146

Eagle, Golden 46
Earth-star, Common 296
Earthworm, Common 172
Earwig, Common 130
Echinocardium cordatum 176
Echinus esculentus 176
Echium vulgare 234
Eel 96
Conger 100
Egret, Little 36
Egretta garzetta 36
Eider 42
Eilema lurideola 112
Elder 188
Eleocharis palustris 266
Eligmodonta ziczac 112
Elm, English 182
Wych 182
Elminius modestus 170
Elymus arenarius 272
Emberiza citrinella 86
schoeniclus 86
Emerald, Downy 126
Large 118
Empetrum nigrum 228
Empid-fly 138
Empis tesselata 138
Ena obscura 158
Enallagma cyathigerum 128
Enchanter's-nightshade 220

Ennomos alniaria 118
Ensis siliqua 164
Enteromorpha intestinalis 286
Ephemera danica 122
vulgata 122
Ephemeroptera 122
Epilobium angustifolium 220
ciliatum 220
hirsutum 220
palustre 220
Epipactis helleborine 262
palustris 262
Equisetum arvense 264
fluviatile 264
sylvaticum 264
Erannis defoliaria 120
Eranthis hyemalis 198
Erica cinerea 228
erigena 228
mackaiana 228
tetralix 228
Erigeron acer 246
Erinaceus europaeus 20
Eriocaulon aquaticum 264
Eriophorum angustifolium 270
vaginatum 270
Eristalis tenax 138
Erithacus rubecula 82
Ermine, White 112
Erodium cicutarium 216
Erophila verna 204
Eryngium maritimum 222
Erynnis tages 108
Erysimum cheiranthoides 202
Esox lucius 96
Euonymus europaeus 186
Eupagurus bernhardus 168
Eupatorium cannabinum 246
Euphorbia helioscopia 216
hyberna 218
paralias 216
peplus 218
Euphrasia officinalis 242
Euphydryas aurinia 106
Eupithecia pulchellata 118
Euproctis similis 112
Eurhynchium praelongum 278
Eutrigla gurnardus 102
Evening-primrose, Common 222
Exidia glandulosa 296
Eyebright 242

Fagus sylvatica 182
Falco columbarius 48
    peregrinus 48
    subbuteo 48
    tinnunculus 48
Fallopia convolvulus 190
    japonica 190
Fannia canicularis 140
Fat Hen 192
Father Lasher 102
Favonius quercus 106
Fennel 224
Fern, Adder's-tongue 278
    Brittle Bladder 276
    Broad Buckler 276
    Hard 276
    Hart's-tongue 276
    Hay-scented 276
    Lady 276
    Maidenhair 276
    Parsley 276
    Polypody 278
    Royal 276
    Rusty-back 278
Fescue, Red 272
    Viviparous 272
Festuca rubra 272
    vivipara 272
Feverfew 248
Ficedula hypoleuca 82
Field-speedwell, Common
    240
Fieldfare 84
Figwort, Common 238
    Water 238
Filago minima 246
    vulgaris 246
Filipendula ulmaria 208
    vulgaris 208
Fissidens taxifolius 280
Flax, Fairy 216
Fleabane 248
    Blue 246
Flesh-fly 140
Flounder 102
Fly, Alder 132
    Horse 136
    Scorpion 132
    St Mark's 136
Flycatcher, Pied 82
    Spotted 82
Foeniculum vulgare 224
Footman, Common 112
    Rosy 112
Forficula auricularia 130
Forget-me-not, Early 234
    Water 234
Formica rufa 144
Fox 22

Foxglove 240
Fragaria vesca 210
Frangula alnus 186
Fratercula arctica 68
Fraxinus excelsior 184
Fringilla coelebs 88
    montifringilla 88
Fritillary, Dark Green 106
    Marsh 106
    Pearl-bordered 104
    Silver-washed 106
Frog, Common 94
Froghopper, Cuckoo-spit
    132
Fuchsia 190
Fuchsia magellanica 190
Fucus serratus 286
    spiralis 286
    vesiculosus 286
Fulica atra 50
Fulmar 34
Fulmarus glacialis 34
Fumaria officinalis 200
Fumitory, Common 200
Fungus, Ear 296
    Honey 290
    Orange-spot 288
    Oyster 290
    Porcelain 290
    Yellow Brain 296
    Yellow Stagshorn 296
Furcula furcula 110

Gadwall 40
Galanthus nivalis 256
Galeopsis speciosa 236
    tetrahit 236
Galium aparine 232
    mollugo 232
    odoratum 232
    palustre 232
    verum 232
Gall, Cherry 142
    Knopper 142
    Marble 142
    Spangle 142
Gallinago gallinago 60
Gallinula chloropus 50
Gammarus pulex 166
Gannet 34
Garganey 42
Garlic, Three-cornered 256
Garrulus glandarius 92
Gasterosteus aculeatus 98
Gatekeeper 106
Gavia arctica 32
    immer 32
    stellata 32
Geastrum triplex 296

Gentian, Autumn 230
    Field 230
    Spring 230
Gentiana verna 230
Gentianella amarella 230
    campestris 230
Geomalacus maculosus
    156
Geometra papilionaria 118
Geranium dissectum 216
    lucidum 216
    molle 216
    pratense 216
    robertianum 216
    sanguineum 216
    sylvaticum 216
Gerris lacustris 130
Geum rivale 210
    urbanum 210
Ghost worm 136
Gipsywort 238
Glasswort 194
Glaucium flavum 200
Glaux maritima 226
Glechoma hederacea 236
Globeflower 198
Globiocephala melas 28
Glomeris marginata 172
Glow-worm 148
Glyceria fluitans 272
    maxima 272
Glyphotaelius pellucidus
    134
Gnaphalium uliginosum
    246
Goat's-beard 252
Goat, Feral 26
Gobio gobio 98
Gobius paganellus 102
Goby, Rock 102
Godwit, Bar-tailed 58
    Black-tailed 58
Goldcrest 80
Golden-saxifrage,
    Opposite-leaved 208
Goldeneye 44
Goldenrod 246
    Canadian 246
Goldfinch 88
Gonepteryx rhamni 104
Good King Henry 192
Goosander 44
Goose, Barnacle 38
    Bean 38
    Brent 38
    Canada 38
    Greylag 38
    Pink-footed 38
    White-fronted 38

Gooseberry 186
Goosefoot, Red 192
Gorse, Common 210
  Western 212
Goshawk 46
Grampus griseus 30
Graphis scripta 284
Graphocephala fennahi
  132
Grass, Blue Moor 274
  Blue-eyed 256
  Cocksfoot 272
  Marram 270
  Quaking 272
  Sea Lyme 272
  Sweet Vernal 270
  Timothy 274
Grass-of-Parnassus 206
Grasshopper, Common
  Field 124
  Common Green 124
  Large Marsh 124
  Lesser Marsh 124
  Mottled 124
Grayling 106
Grebe, Black-necked 32
  Great Crested 32
  Little 32
  Slavonian 32
Green Silver Lines 116
Greenbottle 140
Greenfinch 88
Greenshank 56
Greilada elegans 164
Grimmia pulvinata 280
Grisette, Tawny 290
Gromwell, Common 234
Ground-elder 224
Ground-ivy 236
Groundhopper, Common
  124
  Slender 124
Groundsel 250
Grouse, Red 50
Gudgeon 98
Guelder-rose 188
Guillemot 68
  Black 68
Gull, Black-headed 62
  Common 62
  Glaucous 64
  Great Black-backed 64
  Herring 64
  Iceland 64
  Lesser Black-backed 64
  Little 62
  Mediterranean 62
  Ring-billed 64
Gurnard, Grey 102

Gutweed 286
Gymnadenia conopsea
  258

Haematopota crassicornis
  138
  pluvialis 138
Haematopus ostralegus 50
Hair-grass, Tufted 272
  Wavy 272
Hairstreak, Brown 108
  Green 108
  Purple 106
Halichoerus grypus 28
Halichondria panicea 176
Halimione portulacoides
  192
Hammarbya paludosa 262
Haplophilus subterraneus
  172
Hare, Irish Mountain 22
Harebell 244
Harrier, Hen 48
  Marsh 48
  Montagu's 48
Harvestmen 172
Hawk's-beard, Smooth 254
Hawkbit, Rough 254
Hawker, Brown 126
Hawkmoth, Elephant 110
  Eyed 110
  Hummingbird 110
  Poplar 110
Hawkweed, Mouse-ear 252
Hawthorn 186
Hazel 182
Heart and Dart 114
Heath, Cross-leaved 228
  Irish 228
  Large 106
  MacKay's 228
  Small 106
Heather, Bell 228
Hebrew Character 114
Hedera helix 188
Hedge-bedstraw 232
Hedge-parsley 222
Hedgehog 20
Heliotrope, Winter 248
Helix aspersa 158
Hellebore, Green 196
  Stinking 196
Helleborine, Broad-leaved
  262
  Marsh 262
  Sword-leaved 262
Helleborus foetidus 196
  viridis 196
Helophilus pendulus 138

Helvella crispa 288
Helvella, White 288
Hemlock 224
Hemlock-spruce, Western
  178
Hemp-nettle, Common 236
  Large-flowered 236
Henbane 238
Hepialus humuli 108
Heracleum
  mantegazzianum 224
  sphondylium 222
Herald, The 116
Herb Bennet 210
Herb Robert 216
Heron, Grey 34
Hieraceum pilosella 252
Himanthalia elongata 286
Hipparchia semele 106
Hippophae rhamnoides
  186
Hippuris vulgaris 264
Hirneola auricula-judae
  296
Hirundo rustica 74
Hobby 48
Hofmannophila
  pseudospretella 108
Hogweed 222
  Giant 224
Holcus lanatus 274
  mollis 274
Holly 184
Homalothecium sericeum
  280
Homarus vulgaris 168
Honey-buzzard 46
Honeysuckle 188
Honkenya peploides 194
Hooktip, Pebble 118
Hoopoe 72
Hop 188
Horehound, Black 236
Hornbeam 182
Horned-poppy, Yellow 200
Horse-chestnut 182
Horsetail, Common 264
  Water 264
  Wood 264
Hottonia palustris 226
Hound's-tongue 234
House-fly, Common 140
  Lesser 140
Humulus lupulus 188
Huperzia selago 278
Hyacinthoides non-scripta
  254
Hydra fusca 172
Hydrobates pelagicus 34

Hydrobia ulvae 162
Hydrocotyle vulgaris 222
Hydrophilus piceus 146
Hygrocybe nigrescens 294
Hyoscyamus niger 238
Hypericum androsaemum 218
  elodes 218
  humifusum 220
  perforatum 218
  pulchrum 218
Hyperoodon ampullatus 30
Hypholoma fasciculare 292
Hypnum cupressiforme 280
Hypochoeris radicata 254
Hypogymnia physodes 284

Ichneumon 142
Ilex aquifolium 184
Impatiens balsamifera 218
Inachis io 104
Ink Cap, Shaggy 292
Inula crithmoides 248
Iris pseudacorus 256
Iris, Yellow 256
Ischnura elegans 128
Ivy 188

Jackdaw 92
Jasione montana 244
Jay 92
Jellyfish, Common 174
Jenny, Creeping 226
Juglans regia 182
Juncus bufonis 266
  conglomeratus 266
  effusus 266
  gerardii 266
  inflexus 266
Juniper 178
Juniperus communis 178

Kelp 286
Kestrel 48
King Alfred's Cakes 288
Kingfisher 74
Kite, Red 46
Kitten, Sallow 110
Kittiwake 62
Knapweed, Common 252
  Greater 252
Knautia arvensis 244
Knawel, Annual 196
Knot 54
Knotgrass 190
Knotweed, Japanese 190

Laccaria amethystea 290
  laccata 290
Lacerta vivipara 94
Lacewing 132
Lackey, The 110
Lactarius pyrogalus 296
  torminosus 296
Lady's Smock 202
Lady's-mantle 208
Lady's-tresses, Autumn 262
  Irish 262
Ladybird, 14-spot 150
  7-spot 150
  Eyed 150
Lagenorhynchus acutus 30
Lagopus lagopus ssp.
  scoticus 50
Lamiastrum galeobdolon 236
Laminaria digitata 286
Lamium album 236
  amplexicaule 236
  purpureum 236
Lampetra fluviatilis 96
  planeri 96
Lamprey, Brook 96
  River 96
Lampyris noctiluca 148
Laothoe populi 110
Lapwing 52
Larch, European 178
Larix decidua 178
Larus argentatus 64
  canus 62
  delawarensis 64
  fuscus 64
  glaucoides 64
  hyperboreus 64
  marinus 64
  melanocephalus 62
  minutus 62
  ridibundus 62
Lasius niger 144
Lathraea squamaria 242
Lathyrus japonicus 212
  pratensis 212
Laurel, Cherry 186
Lavatera arborea 218
Laver Spire Shell 162
Leafhopper 132
  Red and Black 132
  Rhododendron 132
Leander serratus 170
Leatherjacket 136
Lecanora atra 284
Leccinum versipelle 294
Ledra aurita 132
Leech, Fish 172

Lemna minor 264
Leontodon hispidus 254
Lepadogaster lepadogaster 102
Lepas anatifera 170
Lepidium campestre 204
Lepiota mastoidea 292
  procera 292
Lepista nuda 290
Leptidea reali 104
  sinapis 104
Leptophyes punctatissima 124
Lepus timidus ssp.
  hibernicus 22
Lettuce, Sea 286
Leucanthemum vulgare 248
Leucobryum glaucum 280
Libellula quadrimaculata 126
Lichen, Black Shields 284
  Crab-eye 284
  Map 284
  Yellow Scales 284
Ligia oceanica 170
Ligusticum scoticum 224
  vulgare 188
Limax cinereoniger 156
  flavus 156
  marginatus 156
  maximus 156
Lime, Common 186
Limnephilus sp. 134
  elegans 134
  marmoratus 134
Limonium humile 230
Limosa lapponica 58
  limosa 58
Limpet, Blue-rayed 162
  Common 162
  River 160
  Slipper 162
Linaria repens 240
  vulgaris 240
Ling 228
Linnet 90
Linum catharticum 216
Liparis liparis 102
Listera ovata 258
Lithobius variegatus 172
Lithospermum officinale 234
Littorella uniflora 244
Littorina littoralis 162
  littorea 162
Lizard, Common 94
Loach, Stone 98
Lobaria pulmonaria 282

Lobelia dortmanna 246
Lobelia, Water 246
Lobster, Common 168
Lobularia maritima 204
Locustella naevia 78
Lonicera periclymenum
 188
Loosestrife, Yellow 226
Lophocolea heterophylla
 282
Lords-and-ladies 256
Lotus corniculatus 214
 uliginosus 214
Louse, Freshwater 166
Lousewort 242
 Marsh 242
Lovage, Scots 224
Loxia recurvirostra 90
Lucerne 214
Lucilia caesar 140
Lugworm 174
Lumbriculus sp. 172
Lumbricus terrestris 172
Lumpsucker 102
Lungwort, Tree 282
Lutra lutra 22
Luzula campestris 266
 sylvatica 266
Lycaena phlaeas 108
Lychnis flos-cuculi 196
Lycia hirtaria 120
Lycoperdon perlatum 296
Lycophotia porphyrea 114
Lycopodium clavatum 278
Lycopus europaeus 238
Lymnaea peregra 160
 stagnalis 160
Lymnocryptes minimus 60
Lysimachia nemorum 226
 nummularia 226
 vulgaris 226
Lythrum salicaria 222

Macroglossum stellatarum
 110
Macropipus puber 168
Macropodia rostrata 168
Macrosiphum rosae 132
Madder, Field 232
Magpie 92
Magpie, The (moth) 118
Malacosoma neustria 110
Male-fern 276
 Scaly 276
Mallard 40
Mallow, Common 218
 Marsh 218
 Musk 218
 Tree 218

Malus sylvestris 184
Malva moschata 218
 sylvestris 218
Maniola jurtina 106
 tithonus 106
Maple, Field 184
Marasmius oreades 290
Marchantia polymorpha
 282
Mare's-tail 264
Marigold, Corn 248
 Marsh 198
Marjoram 238
Marsh-bedstraw, Common
 232
Marsh-orchid, Early 260
 Narrow-leaved 260
 Northern 260
Marten, Pine 22
Martes martes 22
Marthasterias glacialis 176
Martin, House 74
 Sand 74
Matricaria perforata 246
Mayfly 122
Mayweed, Pineapple 246
 Scentless 246
Meadow-grass, Annual
 274
Meadow-rue, Common 200
 Lesser 200
Meadowsweet 208
Meconema thallasiniuim
 124
Meconopsis cambrica 202
Medicago lupulina 214
 sativa ssp. sativa 214
Medick, Black 214
Megachile centuncularis
 142
Megaptera novaeangliae
 28
Melampyrum pratense 242
Melanitta fusca 44
 nigra 44
Meles meles 22
Melica uniflora 274
Melick, Wood 274
Melilot, Ribbed 214
Melilotus officinalis 214
Mellinus arvensis 144
Meloe proscarabeus 148
Melolontha melolontha
 148
Mentha aquatica 238
 arvensis 238
 pulegium 238
 spicata 238
Menyanthes trifoliata 230

Merganser, Red-breasted
 44
Mergus albellus 44
 merganser 44
 serrator 44
Merlangius merlangus 100
Merlin 48
Mertensia maritima 234
Metellina merianae 154
Metrioptera roeselii 124
Metzgeria furcata 282
Midge 136
 Phantom 136
Mignonette, Wild 206
Milfoil, Water 264
Milk-cap, Woolly 296
Milk-vetch, Purple 212
Milkwort, Common 218
 Sea 226
Miller, The 114
Millipede, Flat-backed 172
 Pill 172
Miltochrista miniata 112
Milvus milvus 46
Mimulus guttatus 240
Mink, American 22
Minnow 98
Mint, Corn 238
 Water 238
Minuartia verna 194
Misumena vatia 154
Molinia caerulea 270
Monkeyflower 240
Monodonta lineata 162
Montbretia 256
Moonwort 278
Moorhen 50
Mormo maura 116
Morus bassanus 34
Mosquito 136
Moss, Catherine's 278
 Lawn 278
 Sphagnum 280
 Woolly Hair 280
Motacilla alba ssp. yarrellii
 76
 cinerea 76
Moth, Brimstone 118
 Broom 114
 Brown House 108
 Emperor 110
 Ghost 108
 Muslin 112
 Orange 120
 Peppered 120
 Puss 110
 Swallowtailed 120
 Winter 120

Mother of Pearl 108
Mother Shipton 116
Mouse, House 20
  Wood 20
Mouse-ear, Common 194
  Sticky 194
Mugwort 248
Mullein, Great 238
Mullet, Thick-lipped Grey
  100
Mus musculus 20
Musca domestica 140
Muscicapa striata 82
Mushroom, Field 292
  Parasol 292
  Wood 292
Mussel, Common 164
  Duck 160
  Pea 160
Mustard, Black 202
  Garlic 204
  Hedge 202
  Treacle 202
Mustela erminea 22
  vison 22
Myosotis ramossissima
  234
  scorpioides 234
Myotis daubentoni 24
Myotis mystacinus 24
Myotis nattereri 24
Myrica gale 182
Myrmeleotettix maculatus
  124
Myrmica rubra 144
Myrrhis odorata 222
Myrtle, Bog 182
Mythimna conigera 114
  pallens 114
Mytilus edulis 164
Myxocephalus scorpius
  102

Narthecium ossifragum
  254
Navelwort 206
Nectria cinnabarina 288
Nemacheilus barbatus 98
Nemoura cinerea 122
Neotinea maculata 262
Neottia nidus-avis 262
Nepa cinerea 130
Nereis diversicolor 174
Nettle, Common 190
Newt, Smooth 94
Nicrophorus humator 146
  vespilloides 146
Nightjar 72
Nightshade, Woody 238

Noctua fimbriata 114
  pronuba 114
Notodonta dromedarius
  110
Notonecta glauca 130
Nucella lapillus 164
Numenius arquata 58
  phaeopus 58
Nuphar lutea 200
Nyctalus leisleri 24
Nymphaea alba 200
Nymphalis urticae 104
Nymphoides peltata 230

Oak Apple 142
Oak, Pedunculate 182
  Scalloped (moth) 118
Oak, Sessile 182
Oat, Wild 270
Oat-grass, False 270
Oceanodroma leucorhoa
  34
Ochrolechia parella 284
Octopus vulgaris 162
Octopus, Common 162
Odontites verna 240
Oedemera nobilis 148
Oenanthe crocata 224
  fistulosa 224
  oenanthe 82
Oenothera biennis 222
Old Lady 116
Omocestus viridulus 124
Oniscus asellus 166
Ononis repens 212
Operophtera brumata 120
Ophioglossum vulgatum
  278
Ophion luteus 142
Ophion, Yellow 142
Ophiothrix fragilis 176
Ophrys apifera 258
  insectifera 258
Opisthographis luteolata
  118
Orache, Babington's 192
Orange Peel 288
Orange-tip 104
Orchid, Bee 258
  Bird's-nest 262
  Dense-flowered 262
  Early-purple 258
  Fly 258
  Fragrant 258
  Frog 258
  Pyramidal 258
  Small-white 262
Orchis mascula 258
Orcinus orca 28

Orgyia antiqua 112
Origanum vulgare 238
Ornithopus perpusillus
  214
Orobanche alba 242
  minor 242
Orpine 206
Orthetrum cancellatum
  126
  coerulecens 126
Orthosia gothica 114
Oryctolagus cunniculus
  22
Osier 180
Osmunda regalis 276
Osprey 46
Ostrea edulis 164
Otter 22
Oudemansiella mucida
  290
Ourapteryx sambucaria
  120
Ouzel, Ring 84
Owl, Barn 72
  Long-eared 72
  Short-eared 72
Oxalis acetosella 216
Oxtongue, Bristly 252
  Hawkweed 252
Oxychilus alliarius 158
  cellarius 158
Oxyura jamaicensis 44
Oyster, Common 164
Oystercatcher 50
Oysterplant 234

Painted Lady 104
Palomena prasina 130
Panaeolus sphinctrinus
  292
Pandion haliaetus 46
Panorpa sp. 132
Pansy, Field 220
  Mountain 220
  Wild 220
Panurus biarmicus 86
Papaver rhoeas 200
Pararge aegeria 106
  megera 106
Pardosa lugubris 154
Parentucellia viscosa 242
Parietaria judaica 190
Parmelia caperata 284
Parnassia palustris 206
Parsley, Cow 222
  Fool's 226
Parsley-piert 208
Parsnip, Wild 224
Partridge, Grey 50

Parus ater 86
    caeruleus 86
    major 86
Passer domesticus 90
    montanus 90
Pastinaca sativa 224
Patella vulgata 162
Patina pellucida 162
Paxillus involutus 294
Pea, Sea 212
Peach Blossom 118
Peacock 104
Pear, Wild 184
Pearlwort, Procumbent
    196
Pedicularis palustris 242
    sylvatica 242
Pellia epiphylla 282
Pellitory-of-the-wall 190
Pelvetia canaliculata 286
Penny-cress, Field 204
Pennyroyal 238
Pennywort, Marsh 222
Pentaglottis sempervirens
    234
Pentatoma rufipes 130
Pepperwort, Field 204
Peppery Furrow Shell
    162
Perca fluviatilis 98
Perch 98
Perdix perdix 50
Peregrine 48
Periwinkle, Edible 162
    Flat 162
    Lesser 230
Perla bipunctata 122
Pernis apivorus 46
Persicaria amphibia 190
    bistorta 190
    hydropiper 190
    maculosa 190
Petasites fragrans 248
    hybridus 248
Petrobius maritimus 122
Phalacrocorax aristotelis
    34
    carbo 34
Phalarope, Grey 60
    Red-necked 60
Phalaropus fulicarius 60
    lobatus 60
Phalera bucephala 110
Phallus impudicus 296
Phasianus colchicus 50
Pheasant 50
Pheosia gnoma 110
Philaenus spumarius 132
Philomachus pugnax 58

Phleum arenarium 274
    bertelonii 274
    pratense 274
Phlogophora meticulosa
    116
Phoca vitulina 28
Phocoena phocoena 30
Phoenicurus ochrurus 82
    phoenicurus 82
Pholas dactylus 164
Pholcus phalangioides 154
Pholis gunnellus 102
Phoxinus phoxinus 98
Phragmatobia fuliginosa
    112
Phragmites communis 268
Phryganea striata 134
Phyllitis scolopendrium
    276
Phyllobius pomaceus 150
Phylloscopus collybita 80
    sibilatrix 80
    trochilus 80
Physeter catadon 28
Pica pica 92
Picea abies 178
    sitchensis 178
Picris echioides 252
    hieracioides 252
Piddock, Common 164
Pieris brassicae 104
    napi 104
    rapae 104
Pigeon, Feral 70
Pignut 222
Pike 96
Pimpernel, Bog 228
    Scarlet 226
    Yellow 226
Pimpinella saxifraga 224
Pine, Corsican 178
    Scots 178
Pinguicula vulgaris 242
Pintail 42
Pinus nigra ssp. laricio 178
    sylvestris 178
Pipefish, Greater 100
Pipewort 264
Pipistrellus pipistrellus 24
    pygmaeus 24
Pipit, Meadow 76
    Rock 76
Piptoporus betulinus 288
Pisaura mirabilis 154
Piscicola geometra 172
Placynthium nigrum 284
Plagiochila asplenioides
    282
Plagodis dolabraria 118

Plane, London 184
Planorbis corneus 160
    planorbis 160
Plantago coronopus 244
    lanceolata 244
    major 244
    maritima 244
Plantain, Buck's-horn 244
    Greater 244
    Ribwort 244
    Sea 244
Platalea leucorodia 36
Platanthera bifolia 260
    chlorantha 260
Platanus × hispanica 184
Platichthys flesus 102
Plecotus auritus 24
Plectrophenax nivalis 86
Pleuroptya ruralis 108
Pleurotus ostreatus 290
Plover, Golden 52
    Grey 52
    Ringed 52
Plume Moth, White 108
Pluvialis apricaria 52
    squatarola 52
Poa annua 274
Pochard 42
Podiceps auritus 32
    cristatus 32
    nigricollis 32
Pollachius pollachus 100
Pollack 100
Polydesmus angustus 172
Polygala vulgaris 218
Polygonum aviculare 190
Polyommatus icarus 108
Polypodium vulgare 278
Polypore, Birch 288
    Many-zoned 288
Polyporus squamosus 288
Polytrichum commune
    280
Pondweed, Bog 264
    Broad-leaved 264
    Canadian 264
Poplar, Grey (moth) 114
    Hybrid Black 180
    White 180
Poppy, Common 200
    Welsh 202
Populus alba 180
    × canadensis 180
    tremula 180
Porcellana platycheles 168
Porcellio scaber 166
Porpoise, Harbour 30
Potamogeton natans 264
    polygonifolius 264

Potentilla anserina 210
  erecta 210
  palustris 210
  reptans 210
Prawn, Common 170
Primrose 226
Primula veris 226
  vulgaris 226
Privet 188
Prominent, Iron 110
  Lesser Swallow 110
  Pale 112
  Pebble 112
Propylea 14-punctata 150
Prunella modularis 78
  vulgaris 236
Prunus avium 184
  laurocerasus 186
  spinosa 184
Pseudoips prasinana 116
Pseudopanthera macularia 120
Pseudorchis albida 262
Pseudoscopiones 172
Pseudotsuga menziesii 178
Pteridium aquilinum 276
Pterophorus pentadactyla 108
Pterostichus madidus 146
Pterostoma palpina 112
Puffball, Common 296
Puffin 68
Puffinus gravis 34
  griseus 34
  puffinus 34
Pug, Foxglove 118
Pulicaria dysenterica 248
Pungitius pungitius 98
Purple-loosestrife 222
Purslane, Pink 192
  Sea 192
Pyrochroa serraticornis 148
Pyrola minor 228
Pyrrhocorax pyrrhocorax 92
Pyrrhosoma nymphula 128
Pyrrhula pyrrhula 88
Pyrus communis 184

Quercus petraea 182
  robur 182

Rabbit 22
Racomitrum lanuginosum 280

Radish, Wild 202
Ragworm 174
Ragwort 250
  Oxford 250
Rail, Water 50
Raja clavata 100
Rallus aquaticus 50
Ramalina siliquosa 284
Ramaria stricta 296
Ramshorn, Great 160
  The 160
Ramsons 254
Rana temporaria 94
Ranunculus acris 198
  aquatilis 198
  bulbosus 198
  ficaria 198
  flammula 198
  lingua 198
  omiophyllus 200
  peltatus 200
  penicillatus 198
  repens 198
  sceleratus 198
Raphanus raphanistrum
  ssp. *maritimus* 202
Rat, Brown 20
Rattus norvegicus 20
Raven 92
Ray, Thornback 100
Razorbill 68
Razorshell, Pod 164
Recurvirostra avosetta 52
Redpoll, Lesser 90
Redshank 56, 190
  Spotted 56
Redstart 82
  Black 82
Redwing 84
Reed, Common 268
Reedmace, Great 270
Regulus regulus 80
Reseda lutea 206
  luteola 204
Rest-harrow 212
Rhagio scolopacea 138
Rhagium mordax 150
Rhagonycha fulva 148
Rhamnus catharticus 186
Rhinanthus minor 242
Rhinolophus hipposideros 24
Rhizocarpon geographicum 284
Rhodiola rosea 206
Rhododendron 186
Rhododendron ponticum 186
Rhynchospora alba 266

Rhyssa persuasoria 142
Ribes uva-crispa 186
Ringlet 106
Riparia riparia 74
Rissa tridactyla 62
Roach 98
Robin 82
  Ragged 196
Robin's Pincushion 142
Rocket, Sea 204
Rockling, Five-bearded 100
Roll-rim, Brown 294
Rook 92
Rorippa nasturtium-aquaticum 202
Rorippa palustris 202
Rosa arvensis 210
  canina 208
  pimpinellifolia 210
Rose, Burnet 210
  Field 210
Roseroot 206
Rowan 184
Rubus fruticosus agg. 210
Rudd 98
Ruff 58
Rumex acetosa 190
  acetosella 192
  crispus 190
  hydrolapathum 192
  obtusifolius 192
  sanguineus 192
Rush, Compact 266
  Hard 266
  Saltmarsh 266
  Soft 266
  Toad 266
Russula atropurpurea 294
  claroflava 294
  cyanoxantha 294
  emetica 294
  foetans 294
  ochroleuca 294
  rosea 294
Russula, Blackish-purple 294
  Bright Yellow 294
  Common Yellow 294
  Rose 294
  Stinking 294
Rutilus rutilus 98

Sabella pavonia 174
Sage, Wood 234
Sagina procumbens 196
Sagittaria sagittifolia 254
Salicornia europaea 194

Salix alba 180
  caprea 180
  × *chrysocoma* 180
  cinerea 180
  fragilis 180
  pentandra 180
  viminalis 180
Sallow 180
Salmo salar 96
  trutta 96
Salmon, Atlantic 96
Salsola kali 194
Salticus scenicus 154
Saltwort, Prickly 194
Salvelinus alpinus 96
Sambucus nigra 188
Samphire, Golden 248
  Rock 224
Sand-hopper 170
Sanderling 54
Sandpiper, Buff-breasted 56
  Common 56
  Curlew 54
  Green 56
  Pectoral 56
  Purple 54
  Wood 56
Sandwort, Sea 194
  Spring 194
  Thyme-leaved 194
Sanguisorba minor 208
  officinalis 208
Sanicle 222
Sanicula europaea 222
Sarcophaga carnaria 140
Saturnia pavonia 110
Sawfly, Birch 142
Saxicola rubetra 82
  torquata 82
Saxifraga aizoides 208
  granulata 206
  hypnoides 206
  oppositifolia 208
  stellaris 206
Saxifrage, Meadow 206
  Mossy 206
  Purple 208
  Starry 206
  Yellow 208
Scabious, Devil's-bit 244
  Field 244
Scardinius erythroph-thalmus 98
Scatophaga stercoraria 140
Scaup, Greater 42
Schoenus nigricans 266
Scilla verna 254

Scirpus fluitans 266
  maritimus 266
Sciurus carolinensis 20
  vulgaris 20
Scleranthus annuus 196
Scoliopteryx libatrix 116
Scolopax rusticola 60
Scorched Wing 118
Scorpions, False 172
Scoter, Common 44
  Velvet 44
Scrobicularia plana 162
Scrophularia auriculata 238
  nodosa 238
Scurvygrass, Common 204
Scutellaria galericulata 234
Scyliorhinus canicula 100
Sea Ivory 284
Sea-blite, Annual 194
Sea-buckthorn 186
Sea-hare 164
Sea-holly 222
Sea-lavender, Lax-flowered 230
Sea-lemon 164
Sea-slater 170
Sea-snail, Common 102
Sea-spurrey, Lesser 196
  Rock 196
Sea-urchin, Common 176
Seal, Common 28
  Grey 28
Sedge, Common 268
  Common Yellow 268
Sedge, False Fox 268
  Glaucous 268
  Great Fen 268
  Lesser Pond 268
  Pendulous 268
  Pill 268
  Sand 268
  Saw 268
  Tussock 268
  Wood 268
Sedum acre 206
  anglicum 206
  telephium 206
Selfheal 236
Semibalanus balanoides 170
Senecio jacobaea 250
  squalidus 250
  vulgaris 250
Sericomyia silentis 138
Sesleria albicans 274
Shag 34
Shark, The (moth) 114

Shearwater, Great 34
  Manx 34
  Sooty 34
Sheep's-bit 244
Shelduck 40
Shepherd's-purse 204
Sherardia arvensis 232
Shield Bug, Green 130
  Hawthorn 130
Shoreweed 244
Shoveler 40
Shrew, Pygmy 20
Shrimp, Common 170
  Freshwater 166
Sialis lutaria 132
Sickener 294
Silene acaulis 196
  alba 196
  dioica 196
  maritima 196
  vulgaris 196
Silver Y 116
Silverweed 210
Sinapis arvensis 202
Sinodendron cylindricum 146
Siskin 88
Sisymbrium officinale 202
Sisyrinchium bermudiana 256
Skater, Pond 130
Skimmer, Black-lined 126
  Keeled 126
Skipper, Dingy 108
Skua, Arctic 64
  Great 64
Skullcap, Greater 234
Skylark 76
Slug, Ashy-grey 156
  Common Garden 156
  Dusky 156
  Kerry 156
  Large Red 156
  Leopard 156
  Netted 156
  Shelled 156
  Tree 156
  Yellow 156
Smerinthus ocellata 110
Smew 44
Smyrnium olusatrum 222
Snail, Amber 158
  Brown-lipped 158
  Cellar 158
  Copse 158
  Garden 158
  Garlic 158
  Great Pond 160
  Plaited Door 158

Rounded 158
Strawberry 158
Wandering 160
White-lipped 158
Sneezewort 248
Snipe 60
Jack 60
Snipe-fly 138
Snowdrop 256
Soft-grass, Creeping 274
Solanum dulcamara 238
Sole 102
Solea solea 102
Solidago canadensis 246
virgaurea 246
Somateria mollissima 42
Sonchus arvensis 252
oleraceus 252
Sorbus aria 184
aucuparia 184
Sorex minutus 20
Sorrel, Common 190
Sheep's 192
Wood 216
Sowthistle, Perennial 252
Smooth 252
Sparganium erectum 270
Sparrow, House 90
Tree 90
Sparrowhawk 46
Spearmint 238
Spearwort, Greater 198
Lesser 198
Speckled Wood 106
Spectacle, The 116
Speedwell, Germander 240
Heath 240
Thyme-leaved 240
Spergula arvensis 194
Spergularia marina 196
rupicola 196
Sphaerium corneum 160
Sphagnum sp. 280
Spider, Common Cross
152
Daddy-long-legs 154
Garden 152
House 154
Purse-web 152
Swamp 152
Water 152
Zebra 154
Spike-rush, Common 266
Spilosoma lubricipeda 112
Spindle-tree 186
Spiranthes romanzoffiana
262
spiralis 262
Spirorbis borealis 174

Spleenwort, Maidenhair
278
Sponge, Breadcrumb 176
Spoonbill 36
Spotted-orchid, Common
260
Heath 260
Spring Beauty 192
Springtail 122
Spruce, Norway 178
Sitka 178
Spurge, Irish 218
Petty 218
Sea 216
Sun 216
Spurrey, Corn 194
Squill, Spring 254
Squinancywort 232
Squirrel, Grey 20
Red 20
St John's-wort, Marsh 218
Perforate 218
Slender 218
Trailing 220
Stachys officinalis 236
palustris 236
sylvatica 236
Staphylinus olens 146
Starfish, Common 176
Spiny 176
Starling 78
Stellaria graminea 194
holostea 194
media 194
Stenella coeruleoalba 30
Stercorarius parasiticus 64
Stereum hirsutum 288
Stereum, Hairy 288
Sterna albifrons 66
dougallii 66
hirundo 66
paradisaea 66
sandvichensis 66
Stethophyma grossum 124
Stickleback, Nine-spined
98
Three-spined 98
Stinkhorn 296
Stint, Little 54
Stitchwort, Greater 194
Lesser 194
Stoat 22
Stonechat 82
Stonecrop, Biting 206
Stonecrop, English 206
Stork's-bill, Common 216
Storm-petrel, European 34
Leach's 34
Strangalia maculata 150

Strawberry, Wild 210
Streptopelia decaocto 70
Sturnus vulgaris 78
Suaeda maritima 194
Succinea putris 158
Succisa pratensis 244
Sucker, Cornish 102
Suillus variegatus 294
Sulphur Tuft 292
Sundew, Oblong-leaved
206
Round-leaved 206
Swallow 74
Swan, Bewick's 36
Mute 36
Whooper 36
Sweet-grass, Floating 272
Reed 272
Swift 74
Swine-cress 204
Lesser 204
Sycamore 184
Sylvia atricapilla 82
borin 80
communis 80
Sympetrum sanguineum
126
striolatum 126
Symphytum officinalis
234
× *uplandicum* 234
Syngnathus acus 100
Syrphus ribesii 140

Tabanus bromius 138
Tachybaptus ruficollis 32
Tadorna tadorna 40
Talitris saltator 170
Tanacetum parthenium
248
vulgare 248
Tansy 248
Taraxacum officinale 252
Tare, Hairy 212
Smooth 212
Taxus baccata 178
Teal 40
Teasel 244
Tegenaria domestica 154
Tern, Arctic 66
Black 66
Common 66
Little 66
Roseate 66
Sandwich 66
Testacella scutulum 156
Tetragnatha extensa 154
Tetrix subulata 124
undulata 124

Teucrium scorodonia 234
Thalictrum flavum 200
  minus 200
Thalpophila matura 116
Thecla betulae 108
Thistle, Carline 250
  Creeping 252
  Marsh 252
  Meadow 250
  Melancholy 250
  Musk 250
  Slender 250
  Spear 250
Thlaspi arvense 204
Thongweed 286
Thorn, Canary-shouldered 118
Thrift 230
Thrush, Mistle 84
  Song 84
Thuidium tamariscinum 280
Thyatira batis 118
Thyme 238
Thymus polytrichus 238
Tiger, Garden 112
  Ruby 112
Tilia × vulgaris 186
Timarcha tenebricosa 150
Tipula maxima 136
  paludosa 136
Tit, Bearded 86
  Blue 86
  Coal 86
Tit, Great 86
  Long-tailed 86
Toad, Natterjack 94
Toadflax, Common 240
  Ivy-leaved 240
  Pale 240
Toothwort 242
Topshell, Toothed 162
Torilis japonica 222
Tormentil 210
Tortoiseshell, Small 104
Tortula muralis 280
Tragopogon pratensis 252
Tree, Strawberry 188
Treecreeper 86
Trefoil, Birdsfoot 214
  Greater Birdsfoot 214
  Hop 214
Tremella mesenterica 296
Trichia striolata 158
Trichius fasciatus 148
Trichoniscus pusillus 166
Trifolium arvense 214
  campestre 214
  pratense 214

repens 214
  scabrum 214
Triglochin maritima 244
Tringa erythropus 56
  glareola 56
  nebularia 56
  ochropus 56
  totanus 56
Triturus vulgaris 94
Trivia monacha 162
Troglodytes troglodytes 78
Trollius europaeus 198
Trout, Brown 96
True Lover's Knot 114
Tryngites subruficollis 56
Tsuga heterophylla 178
Turdus iliacus 84
  merula 84
  philomelos 84
  pilaris 84
  torquatus 84
  viscivorus 84
Turnstone 58
Tursiops truncatus 30
Tussilago farfara 250
Tussock, Nut-tree 116
  Pale 112
Tutsan 218
Twayblade 258
Twite 90
Typha latifolia 270
Tyria jacobaeae 112
Tyto alba 72

Ulex europaeus 210
  gallii 212
Ulmus glabra 182
  procera 182
Ulva lactuca 286
Umber, Mottled 120
Umbilicus rupestris 206
Underwing, Broad-bordered Yellow 114
  Large Yellow 114
  Red 116
  Straw 116
Upupa epops 72
Urchin, Heart 176
Uria aalge 68
Uroceras gigas 142
Urtica dioica 190
Utricularia vulgaris 264

Vaccinium myrtillus 228
  oxycoccos 228
  vitis-idaea 228
Valerian, Red 242
Valerianella locusta 242
Vanellus vanellus 52

Vanessa atalanta 104
  cardui 104
Vapourer, The 112
Verbascum thapsus 238
Veronica anagallis-aquatica 240
  beccabunga 240
  chamaedrys 240
  officinalis 240
  persica 240
  serpyllifolia 240
Verrucaria maura 284
Vespula germanica 144
  vulgaris 144
Vetch, Bush 212
  Common 212
  Kidney 214
  Tufted 212
  Wood 212
Vetchling, Meadow 212
Viburnum opulus 188
Vicia cracca 212
  hirsuta 212
  sativa 212
  sepium 212
  sylvatica 212
  tetrasperma 212
Vinca minor 230
Viola arvensis 220
  lutea 220
  odorata 220
  palustris 220
  riviniana 220
  tricolor 220
Violet, Marsh 220
  Sweet 220
  Water 226
Viper's-bugloss 234
Vole, Bank 20
Volucella bombylans 140
Volvariella speciosa 292
Vulpes vulpes 22

Wagtail, Grey 76
  Pied 76
Wahlenbergia hederacea 244
Wainscot, Common 114
Wall-rue 278
Walnut, Common 182
Warbler, Garden 80
  Grasshopper 78
  Reed 80
  Sedge 80
  Willow 80
  Wood 80
Wasp, Common 144
  Field Digger 144
  German 144

Giant Wood 142
Ruby-tailed 142
Sand Digger 144
Water Boatman 130
Lesser 130
Water Scorpion 130
Water-cress, Fool's 226
Water-crowfoot, Chalk
Stream 198
Common 198
Pond 200
Round-leaved 200
Water-dropwort, Hemlock
224
Tubular 224
Water-flea 166
Water-lily, Fringed 230
White 200
Yellow 200
Water-pepper 190
Water-plantain, Common
254
Water-speedwell, Blue 240
Watercress 202
Wax-cap, Blackening 294
Waxwing 78
Weevil 150
Hazel 150
Weld 204
Whale, Cuvier's Beaked 30
Finback 28
Humpback 28
Killer 28
Long-finned Pilot 28
Minke 28
Sperm 28

Wheatear 82
Whelk, Common 164
Dog 164
Whimbrel 58
Whinchat 82
White, Green-veined 104
Large 104
Réal's Wood 104
Small 104
Wood 104
Whitebeam 184
Whitethroat 80
Whiting 100
Whitlowgrass, Common
204
Wigeon 40
Willow, Bay 180
Crack 180
Grey 180
Weeping 180
White 180
Willowherb, American
220
Great 220
Marsh 220
Rosebay 220
Winter-cress, Common
202
Wintergreen, Common
228
Witches' Butter 296
Wood-rush, Great 266
Woodcock 60
Woodlouse, Common
166
Pill 166

Woodpigeon 70
Woodruff 232
Woodrush, Field 266
Worm, Peacock 174
Slow 94
Wormwood 248
Sea 250
Woundwort, Hedge 236
Marsh 236
Wrack, Bladder 286
Channeled 286
Egg 286
Serrated 286
Spiral 286
Wrasse, Corkwing 100
Wren 78

Xanthoria parietina 284
Xanthothoe montanata
118
Xylaria hypoxylon 288
Xysticus cristatus 154

Yarrow 248
Yellow, Clouded 104
Speckled 120
Yellow-rattle 242
Yellow-tail 112
Yellow-wort 230
Yellowcress, Marsh 202
Yellowhammer 86
Yew 178
Yorkshire Fog 274

Ziphius cavirostris 30
Zygaena trifolii 108